Multi-Tiered Systems of Support in Secondary Schools

The Definitive Guide to Effective
Implementation and Quality Control

Alison G. Clark and
Katherine A. Dockweiler

Routledge
Taylor & Francis Group

NEW YORK AND LONDON

First published 2019
by Routledge
52 Vanderbilt Avenue, New York, NY 10017

and by Routledge
2 Park Square, Milton Park, Abingdon, Oxon, OX14 4RN

Routledge is an imprint of the Taylor & Francis Group, an informa business

Library of Congress Cataloging-in-Publication Data
Names: Clark, Alison G., author. | Dockweiler, Katherine A., author.
Title: Multi-tiered systems of support in secondary schools : the definitive guide to effective implementation and quality control / Alison G. Clark and Katherine A. Dockweiler.
Description: New York, NY : Routledge, 2019. | Includes bibliographical references and index.
Identifiers: LCCN 2018042253 (print) | LCCN 2018045662 (ebook) | ISBN 9780429023712 (E-book) | ISBN 9780367086787 (hbk) | ISBN 9780367086794 (pbk) | ISBN 9780429023712 (ebk)
Subjects: LCSH: Student assistance programs. | Counseling in secondary education. | Youth with social disabilities—Education (Secondary) | Academic achievement.
Classification: LCC LB3430.5 (ebook) | LCC LB3430.5 .C53 2019 (print) | DDC 373.2–dc23
LC record available at https://lccn.loc.gov/2018042253

ISBN: 978-0-367-08678-7 (hbk)
ISBN: 978-0-367-08679-4 (pbk)
ISBN: 978-0-429-02371-2 (ebk)

Typeset in Bembo
by Wearset Ltd, Boldon, Tyne and Wear

In memory of Esther Reva Gresen. – AC

This book is dedicated to the educators who do not believe themselves to be leaders; there is a leader in each of you, you just need to access your voice. – KD

Contents

Illustrations

Figures

Table

Foreword

In 1647 the "Old Deluder Law" was enacted in Massachusetts to promote education among the common people. The first phase of the Law revealed its real purpose to forestall Satan, the Old Deluder, from capturing the souls of the populace by depriving them of the opportunity to study the scriptures. By the close of the American Revolution, a growing nation demanded an educated populace. Formal education helped citizens attain material wealth and status in their communities. As the United States grew over the following 100 years, schooling became increasingly necessary for successful industrialization, business methods, scientific achievements and government operations. In the early 1800s, many State Boards of Education were enacted. On July 3, 1839, three young women reported for the first formal, teacher training program. Today there are over 250 colleges in the United States with more than 150,000 students preparing for public and private service teaching primary, secondary, graduate and postgraduate students.

As America charged into the twentieth century, the United States assimilated more and more immigrants. Education served a paramount role in helping people from a wide diversity of cultures learn American customs. The role of formal education became increasingly important, helping millions of immigrants integrate successfully into our society. Further, mandatory education was used to prevent children from entering the workforce absent an education, being taken advantage of and economically deprived.

As we have entered the twenty-first century, the role of education is again shifting. Rote, drill, memorization, repetition and regurgitation of factual information have taken a back seat to thinking, reasoning and executive functioning. Every member of our society has at his or her fingertips the knowledge of the world. Further, this knowledge can be easily "Googled." We must change our mindsets about education. We can no longer educate children as we have over the past 250 years and pretend that we are doing something new simply because we have introduced technology into the classroom. Education must find its way from a soft science filled with belief, unproven ideas and misguided enthusiasm to a scientist practitioner model in which educators develop, test, modify and implement effective educational strategies to help today's students maximize their acquisition of knowledge while simultaneously developing their capacities for thinking, reasoning, problem solving, stress hardiness and resilience.

As educators and school administrators continue to feel the pressure of high-stakes testing on educational practices and strategies, there is an accumulating awareness that the social/emotional dimension of students' lives is equal to if not more critical than academics. Unfortunately, rather than embracing the need to "educate the whole" student, a dichotomy has emerged prompting some educators to perceive that nurturing a student's emotional and social health is somehow exclusive from the task of academic instruction (Brooks, 2004). However, strengthening a student's self-esteem, resilience, stress hardiness and emotional well-being is not an extra curriculum. A student's sense of belonging, security and self-confidence provides the essential foundation for enhanced learning, motivation and self-discipline required for an educational atmosphere capable of instilling a resilient mindset in every student. The healthy future of educational institutions is dependent upon their capability to provide social and emotional support hand-in-hand with academic education (Weist, 2003). A sustainable school environment must be capable of meeting the social, emotional and academic needs of all students (Elias, Zins, Graczyk, & Weissberg, 2003).

Schools of the future must be capable of simultaneously evaluating and understanding the impact of causal attributions on beliefs about student behavior and required interventions; the manner in which direct and indirect services are combined; the impact of causative beliefs and academic standards on teachers' and administrators' perceptions of effective interventions; and the opportunity for ongoing support from the many consultants and resource personnel available in secondary schools. Educational interventions implemented with high integrity based on research proven data are more likely to lead to successful outcomes. Increasingly, behavioral, academic and emotional challenges impact a significant percentage of the school population. Yet only a small percentage of these are served through the Individuals with Disabilities Educational Improvement Act (2004).

Nearly 50 years ago, Kounin (1970) suggested that teachers in both well and poorly managed classrooms respond similarly to student behavior. However, teachers of well-managed classrooms are much more efficient in monitoring student attention and performance structuring school-wide activities and implementing classroom rules and procedures (Gettinger, 1988). Classroom consultation has become an increasingly popular means of providing cost effective assistance to teachers and students. Research in this area has steadily increased over the past 20 years. Recent trends in education to deal with problems as they occur rather than through a special education maze, place an even greater emphasis on in-vivo consultation and intervention. When consultants join consultees by framing interventions in a way that is in line with the consultees' mindset and classroom system, effective change occurs. Consultation involves more than simply providing intervention strategies. Consultation is an ongoing process best implemented by knowledgeable, and available, support staff.

The body of existing science concerning effective practices and the important impact teachers have upon students acquisition of knowledge, capacity to think and problem solve, and stress hardiness is well-demonstrated in the scientific, educational, psychological research over the past 20 years. For example, teacher behaviors toward students have been found to create classroom conditions in which negative beliefs are minimized and students demonstrate higher math and science achievement (Griggs et al., 2013). Self-regulation in the classroom is enhanced when teachers deftly combine cognitive and affective behavioral/

teaching strategies, provide a higher ratio of approving to disapproving comments toward students, utilize a positive emotional tone, spend the greater proportion of their time guiding and teaching versus managing and supervising (Fuhs et al., 2013). Finally, high-quality classroom environments are created by teachers who provide students with effective organizational strategies, emotional and instructional support (Curby et al., 2011).

Our challenge is to create a viable and sustainable educational system building on the system we have shaped over the past 250 years with an appreciation of what the future holds for our citizens. A sustainable school environment must be capable of meeting the present social, emotional and academic needs of all students while simultaneously setting goals for academic, citizenship and life skills for the future. Daniel Siegel points out in his book, *The Developing Mind* (2012), "we are the architects of the way in which experience influences genetically pre-programmed but experienced, dependent, brain development." Our innate drive to help, to achieve mastery, be connected to others, treat others and be treated by others fairly, to be motivated by intrinsic rather than extrinsic consequences, and to be instinctually optimistic are all qualities of the human species that can and must be integrated into the educational system we are building for the next 100 years.

With this foundation in place, it is my honor to author this Foreword to *Multi-Tiered Systems to Support in Secondary Schools.* With nearly 40 years of combined experience, Alison Clark and Katherine Dockweiler have created a valuable desk reference and resource for psychologists, educators and allied health professionals working within secondary schools. This volume arises from the increasing recognition that a significant group of secondary school students struggle as the result of mental illness, academic challenges, family conflicts, poverty and illness. It is still the case that the most in need are often provided with inadequate or ineffective resources. This volume builds on Clark's and Dockweiler's experiences by providing a new theory of multi-tiered support as the foundation for school-wide service implementation. LIQUID (Leadership, Inclusiveness, Quality control, Universality, Implementation feedback looping and Data-based decision making) is designed to address the inequities that are rampant in secondary schools. This volume provides a nexus for leadership and inclusivity. It is increasingly recognized that multi-tiered systems of support must form the foundation of effective services for youth struggling in all walks of educational experience. As Clark and Dockweiler point out, it is their hope that this volume empowers educators' advocacy and guides them to make the critical changes necessary in our educational system. In doing so, we will prepare every student for their future and ours.

Sam Goldstein, PhD

References

Brooks, R. (2004). To touch the hearts and minds of students with learning disabilities: The power of mindsets and expectations. *Learning Disabilities: A Contemporary Journal, 2,* 9–18.

Curby, T. W., Rudasill, K. M., & Perez-Edgar, K. (2011). The role of classroom quality in ameliorating the academic and social risks associated with difficult temperament. *School Psychology Quarterly, 26*(2), doi:10.1037/a0023042.

Elias, M. J., Zins, J. E., Graczyk, P. A., & Weissberg, R. B. (2003). Implementation, sustainability and scaling up of social, emotional and academic innovations in public schools. *School Psychology Review, 32*, 303–319.

Fuhs, M. W., Farran, D. C., & Nesbitt, K. T. (2013). Preschool classroom processes as predictors of children's cognitive self-regulation skills development. *APA PsychNet Direct*, 347–359, doi:10.1037/spq0000031.

Gettinger, M. (1988). Methods of proactive classroom management. *School Psychology Review, 17*, 227–242.

Griggs, M. S., Rimm-Kaufman, S. E., Merritt, E. G., & Patton, C. L. (2013, July 29). The Responsive Classroom Approach and fifth grade students' math and science anxiety and self-efficacy. *School Psychology Quarterly*. Advance online publication, doi:10.1037/spq0000026.

Individuals with Disabilities Educational Improvement Act (IDEIA) of 2004. Pub. L. No. 108–446, 20 U.S.C. §1400 *et seq* (2004).

Kounin, J. S. (1970). *Discipline and group management in the classroom*. Melbourne, FL: Krieger.

Siegel, D. J. (2012). *The developing mind* (2nd ed.). New York: Guilford Press.

Weist, M. D. (2003). Commentary: Promoting paradigmatic change in child and adolescent mental health and schools. *School Psychology Review, 32*, 336–341.

Acknowledgments

Thank you, Gary, Noah, Remi, and my entire family for love, support, and encouragement. I would also like to thank Lisa Laura Medina, Dr. Christy K. Beaird, the entire Clark County School District Psychological Services staff, Robert Weires, the staff of Mario C. and Joanne Monaco Middle School 2011–present, and all my professional supervisors and mentors, including Ron Jordan (in memory), Melinda Hauret, Laurie Walz, Catherine C. Gardner, and Dr. Jo Velasquez. A special thank you to the "B.F. Skinner of school psychology," James (Jim) M. Jones, for contributing to the field of school psychology with brilliant insights in student behavior–teacher interactions and discoveries in selective attention, school-based social-emotional-behavioral modification techniques, and leadership excellence, while proving to be one of the greatest professional mentors of all time. – AC

It is with great appreciation and affection that I would like to thank my husband Paul, our children Audrey and Beau, and my parents Greg and Vicki for their unconditional patience, support, and love. "Make no little plans; they have no magic to stir men's blood…. Make big plans, aim high in hope and work." Daniel Burnham 1846–1912. – KD

We would also like to express deep gratitude to Dr. Sam Goldstein for writing our Foreword, and Dr. Randy Sprick, Catherine Gardner, Dr. Tonia Holmes-Sutton, Dr. Katherine Lee, Jim Jones, and Meredith Smith for reviewing our book and believing in our work.

Introduction

Trying to prevent adverse outcomes for students sometimes feels like trying to hold back the ocean; challenges flow too deep and feel too vast for educators to make an impact. School violence, mental illness, and student failure are complex multi-layered problems that are compounded by poverty, inequitable services for the most-needy, and lack of civic education and responsibility. Education continues to be a key social justice issue in our lifetime. With zero tolerance and mandatory retention policies that disproportionately impact students of color, English language learners, and students living in poverty, the school-to-prison pipeline is bursting. Especially with fewer supports and funding, there are extreme pressures on public school systems to "figure it out" for every student to succeed in their education; because if they do not, many of our failing students are on the path to prison. Educators may not be able to hold back the entire ocean of adverse outcomes for children in society, though socially just practices in schools can help students from all backgrounds to not only keep their heads above water but to learn how to ride the waves and be resilient in the face of tsunamis.

With nearly 40 years of combined observations, data collection, and experience working in the fifth largest school district in the United States, we have developed a new theory, LIQUID, to address the inequities that exist not only in large urban school districts, but also small rural school districts and every kind in between. Integrating the constructs of leadership, inclusivity, quality control, universality, implementation and feedback looping, and data-based decision making, and applying it as a lens in which to provide multiple tiers of support for students, we can proactively provide racially and socially just educational services to our students.

Multi-tiered systems of support (MTSS) is foundational for successful student outcomes, the equalizer to providing a socially just education for all students, and the framework for eradicating the school-to-prison pipeline. We intend to answer the question of *how* to successfully implement MTSS with fidelity so schools can begin addressing these inequities while building program capacity. Ideally, MTSS would be adopted into public policy, as it proves to be the most effective way to allocate resources and maintain services and supports for school children. School administrators need clear guidelines on implementation standards to improve effective program delivery and accountability. The organizational psychology principles required to operate functional MTSS at most schools are misunderstood, under-estimated as necessary, under-implemented, and largely disregarded. MTSS is not a pathway to special education eligibility, though it can get there.

MTSS is a resource allocation framework for stakeholders, especially school administrators, to map out school resources and build the systems and processes required to support those functions at each tier. It strives to support the needs of all school children and educators through climate and culture.

One of the best predictors of MTSS success on a school campus is the relationship between the school principal and the school psychologist. Without a doubt, school psychologists are some of the most knowledgeable experts in MTSS in schools. Talented individual practitioners of school psychology in addition to open-minded administrators and educators are the magic combination to unlocking MTSS potential on a school campus. If administrators actively buy into the MTSS framework they seem more likely to value the expertise and input of the school psychologist; just as, if administrators do not buy-in to the framework, they may be less likely to value the input of their school psychologists. As mental and behavioral health needs in schools grow, school administrators and school psychologists need to work more closely together, as never before, because MTSS is an important part of the solution.

On October 1, 2017, our local community fell victim to the most deadly mass shooting in the United States at the Route 91 Harvest Music Festival in Las Vegas, Nevada. As mental health first responders reassigned from school district duties to the County in a state of emergency, we experienced crisis response first hand on a grand scale. That devastating night caused trauma and despair across our home town; yet was mixed with countless acts of generosity to assist victims through donations, blood drives, food and water deliveries, and offers of mental health supports from trauma specialists calling from across the country. Our community united in facing the crisis with humanity and compassion, and we felt deeply honored to help our strong community through the dark hours and days that followed.

At the time, we struggled with the massive damage done to our community, the senselessness of the tragedy, and wondered what the signs of the shooter's path to attack were and who knew about it beforehand. We believed more than ever that MTSS implemented effectively in schools could help prevent future school shootings and school violence. As the horrors of the Parkland school shooting at Marjory Stoneman Douglas High School unfolded a few months later during the National Association of School Psychologists' national conference in Chicago on Valentine's Day, 2018, we joined in solidarity with thousands of other school psychologists and the Florida community to share in grief while processing the devastation and trauma. That day we knew, without a doubt, that we have the individual and collective power to be a part of the solution, knowing that our work is more urgent than ever.

This textbook is intended to provide schools with guidelines on how to meet the leadership and organizational demands of implementing multiple tiers of support in secondary schools. It is intended as a companionship guide to all stages of MTSS implementation. Situational examples are shared based on field experiences with successes and failures of MTSS implementation science from real schools. Schools must become smart organizations. Our hope is to encourage and empower all educators to access their voice and engage in advocacy to influence policy and practices that impact schools, educators, students, and communities. If educators do not speak up, who will?

Chapter 1

New Foundations for Multi-Tiered Systems of Support

Key Terms

Social Justice
Multi-Tiered Systems of Support
Implementation Science
LIQUID Theory
Ecosystem
Counterintuitive Cultures

Chapter Concepts

In this chapter, readers will learn:

1. The intersection of multi-tiered support systems and social justice.
2. How to use this practice guide to implement sustainable MTSS programming for academics, behavior, and mental health.
3. How to reframe organizational thinking and consider multiple perspectives.
4. The key tenets of a new theoretical model to ground MTSS implementation: LIQUID.
5. How to avoid counterintuitive practices.
6. Legal, perceptual, and value aspects of MTSS.

Working in schools has never been more challenging for educators than right now. Zeitgeist of the times is putting more pressure on public schools to perform miracles like never before with fewer resources and higher stakes when systems fail. Corporate interest campaigns have successfully damaged public perception of public schools, allowing for-profit schools to make significant dents in redirecting federal funding and general support away from public schools in state and national policies, without providing better outcomes. Schools are expected to provide greater service delivery to students, who have more needs than ever, while competing for funding that is inadequate to meet those needs. Civil rights in schools are precarious. Safety for students and staff at schools can no longer be taken for granted. Public education is on the verge of existential crisis, and time will tell whether the public education sector can figure out how to meet the evolving needs of children, while making education more effective and relevant. The challenge will be for public education to effectively address these needs before the corporate world perfects the illusion that it can do it better, and in the process of convincing the public it is a good idea, they take away students' rights to a free appropriate public education.

Socially just practices in schools, at the individual and group levels, must include respect, equity, and access to all of a school's resources and benefits (Shriberg, Bonner, Sarr, Walker, Hyland, & Chester, 2008). This *social justice* occurs when all children, from all different backgrounds, regardless of socioeconomic background or demographic characteristics, are valued in a school community and have access to a relevant education. Current educational realities demand that teachers stop teaching a curriculum for the masses, and start teaching differentiated curriculum to real students, with real challenges (Quintero, 2017; Rodriguez, Loman, & Borgmeier, 2016; Jimerson, Burns, & VanDerHeyden, 2016; Lane, Carter, Jenkins, Dwiggins, & Germer, 2015; Sprick, 2013). The *Multi-Tiered Systems of Support* (MTSS) framework is a socially just approach to providing equitable access and support to all students in the educational setting. Further, it can be differentiated for real schools to address real student challenges; MTSS "is an evidence-based framework for effectively integrating multiple systems and services to simultaneously address students' academic achievement, behavior, and social-emotional well-being" (National Association of School Psychologists, 2017, para. 1). MTSS is an ideal framework for school systems because it relies on quality universal instruction and preventative proactive methods, while providing increasingly strategic supports for students as their needs become more severe. This book will demonstrate how MTSS is a recipe that can be replicated across schools with enough flexibility to adapt to the uniqueness of each school and their teams.

This unique approach to the implementation of MTSS in secondary schools is much like a bull's approach to organizing a china shop. Necessity is the mother of invention, so a system was devised that crashed through much of the pre-established notions of what could and could not be accomplished. Through feedback looping and program evaluation, this approach to quality control of effective multi-tiered systems of support in secondary schools lends itself to re-evaluation and refinement each school year (Yuen, Terao, & Schmidt, 2009; Hanson, 2003). This guide is intended as a road map for state Departments of Education, District Superintendents, professors, administrators, principals, school psychologists, teachers, and other motivated educators who are attempting to implement real school change and ultimately increase achievement, promote student well-being, and improve promotion and graduation rates, especially for at-risk students. It requires confidence at the leadership level of decision making because change is not always welcome in the ranks. Change is hard to come by. The main questions for beginning this journey are: where do you want to go and where do you start?

Schools bear the brunt of responsibility for student outcomes, regardless of students' environmental challenges and the practical realities of adequately educating every student who has experiences beyond the control of educators. Many stakeholders understand *why* they need MTSS to expand supports for students, but most are unable to define *what* to implement or *how* to implement MTSS at the secondary level. Research is clear that MTSS models are a necessity for adequately addressing our students' needs on an individual level as well as a systems level (Bamonto-Graney & Shinn, 2005; Shinn, 2007; Sprick, 2009; Shinn & Walker, 2010; Sprick, 2013; Sink, 2016; Rodriguez, Loman, & Borgmeier, 2016; Jimerson et al., 2016; Francis, Mills, & Lupton, 2017). However, at the secondary level, these practices are rarely implemented, let alone implemented systematically and with fidelity.

This practical guide was developed to help educators make manageable changes at their secondary schools in accordance with public policy and best practices. It was also designed as a therapeutic guide to accompany educational leaders and professionals on the difficult journey of transforming their secondary campuses in multiple stages to allocate resources among the three tiers. Embedded throughout are Connection to Practice examples, Voices from the Field narratives from real educators, and Exercises to help guide teams through the MTSS process. The process required to instill new practices and systems, especially in large bureaucratic settings, is always fraught with barriers that require creative problem solving to address culture changes, implementation fidelity, and relationship issues among staff members that can be improved by consulting implementation science, which promotes the systematic application of data and research into practical use by professionals, and into public policy. (Bryk, Gomez, Grunow, & LeMahieu, 2016). *Implementation science* incorporates the integration, application, and refinement of evidence-based practices in the field. Creating a climate to improve achievement is not easy in any school, let alone in schools with significant risk factors. Creating and sustaining MTSS in secondary schools to systematically address the needs of all students is not for the faint of heart. Practitioners may be in the process of implementing tiered supports or they may be starting on a new path because school achievement is not what it could or should be. *Schools are complex organizations that are inherently resistant to change.* A wise master educator often emphasized with novices that one can lead a horse to water and CAN make it drink; however, if the horse does not drink, one cannot blame the horse.

From a managerial standpoint, if the sale is not made, it is not the customer's fault the salesman did not close the deal. It is the job of school administrators, the leadership team, and motivated educators to get staff and stakeholders on board and engaging with best practices through MTSS. It is up to schools to work more like smart organizations: using the skills of highly talented individuals in teams to operate efficiently and learn together to adaptively grow an organization and best practices by leveraging tools, information, knowledge, relationships, and collaborative experiences. Administrative leadership of smart teams must recognize that schools, like any other organization, are institutional in nature with political influences that impact change (Meijer & Bolívar, 2015).

What Are Multi-Tiered Support Systems?

As mentioned earlier, MTSS is an ideal framework for school systems because it relies on quality universal instruction and preventative proactive methods, while providing increasingly strategic supports for students as their needs become more severe. Built on the familiar foundation of the tiered Academic MTSS framework, the Behavior and Mental Health model is an extension of the same schema.

There are numerous books and references as to why a multi-tiered support system is a best practice, and readers are directed to peruse explicit practitioners' texts, including the comprehensive list of over 100 MTSS and related resources compiled by Shinn (2013), for further information. For practitioners who are already on board with intentions to implement a multi-tiered support system at a school, but are not really sure how to put the processes in action, this is the right place to get inspired by practices that have been tried and were successful. Elementary multi-tiered support systems are an established practice and are generally more universally accepted than secondary multi-tiered support systems, but evidence is clear that MTSS is best practice at all grade levels. Figure 1.1 is a visual representation of the multiple-tiered support system. This book will comprehensively

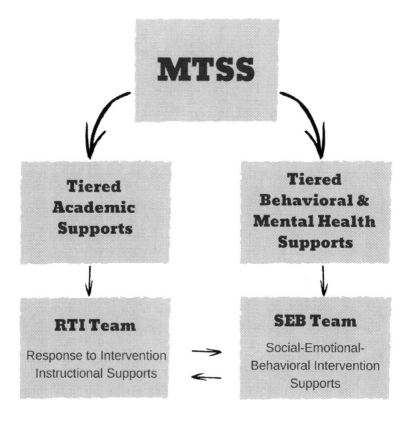

Figure 1.1 Multi-Tiered System of Support.

Note
RTI and SEB each have their own tiers of support and decision points. Systemic implementation includes evidence-based practices and procedures that must be followed with fidelity, at each Tier, to ensure universally consistent instruction and behavior management.

review the components essential to both Academic MTSS, also referred to as "response to intervention" (RTI), as well as Behavioral and Mental Health MTSS, also referred to as "social-emotional-behavioral" (SEB) intervention. This includes review of the tiered model, assessment, data-based decision making, and collaborative problem solving.

Not all schools require the same amount of intensity or the same scope of opportunities, depending on the student population. As described in the Safe and Civil Schools (Sprick, Booher, & Garrison, 2009; Sprick, 2009, 2013) approach, higher-needs classrooms' risk factors indicate the need for more intensive classroom structures; and higher-needs schools need more intensive structure for tiers of support. The higher the needs of the student population, the higher the structure that is needed to support them. The lower the needs, the lower the structure needed. In reading this text, you will learn how to determine whether your school is low-, medium- or high-needs, and then be guided through the steps to create a team to make the best decisions for students on your campus. Processes will be outlined to help teams create levels of support that grow with a team's and school's needs, which have checks and balances based on a model of continuous improvement.

Organizational Framing

Bolman and Deal (2017) assert that there are four different perspectives from which organizations can be viewed in order to understand how they work: structural, human resource, political, and symbolic. Structural is rooted in sociology and is metaphorically represented as factories, human resource is rooted in psychology and is represented as extended families, political is rooted in political science and is represented as jungles, and symbolic is rooted in anthropology and is represented as temples. Viewing organizational operations through each distinct lens is a powerful tool in which to examine systems and practices from diverse angles simultaneously to understand the whole picture of how an organization operates. Each perspective may impact leadership challenges, reframed as opportunities to grant authorship, love, power, or significance within the corresponding organizational ethics of excellence, caring, justice, and faith, respectively.

When schools are viewed through the structural frame with the goal of excellence, there is an expected hierarchy with rules, assigned roles, procedures, and systems. When schools are viewed through the lens of human resource with the goal of caring, unique individuals must be validated through interpersonal relationships and a shared sense that the collective health of the organization is a main priority. In schools viewed through the political frame with goals of justice and power, educators are motivated by leaders' power sharing and can be incentivized to concentrate efforts on shared purpose, with fairness as the currency. Lastly, in schools viewed through the symbolic lens, with the goal of faith and significance, culture is aligned with values and tradition rooted in stories, school spirit, and greater purpose. These leaders provide ceremony and promote faith in sacred shared beliefs within the organization.

When building MTSS at a school, all four leadership frames must be considered, beginning with structure. Bolman and Deal (2017) make a case that differentiation and integration are opposite sides of the same coin of structure, requiring individuals with specialized roles and responsibilities grouped into working units, to effectively coordinate efforts laterally (within and across teams) and vertically (up the hierarchy). The more complex the system, such as implementation of MTSS, the clearer the roles, responsibilities, and procedures must be to meet the needs of individuals and the collective.

Theory

In addition to supporting MTSS as a practical framework that can be used to differentiate student need and to provide interventions, this text also offers a theoretical approach in which to view MTSS. This new theoretical approach is referred to as LIQUID and consists of the conceptual notions of *L*eadership, *I*nclusiveness, *Q*uality control, *U*niversality, *I*mplementation and feedback looping, and *D*ata-based decision making.

Spanning more than 20 years, the researchers collected observations, staff interviews, student performance data, and MTSS artifacts; and analyzed the data at iterative cycles using the qualitative procedure of emerging design grounded theory (Glaser, 1992), to hone and refine their theory until saturation was achieved (Bernard & Ryan, 2010). Grounded theory research "is a systematic, qualitative procedure used to generate a theory that explains, at a broad conceptual level, a process, an action, or an interaction about a substantive topic" (Creswell, 2008, p. 432). In this case, the substantive topic was the constructs necessary for successful MTSS implementation and sustainability. Structuring implementation and sustainability through the commonalities of a theory can enhance fidelity and ensure quality of the tiered program.

Glaser (1992) proposes a flexible approach to grounded theory research consisting of conceptual notions versus stringent codes or visual representations that must be forced into set categories. Moreover, he suggests grounded theory must align with four criteria: fit, work, relevance, and modifiability. The theory must fit the reality of those that it serves and it must work to explain variations of participant (e.g., administrator, teacher, student) behavior. If both conditions of fit and work are met, then the theory has relevance. Finally, the theory must be modifiable and be malleable to change as new data become available. The LIQUID theory meets these four conditions and is described in greater detail in the following section.

LIQUID Model

The LIQUID Model is a new theoretical construct to frame essential components in implementation of MTSS to promote academic, mental, and behavioral health in elementary and secondary schools. The LIQUID Model was designed as a tool to assist in customizing MTSS for individual schools with unique needs and demographics; just as liquid fits the shape of any container. Across the three intervention tiers, the foundation of solid academic, mental, and behavioral health supports at a school rests on six micro and macro factors: leadership, inclusiveness, quality control, universality, implementation and feedback looping, and data-based decision making.

Borrowing from the configuration of an atom, Figure 1.2 illustrates how LIQUID components orbit and overlap to build and sustain the system. Each

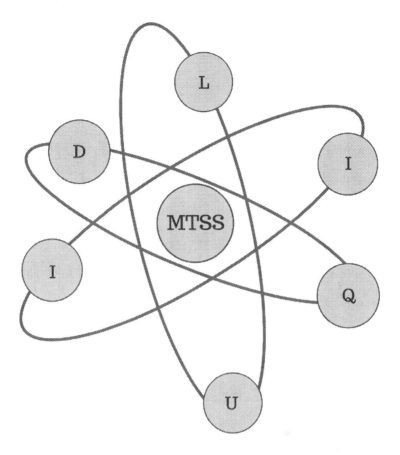

Figure 1.2 Visual Representation of the Theoretical LIQUID Model.

Note
MTSS = Multi-Tiered System of Support, L = leadership, I = inclusiveness, Q = quality control, U = universality, I = implementation and feedback looping, and D = data-based decision making.

L-I-Q-U-I-D are "electrons" that orbit the MTSS "nucleus." As learned in chemistry, all physical matter is constructed of atoms, and electrons are essential components that balance the nucleus. The theoretical model of LIQUID must be present to balance MTSS. The MTSS chemical equation would not work without any of the six "electrons." H_2O requires two hydrogen atoms and one oxygen to be present in the right proportion to form water, the same is true for MTSS. MTSS cannot be formulated and implemented successfully if the six elements of leadership, inclusiveness, quality control, universality, implementation and feedback looping, and data-based decision making are not present in the requisite proportions for a particular school. These elements are woven together and continually influence one another.

Leadership

This team-based approach to improving academic, mental, and behavioral health of students on a school campus begins with the leadership of the primary school administrator and a comprehensive vision for all three tiers. *Having a clear understanding of the relationships and differences between the tiers, how to effectively implement each tier of support, and how to allocate school resources to grow and sustain each tier is required.* If the primary school administrator makes implementation of MTSS a priority, and is willing to actively solve problems to overcome barriers, then MTSS can flourish in a school and systems issues can be resolved, while improvements are continually made and the integrity of the framework is sustained. Due to the complex systems and professional roles that are required to successfully execute MTSS, practices and procedures must be clear and monitored for fidelity, with corrective practices put into effect as necessary by the school leader. School principals must be willing to utilize the master calendar to drive MTSS scheduling requirements, select and endorse evidence-based supports and structures, monitor and enforce fidelity of evidence-based practices, and provide guidance and visible support for educator leaders on campus working in smart teams who are actively solving problems for students on campus.

Effective school leaders empower change agents and can redesign learning environments (VanWynsberghe & Herman, 2015). Ultimately, school leaders serve as role models, problem solvers and decisive enforcers to publicly, visually, and materially support MTSS implementation at all phases, with issues large and small. Leaders should be willing to plan, prioritize, lead, and supervise all MTSS functions and processes. MTSS budgeting must be embedded in the school improvement plan, especially to invest in human capital and to symbolically lead the cultural shift on a school campus. Finally, school leaders must engage in ongoing reflection to evaluate and revise practices, continuously improve staff competencies with professional development experiences, and sustain the supports needed to implement functional programs. Leadership is the foundation of MTSS, and if this domain is not strong, anything built at any tier will be on shaky ground. If administrators are not leading, or at least actively supporting, an MTSS framework, practitioners must start here and try to get that horse to drink; help principals solve their problems by connecting administrative priorities with effective solutions that align with MTSS.

Inclusiveness

Making school relevant for everyone at the micro- and macro-level is paramount. An inclusive school is welcoming and accessible to all staff, students, and families, not just those who are represented by the cultural majority. Culturally competent practices at schools are based on understanding, acceptance, respect for and celebration of, diverse individual, group, and community values, languages, beliefs, principles, and customs (Jones, 2009; Pratt-Johnson, 2006). Cultural competence requires educators to be aware of their own biases and to include students' cultural diversity in a positive manner through all aspects of learning. Educators should have the disposition and skill to learn from other cultures and effectively include other individuals and groups from all backgrounds in all aspects of the school environment.

Teaching students where they are, validating where they are from, and having supports in place for all students at all levels to help them get where they need to go is the epitome of school inclusiveness. Schools demonstrate strength when working with diversity and viewing challenges as opportunities to improve service delivery to all students. There is a place for every person and group in an inclusive school because everyone fits in. Inclusiveness is the primary purpose of MTSS.

Quality Control

Fidelity, integrity, and accountability at the individual level of implementation of MTSS adds up to fidelity, integrity, and accountability at the collective level. Micro-level assuredness that procedures and processes are being followed every time, for every student, as well as macro-level assuredness that practices are evidence-based and are shaped by data-based improvement measures, go hand in hand. Essential elements are required to meet the minimum standards of MTSS implementation that cannot be compromised and still considered to meet those same standards. Quality control means so much more than checking a box on a checklist to indicate whether a standard is present or not at a school. It embodies the spirit of the LIQUID Model to frame practices through different lenses to get multiple angles of the same problems leading to better solutions when systematically implementing tiers of support at a school to meet the needs of all students and staff, regardless of the population or risk factors of the school. Research demonstrates that large changes and school reforms *can* be implemented with fidelity, perhaps more so than small changes (Anderson, 2017).

Confidence in a product or service is achieved when the product or service has been repeatedly tested for effectiveness, and the consumer knows that any defect with the product or service will be replaced or corrected by guarantee. Quality control in MTSS is achieved when school leaders have a comprehensive vision and are willing to actively support implementation of MTSS, when educational practices are evidence-based and implemented with fidelity, and there is confidence that students are able to access instructional opportunities at the level of intensity they need, when they need it, by having processes in place to systematically address individual problems and systems problems within the organization. Quality control in MTSS relies on strong leadership, specific standards to which educators are held accountable, and corrective practices embedded in school culture; checks and balances built in the design of the systems to cyclically reflect on current practices then make revisions in response to data-based outcomes. School leaders are ultimately responsible for enforcing quality of school practices, even when there are policy issues that lie beyond the control of site-based administrators.

Universality

Universal means everyone. The universal tier, the foundation of high-quality instruction using evidence-based practices, is the most important tier in MTSS because it impacts *all* children on campus (National Association of School Psychologists (NASP), 2016). If every student gets quality instruction of developmentally appropriate academic, social, emotional, and behavioral curriculum, most students will positively respond, thus preventing undesirable outcomes most of the time. Expensive targeted solutions, added on top of poor universal instruction for underperformers without addressing root causes, including implementation fidelity issues in delivering curriculum, are much less effective than addressing the actual problem. If a higher number of students are having difficulties than reasonably expected, then evaluating and revising universal practices will have the greatest impact.

Universal practices are designed to maximize opportunities for all students to benefit from instruction, with a direct link to inclusive practices. All students are able to receive the intensity of support they require, starting with universal benchmarking, checking regularly for symptoms of underachievement and social-emotional-behavioral issues that may be indicative of greater overarching challenges that require timely treatment with more intensive targeted instructional experiences. Healthy lifestyle, getting regular health check-ups, and getting timely treatment to address minor ailments and illness is sound preventative and maintenance health advice for everyone; as quality instruction, quarterly academic and social-emotional-behavioral screenings, and getting timely treatment to address underachievement and underperformance in school is sound preventative and maintenance health advice for all students in school. Multi-tiered support systems provide levels of care for students, beginning with healthy universal instructional practices, and including built-in processes to examine practices at all three tiers. Systems that reinforce quality universal instruction and allow for increasingly intensive treatments, supports, and services available in a timely manner to every student who needs it, every time, captures universality in a school setting.

Implementation and Feedback Looping

Fidelity of implementation of evidenced-based practices at the micro-level makes a huge impact at the point of service delivery and student outcomes. Macro-level fidelity is essential to impact the long-term capacity and sustainability of an initiative. Efficacy of a practice cannot be strategically evaluated if the practice is not being implemented with integrity and fidelity. Implementation of new practices requires leadership for close supervision and correction of implementation fidelity issues. *Macro-level review and revision of the micro-level steps of quality control within a continuous improvement model is required.* Using a team-based approach will allow for collaborative responsibility in providing feedback and defining actionable steps to hone the effectiveness of MTSS on a school campus. The answers to almost all problems on a school campus are within the educators who work on that campus. Working collectively for shared purposes in smart teams, and accepting divisions of labor which are visibly and publicly reinforced to grow better practices by school leadership, will increase probability of successful implementation of new MTSS processes and procedures. Ultimately, practices that help make educators' jobs easier, like providing structured opportunities for interventions, eliminating excessive documentation or paperwork and increasing automaticity of data collection, will increase motivation to sustain and improve future practices.

Feedback looping relies on examination of cause and effect processes, observing measurable outputs that lead to new input variables implemented in efforts to positively impact the system (Hanson, 2001, 2003; DiMaggio & Powell, 1991). A system is only as strong as its reflective practices and flexibility to respond adaptively to outcome data and new information in determination of continuing or changing current practices moving forward. A sustainable feedback loop includes many relevant sources of quantitative data, including achievement data, discipline data, graduation rates, as well as qualitative data, including teacher and parent/caregiver surveys. MTSS by design is a layered network with procedures for appropriate application within each layer. Iterative reflection and evaluation can reduce barriers while streamlining processing and increasing efficiency and effectiveness. These iterative reflections can be formative as well as summative. Having systems in place to provide formative and summative feedback helps MTSS teams make better data-based decisions in continuous improvement practices of implement–review–revise cycles.

Data-Based Decision Making

Outcome data usually tells the truth about whether educational practices are working or not, though it may not tell the whole story; follow the data across multiple data sources to get the best understanding of trends and variables that impact trends. Triangulating data using a variety of sources to provide information to make decisions for students will only result in better decisions, including but not limited to improving the quality of implementation of instructional practices at the three tiers, successfully building and sustaining MTSS landmarks to support how systems acquire, process, and access data for decision making, positively impacting school culture, and crystallizing staff procedures and team processes systematically. Chapter 11 offers an MTSS Evaluation Frequency and Intensity Framework to guide teams through the data-analysis process. Data collection, repeated measurements, and documentation requirements must be automated as much as possible to sustain practices with any semblance of fidelity, especially on large secondary campuses. With feedback looping, MTSS teams use data to initiate targeted treatment in a case management model. Data is used to determine whether to intensify or reduce intensity of interventions for students to successfully respond to instruction. Data may be formative or summative, and may include but not limited to: observational, curriculum-based measurement, standardized, attendance history, enrollment history, grades, parent input, dean's database, discipline reports, and universal screenings. School administration and MTSS team members must engage in reflective practices to review micro- and macro-trends, track systems issues, and make adjustments based on data-based outcomes.

Who Are Our Students?

There are many reasons why students don't achieve. Many of those factors are beyond control of the school such as high rates of poverty, hunger, second language and cultural factors, high rates of absenteeism, teenage pregnancy, history of abuse and/or trauma, drug use, lack of parent involvement, dysfunctional family systems, and other socioeconomic and psychosocial factors. School climate, diverse opportunities, and quality teaching practices are about the only factors schools have control over that lead to improved educational outcomes for individuals and groups of students.

Public schools are required to meet all the needs of all students. *Judging the success of an entire school population can be misleading because there are constantly successes and failures going on with every student, every day.* Some students are more difficult to help because of their complex multi-layers of problems. Educators who have experienced success with hard-luck cases find those successes the crowning achievements of their careers in education. To save one child is noble and worthwhile, indeed. However, public schools are challenged with saving all children who cross the threshold of enrollment. Regardless of what challenges students have, the job of all educators in a public setting is to provide them with an appropriate education. Though, the current definition of "appropriate" education in an ever-changing society, with global competition and rapidly evolving technology, is proving to require adaptation to struggle in its relevance.

Most parents can attest to the challenges of raising their own children if they are being genuinely honest. To be responsible for the well-being and futures of hundreds, and even thousands, of other peoples' children can be a crushing responsibility, especially from an administrative standpoint. In the educational sense, *ecosystems* are the confluence and interaction of all persons on a campus who influence student growth, guide development and experiences. The federal ecosystem, the ecosystem of states, the local school district ecosystem, the school ecosystem, the family ecosystem, and the classroom ecosystem all contribute to educational outcomes for students. Administrators can never underestimate the power of the classroom ecosystem. Quality education really boils down to the skill of the educators working directly with children.

Teachers deserve true affection, respect, and admiration for their efforts and accomplishments in raising other people's children to be educated citizens. Most teachers are very well-meaning individuals doing the best they can. Secondary teachers not only have to be masters of curriculum, but also masters of behavior management. They need ninja warrior-like skills to manage up to 50 students at a time, while keeping them engaged, on-task, and productive. Teachers must teach students information they may or may not be prepared to learn for a variety of different reasons. Teaching is a *high-level skill*, which cannot be emphasized enough. Teachers have to think in terms of players on a chess board, where their success in the classroom depends on the efficacy of the battle plan and flexibility to adapt, reorganize, and push through. They must understand rules of engagement enough to manipulate variables in the environment to elicit positive pro-academic behavior. Teaching requires constant creative problem solving.

Counterintuitive Cultures

Sometimes, practices in education are counterintuitive. *Counterintuitive cultures* arise when practices in the field are producing results opposite to that which is desired. Sometimes our solution to address a problem does not fix the problem, rather it creates different problems or intensifies the existing one. For example, in order for teachers to increase the probability of students behaving correctly in class there needs to be much more positive attention than negative attention given to students. Positive attention occurs during or directly after a student behaves in a prosocial or pro-academic way. Negative attention occurs during or directly after a student behaves in an anti-social or anti-academic way. Positive attention increases the probability of positive, prosocial behavior. Negative attention increases the probability of negative, anti-social behavior. Whichever type of behavior you pay more attention to, is the type of behavior you are going to get more of (Jones & Kepner, 2007).

A common mistake that teachers make is when they move in proximity to a student who is off-task and talking. Depending on the function of the student's behavior, this teacher response may not be the best fit to correct the behavior. It would seem that standing next to the student would be a negative consequence for talking during a teacher-led activity and would reduce the probability of that student disrupting the class. However, when a student is repeatedly given attention for being off-task, rather than when he or she is on-task, that student (and every other student in the room) is taught that when a student disrupts teacher-led instruction the student gets more attention and power to disrupt (and controls the movement of the teacher). Repeated proximity, or negative reinforcement, to an off-task student from the teacher actually increases the probability of that student disrupting the class again (Jones & Kepner, 2007). As mentioned, best practices can be counterintuitive.

The teacher has a better chance of improving behavior if he or she gives more *selective* attention to those seated around the disruptive student by praising the on-task peers for following classroom rules: listening respectfully when someone else is talking, raising their hands to speak, and waiting to be called on by the teacher before speaking (Jones & Kepner, 2007). Not only does that draw attention to other students' on-task behavior, but it shows other students who are off-task what they need to do to get more attention from the teacher. Most importantly, the target student must be given positive attention for following the rules as well, especially if she changed her behavior in response to the differential reinforcement given to others. Over time, through shaping, students in the classroom are more likely to use prosocial and pro-academic behaviors to get teacher attention (Jones & Kepner, 2007). Unfortunately, not all behavior problems are so simple, and this was an oversimplified example of one of the many principle components of an effective behavior management system that is found in the context of a positive, proactive classroom culture.

The classroom is a microcosm of school-wide culture. Just as positive attention in the classroom grows more positive behavior from students, positive attention to school-wide teacher competencies from the school administrator can draw attention to best practices in teaching, thus cultivating more effective teachers. There are always good and not-so-good practices going on in a school at any given time, like in any company or workplace. There are resisters and problem solvers. How do the problem solvers get rewarded, while retooling practices to address the resistance? Positive perceptions of school improvement may be achieved with positive reinforcement and success when using evidence-based practices.

Meaningful Change and the Law

When examining ways to grow best practices at a school to meet the most immediate needs, those processes directly and inadvertently generate solutions to address less immediate needs. Or in some schools, more pressing problems will reveal themselves that will lead to an even greater appreciation for, and validation of, effective processes being in place to tackle the issues. Change must occur from the top down as well as the bottom up, and that means there will be numerous moving parts at all times. Unlike many moving parts that do not work well together, and sometimes work counterproductively, implementation of MTSS processes can work synchronously with adaptability to respond to the characteristics and unique needs at any school.

It is very challenging, and can be downright frustrating, to try to make meaningful changes at the school level. Schools are, by nature, bureaucratic institutions that have endless rules and regulations written and challenged by layers of federal and local government, advocacy groups, lawyers, court orders, Supreme Court rulings, and acts of Congress (Bolick, 2016; Robinson, 2015; Hallonsten & Hugander, 2014; Powell & DiMaggio, 1991). Changing rules and regulations requires tenacity and patience, and it is easy to give up. Making an impact at the top levels of bureaucracy takes strategy, perseverance, and many Ibuprofen. However, these are necessary evils in order to advance through numerous levels of bureaucratic decision making. Leaders must be convinced, as well as compelled to act, in which case buy-in must be had, if there is any chance that changes will actually occur at a school (Anyon, Nicotera, & Veeh, 2016).

Fortunately, the current education law passed by Congress in December 2015, the Every Student Succeeds Act (ESSA) (built on the No Child Left Behind Act),

---

Box 1.1

Voice from the Field

In my own school district, I spent the first half of my career as a school psychologist in elementary schools, developing student intervention teams and training teachers and staff in best practices in intervention implementation, data collection, and reporting. The second half of my career included attempts to implement such processes at the secondary level with varied levels of success. Thanks to focused leadership and policy advocacy, intervention protocol was added to our state educational policies, administrative codes, and school procedures in the early 2000s. Throughout my career, intervention teams have become part of the fabric of a majority of elementary schools in our school district, with dramatic levels of variability in stages of implementation. In secondary schools, only a few school administrators earnestly tried to invent MTSS at their schools. The skill level of the building principal, including successful prior experience in one or more parts of implementation of MTSS, and the quality of educators empowered to be change agents in propelling MTSS forward by crafting supports based on the needs of the school, staff, and population, were directly correlated to how well those teams implemented MTSS, ranging from not at all to highly functional.

entreats us to provide multi-tiers of support to students in a school setting. Disability education law requires that some eligibility categories for special education require interventions prior to eligibility determination, and ESSA recognizes MTSS supports as a viable use of federal funding to support programming for students (NASP, 2017). Interventions must be implemented with fidelity, with corresponding documentation of research-based methods and response to intervention data. However, the level of compliance with the spirit of the law is dependent on the knowledge and skill level of the building principal and the quality of the team of educational professionals on campus.

Comparing Practices

Even though some elementary schools understand and use intervention processes, many do not, despite best practice recommendations to train and support schools in doing so. On the other hand, many secondary schools do not provide systematic intervention opportunities at all, let alone documentation of teacher efforts to remediate skills deficits. Secondary school teachers often report that the MTSS model cannot be done in a secondary setting; it seems to be widely accepted that MTSS in secondary schools is unrealistic. There are mountains of obstacles to making changes in a bureaucracy like a large school. Many well-intentioned secondary educators give up on system-wide changes in the face of repeated failures to achieve implementation of MTSS processes without school leadership making MTSS implementation explicit, and they settle for personal efforts by individual teachers on a small scale. Small scale is valiant, but system-wide compliance with federal education law and state policy is better. Many educators do not understand the step-by-step mechanics to implementing the science of change in secondary schools to support a multi-tiered support system, and they make the thinking error that it is too complicated and fraught with bureaucracy to systematically implement. *It is true that MTSS is a comprehensive system, which is why it is important to break it into bite-sized pieces that seem doable instead of impossible.*

School psychologists have been supporting MTSS implementation and policy efforts for years (NASP, 2017). Professional shortages and logistical practicalities, among other factors, restrict school psychologists' practice to only testing students suspected for special education eligibility. This is problematic for many reasons, not the least of which that it is a colossal waste of qualified mental health support, child wellness advocacy, and mental and behavioral health leadership on school campuses. School psychologists may find their roles limited, or perhaps allow themselves to be limited in their roles.

Some special education disabilities require documented, evidence-based interventions and the burden of proof for eligibility lies with the school psychologist. In turn, school psychologists often are faced with making data-based decisions without sufficient data or guarantee of implementation fidelity of interventions. It is natural for school psychologists to be involved in leadership efforts in implementation of MTSS in a comprehensive framework of academic, social, emotional, and behavioral educational supports; they are highly specialized child advocates and mental health care providers already embedded in school systems, though oftentimes their expertise is underutilized by administrators. Many school psychologists spend much of their time completing clerical and repetitive paperwork that could be accomplished by an assistant at a fraction of the cost, freeing up these highly specialized children's advocates and mental health care providers in schools to focus on more direct student care and participation in roles and functions of overlapping smart teams of MTSS.

Having MTSS in place helps with other challenging problems, including reducing over-identification of minority students for special education programming and discipline referrals. Routine program evaluation may highlight issues that intersect and create barriers, such as how intervention scheduling may impact graduation requirements in high school. School counselors must be mindful of credit attainment and how those additional instructional supports are accessed, which can have unintended consequences. Beware of mistakes that are counter-intuitive. By only focusing on remedial skills, lowered expectations for students may result in students leaving school without graduating. It is well-established that children who do not have a high school diploma face considerably more financial difficulty and career limitations than those who have graduated (Tyler, 2004). It is paramount to teach students how to be successful and independent so they can pursue their life goals with as much preparation as possible. Many require remedial skills, but all require the opportunity to graduate, regardless of risk factors.

It took an act of Congress to allow the use of research-based intervention as part of the eligibility determination process for some disabilities, such as specific learning disability, and to remove the severe discrepancy mandate (Assistance to States for the Education of Children with Disabilities, 2010). Public schools are required to provide opportunities for increasingly intensive levels of support to struggling students, depending on documented need and documented response to interventions. It is up to individual schools to figure out how to implement best practices with their schools' needs, population, and budget in mind; however, the framework of MTSS in secondary schools is largely misunderstood and necessary components underestimated. The LIQUID Model organizes the components that impact MTSS fruition: leadership, inclusiveness, quality control, universality, implementation and feedback looping, and data-based decision making. Every instructional practice, team operation, procedure, system, and decision should be evaluated through each lens of LIQUID to identify strengths and weaknesses, and areas in need of improvement.

Change does not come easily whether that be in a low-, medium-, or high-risk school. The process for creating a decision-making model at a school is explained in the following chapters, and each administrator and educational leader will determine how much change can occur, how quickly those changes can be implemented, and what will be supported and enforced at any one time. Effective leadership in this process requires clear expectations, creating space and time for the tiers of support to develop, funding of resources, highly positive reinforcement of staff and students, community involvement, and a lot of patience. In all cases, change will not occur as quickly as expected or exactly as envisioned.

Measuring a school's success based on aggregate student achievement data can be helpful, yet it can also be misleading. In a previous example, the hard-luck student who seemed to have no chance of graduating but then turned it around and was able to achieve this honor will always be considered a success for that school, regardless of the school aggregate indicators. But understanding the realities of the political climate, and the high expectation that every student will graduate, is a challenge indeed. In reading this book, rather than becoming discouraged by the complexity of processes and procedures, readers are challenged to become more motivated. School leaders and educators will learn how to lead their horses to water and make them drink. And if the horses do not drink, the horses will not be to blame; nor will the stakeholders who do not understand the need to do anything differently, the educators who do not want to add more responsibilities to their jobs, or the students who choose to fail by putting in no effort and giving up on themselves. If the horses are not drinking, then the leadership team must reassess organizational frames, improve relationships with resistant stakeholders and validate their input, and systematically determine which opportunities must be developed to increase buy-in and, ultimately, output.

Perception and Value

Poverty and family culture have a significant impact on students' regard toward school. Students may not have good role models in the home, or in the community, and may have never learned appropriate school behavior, let alone a love of learning. Other students have beaten the odds and succeeded in spite of lack of opportunities and resources. *School cultures that embrace cultural differences and provide appropriate learning experiences for all students, regardless of their needs, have the greatest chance for the best outcomes.* For example, high-achieving, high-risk schools share nine commonalities. These nine commonalities are: (1) a culture that emphasizes high expectations; (2) supportive and respectful relationships between stakeholders; (3) a focused academic intent; (4) systematic formative and summative assessment of students; (5) team based decision-making structures; (6) functions and processes; (7) a principal who supports equity; (8) strong staff motivation, perceived efficacy, and work ethic; and (9) reallocation of staffing supports in a coordinated fashion (Kannapel, Clements, Taylor, & Hibpshman, 2005). There are numerous examples of what is needed to turn a low-achieving school into a better achieving school, but it is not always clear how to get started, build momentum, and sustain effective practices. The only way to eat is one bite at a time. Changing educational practices is no different and also requires taking one small bite after another.

Start with perception. How is success defined? Are celebrations allowed if things are moving in the right direction toward the goal, or is celebration supposed to happen only after the goal is achieved? The number of students passing or failing is an indicator of a school's efficacy, though grade inflation and inconsistent grading policies across teachers and schools may make those numbers unreliable indicators of school success. Proficiency tests are also popular measures of a school's success, but what about students who are not good test takers, limited English proficient, or have disabilities and are unable to pass these tests? Are they all failures? When educators address one issue at a time, they need to find ways to celebrate small achievements, which lead to big achievements over time for individual students and whole schools. *Celebrations must occur at every opportunity, and positive attention given when incremental improvements are attained.* There are no successes without failures, as any great inventor will tell you, so ultimate success goes back to building on what works and letting go of ineffective practices.

The value and emphasis must be on the process, not the outcome. The outcomes will then drive future changes to the process and additional areas of need can be addressed. Schools must constantly adapt to the growing needs of students and the realities of the school's teaching climate. Some of the factors that contribute to a school's teaching climate include resource funding, administrative support, and corrective procedures for misbehaving students. Teachers have no control over the raw materials, the students, in their classrooms, which is why the business model of producing widgets does not compare. Factors such as grade-level preparedness, level of age-appropriate behavior, and family support fall into this nebulous uncontrollable realm. When working to produce widgets, inputs can be controlled, thus there are quality control efforts in the input and output. When working with students, they come with their own unique sets of inputs and success cannot be measured in terms of uniform product development but in terms of individual growth, which depends on where they start. Educators impact the development of individual children every single day, and each child is precious and unique.

Once a school has been identified as requiring high, medium, or low structure, processes explained in this customizable guide can be expanded and adapted to meet the needs of individual school sites and populations. The recommendations herein may be challenged; however, be warned that a recipe will not come out the same if one picks and chooses which ingredients in the recipe to use, or not use. MTSS aims to ensure that all areas of student needs are systematically addressed, measures taken, and outcomes monitored. If the cake does not rise the way it was intended, then the recipe will have to be followed more closely. How do schools make the most meaningful changes most quickly? Does the school culture have to change first, or instructional practices? Understanding the cumulative variables that contribute to school outcomes will help teams better understand school needs and identify manageable steps moving forward. Any attempt to make change at the cultural level or the practical level is, most likely, better than no attempt. But again, the caution is that if the cake does not rise, and one did not follow the recipe, one cannot blame the recipe.

The Process

This book moves beyond traditional books that discuss what MTSS is; and delves into the *how* of implementing changes at a school. It will serve as validation of the challenges that educators face on this transformational journey and may be of some solace during the difficult times when things do not seem to be going as planned. What happens so often in education is that when something does not work fast enough, the baby is thrown out with the bath water. Then multiple new babies are adopted all at once, and when they do not produce change fast enough all the new initiatives are abandoned for something else. Change is always a constant in the field of education in terms of procedures, paperwork, assessment, and service delivery, but oftentimes feels like nothing really ever changes. Before schools throw away any more babies, this guide can assist teams in systematically evaluating where they are in terms of MTSS implementation and development; what they have, what they want and need, and where they are going in providing differential opportunities to learners with diverse needs that can be grown incrementally and systematically.

School-based teams must come up with the best solutions for their campuses with the resources that they have, and this book will guide teams through a series of exercises to evaluate their individual needs. Using the continuous improvement model, teams must be constantly re-evaluating and reassessing what works and what does not work, continuing with what works, and trying new methods to address what is not working. Teams might find improvements in some areas but not in others, and then it may become evident that some structures and practices must be addressed first to impact growth in other targeted areas. For example, teams may strive to improve teachers' instructional practices in terms of content mastery and quality teaching, but if their classroom management skills are lacking, increased student achievement may not pan out. The type of interventions needed on a campus depends on whether a large number of students are struggling in a subject area or a smaller subgroup. Analyzing data systematically will help school leaders prioritize needs and implement practices that have the best chance of impacting the most students. Once basic instructional gaps are addressed at Tier 1, Tier 2, and Tier 3, intervention opportunities can be better designed and outcomes can be better evaluated, leading to better instructional practices.

Behavioral and Mental Health MTSS seems to be much more difficult to implement on school campuses than Academic MTSS instructional supports. Several factors contribute to this phenomenon including access and funding. To begin with, formal, universal Tier 1 social-emotional and behavioral instruction typically ends with elementary school. Also, targeted social-emotional and behavioral learning experiences are underfunded and under-implemented, which often leads to disruptive students being blamed and punished without getting treatment. This pattern leads to a series of questions. Who is teaching students to do better? Who is teaching teachers to do better? How will these "problem students" ever learn how to be independent or contributing members of society without having multiple opportunities and consistent support to learn correct behavior? How can schools begin to interrupt the school to prison pipeline?

Adding social-emotional learning and positive behavioral instructional supports is part of the multi-layered recipe to making a multi-tiered support system wedding cake that marries best practices systematically. When does each ingredient get introduced on each level? That depends on each school, their team, and their school's needs and resources. Just know that the ingredients must be in there, added at some point, or the cake will not rise and a comprehensive multi-tiered support system will not nourish all students and staff.

The journey to implementing best practices in schools, which requires system-wide change, is fraught with resistance to change. Most educators are not necessarily happy when change is presented. It requires a new way of thinking, a new way of acting, and an open attitude to make the effort. The trickle-down effect of negative attitude to change is often transparent in a school setting. If the administrator of the school is not excited about making required changes, the teachers will not be excited, nor will the students or the parents. Bad attitude is contagious, as any classroom teacher can attest. If a school administrator is being directed to change without buying into the big picture, educators will be less likely to adopt those changes with integrity.

Sometimes, change is implemented on paper, but not in true practice, and is referred to as "the smoke and mirrors effect." Leaders on campus talk about systems changes as if they have occurred when, in fact, they have not. Principals may think that they have the MTSS framework in place but, in truth, they do not. Many of these schools have a remedial class, or two, a progressive discipline plan, and nothing more, with no team actively solving problems within a comprehensive system. When understanding of MTSS is unclear and access to academic and behavioral supports restricted, MTSS is an illusion.

On the other hand, if the system is too laborious and falls only on a few well-meaning teachers, the system becomes unfair. If only some of the educators have embraced change and others have not, the ones who are not working to implement real change can spread ill will like a bad rash. Those doing the hard work of adopting new ways of thinking and acting are going to feel punished because there is no consequence for those who are not doing their due diligence. Another problem arises when teachers and other professionals receive no overt rewards for working the program and are treated the same as the teachers and professionals who are *not* working the program. This creates a culture of resentment. And when the cake does not rise because the recipe is not being followed, the school staff members who did not follow the recipe are validated because the new processes did not work, and the teachers who were open to change are resentful because they did everything they could do and no-one else was held accountable.

This guide will have a significant impact on readers' schools and will offer incremental steps toward meaningful changes. This is a process guide based on experiences in the field of school psychology. It is a process book that includes content of established best practices, designed to bridge the gap between best practices and actual practices with specific recommendations to lasting systemic change and increasing positive outcomes for students. Readers may not agree with all recommendations to the point that they may seriously disagree. Readers are encouraged to be mindful of emotional responses when reading through this guide to examine gut instincts and implicit bias, and address mindset and thinking patterns that may interfere with solution-based activities. This book will not be therapeutic, or professionally encouraging, if readers are not monitoring and tracking their feelings. Practitioner feelings about how things are going qualitatively is important, just as important as the quantitative outcomes.

This process is not a stagnant set of boundaries but a streaming river of opportunity. Some recommendations might be applicable or appealing, and some not. Goals of this guide are to inspire, educate, and promote site based problem solving. Feel free to disagree, just know that readers' thoughts and beliefs may be challenged so that they can make better decisions for their school growth, which ultimately leads to better results for their students. If readers have a strong reaction to a statement or recommendation, question why. Do some examples hit too close to home? Do readers feel like they need to defend their current practices? If the answer to either of these questions is yes, please consider recommendations in the nature in which they are intended, to assist schools and individual professionals in making the most of their multi-tiered support system.

Ultimately, it is school practitioners and their teams who are responsible for decision making on behalf of their students and making the process work with their school's needs in mind. Try to build upon, modify, and create methods to meet the needs of unique school climates. To start, the focus will be to determine the needs of individual schools and build their MTSS team, two of the biggest steps in the process. Then readers will establish their school supports in terms of basic resources, training, and scheduling. Examples of the evolution of practices at real schools will be illustrated, as well. Be aware that improving student and staff engagement, school culture, and addressing special needs populations require additional resources, training, and scheduling. Extra components added to the mix take additional time and patience to implement. Readers may not feel they need to address all components of the recipe based on the needs of their school, but those areas should be regularly evaluated and monitored nonetheless. Practitioners might not presently focus on a component, though they may find that they do indeed need to address it down the road based on outcome data.

Processes to make changes that can be implemented in both middle schools and high schools are addressed, as well as specific modifications for high schools. The process is the same, but the outcomes will be different. Therapy is what individuals make of it. Readers are encouraged to consider these processes and take away what is needed to make sustainable improvements to student supports and services. For now, readers are encouraged to let go of defending what they have in place and start thinking about how to include more practices that work in a new or improved infrastructure. It takes courage and confidence for school leaders and educators to take schools to the next level by embracing the practice of a multi-tiered support system and applying it their schools.

This is a guide to help administrators, and other motivated educators, with evaluating the needs of specific school sites and generating realistic recommendations that can be implemented to make positive school changes to impact schoolwide achievement. There are interactive exercises designed to strategically plan for school change. Every school is its own kingdom with its own ruler, its own citizens, and its own culture. Every school has its own personality, quality of teachers, resources, funding for resources, diverse student populations, and varying degrees of family engagement and support. There are commonalities between effective programs, but each school must find its own way. That said, there are questions to be asked that can lead to the right decisions at the right time for a school site.

Every school has access to the solutions to their own problems, and practitioners and their school teams have ideas how to improve instructional quality and outcomes for their students. School leaders and administrators benefit from guidance on how to be their own best resource. If principals are lucky, they have talented and experienced educators on their staff guiding their school and already implementing MTSS successfully because of their hard work, dedication, and reflective practices. If educators have not had the amount of success in implementation of MTSS they wish for at their schools, want to fine-tune the MTSS process, or are just getting started, this book is the definitive guide to building and sustaining MTSS. Every school team has the solutions to their own problems. This guide will elicit those solutions.

Exercise 1.1

Reflection Journaling

- Take a moment and reflect on how you feel about this journey to build MTSS at your school.
- Write about any doubts or fears you may have.
- Write down the benefits of embarking on this path to ensure there are supports for all learners at your school.
- Imagine your school in a year and write about what that will be like in terms of improvements.
- Now imagine your school in five years and what that might be like and write a few sentences about what outcomes you would expect.

References

Anderson, E. R. (2017). Accommodating change: Relating fidelity of implementation to program fit in educational reforms. *American Educational Research Journal, 54*(6), 1288–1315.

Anyon, Y., Nicotera, N., & Veeh, C. A. (2016). Contextual influences on the implementation of a schoolwide intervention to promote students' social, emotional, and academic learning. *Children & Schools, 38*(2), 81–88.

Assistance to States for the Education of Children with Disabilities, 34 CFR §300.307 (2010).

Bamonto-Graney, S., & Shinn, M. R. (2005). Effects of Reading Curriculum-Based Measurement (R-CBM) teacher feedback in general education classrooms. *School Psychology Review, 34*(2), 184–201.

Bernard, H. R., & Ryan, G. W. (2010). *Analyzing qualitative data: Systematic approaches.* Thousand Oaks, CA: Sage Publications.

Bolick, C. (2016). Jump starting K-12 education reform. *Harvard Journal of Law & Public Policy, 40*(1), 17–25.

Bolman, L. G., & Deal, T. E. (2017). *Reframing organizations: Artistry, choice, and leadership* (6th ed.). San Francisco, CA: Jossey Bass.

Bryk, A. S., Gomez, L. M., Grunow, A., & LeMahieu, P. G. (2016). *Learning to improve: How America's schools can get better at getting better.* Cambridge, MA: Harvard Education Press.

Creswell, J. W. (2008). *Educational research: Planning, conducting, and evaluating quantitative and qualitative research* (3rd ed.). Upper Saddle River, NJ: Pearson Education.

DiMaggio, P. J., & Powell, W. W. (1991). The iron cage revisited: Institutional isomorphism and collective rationality in organizational fields. In P. J. DiMaggio & W. W. Powell (Eds.), *The new institutionalism in organizational analysis* (pp. 63–82). Chicago, IL: University of Chicago Press.

Every Student Succeeds Act of 2015, 20 U.S.C. (2015).

Francis, B., Mills, M., & Lupton, R. (2017). Toward social justice in education: Contradictions and dilemmas. *Journal of Education Policy, 32*(4), 414–431.

Glaser, B. G. (1992). *Basics of grounded theory analysis: Emergence vs. forcing.* Mill Valley, CA: Sociology Press.

Hallonsten, O., & Hugander, O. (2014). Supporting "future research leaders" in Sweden: Institutional isomorphism and inadvertent funding agglomeration. *Research Evaluation, 23*, 249–260.

Hanson, M. (2001). Institutional theory and educational change. *Educational Administration Quarterly, 37*(5), 637–661.

Hanson, M. (2003). *Educational administration and organizational behavior*. Boston, MA: Allyn & Bacon.

Jimerson, S. R., Burns, M. K., & VanDerHeyden, A. M. (Eds.) (2016). *The handbook of response to intervention: The science and practice of multi-tiered systems of support*. New York: Springer.

Jones, J. (Ed.) (2009). *The psychology of multiculturalism in the schools: A primer for practice, training, and research*. Bethesda, MD: National Association of School Psychologists.

Jones, J. M., & Kepner, J. A. (2007). Learning to use selective attention: How and why. In R. P. Cantrell & M. L. Cantrell (Eds.), *Helping troubled children and youth* (pp. 265–279). Memphis, TN: American Re-Education Association.

Kannapel, P. J., Clements, S. K., Taylor, D., & Hibpshman, T. (2005). *Inside the black box of high-performing high-poverty schools*. Lexington, KY: Prichard Committee for Academic Excellence. Retrieved from www.prichardcommittee.org/wp-content/uploads/2013/02/Inside-the-Black-Box.pdf.

Lane, K. L., Carter, E. W., Jenkins, A., Dwiggins, L., & Germer, K. (2015). Supporting comprehensive, integrated, three-tiered models of prevention in schools: Administrators' perspectives. *Journal of Positive Behavior Interventions, 17*(4), 209–222.

Meijer, A., & Bolívar, M. P. R. (2015). Governing the smart city: A review of the literature on smart urban governance. *International Review of Administrative Sciences, 82*(2), 392–408.

National Association of School Psychologists (2016). *Engaging school psychologists to improve multi-tiered systems of support*. Bethesda, MD: Author.

National Association of School Psychologists (2017). *ESSA and multitiered systems of support for school psychologists*. Bethesda, MD: Author. Retrieved from www.nasponline.org/research-and-policy/current-law-and-policy-priorities/policy-priorities/the-every-student-succeeds-act/essa-implementation-resources/essa-and-mtss-for-school-psychologists.

Powell, W. W., & DiMaggio, P. J. (1991). *The new institutionalism in organizational analysis*. Chicago, IL: University of Chicago Press.

Pratt-Johnson, Y. (2006). Communicating cross-culturally: What teachers should know. *The Internet TESL Journal, 12*(2). Retrieved from http://iteslj.org/Articles/Pratt-Johnson-CrossCultural.html.

Quintero, E. (Ed.) (2017). *Teaching in context: The social side of education reform*. Cambridge, MA: Harvard Education Press.

Robinson, S. (2015). Decentralisation, managerialism and accountability: Professional loss in an Australian education bureaucracy. *Journal of Education Policy, 30*(4), 468–482, doi:10.1080/02680939.2015.1025241.

Rodriguez, B. J., Loman, S. L., & Borgmeier, C. (2016). Tier 2 interventions in positive behavior support: A survey of school implementation. *Preventing School Failure: Alternative Education for Children and Youth, 60*(2), 94–105, doi:10.1080/1045988X.2015.1025354.

Shinn, M. R. (2007). Identifying students at risk, monitoring performance, and determining eligibility within RTI: Research on educational need and benefit from academic intervention. *School Psychology Review, 36*(4), 601–617.

Shinn, M. R. (2013). *Secondary version: References for professional development for multi-tiered system of services and supports*. Retrieved from www.tnspdg.com/pdf/RTItraining/2/Shinn%20Secondary%20Readings%20and%20Resources.pdf.

Shinn, M. R., & Walker, H. M. (Eds.) (2010). *Interventions for academic and behavior problems in a three-tier model, including Response-to-Intervention* (3rd ed.). Bethesda, MD: National Association of School Psychologists.

Shriberg, D., Bonner, M., Sarr, B. J., Walker, A. M., Hyland, M., & Chester, C. (2008). Social justice through a school psychology lens: Definition and applications. *School Psychology Review, 37*, 453–468.

Sink, C. A. (2016). Incorporating a multi-tiered system of supports into school counselor preparation. *The Professional Counselor, 6*(3), 203–219.

Sprick, R. A. (2009). *CHAMPS: A proactive and positive approach to classroom management* (2nd ed.). Eugene, OR: Pacific Northwest Publishing.

Sprick, R. A. (2013). *Discipline in the secondary classroom: A positive approach to behavior management* (3rd ed.). Hoboken, NJ: John Wiley & Sons.

Sprick, R., Booher, M., & Garrison, M. (2009). *Behavioral response to intervention.* Eugene, OR: Pacific Northwest Publishing.

Tyler, J. H. (2004). Does G.E.D. improve earnings? Estimates from a sample of both successful and unsuccessful G.E.D. candidates. *ILR Review, 57*(4), 579–598.

VanWynsberghe, R., & Herman, A. C. (2015). Education for social change and pragmatist theory: Five features of educative environments designed for social change. *International Journal of Lifelong Education, 34*(3), 268–283, doi:10.1080/02601370.2014.988189.

Yuen, F. K. O., Terao, K. L., & Schmidt, A. M. (2009). *Effective grant writing and program evaluation: For human service professionals.* Hoboken, NJ: John Wiley & Sons.

Chapter 2

Evaluating Your School's Needs and Building Your Team

Key Terms

Cultural Change
Smart Teams
Human Capital
LIQUID Model
Neo-Institutional Theory
Universal Screening
Benchmarking
Progress Monitoring
Rate of Improvement
Strategic Opportunism

Chapter Concepts

In this chapter, readers will learn:

1. To engage in culture change at their schools through perception shifting.
2. To adopt a new MTSS leadership paradigm through the conceptual lens of the LIQUID Model.
3. The basic sociopolitical realities of our education system.
4. The basic components of a successful MTSS program.
5. Entry points to begin MTSS program implementation.

There Is No "No" in Yes

School change is a slow and laborious process. Many urban school campuses have large staff and student populations. When a secondary school has 75 plus teachers, with 75 plus support staff members, and 1,300 to 4,000 students, organized chaos is reliant on systems in place. Instantaneous incorporation of new practices in a large school setting is highly improbable. It takes time for practices to become accepted by school staff members, and it takes a high level of supervision and quality control to model professional standards, monitor professional performance, and provide corrective feedback to insure implementation fidelity. Implementation outcome data indicates less than 5 percent of school teachers notified of new procedures implement those procedures with integrity initially (Colter & Gibbons, 2018). Selling the value of evidence-based practices to educational professionals opens the door to improved compliance but does not necessarily sustain the practices. Introducing changes incrementally within the framework, providing continuous follow-up training, and engaging in feedback looping is required to increase competence in new school practices. Making replicable and positive changes through MTSS in large urban school settings is possible, regardless of the obstacles.

Varying circumstances may impede the development of a multi-tiered support system in secondary schools. And yes, changing a large school system is difficult. However, there is no "no" in yes. There's no "I" in team, and there's no "no" in yes. If the principal at a school decides to commit to growing a functional multi-tiered support system, commitment must be absolute; not partially, not a pilot study, not just for some students, but a total cultural change that impacts everyone. Culture is "the individually and socially constructed values, norms, and beliefs about an organization and how it should behave that can be measured only by observation of the setting using qualitative methods" (Hall & Hord, 2006, p. 20). Therefore, in a school setting, *cultural change* is the observable shift toward new standards, attitudes, and behavior.

In this chapter, readers will understand the premise behind this cultural change and will be introduced to actionable steps that will guide administrators and other motivated educators through the processes of evaluating school needs and building a smart team to grow MTSS at a secondary school (Cunliffe, 2017; Duffy, 2015; VanWynsberghe & Herman, 2015; Naraian & Oyler, 2014; Wilson, 2014). These smart teams are unique in their composition, emotional intelligence and task delegation that make them efficient and effective. *Smart teams* are comprised of individuals who contribute equally to the task at hand, are adept at reading the complex emotional states of others, and tend to have a greater number of female team members than males (Woolley, Chabris, Pentland, Hashmi, & Malone, 2010).

The MTSS framework can be represented by the overlapping non-negotiable variables of Leadership, Inclusiveness, Quality control, Universality, Implementation and feedback looping, and Data-based decision making (LIQUID). *Each variable must be infused in all aspects of the framework to ensure success of MTSS at a school.* The LIQUID Model is the standard in which to compare all phases of the MTSS process. If MTSS is spearheaded and actively supported by leadership, educational practices are inclusive, there are quality control measures to ensure that processes are set up to regularly monitor outcomes and correct practices that are not working, universal practices are in place to support the academic and social-emotional and behavioral health of all students, with universal screening measures to identify all underachievers for early intervention, implementation of tiered supports are in place with fidelity checks and feedback looping processes embedded in automated systems, and data-based decisions are regularly made to improve student outcomes, then MTSS at a school may be running at peak efficiency. If one or more of these variables cannot be seen, heard, or experienced in one or more MTSS practices, then school teams will be able to identify the weak links to effectively match solutions to the right problems.

Taking the lead to implement MTSS requires changing perspectives of school staff by using an evidence-based, best practices cultural shift that will impact everyone on a school campus. Most industries make decisions based on various sets of data, production data, efficiency data, or user data; education is one of the few fields where best practices are suggested but are largely optional (Ladd & Fiske, 2008). This lackadaisical approach is challenged in this book and removes the option of implementing poor policies and programs not backed by evidence-based practices.

The field of medicine also relies on standards and best practices that are critical. Not all medical professionals comply with updates to professional standards, even in the most obvious cases. In 1847, a Hungarian doctor, Ignaz Semmelweis, discovered the benefits of handwashing and disinfecting instruments in a chlorinated lime solution. By instituting these two simple practices in the hospital where he was working, he was able to reduce the mortality rate of his patients from approximately 16 percent to approximately 3 percent (World Health Organization, 2009). Even with overwhelming data to support the effectiveness of the new practices, physicians were largely opposed to such methods, as they took offense to a peer pointing out the errors of their ways. In 1867, a British doctor, Joseph Lister, contributed to the knowledge base of antiseptic science with his application of germ theory and his discoveries surrounding wound care, further reducing mortalities and improving surgical care (Pitt & Aubin, 2012). However, it wasn't until the mid-1870s that handwashing and disinfecting became best practices in medicine. And it wasn't until a century later, the 1980s, when national standards were set in the United States for hand hygiene in health care (World Health Organization, 2009). Presently, one would think that there are no valid arguments for a physician to not wash his or her hands before touching a patient because it has been best practice in medicine for almost 150 years; however, it is estimated that up to 50 percent of providers currently fail to do so (Goldmann, 2006). Educators can learn from medicine's lag in implementation of best practices and recognize it as a call for transformational leadership and an opportunity to become a smart organization (Guerro, Fenwick, & Kong, 2017; Hanson, 2003). In education, when data exists to support a best practice that will benefit all students, it is worth investigating ways to implement it without extraneous delay. *All students have the capacity to learn but not all have the resources to realize their potential.*

A key feature of evaluating needs of a school and building a smart team rests with the human capital aspects of tier implementation. *Human capital* includes the competencies, value, and knowledge professionals on campus bring to the table. Hiring professionals with necessary capital who also buy into the administrator's vision for MTSS, including releasing those who resist it, is a foundational component of organizational change and building an MTSS team (Anyon, Nicotera, & Veeh, 2016; Foorman, 2016; Freeman, Miller, & Newcomer, 2015; McCarthy, Lambert, Lineback, Fitchett, & Baddouh, 2015; Meyer & Behar-Horenstein, 2015; Pinkelman, McIntosh, Rasplica, Berg, Strickland-Cohen, 2015; Hall & Hord, 2006). In addition to competence and buy-in, staff motivation should never be underestimated as an essential ingredient of systems change. Implementation of new programs are most successful when administrators are inclusive and active in the change process, and all individuals on campus support the change efforts.

LIQUID Considerations

Following the new LIQUID Theory for MTSS, the LIQUID Model allows smart teams to analyze MTSS framework components and strategically evaluate how system processes are affected by each variable; which also reveals the effectiveness of structures that support functions, and how well processes are organized, implemented, monitored, adapted, and supported. If each element is not adequately supporting the other elements, the system will not run synergistically and desired measurable student achievement outcomes will be less likely. Current and future educational practices must be appraised through each lens of LIQUID. *The LIQUID Model offers tangible milestones for critical exploration and problem solving to improve team building, operationalization of team functions, and growing site-based capacity of MTSS.* It synthesizes the core features of the most popular multi-tiered model that will result in positive outcomes for students. For every required landmark and systemic practice to grow, in efforts to build and refine tiers of support on a school campus, each component of the LIQUID Model must be considered and questions asked:

1. Leadership: How well will the school's administration lead and support each landmark or practice in MTSS, monitor fidelity of implementation, and correct ineffective practices? How visible is leadership and support of MTSS practices?
2. Inclusiveness: Is the implementation of a landmark or practice truly inclusive? What evidence is there to support that is true or not? Have implicit biases been taken into active consideration? What evidence is there that practices are socially just? How are socially just practices being measured?
3. Quality Control: How is quality of a system or practice assured? How are processes monitored for efficacy? How often? How do improvements get made, who decides, and when? Are practices working? What evidence exists to support functional practices? Are all sources of information reliable? What evidence is there that practices are implemented with fidelity? Are the right things being measured?
4. Universality: How do school practices impact every student on campus, directly and indirectly? Has every student been counted? How do practices evolve to better meet the needs of all children? How do we teach critical thinking and provide social-emotional, and behavioral experiences that infuse instruction in communication, problem-solving, and resilience as preventative medicine, like immunizations and healthy nutrition? How are all students being actively monitored to check their educational health periodically to intervene at the earliest opportunity, if not by universal benchmarking? Is there universal access to instructional supports to all students who may benefit from them?
5. Implementation and Feedback Looping: Are practices being implemented as intended? Why or why not? How do we know? What are barriers to implementing supports that are needed at a school? Who is doing it well already? What actionable steps can be taken to improve selection of research-based curriculum and implementation fidelity? How does the team get feedback, qualitative and quantitative, for discussion and decision making? How often?

How responsive is the team to modifying supports and service delivery when data support the need to do so? How to select what are next steps based on feedback loop? Who ensures every school professional does their part?

6. Data-Based Decision Making: What does the data tell us? What are the trends? Is instructional service delivery working? Does it work in some instances and not others? Are qualitative and quantitative data consistent? Why or why not?

In shifting the leadership lens, we must also shift the practitioner lens. Students are challenging educators to create more relevant and holistic learning experiences personalized to meet individual abilities and needs, while policy makers are focused on other outcomes such as passing accountability standards based on high-stakes testing. The students in classes now are not the same students of the past, as technology has advanced the access to information sources a million-fold. Inexpensive electronic devices can store more information than could ever be memorized, yet even with immediate access to information and knowledge, our students think critically less and less. Our children have more "friends" on social media and fewer social skills and interpersonal relationships. They are unique individuals but are required to have identical studies and pass the same materials at the same rate, or they are deemed failures, regardless of their circumstances.

Thirty-five years ago, it was argued that bureaucratic structuralization had extended from the competitive marketplace to the professions (DiMaggio & Powell, 1983). Since then, schools, and the field of education, have continued to operate as bureaucratic structures and have become even more homogenous, not adapting to unique and diverse environmental demands. In other words, macro-level systems have been put in place without taking into consideration the diverse characteristics at the micro-level, such as individual schools, communities, and families. This *institutional isomorphism* may not be driven with a goal toward organizational efficiency, or use of best practice, but rather, they may be driven by coercive, mimetic, and normative processes (DiMaggio & Powell, 1983). For example, schools are increasingly having demands placed on them from the outside, which hinders their ability and initiative to adapt and be reflexive. Conversely, districts repeatedly have mandates put on them from the state forcing them to align with some standard, thus making both districts and schools more homogenous. When these external sources have the power to dictate the narrative and the mandates, decision making at the lower levels is compromised. According to neo-institutional policy research, organizations may increasingly be concerned with goals of power rather than efficiency, and arguably, best practice (Dockweiler, Putney, & Jordan, 2015).

In the school setting, this isomorphism and lack of adaptive responsiveness poses new challenges for school leaders. The MTSS program is a valiant effort to teach differentiated curriculum to real students, and administrators can promote this institutional shift through adopting MTSS practices that are designed and evaluated by the LIQUID Model standards, to have the most positive impact on a school's culture. *Neo-institutional theory* is a sociopolitical lens in which to view how organizations interact and how they impact society. Understanding that while schools may operate as bureaucratic structures, empowering school leaders to engage autonomously, shifts the paradigm away from homogenous decision making to individual decision making on behalf of students. One way to support responsiveness to environmental and individual student demands is through establishing an MTSS program.

Using a team-based model of decision-making, four necessary components of MTSS programs will be reviewed in-depth: appraisal of the team's multiple tiers of support, human capital support, data-based decision making, and collaborative problem solving (Sprick, 2013, 2009; Shinn & Walker, 2010; Shinn, 2007). These four components must be underscored by administrative backing and are essential to maintaining efficacy and quality control of an MTSS program.

Multiple Tiers of Support Appraisal

Using a tiered support system can make it difficult for a team to determine where to focus its efforts. With Tier 1 universal instruction, Tier 2 targeted instruction, and Tier 3 intensive instruction, where does a team start? Many school teams believe it makes sense to start with Tier 3 because that is where the neediest students are who require the most intense instructional and behavioral supports. If a team has a strong, established MTSS foundation and a history of success with the tiers, this may be an appropriate place to begin. However, for the majority of teams, they have not reached this level of efficiency and quality control and will need to focus their efforts at the bottom of the triangular framework first with Tier 1.

Universal screening, benchmarking, progress monitoring, and rate of improvement are central tenants of a multi-tiered support system. *Universal screening* is administered to all students to determine their current level of performance in any given domain. *Benchmarking* is conducted at set intervals throughout the year to provide a snapshot of a student's performance. *Progress monitoring* is conducted at regular intervals, such as monthly or weekly, to build into the overall portfolio of student progress in response to the interventions provided. *Rate of improvement* is the student's actual rate of improvement and is contrasted against a goal rate of improvement to make decisions about adequacy of progress. For more detailed explanations of each component, and how to conduct them, it is encouraged that explicit practitioner texts be consulted.

Many assessments use a normal distribution to determine student performance with standard deviations representing how significant a student's deficits or strengths are. The greater the deviation below the mean, the greater the need for intensive interventions. The greater the deviation above the mean, the greater the need for enrichment opportunities. For representation purposes, the estimations presented within each tier are based on percentile performance along the normal curve. In doing so, students can easily be divided based on benchmark assessments to determine the requisite level of instructional intensity needed to accomplish core curriculum success and credit requirements. Depending on a student's performance (see Figure 2.1), they will fall within Tier 1, Tier 2, or Tier 3 (Shinn, 2007).

Data consistently supports that students who fall above the 25th percentile will respond well to universal Tier 1 instruction. The majority of students respond to universal evidence-based classroom instruction provided within the general education setting and will not require more intensive supports. These students typically fall above the 25th percentile on benchmark assessments such as

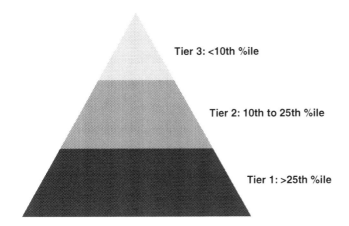

Tier 3: <10th %ile

Tier 2: 10th to 25th %ile

Tier 1: >25th %ile

Figure 2.1 Multiple Layers of Support.

AIMSweb (Pearson, 2015). Each tier represents a layer of instruction, and at Tier 1, students only receive one layer: high-quality universal core curriculum.

Some students require Tier 2 targeted instruction to ensure success in the general education setting. Students who fall below the 25th percentile on benchmark assessments may be appropriate for Tier 2 interventions based on team decision criteria (Shinn, 2007). These students benefit from weekly intervention and monthly progress monitoring to measure response to the interventions provided. These Tier 2 interventions should transpire for a specific number of minutes a week outside the core curriculum, for example 180 minutes, and with a student to teacher ratio of approximately 6:1. At Tier 2, students receive two layers of instruction: high-quality universal core curriculum and small group intervention.

A very small portion of students require Tier 3 intensive, individualized academic instruction provided in a specially designed intervention setting. These students fall below the 10th percentile on benchmark assessments such as AIMSweb (Pearson, 2015). Students who fall within Tier 3 benefit from intensive instruction with a teacher *in addition to* Tier 2 interventions *and* the core curriculum, with progress monitoring occurring weekly. These Tier 3 interventions are recommended to occur for a specific number of minutes, for example 90 minutes weekly, outside Tier 1 and Tier 2 with a student to teacher ratio of approximately 3:1. At Tier 3, students receive three layers of instruction: high-quality universal core curriculum, small group intervention, and intensive instruction.

Many urban secondary schools are not going to start with the traditional 75 percent of students in Tier 1, 20 percent of students in Tier 2, and 5 percent of students in Tier 3. This 75–20–5 triangle model is more realistic for schools who have established MTSS programs or who have lower-risk student populations. For many high-risk schools starting out, it is not unrealistic to have more of a 25–50–25 diamond model. No matter what model a team is driving, they can still have a successful journey and reach their MTSS goal destination.

A shift in distribution from a 25–50–25 diamond model, or 10–40–50 upside-down triangle model, to a 75–20–5 triangle model requires creative and persistent changes over time, and will continue to require incremental growth. Depending on the needs of a school and the demographics of their student population, a traditional triangle model may be too high a goal. In these extreme high-risk schools, a 33–34–33 rectangle model may be more realistic and sustainable.

Through leadership fidelity checks (Chapter 4) and program assessment and feedback looping (Chapter 11), teams must continuously use formative and summative measures to evaluate the effectiveness of their MTSS implementation. The Voices from the Field boxes illustrate examples of schools which have made incremental changes to shift the weighted distribution of their model to increase student success at Tier 1 through ongoing reflection and analysis. Some of these examples include bolstering Tier 1 universal instruction through intensive teacher trainings in effective instructional practices, providing continuous subject-level collaboration opportunities for teachers, funding intervention resources and teaching positions, and investing in human capital.

For teams who are unsure of the functional aspects of how to set goals, how to deliver an intervention lesson, how to progress monitor, and how to record progress monitoring data, it is suggested that further resources be sought. While this book will provide teams with the macro-operational aspects of how to implement MTSS in secondary schools, it does not delve into the micro-functional aspects of how to deliver the specific interventions at each tier. Both the high-level operational components and the more minute functional components are essential to MTSS program success.

All things considered, progress monitoring data should demonstrate a growth trajectory that suggests a student is on track to closing their achievement gap. Students in Tier 1 who do not receive additional supports are typically able to achieve one year of academic growth per year. Students in Tier 2 and Tier 3 need aggressive goals and their target rate of improvement should be up to twice the typical growth rate of Tier 1 students. If a student does not respond adequately to Tier 3 supports (as demonstrated by a poor rate of learning and a low level of performance) over time, and the team suspects the presence of a disability, the MTSS team will submit the referral for special education testing to the Multidisciplinary Evaluation Team.

MTSS teams must ensure that they are diligent about their intervention implementation and documentation which ensures quality control, as special education law requires documentation of research-based interventions and response to instruction data prior to identification of some educational disabilities. Through embodiment of the LIQUID Model, MTSS teams will not view Tier 3 as a track to special education eligibility. Students in Tier 3 require substantial resources to be successful, and some of these students may eventually qualify for special education support. However, teams must also consider exclusionary factors as part of their decision making so they are not contributing to the over-identification of students in special education. Teams should strive for quality control to avoid this over-identification of students, particularly minority students and English language learners (Kincaid & Sullivan, 2017; Sullivan, 2011). Historically, these are two groups that are consistently overrepresented in special education.

In education, social justice isn't just about validating cultural beliefs and acknowledging different holidays and traditions. Conceptual clarity for what a socially just education system looks like is needed and can lead to better policy making with fewer inequities for students (Francis, Mills, & Lupton, 2017). Education has the potential to be the true equalizer and to provide unlimited opportunity for all. Yet not all children have access to high-quality instruction, or high-quality instructors who understand individualized differences and have the tools, resources, and systemic support to have inclusive classrooms. Justice is when all children, from all different backgrounds, regardless of socioeconomic background, belong in a school community and have access to a relevant education. *All* students would benefit from individualized growth plans, quite frankly, not just the ones who are low performers, who are from low socioeconomic backgrounds, or who have special needs.

Box 2.1

Voice from the Field

My principal at Jackson Middle School implemented a successful MTSS program. After our initial construction of structures, functions, and processes to support the model, our principal realized through data analysis that Tier 1 instruction was clearly not effective in our 6th grade English Language Arts (ELA). A byproduct of the lack of quality teaching at Tier 1 created stress on supports needed for a greater number of students in Tiers 2 and 3. Our principal knew that our 6th grade students were suffering from a lack of quality basic instruction in ELA and would fall further behind without corrective action. After evaluating the curriculum, he took steps to replace outdated instructional tools with newer research-based curriculum that supported best practices. Ultimately, the 6th grade ELA teachers who did not respond adequately to training efforts to improve their instructional delivery were transferred to other positions. More effective teachers replaced less effective teachers. Results the following school year supported the shake-down and build-up of the new 6th grade ELA team through outcome data, which demonstrated administrative commitment to providing quality instruction universally to all students.

Human Capital Support

The second component of a successful MTSS program is human capital support. Sometimes school leaders must take drastic measures to impact outcomes and, most likely, those measures will impact teachers' performance. If school leadership is strong, the curriculum is solid, and achievement is not improving as evidenced by evaluation data, then the scrutiny, and bulk of administrative support, must be placed on teaching practices. The important take-away is that a school *must* evaluate Tier 1 instruction, curriculum tools, and efficacy of implementation before it can be determined whether a student is failing. *It may be the established system that is failing the student.*

Let's extrapolate the 75–20–5 triangle model to instructional supports for teachers. Teachers are similar to students in that they also require supports to varying degrees in order to be successful in the classroom (McCarthy, Lambert, Lineback, Fitchett, & Baddouh, 2015; Meyer & Behar-Horenstein, 2015). Factors such as their background, education level, and innate ability to differentiate their instruction, will all impact the type and intensity of supports a teacher will require to teach successfully within a school with MTSS. The triangle ideal probably does not hold true for teachers-as-learners in many schools, especially in lower income, high-risk schools that are harder to staff with highly qualified teachers, which typically have a high percentage of substitute teachers or teachers with limited experience. Depending on the composition of a school's teachers, the distribution of teacher supports may more closely resemble a 33–34–33 rectangle model or 25–50–25 diamond model.

Box 2.2

Voice from the Field

When we began using an MTSS model at Park Middle School, about half of the teachers were able to support and work with the model right off the bat. With clear expectations explained by our administrator, and some convincing to "buy in," many teachers were motivated to change their instructional practices to meet all students' needs. These teachers were willing to modify their practices because they were highly competent and always willing to try different things to improve their teaching. These teachers were motivated to access additional supports for their students and were engaging in reflective and reflexive practices. About a quarter of teachers needed some targeted trainings, additional supervisor support, high ratio of positive reinforcement, and convincing to "buy in" because they either lacked skills, motivation, or both. That left about a quarter of the teaching staff requiring intensive instructions and explicit demands from their supervising administrators before they put effort into differentiating instruction, implementing instruction with integrity, or "buying-in" to the school plan of multi-tiered supports. The attitude of these teachers was difficult to change. They largely believed that *they* did not have to change, the *students* had to change. Such perceptions were unrealistic and unproductive and did not serve the students, teachers, or school well.

In order to see change and success, the perception of educators as teaching the curriculum must shift to a paradigm of teaching curriculum to *real* students, with *real* challenges. Our schools are filled with students living with issues of poverty, food insecurity, homelessness, abuse, parental abandonment, addiction, trauma, and worse. One size does not fit all, in any scenario, and a differentiated model of support is essential. Teachers have taken over extended roles in society because of students' lack of access to basic needs, health care, mental health support, involved parenting, positive role models, and quality emotional support. Collectively, teachers are required to be more than teachers.

Teachers are learning to make data-based decisions to impact their quality of instruction on a daily basis. For many of our students, these decisions may include referrals to community-based agencies to support students in their homes in order to obtain basic needs such as food, housing, mental health, and medical care. *Basic needs are the true Tier 1 of appropriate instruction because if food, housing, and health security are not addressed, more intensive interventions will be much less effective.* In schools that have a large population of students without access to basic needs, a logical step would be for those schools to engage community partnerships to fill the void for those students and families (VanWynsberghe & Herman, 2015).

Changing human behavior is not an easy task and school professionals are no different. Research on the psychology of organizational change in education repeatedly demonstrates that behavioral change of teachers is challenging, hard to enforce, and even more difficult to measure as successful (VanWynsberghe & Herman, 2015; Hanson, 2003). Some schools might have amazing talent and have all highly adept and adaptable teachers who will make the transition from maintaining few supports to actively working toward comprehensive supports without skipping a beat when directions change. Transitioning adult behavior collectively in a common cause of comprehensive supports for all students in a secondary school is not likely to happen without bumps in the road. In utilizing this book, and the exercises embedded within, teams will be well on their way to successfully gliding over the potholes on their journey ahead.

Data-Based Decision Making

The third component of a successful MTSS program is data-based decision making. In reviewing the tiered model, data-based decision making must start with Tier 1. Universal instruction at Tier 1 is the cornerstone of a tiered support model and is the place to begin laying a foundation. Otherwise, how can the efficacy of Tier 2 and Tier 3 instruction be evaluated when universal instruction is not being provided with fidelity? There are five imperative steps administrators must take to ensure fidelity of Tier 1 practices.

1. Review the research regarding highly effective curriculum to ensure that Tier 1 instruction is based on best practices.
2. Ensure that curriculum is being implemented with integrity and fidelity. If a holistic program sequences lessons, ensure that the lessons are being delivered in order as prescribed.
3. Establish opportunities for staff to be engaged in continuous professional learning to keep teachers abreast of best practices and provide opportunities for guided practice.
4. Provide continuous collaborative opportunities for subject level planning with a constant feedback loop to the school's leadership team.
5. Monitor teachers through observations and administrative conferences to get feedback about curriculum, assessment, and instruction.

If the foundation of universal instruction is not solid, these five criteria will need to be reassessed and addressed to ensure they meet the standards of stable and quality Tier 1 instruction. If it has been determined that the established Tier 1 universal curriculum is evidence-based and is being implemented with fidelity, and students are still failing, what is next?

If the problems do not lie with administrative support, engagement, or reinforcement of teachers implementing Tier 1 instruction with fidelity, the next step is to examine processes and procedures. Are the wheels spinning but the car is not moving? How do students access the best opportunities to obtain targeted and intensive instruction through Tier 2 and Tier 3? The answers depend on the leadership, resources, and staffing available at individual schools. *Limitations must be viewed as opportunities, not challenges, to help shift the mindset of the school.* Schools may face many opportunities including those of funding, team creativity, and minimizing staff resistance toward change. While a portion of the staff will be resistant, overcoming resistance provides the administrator with an opportunity to clearly outline the vision, set explicit expectations, establish open lines of communication with staff, and establish a system of continuous improvement.

Collaborative Problem Solving

The final component of a successful MTSS program is collaborative problem solving. *Effective MTSS programs rely on constant, iterative problem-solving cycles that involve the talents of a variety of team members and stakeholders.* These smart MTSS organizations share hard and soft knowledge school year to school year with new team members through "written record, organizational culture, socialization, in-service training, and imitation" (Hanson, 2003, p. 290). Hard knowledge is categorized by the processes, programs, and structures ingrained in an organization. Soft knowledge includes the values, perspectives, and attitudes of the organization's members. This evolving organizational memory is strengthened by constant reflection and review of how to improve both hard and soft knowledge.

Administrators must build relationships with their leadership team and staff for successful problem solving and collaboration. The speed and success in making inroads to achieve this often depends on the school climate, which is most often driven by the school principal. On a school campus, there are several established social systems, some formal and some informal (Hanson, 2003). The MTSS team operates as a formal social system while the group of teachers who walks together at lunch is an informal social system. Depending on the social system, the approach for obtaining buy-in and collaboration may differ. Regardless of the approach, this is a prime opportunity for the administrator to build the school climate around supportive MTSS practices.

For a secondary school wishing to implement a multi-tiered support system, the first question to ask is, what are the bare essential elements of MTSS that can be established most quickly and effectively? The answer to that question depends on the administrator's commitment to implementation, the school's population, and various risk factors a school faces. It also depends on the status of the team with regard to the four required components of an MTSS program: multiple tiers of support appraisal, human capital support, data-based decision making, and collaborative problem solving.

When it is broached to school staff that it will be implementing an MTSS program, many questions arise. Common questions include:

- How can multiple layers of support be built in schools?
- Which assessment tools do teams use to assess growth?
- How often are students assessed?
- How do students access the layers of support at the school?
- When do teams make data-based decisions?

- How do teams decide when there is enough intervention data to refer a student to the multidisciplinary team for special education evaluation and support?
- How does the collaborative problem solving approach work?

Patience is requested of teams as the problem solving processes evolve. As the MTSS program is built, discussion points are brought up to administrators and their leadership teams to begin addressing the various opportunities on their campuses. There are several common steps in a classical decision-making process (Hanson, 2003, pp. 63–64):

1. Recognize, define, and situate the problem in relation to program goals.
2. Analyze and evaluate the problem.
3. Establish criteria and standards by which a solution will be evaluated or judged as acceptable and adequate to the need.
4. Define the alternatives.
5. Collect data on each alternative.
6. Apply evaluative criteria to each alternative.
7. Select the preferred choice.
8. Implement the choice.
9. Evaluate the results.

Starting Points

Before delving into meaty questions, some basics will be addressed to help drive solutions, which will depend on the risk-level and needs of a school. The needs of each school and the student population will determine the level of support structure needed. Every school is unique and each will require a differentiated approach within the tiered paradigm. Low socioeconomic schools experience challenges associated with poverty. Students in higher socioeconomically advantaged schools most often have their basic needs met but also have the challenges faced by all students, such as learning problems, social and behavioral problems, mental health issues, trauma, and family issues that require supports and interventions. When generalizing risk factors, schools greatly require structures to be in place to systematically evaluate and monitor students' academic and behavioral achievement, and support a decrease in the likelihood of recidivism (Taskiran, Mutluer, Tufan, & Semerci, 2017; McKee & Caldarella, 2016; Barrett & Katsiyannis, 2015). Effective instruction has to fit the needs of community as well as the classroom population.

The School Risk Assessment Survey (SRAS) can be used by school teams to determine where their school falls along the risk continuum: high, medium, or low (see Figure 2.2). This informal survey is used as a reference to get an idea of the general need and risk-level of the school. At this time, school leaders will want to complete the SRAS.

The SRAS can be used by school teams to determine where their school falls along the risk continuum: high, medium, or low. In general, if the school community identifies with 1–5 of these challenges, the school is probably in the low-risk category. If the school community identifies with 6–11 of these factors, the

School Risk Assessment Survey

Put a checkmark next to all of the risk factors below evident in your school building and circle the corresponding risk level.

_____ Poverty   _____ Second language factors

_____ Hunger   _____ Low funding for education

_____ Transience   _____ Student safety

_____ Absenteeism   _____ Teacher burn-out rate

_____ Family involvement   _____ Negative school culture

_____ Family issues   _____ Learning problems

_____Student motivation   _____ Social/behavioral problems

_____ Overcrowded classrooms   ——— Developmental issues

_____ Teaching quality   _____ Community risk factors

Low-risk	Medium-risk	High-risk
1–5 factors	6–11 factors	12+ factors

Figure 2.2 School Risk Assessment Survey.

school is probably in the medium-risk category. If the school community identi-fies with 12 or more of these risk factors, it is probably safe to say that the school can count itself in the high-risk category. Keep in mind that there are always high-risk students in low-risk and medium-risk schools, and vice versa.

Why does it matter how many risk factors a school has when determining the needs of its students? _High-needs students need higher levels of support to succeed as a matter of equity._ Higher-needs schools require team processes that consist of more manpower, more resources, and more data to make better decisions. Higher-needs schools face more opportunities to remediate skill deficits. Lower-needs schools have fewer students in need, but make no mistake, they still require checks and balances to support low-achieving students. Teachers should be able to access supports to help high-needs students, regardless of the socioeconomic status of the school. The more immediately school teams can identify student needs and put interventions in place, the better chance the students have to improve and become successful learners and, ultimately, independent successful adults. Most teams already have a general idea about the implementation challenges they face. But, again, the barriers must be properly identified and be viewed as opportunities if there is any chance of overcoming them.

Change from the bottom up has some advantages and may come in the form of increasing teacher leadership on a small scale or helping a targeted number of students. There are instances where grassroots efforts lead by teachers at the bottom have garnered attention from administration and resulted in lasting systemic change. These grassroots efforts lead to high levels of buy-in from staff that is essential to the change process (Pinkelman et al., 2015). However, lasting school change is most likely to occur from the top down through strategic opportunism (Isenberg, 1987). *Strategic opportunism* is a term borrowed from the business world that simply means the leader is able to adhere to the long-term vision, for example higher student achievement, while remaining flexible enough in the short-term to take advantage of opportunities that arise to support and help meet the long-term vision, for example implementing a model of support consisting of multiple tiers.

The most significant change in the educational practices at a school will not occur through democracy, unfortunately. *Change will require the focused leadership of the school principal who can make decisions for the entire school staff and who can ensure change with guided enforcement and implementation of policies.* The administrator will make things happen through scaffolding, supervision, and evaluation of staff and programs. If a team would like to implement an MTSS framework but the school principal is not willing to take leadership, or at the very least support a team of leaders, there are two choices: wait until the principal is convinced and is on board, or accept the fact that the team's best efforts may result in limited cultural change. In this case, teams can reframe the restricted support as an opportunity to collect data through a pilot study, by improving professional learning opportunities, or helping a small number of students at a time.

Exercise 2.1

MTSS Team Development Mirror Exercise

At this point in the process, the individual or team of individuals driving the MTSS initiatives on a campus will want to complete the MTSS Team Development Mirror Exercise. This exercise is a recommendation for you to look in the mirror. You are the first step in your school's change by picking up this book and using it to guide your actions in regards to implementing a multi-tiered support system at your school. As you look in the mirror ask yourself if are you the only one in the picture that desires this change at your school and who else believes it's a good idea. If you are the leader at your school, and you're standing alone in that mirror, then know that you are going to have to cultivate and train a team of people that can help you attain your vision for your school. If you are a motivated educator, such as an assistant principal, dean, teacher, specialist, or school psychologist, and the primary administrator is not standing in that mirror next to you when you look at the reflection, then understand that your vision has a much smaller chance of obtaining fruition in a natural timeline. The more engaged and motivated the primary administrator, the greater the likelihood of MTSS programming success.

- Look in the mirror and describe what you see. Use kind words to describe yourself.
- Close your eyes and think about what your intentions are for your school. Set your intentions in simple sentences in your mind (i.e., I want to improve achievement or I want to improve school-wide behavior). Make it global in nature and decide what you want. Now open your eyes and speak your intentions to yourself, as in a mirror. Write your intentions down.
- Be honest with yourself. Why do you want those things listed above? Do you have a passion for teaching? Helping children? Do you enjoy leading? Are you seeking experience for a promotion? Think about your own motives because self-awareness will help you keep your eyes on the big picture and help you understand how to motivate others to join your vision.
- List your motives now. Reflect how your motives will benefit students and teachers.
- Think about who else shares your intentions at your school. List the names of personnel and staffing positions at your school who you are certain share your intent already and have the skill set to help you pull it off. This list will seed your decision-making team.
- Who is missing? List the people or staffing positions missing from above list that you want or need to be on board your team.
- Why aren't those staff members backing you? What do you think you can do to get the missing staff members to buy in? Other questions you may want to answer could include: Who is the biggest obstacle to change in attitude and/or practice? Who has a strong voice on your campus who could help you win over others? Who do you need to win over first?

After the MTSS Team Development Mirror Exercise Form has been completed, leaders will have a detailed vision of the intent for their school and they will know who shares, and does not share, that intent. Leaders may rejoice in knowing that their intentions are clear. Knowing where the train is going and who is on board is half the battle. The people who are not on board or yet convinced of leaders' intentions are going to know how much of a priority those intentions are as they are empowered and tasked with specific team functions and asked to delineate processes to meet the needs of all students. Leaders must continually reflect on their intentions and who will help them reach the goals by actively overcoming hurdles to the finish line.

Set this list aside for later reference.

Exercise 2.2

Evaluate Leadership Commitment to the Process

The first question administrators who are implementing, or who are considering implementing, a multi-tiered support system in their school should ask themselves is how important is it to them? Is this something they really believe will help their students?

On a scale of 1–10, how important is implementing a multi-tiered support system at your school?

Not Important	1	2	3	4	5	6	7	8	9	10	Very important

How can you increase your commitment, motivation, and dedication to implementing MTSS? Additional awareness to lend comfort? Diversifying the skill sets of educators on staff to enhance effectiveness? Increasing personal knowledge and professional development of MTSS?

Teacher Effectiveness

All professionals on a school campus have strengths and weaknesses. The leaders and experts in one subject may not be the ones selected to lead and guide practice in another. For this exercise, think about the strengths of the teachers on campus, with 1 being those teachers with the most opportunity to grow and 10 being the most accomplished teachers. Consider who needs to be on the MTSS leadership decision-making team, and think of at least two teachers per grade level, in addition to specialists, who can serve as leaders in decision making. The level of importance for implementing MTSS in a school should match with the level of teacher strength on the team. If a principal estimates the importance of MTSS at a high level, between 7 and 10, then he or she should match the skill level of teachers on the decision-making team with the importance level of the system. If the team is stacked with teachers in the 3 to 4 level range, that probably is the highest level of quality in results the team will get.

If school leaders believe they get what they pay for then why would they put less accomplished teachers on such an important committee that will shape instructional practices and culture at their school? While it is easy to burn out the best teachers with multiple functions, it is crucial to stack the MTSS team with competence from the start. Less accomplished teachers can get up to speed after MTSS is running well, but schools will need the best problem solvers on their MTSS team, especially at first. If administrators think that this committee has an importance level of 7 or above, they cannot afford to assign less accomplished teachers.

If the leadership team believes MTSS to have an importance level of 7 or above, then they need to assign committee members with a ranking of 7 and above to the team. *Pick your top performers, best thinkers, and best problem solvers on the team.* Go ahead, select the 9 and 10 level teachers for the team. They are role models and leaders for the whole school. They know how much work it is to do what they are asking other teachers to do, and they do exemplary work, going above and beyond with students, and with a positive attitude. The problem with picking the best teachers and problem solvers to be on this team is they are often over-used and inundated with doing all the work on campus that others cannot or will not do (i.e., all the little pet projects that need to get done along with some quasi-administrative responsibilities), as well as all the other things they volunteer to do to make the school days run smoothly for students. This committee commitment really has to be the most important in terms of extra duties outside of the classroom that those teachers have because it is very time consuming. In order to build capacity and sustainability of MTSS, all teachers on campus must feel supported and be given opportunities to improve their skills within the MTSS framework. Without this growth, the teacher leaders on campus will burn out and the entire system will falter.

Exercise 2.3

- Who are your strongest (e.g., levels 7, 8, 9, and 10) teachers by grade level and/or subject?
- Who are your specialists? What are their positions? Are they on board with MTSS?
- Are the people listed in this exercise many of the same listed on Exercise 1 that share your vision? Why or why not? How can relationships between stakeholders improve to get buy-in?

Combine your responses from Exercises 2.1 through 2.3. Review the School Risk Assessment Survey results and begin problem solving. Organize the list by grade level, with at least two teachers per grade level, and try to have math and ELA subject levels represented as well. These are the staff members who will require training and administrative support to plan the structure and function of MTSS at your school. Congratulations! You have an MTSS team. Now you have to convince them of their power to lead this endeavor and train them in the basic duties and responsibilities of leading this extremely important school improvement team. You have committed your best resources to the team in form of human capital, now show your commitment to the team and the rest of the school community.

References

Anyon, Y., Nicotera, N., & Veeh, C. A. (2016). Contextual influences on the implementation of a schoolwide intervention to promote students' social, emotional, and academic learning. *Children & Schools, 38*(2), 81–88.

Barrett, D. E., & Katsiyannis, A. (2015). Juvenile delinquency recidivism: Are Black and White youth vulnerable to the same risk factors? *Behavioral Disorders, 40*(3), 184–195.

Colter, W. A., & Gibbons, K. A. (2018, February). *Creating thirsty horses: Three keys to increasing implementation fidelity.* Paper session presented at the National Association of School Psychologists Annual Conference, Chicago, IL.

Cunliffe, R. H. (2017). Conflict resolution classrooms to careers: An emergent theory of change with implications for a strategy in peace education. *Journal of Peace Education, 14*(2), 235–252, doi:10.1080/17400201.2016.1278165.

DiMaggio, P. J., & Powell, W. W. (1983). The iron cage revisited: Institutional isomorphism and collective rationality in organizational fields. *American Sociological Review, 48*(2), 147–160.

Dockweiler, K. A., Putney, L. G., & Jordan, T. S. (2015). Enhancing the policy analysis process: Case studies using the Layers of Analysis Framework. *Journal of Ethnographic and Qualitative Research, 10*(4), 87–103.

Duffy, M. (2015). Education, democracy and social change: Venezuela's education missions in theory and practice. *Journal of Education Policy, 30*(5), 650–670, doi:10.1080/02680939.2014.981868.

Foorman, B. (2016). Introduction to the special issue: Challenges and solutions to implementing effective reading intervention in schools. In B. Foorman (Ed.), *Challenges to Implementing Effective Reading Intervention In Schools. New Directions for Child and Adolescent Development, 154,* 7–10.

Francis, B., Mills, M., & Lupton, R. (2017). Towards social justice in education: Contradictions and dilemmas. *Journal of Education Policy, 32*(4), 414–431.

Freeman, R., Miller, D., & Newcomer, L. (2015). Integration of academic and behavioral MTSS at the district level using implementation science. *Learning Disabilities: A Contemporary Journal, 13*(1), 59–72.

Goldmann, D. (2006). System failure versus personal accountability: The case for clean hands. *The New England Journal of Medicine, 355,* 121–123, doi:10.1056/NEJMp068118.

Guerro, E. G., Fenwick, K., & Kong, Y. (2017). Advancing theory development: Exploring the leadership-climate relationship as a mechanism of the implementation of cultural competence. *Implementation Science, 133,* 1–12, doi:10.1186/s13012-017-0666-9.

Hall, G. E., & Hord, S. M. (2006). *Implementing change: Patterns, principals, and potholes* (2nd ed.). New York: Pearson Education.

Hanson, M. (2003). *Educational administration and organizational behavior.* Boston, MA: Allyn & Bacon.

Isenberg, P. (1987, March). The tactics of strategic opportunism. *Harvard Business Review.* Retrieved from https://hbr.org/1987/03/the-tactics-of-strategic-opportunism.

Jimerson, S. R., Burns, M. K., & VanDerHeyden, A. M. (Eds.) (2016). *The handbook of response to intervention: The science and practice of multi-tiered systems of support.* New York: Springer.

Kincaid, A. P., & Sullivan, A. L. (2017). Parsing the relations of race and socioeconomic status in special education disproportionality. *Remedial and Special Education, 38*(3), 159–170.

Ladd, H. F., & Fiske, E. B. (Eds.) (2008). *Handbook of research in education finance and policy.* New York: Routledge.

Lane, K. L., Carter, E. W., Jenkins, A., Dwiggins, L., & Germer, K. (2015). Supporting comprehensive, integrated, three-tiered models of prevention in schools: Administrators' perspectives. *Journal of Positive Behavior Interventions, 17*(4), 209–222.

McCarthy, C. J., Lambert, R. G., Lineback, S., Fitchett, P., & Baddouh, P. G. (2016). Assessing teacher appraisals and stress in the classroom: Review of the classroom appraisal of resources and demands. *Education Psychology Review, 28,* 577–603.

McKee, M. T., & Caldarella, P. (2016). Middle school predictors of high school performance: A case study of dropout risk indicators. *Education, 136*(4), 515–529.

Meyer, M. M., & Behar-Horenstein, L. S. (2015). When leadership matters: Perspectives from a teacher team implementing response to intervention. *Education and Treatment of Children, 38*(3), 383–402.

Naraian, S., & Oyler, C. (2014). Professional development for special education reform: Rearticulating the experiences of urban educators. *Urban Education, 49*(5), 499–527.

Pearson (2015). *AIMSweb software guide version 2.5.10.* Retrieved from https://aimsweb2.pearson.com/aimsweb-frontoffice/helpsupport/help/aimsweb_software_guide2510.pdf.

Pinkelman, S. E., McIntosh, K., Rasplica, C. K., Berg, T., & Strickland-Cohen, M. K. (2015). Perceived enablers and barriers related to sustainability of school-wide positive behavioral interventions and supports. *Behavioral Disorders, 40*(3), 171–183.

Pitt, D. P., & Aubin, J. M. (2012). Joseph Lister: Father of modern surgery. *Journal of Canadian Surgery, 55*(5), E8–E9, doi:10.1503/cjs.007112.

Quintero, E. (Ed.) (2017). *Teaching in context: The social side of education reform.* Cambridge, MA: Harvard Education Press.

Rodriguez, B. J., Loman, S. L., & Borgmeier, C. (2016). Tier 2 interventions in positive behavior support: A survey of school implementation. *Preventing School Failure: Alternative Education for Children and Youth, 60*(2), 94–105, doi:10.1080/1045988X.2015.1025354.

Shinn, M. R. (2007). Identifying students at risk, monitoring performance, and determining eligibility within RTI: Research on educational need and benefit from academic intervention. *School Psychology Review, 36*(4), 601–617.

Shinn, M. R., & Walker, H. M. (Eds.) (2010). *Interventions for academic and behavior problems in a three-tier model, including Response-to-Intervention* (3rd ed.). Bethesda, MD: National Association of School Psychologists.

Sprick, R. A. (2009). *CHAMPS: A proactive and positive approach to classroom management* (2nd ed.). Eugene, OR: Pacific Northwest Publishing.

Sprick, R. A. (2013). *Discipline in the secondary classroom: A positive approach to behavior management* (3rd ed.). Hoboken, NJ: John Wiley & Sons.

Sullivan, A. L. (2011). Disproportionality in special education identification and placement of English language learners. *Exceptional Children, 77*(3), 317–334.

Taskiran, S., Mutluer, T., Tufan, A. E., & Semerci, B. (2017). Understanding the associations between psychosocial factors and severity of crime in juvenile delinquency: A cross-sectional study. *Neuropsychiatric Disease and Treatment, 13*, 1359–1366.

VanWynsberghe, R., & Herman, A. C. (2015). Education for social change and pragmatist theory: Five features of educative environments designed for social change. *International Journal of Lifelong Education, 34*(3), 268–283, doi:10.1080/02601370.2014.988189.

Wilson, H. W. (2014). *The reference shelf: Embracing new paradigms in education.* Amenia, NY: Grey House Publishing.

Woolley, A. W., Chabris, C. F., Pentland, A., Hashmi, N., & Malone, T. W. (2010). Evidence for a collective intelligence factor in the performance of human groups. *Science, 330*(6004), 686–688.

World Health Organization (2009). *WHO guidelines on hand hygiene in health care: First global patient safety challenge clean care is safer care.* Geneva, Switzerland: Author.

Chapter 3

Invest in Resources at Your School

Key Terms

Education Malpractice
Controlled Chaos
Fidelity
Access
Overcorrection
Growth Model
Three-Pronged Motivation Approach
Triangulating

Chapter Concepts

In this chapter, readers will learn:

1. The current realities facing today's education field.
2. The need for a shift in the social perspective of an educator's value.
3. The critical need for proactive and adequate allocation of fiscal resources.
4. The benefit of evidence-based assessment tools for universal benchmarking and progress monitoring.
5. The importance of data-based decision making and how to triangulate data sources.
6. The demand for research-based interventions and fidelity of implementation.

In this chapter, the realities of today's education field will be discussed, as well as the need to shift the social perspective of educators' value. The critical resources of fiscal allocation, assessment tools, data-based decision making, and research-based interventions are also examined. This chapter "gets real" about current teaching conditions, including socioeconomic challenges, outdated compensation and professional learning systems, and the unrealistic expectations and demands that are often placed on teachers' time (Preiss, 2015; Wilson, 2014; Odden & Picus, 2014; Odden, 2012; Ladd & Fiske, 2008). The demands placed on educators have increased over the past decade due to the continued growth of the accountability movement and the expanding needs of our students, but the infrastructure to support these professionals have remained stagnant.

Social perceptions of the teaching field are discussed and current shifts are presented that support the modernization and elevation of the teaching profession, led by the efforts of the 40 "TeachStrong" coalition partners, including but not limited to, the Center for American Progress, Teach for America, The Education Trust, ASCD, Council of Chief State School Officers, Learning Forward, and the National Board for Professional Teaching Standards (Preiss, 2015). This coalition focuses on research and supports nine campaign principles to strengthen the entire teaching continuum, including the highest set of rigorous standards for accomplished teaching, National Board Certification, as developed by the National Board for Professional Teaching Standards (National Board for Professional Teaching Standards, 2016a; Preiss, 2015; Layton, 2015; Martin, Partelow, & Brown, 2015; Sawchuk, 2015; Ladd & Fiske, 2008). Leveraging relationships with stakeholders will be introduced with further discussion included in Chapter 12.

Realities of Today's Education Field

Working within the field of education is a noble endeavor. Whether serving as a teacher, school psychologist, school nurse, teacher's aide, or in any other capacity, these professionals dedicate their lives to improving the quality of life for students, communities, and society. Educators invest in their own educational and professional learning throughout their careers costing them much of their hard-earned income. Many endure economic hardships themselves including paying back student loans, surviving student-teaching and internship experiences for little to no pay, and existing at barely a living wage at the bottom of a school district's pay scale for years before reaching a minimum economic comfort level. Political climates impact teachers' daily functions depending on the emphasis of the day, whether that be high-stakes testing, mandatory Common Core State Standards (2010) instruction, or negative media bias regarding the education establishment in general or teachers' job security and benefits specifically. Teachers are often among the best role models in a child's life. Teachers help our children learn, guide them through critical thinking development, and nurture them through their formative years. Almost everyone can think of a teacher or caring adult at school who changed their lives for the better; one who deserves great praise.

Of course, there are also less effective educators. In all professions, there are individuals with uncertain intentions and lower expertise. In addition to less effective educators, there are ineffective practices that negatively impact children. There is no excuse for individual educators' apathy, malpractice, or outright abuse in the workplace. Case in point: states that allow legal corporal punishment in schools and allow adults in education to engage in abusive and harmful practices toward children. Institutionalized abuse has negative consequences that can last a lifetime for students. Some of these professionals can be rehabilitated with the appropriate training. Still, there are educators who will continue to engage in education malpractice and are not able to transfer from punitive to proactive practices. Such individuals should be monitored closely in the presence of children and be encouraged to leave the profession, in accordance with employee contracts and state laws. *Education malpractice* is the preventable adverse impact on a student through educator negligence or incompetence that goes against evidence-based practices.

Corporal punishment is a longstanding social construct used to physically command obedience and respect from children (Freeman, 2010; Foucault, 1995). Forms of physical abuse have historically provided parents with legal protections; however, children have not been afforded the same protections should they return the abuse to their parents (Freeman, 2010). As early as 1641 it was recognized in the Massachusetts *Body of Liberties* that parents should not use excessive severity in the punishment of their children (Pleck, 2004). This same law also provided children the right to report to authorities any instances of excessive punishment. While this early recognition of children's rights is encouraging, there is no documented evidence that any complaints were made or cases heard (Pleck, 2004).

In the centuries that ensued, and as education systems evolved in the United States, this allowance and social acceptance of corporal punishment has extended to its use in classrooms by teachers and administrators. Historically and presently, evidence does not support that corporal punishment is an effective way to model desired prosocial behavior (Straus, 2010; Foucault, 1995). Indeed, international research confirms that corporal punishment causes a high degree of emotional harm to children, with the level of internalized behaviors, specifically anxiety and depression, directly correlated to the intensity of the abuse (Gershoff, 2010). The negative repercussions of harsh punishment include increased student behavioral problems, decreased academic achievement, clinical depression, trauma, and suicidal ideation, among other devastating impacts for children (Asghar, Munawar, Muhammad, 2015; Tong, Shinohara, Sugisawa, Tanaka, Watanabe, Koeda, & Anme, 2015).

Minority students and those with disabilities are disproportionately targeted with the harshest forms of discipline (Sparks & Harwin, 2016). In a socially just school culture, adults never destroy children's trust by hurting them physically and emotionally; without doubt, *the opposite must occur, with adults protecting children from hurt and guiding them during vulnerable years with care and purpose.* Concerned citizens should advocate against such practices by writing their congressional representatives and state legislators to have corporal punishment in schools outlawed in state policy. Educators practicing corporal punishment are not necessarily bad people, but may be habituated to horrific abuses. In such cases, the abuse has become normalized, but that does not make it acceptable. Intentionally inflicting pain on children for teaching purposes will *never* be a valid teaching method or ethical practice.

Moving away from educational practices that do not work, at best, and are harmful to students, at worst, teachers are under a lot of pressure to demonstrate measurable growth in their students. In some school districts, resources are scarce and their materials and technology are outdated due to budget constraints. In other districts, the constant mandating for updated curriculum, continual cycles of different types of testing, teacher documentation requirements, and school accountability reporting take up a staggering amount of teaching time that could be otherwise spent on meaningful learning activities. *Teachers must balance what they are mandated to do by state laws and district procedures, with what they need to do to reach all students.* Teachers must have access to appropriate tools and continuing opportunities to improve their teaching methods in order to increase positive outcomes for students.

Being an educator is hard work, arguably one of the hardest working professions. Educators have a future of modest pay, which is just the beginning of the challenges they will face along their career paths. For example, teachers might be expected to teach curriculum that may not be developmentally appropriate for their students, they may not have the preservice training, job support, or resources to adequately address student behavior difficulties, and they will have to accept varying levels of parent and community support. However, most educators are committed to improving the skills of their students. Some are more skilled than others at managing the demands for higher achievement in the classroom despite all the risk factors that impact achievement. Some educators prefer to work with students who have knowledge gaps or learning problems. Working with children who do not learn the prescribed way, or at the expected speed, requires creative adaptation to engage those learners and fill in those gaps. Some educators find those same students difficult to reach and are taxed by the amount of time and energy that must be devoted to the higher-needs students. Overcrowded classrooms, lack of adequate resources, and working over recommended ratios are also challenges to overcome. Educators are sometimes blamed, and receive negative consequences, as a result of poor student outcomes over which they had limited control. Despite all the difficulties, many educators still consider being an educator the best job in the world.

However, educators are people too, and they fulfill many life roles including parent, spouse, and caregiver for aging parent(s), in addition to roles and responsibilities in community service. They have busy lives with personal interests, projects, family duties, and health issues. Educators have a lot of responsibility, but not a lot of control over factors that impact students. Educators must manage their time wisely in order to have a life of their own and a successful career concurrently; a high percentage work multiple jobs to make ends meet. Many spouses and families will attest that their husband or wife, mom or dad, brings too much work home and spends too much time thinking about their students and work outside of work hours. Daily physical and emotional exhaustion can negatively impact an entire family unit. Educational leaders must be very cognizant of the realities of educators when asking them to do anything more or differently.

Exercise 3.1

Educator Challenges and Opportunities Survey

- Take a moment and reflect on the challenges educators at your school are likely to experience. Write them down and be as specific as possible.
- Write some possible solutions and supports that may help educators with those challenges.

Share these notes in discussion with the school's leadership team. Pick one issue at a time and address it with the school's staff. Try possible solutions and wait for feedback. Some issues are beyond quick fixes; however, if a listed problem has an obvious solution on your campus, make it happen as soon as feasible. *Positive results increase goodwill and trust, which goes a long way toward educator morale.*

Social Perspectives and Educator Value

Budgets are tight and job security is scarce in many school districts across the nation due to unreliable funding. Compounded by issues of teacher shortages, school psychologist shortages, and staffing difficulties in all education related professions, schools are grappling with how to adequately fill vacancies to meet the needs of its students. Nationwide, many of the large, at-risk school districts report significant shortage numbers. In the School District of Philadelphia there were 190 teaching positions open in the 2016–2017 school year (Yaffe, 2016), and in Clark County School District (Las Vegas, Nevada), the number of open teaching positions pushed 1,000 during that same time period (Gonser, 2016). In both districts, the shortages reported are a significant percentage of their local teaching force, which leave thousands of students without a licensed teacher. State Departments and individual school districts are devising creative strategies to address this chronic shortage through incentive programs, partnerships with local teacher training programs at colleges and universities, and hiring substitute teachers and non-licensed teachers (Gonser, 2016; Yaffee, 2016).

Teaching is a skill that cannot be approximated by only having knowledge of a subject matter. For example, just because someone knows how to read does not mean that person knows how to effectively teach reading to someone else, let alone to classes of 30 to 40 children. State and national educational policies attacking the teaching profession and replacing qualified licensed teachers with untrained individuals will not produce good outcomes for vulnerable children who desperately need strong teachers. Students benefit the most from highly trained and accomplished teachers (National Board for Professional Teaching Standards, 2016b).

Coast to coast there is also a shortage of school psychologists who can assist school teams and help implement evidence-based MTSS programs and support students' academic and mental-behavioral health needs (National Association of School Psychologists, 2017). Oftentimes, the ratio of school psychologist to students is as high as 1:3,500 (Nevada Association of School Psychologists, 2018), or five to seven times over the National Association of School Psychologists recommended ratio for comprehensive services of 1:500–700 (National Association of School Psychologists, 2010). Lack of sufficient training programs contributes to this shortage, as does the inadequate compensation in some districts, which makes recruitment in these districts near impossible. Districts that have the greatest numbers of high-risk students would benefit most from the expertise and professional services of more school psychologists and greater access to mental health services in schools. Technology will have to be a vital element of psychological services and mental health supports in rural school districts, which can telecommute many of these services to their schools with proper funding.

In looking at the value of teachers in society, popular media glorifies some professions over others. The professional athlete is one such occupation, which sends a message to children that the athlete is far more valued than the educator. This is evidenced by pay and social status and the various methods that the media uses to influence the public (Smith & Sanderson, 2015; Hathorn, 2013). It also leads some students to the faulty conclusion that education is not a valuable profession, and education in general is not worthwhile.

Some struggling students believe they do not need an education because they plan to be professional athletes. Teachers may try to educate the student about the realities of this plan by asking them how they are going to get on a professional team, let alone stay on one, if they don't come to practice or games on time (because they don't get to class on time or at all). In addition, the students with star-studded dreams often don't practice (do their homework), are never prepared (bring required equipment), and tend to put in very little effort with a bad attitude (poor behavior toward teachers and peers). These students must be told with honesty that their professional coach would fire them before they got in the game, no matter how much natural talent they had, because they are not team players and have poor work ethic. Teams count on each member of the team to do their part, and if a team member does not do his or her part, the coach will not let that person play on the team. Therefore, if past and current behavior are the best predictors of future behavior, how can students reasonably expect skill and discipline from themselves at a later date without putting effort into it now?

The same question could be asked about the future of education. If an investment in teachers is not made, in their training and ongoing professional learning and supports, how can they be expected to produce dividends in terms of successful teaching practices and positive educational outcomes for students? The short answer is that a plan that expects teachers to succeed without adequately preparing and supporting them will likely fail, just as the student expecting to become a professional athlete without putting in the discipline and team work will likely fail.

There must be a cultural shift to reject the ever-increasing burdens that educators are saddled with. Until the paradigm shifts away from requiring more work from teachers without adequate supports, teacher burnout will persist. Teachers principally leave the profession due to high emotional stress as a result of low supports. Society has perpetuated this injustice by accepting the present reality of increased work demands without increased support, at the expense of our teachers and students. Systemically, the field of education must rise in the esteem of the populace to break with the current model and replace it with one that justly supports the workers it employs. Adequate supports should be provided for all educators, and hard workers and strong performers in education should be rewarded. *School leaders can begin to shift the paradigm by fostering a culture of validation for quality work.*

Educators do a lot of extra work after school as it is. If school leadership is looking to start up a committee, especially on a middle school or high school campus, it must value the educators' time. Organizational demands and responsibilities of MTSS are not likely to get done during the school day because of teaching duties and other job requirements. No one really wants to hear that. The public often thinks educators should put in extra time out of the goodness of their hearts, and that extra work is just part of the job; however, lack of validation destroys educators' motivation and quality of effort over time. Either compensate educators' time after school, or decrease their teaching or work load during the day so they can work on their additional demands and responsibilities. Think of a scale, both sides must be in proportion in order for the scale to balance. If a salaried employee is compensated for eight hours on one side of the scale, the corresponding duties should balance on the other side. If the duties side becomes increasingly loaded, the compensation side should also have a proportionate quantity added to maintain the balance. A balance must be found between duties and compensation in order to maintain an appropriate and functional level of stress and to prevent teacher burnout.

Many, many educators suck it up and sacrifice their personal time for the greater good. Good bosses know that uncompensated work is not reasonable and leads to discontent and burnout, as does poor job training, poor organizational understanding, poor peer support, and limited forward career movement (Taormina & Law, 2000). A culture deprived of support and full of resentment must be avoided. Educators should be compensated for working additional hours past contract time on behalf of students. *Educators are trained professionals and should be compensated accordingly.* This point cannot be stressed enough. If there are grants or extra monies that can be (re)allocated for the MTSS team's additional work time, they should be paid for extra duty; or a way should be found to compensate their time if additional funds are not available. Adjust the school budget to make the most out of schools' most valuable assets: its educators. Schools must have basic supplies and technology; however, the adaptable, creative, and unlimited potential of educators can be more effective and a better investment than more computers or any other gadget. Bottom line: an educator actively solving problems for a student will always be that student's best resource.

It is extremely motivating for educators to earn more money or banked hours time for all the extra work that is required to make a multi-tiered support system model effective at a school. As important as it is to provide incentives and positive reinforcement to students, the same holds true for teachers and other educators who work with students. Educators frequently feel overburdened; many are not going to be thrilled to be on another committee, at least in the beginning. One-third of teachers leave the profession within the first five years because being a teacher is not easy (Farmer, 2017). Many of them will not be grateful for the extra burdens that go along with the team responsibilities of MTSS at first. It is important to remember that the workers experiencing the most emotional and occupational stress are going to burn out first (Farmer, 2017; Mérida-Lopez & Extremera, 2017). If administrators can somehow lighten educators' load in some way or give them extra duty pay, they must. It is the right thing to do and is a key element of the LIQUID Model, starting with leadership. Effective leaders equitably support and compensate workers. Supported educators are more likely to work harder with a more positive attitude, which falls under quality control because they are more likely to take greater pride in doing a good job and implementing best practices with integrity. Taking care of staff members creates a culture of taking care of everyone in the school community. Actively supporting educators also addresses inclusiveness and social justice because educators have the tools and training to teach all learners, and are motivated to teach all students, no matter how diverse their needs. Educators working in higher-needs schools should get paid more to work in communities with the most challenges in order to entice the strongest teachers to work in the most at-risk neighborhoods, giving students living in poverty access to the best educators and best chance to rise above their circumstances.

By adequately compensating educators, administrators will get what they pay for. Paying MTSS team members for their extra duties will increase the likelihood that they will give these important tasks the time, attention, and effort they require. If administrators expect educators to add more work to their day without compensation, the educators will squeeze it in somehow, but the quality of effort and the quality of outcomes will be pinched as well. Very few educators are not willing to work for extra pay. It is common sense. *As a society, the unrealistic expectation of more work for salaried employees without compensation must be part of the new paradigm shift.* Stop taking advantage of salaried educators. Educators deserve better, and so do students.

Another social shift that must happen in education is the negative perception that change equates to more work and could be a waste of time and effort. This thinking is not productive and is an opportunity for teacher-leaders to educate their peers about the positive impact of MTSS programs. The education leaders and change agents on campus are putting their necks on the line with their peers when asking them to make changes. Many educators don't like change, often perceive it as extra work, and may not be very appreciative or excited about the hard work to come. Planning and implementation of instructional supports requires change of minds, hearts, and practice.

Oftentimes, practice must change first, long before people change their minds about how much they value the new practice. And the value of the new practice must be felt to be beneficial over time to promote a change of heart. It is easier to change what you *do* than how you *feel*, and people do better when they feel better. If administrators wait for everyone to feel like changing before implementing changes, they will definitely be waiting a long time. The majority of educators might not be on board with the change at first. With school initiatives constantly coming and going, they might figure, "this too shall pass." The school's education leaders are going to be on the front lines defending challenges from colleagues who are not thrilled about new practices. Peers will have to be won over first in order to change their minds and hearts. It is imperative that school principals give clear directives and are willing to enforce the MTSS plan through follow-up supervision and support to the education leaders as they work to implement the administrator's vision, for this is the only real chance of consistent implementation of the new practice (Forman & Crystal, 2015; Meyer & Behar-Horenstein, 2015). When education leaders are valued and compensated, a powerful message is sent to the entire school staff that the school principal supports educators with more than words and is willing to reward the most effective educators implementing best practices for best student outcomes.

Allocating Fiscal Resources

Fiscal allocation specifically addresses the two key domains of business plan development and compensation to educators. A common theme heard from colleagues who work in secondary schools is that MTSS does not work because it is too difficult to require teachers to implement differentiated instruction with large numbers of students, and that teachers are already asked to do too much and they cannot, or will not, do it. The process will not work when educational leaders do not follow the recipe. Of course, in those instances, the recipe is blamed when the cake does not rise. And the cake will never rise as long as school leaders do not put the right ingredients in to make it work.

Shifting the perspective to view MTSS implementation through another lens, MTSS can be viewed from the angle of a business model for providing appropriate educational services to diverse students in diverse populations. The chief executive officer (CEO) of the school, the school principal, is in charge of all business in his or her school. The business of schools is to teach *every* child. The only flaw in the educational business model is that children are not widgets. Educators can't return or disregard children when they arrive with gaps and do not function as the curriculum demands. If the business of school is to teach every child, and every child does not develop or learn uniformly, then there must be a systematic way to evaluate children's individual needs, provide timely remediation to address their deficits, and provide that support for as long as it is needed. MTSS is that business plan for education and will facilitate the delivery of quality instruction to every child and will guide data-based decisions to maximize school success.

In which business industry would a business plan unsupported by the CEO actually be successful? Probably none. How many successful business owners start a business without a plan? Probably none. MTSS is a research-based business plan, and like every other business plan, it probably won't be that effective without the CEO, the school principal, leading the vision of the plan and actively working to solve problems that may impact the plan's fruition.

School administrators have an immense responsibility to an enormous number of people. School campuses are controlled chaos in which some level of disorderliness is expected and accepted. *Controlled chaos* is a term borrowed from the biology, engineering, and life sciences fields that recognizes some or whole segments may be disorganized, yet can be controlled within given parameters (Uversky & Dunker, 2008). School principals have much on their plates and are responsible for everything on those plates. There are a lot of moving parts at any given moment in a large secondary school that require administrative attention. The MTSS process may feel overwhelming and undoable if the principal does not feel like they have time to address issues comprehensively with their current workload, or if they do not see the value in investing in the process with time, money, and active support. However, the benefits of an established MTSS will long outweigh the upfront inconvenience of extra work to lay the foundation. Once MTSS is up and running, it's like a well-oiled machine, and administrators will have to spend much less time reacting to problems, since they are being addressed proactively with supports in place for every student on campus. *Like money in the bank, the bigger deposit you put down the more interest you are going to earn.*

The leaders on a school's MTSS team are campus role models who work tirelessly to be the problem solvers for everyone; from the neediest students to the neediest educators, they help to identify practices that do not work and recommend fixes and work-arounds. They are ideally the strongest staff members in implementing effective instruction in the classroom for students. Depending on whether the leadership is for the Academic MTSS team or the Behavior and Mental Health MTSS team, the need to adequately compensate remains. Help these educators feel like valued professionals. Value their expertise and time, and pay them extra for all the extra work and burdens they will have. In truth, administrators may not be able to fully compensate their MTSS team members for the extra hours of work they do, but they must make a good faith effort. Pay them, and appreciate the value they bring to the school and community.

In the end, educators will want to be on this committee because they will have power to make positive changes for students. Financially rewarding these educators for the extra work they do will empower them, and will send a strong message to other staff members that these educators work to make the school principal's expectations come to fruition and have complete administrative backing. The MTSS team members are the leaders in implementing the boss's will to improve educational opportunities for all students, and all educators will be expected to change their instructional and professional practices accordingly.

Students are unpredictable. One in five children present with mental illness (Merz, 2017; National Association of School Psychologists, 2017), and students with emotional and behavioral disorders are an underserved and underfunded population (Ennis, Blanton, and Katsiyannis, 2017). Many more than that will display symptoms of a mental illness, depending on the risk factors and situational trauma they may be exposed to (Souers, 2017). No matter how many supports a school has in place, something will happen that exceeds what the school staff thought it was prepared for. When a problem solving process is in place with effective team work, those teams will be able to handle any problems that come up. The team approach of both the business model and health care model is well established and celebrated, and must be implemented in education as well. Ideally, educators with varying perspectives and experiences can each contribute to the solutions of a team problem. Children's problems must be addressed systematically, as part of a team approach, in every school to teach every child. Teams learn to adapt and grow from experience. Once teams are trained to work together they will be able to work more efficiently, which will give their administrators more time to attend to other pressing matters. MTSS is money in the bank with compound interest. Compensating educators validates them, which goes a long way toward that initial deposit, and those educators will be a greater asset in solving problems on their school campus.

Exercise 3.2

Administrator Challenges and Opportunities Survey

- Take a moment and reflect on some administrative challenges on your school campus that could be addressed by your team. Be as specific as possible. After you have generated your list of challenges, rank them by priority level. Save this list to discuss with your team.
- Brainstorm funding ideas to compensate your educators. Title I funding sources are flexible in terms of funding interventions for at-risk populations. Higher socio-economic schools can consider fundraisers and parent-teacher-association donations. All should consider grants and reallocation of other sources.

Assessment Tools

Invest in a school's teachers, specialists, and support staff; human capital is a school's best asset. The investment doesn't stop there, naturally. Administrators must also invest in the tools required to get the job done. First, administrators must measure where they are and decide where their school is going. Then, they need to invest in intervention tools and training opportunities for staff in how to use the methods with *fidelity*, or accuracy and quality. Overall, an entire school needs to invest in MTSS development and processes to be able to make data-based decisions for its students.

To make the right decisions, an investment must be made in selecting the right tools. One exemplary tool, AIMSweb, is very popular and highly recommended for schools implementing MTSS, as it screens all students using universal benchmarking to get a quick look at students' academic fluency skills at their given grade level (Pearson, 2015). Evidence-based progress monitoring and strategic monitoring tools are priceless when it comes to the data they generate, which helps teams make decisions about the effectiveness of instructional practices and whether students are adequately responding to interventions (Shinn, 2007). In all schools, especially those with large populations, universal screening makes sense. Students often get lost in the shuffle if they depend on individual teacher referrals to support their needs.

For example, in urban secondary schools it is not uncommon for a teacher to have 200 or more students on their caseload. It can become very burdensome to put the entire responsibility for identification and remediation of failing students on classroom teachers alone. There are some extremely resourceful, talented, and creative teachers who are responsive to students' academic needs and help students close their achievement gaps. However, students with Tier 2 and Tier 3 needs may fail repeatedly, over long periods of time, before someone intervenes. Oftentimes, it is one caring and persistent teacher who speaks up, a concerned parent, or school counselor, who manages student schedules and credit status, to advocate for additional supports for a student. Typically, this advocacy is in the form of requesting special education testing because the school lacks systemic processes of tiered supports or parents do not really understand what they are asking for; they just know their child needs help. School counselors are often limited in helping students obtain remedial supports given the nature of their role and the availability of resources on the school campus and within the community.

If teachers and itinerant specialists perceive MTSS as more work than they feel it is worth, especially on top of their already busy schedules, they are not going to refer students very often, let alone systematically. Even in elementary schools, which often have smaller class sizes, teachers are hesitant to refer students for interventions and monitoring. Low performing children in schools with limited resources and opportunities for remediation may be less likely to get intensive help and referred for supports because the burden of proof falls solely on over-burdened classroom teachers. These issues quickly become an issue of student *access* to remedial education and becomes another barrier to social justice. Access to, and benefits of, all a school's resources is one component of a socially just system, along with respect and fairness (North, 2006). Teachers expected to provide interventions during their "free time" are hard-pressed to implement quality interventions with fidelity and document accordingly.

Universal benchmarking allows administrators to take a snapshot of the student population and quickly identify students who may be at risk for school failure (Freeman, Miller, & Newcomer, 2015; Gill, Borden, & Hallgren, 2014; Shinn, 2007). There are other indicators that must be cross-referenced, or triangulated, because snapshots are not always accurate. Other indicators could include grades, behavioral history, dean's database, parent and teacher reports, attendance history, criterion referenced tests, English language fluency assessments, and enrollment history. When data across sources consistently identifies a student as requiring interventions, then the student can be quickly placed in remedial programs. Students with conflicting data would be discussed by the team, and other factors could be addressed. Such solution-based discussions may include offering incentives for completing homework, which can be implemented before placing the student in an intervention class that he or she may not really need. Universal benchmark scores also come in handy when students arrive at a school with little to no history of their data. Whether your school is high-risk or low-risk, benchmarking at regular intervals is strongly recommended because it helps the school team identify low performing students as soon as possible and allows the team to schedule them into the needed classes immediately, not a semester later wasting time and opportunity for those students. With regular benchmarking, low performing students are also picked up throughout the year, which is critical as many school populations have a high transiency rate and the students beginning the year will not necessarily be the same ones at the end of the school year.

Box 3.1

Connection to Practice

Weigh Yourself

Behavioral change is not easy. For example, the behavioral changes required for losing weight are difficult. Making healthy food choices and exercising every day is not easy to do, as is evidenced by the obesity epidemic in western civilization. Most consumers already know that a healthy weight is based on access to healthy foods, portion control, and daily exercise, but how many diet books are there on the market selling a different way to get thin fast?

As public consumers, success is desired to happen quickly, with efforts materialized in positive results instantly. How long will it take an individual to lose enough weight to wear a size 4? Of course, it depends on how large the person is to begin with. If she went from a size 22 to a size 16 in one year, most people would consider her diet a success even though she didn't reach her goal of a size 4 by that time. Data would support continuing with the successful behavioral changes made. A data-based decision could be to continue with the plan as is, or parts of it could be reviewed and revised to try for quicker results.

Conversely, if a man started at a size 40 pant size and went up to a size 52, most people would tell him to go on a different diet because the data do not indicate that his behavioral practices were leading to a smaller clothing size, or ultimate weight loss. He might even need more intensive support to help keep him on track, like Weight Watchers or Jenny Craig, with weekly weigh-ins, nutritional advice, pre-made food, and counseling to guide him through the emotional and behavioral challenges of overeating. If he can't achieve success with what interventions he has implemented, he might require working with a team of specialists. Such an approach may consist of meeting with a doctor specializing in weight loss, planning with a nutritionist, hiring a chef to make healthy foods, and getting a personal trainer to motivate him daily to engage in cardio and weight-lifting exercises. If he were morbidly obese, he might even consider gastric bypass surgery when other efforts have failed.

Most people cognitively understand "best practices" in weight loss (i.e., eat healthy foods, limit portion size, exercise daily), but what works for one person may not work for another. The intensity of intervention required depends on how overweight one is to begin with, genetic and health issues, emotional and cognitive behavioral issues, motivation, willpower, and how that person will be supported in daily behavioral changes in his or her environment. The intensity of interventions should increase when lesser intensity interventions have failed. The same is true for educational practices.

Educational progress is like weight loss in more ways than one. Educators want spectacular improvement with quick results. However, expecting instant success by getting students at or above grade level in a week, or even one year, is just as unrealistic as expecting a woman to go from a size 22 to a size 4 in the same amount of time. It could happen, but dramatic results are not the realistic norm. There are many methods to reach success academically but the basics remain the same. Using Maslow's research (1943) as a baseline, students must have a sense of belonging, and they require consistent, engaging, quality instruction led by qualified teachers.

Each education leader has their own ideas about what good teaching is and is not. Most educators have experience with students who do not respond to quality instruction as planned. Like weight loss, some need more help than others to follow a diet and exercise plan, or the problem is so severe it may require bariatric surgery. Before performing "surgery" on students, or cutting them out of general curriculum to go to a special education class, less intense interventions should be tried first to see if they work.

Struggling students should have the opportunity to learn the skills they do not possess in order to gain the necessary building blocks to stabilize their educational foundations. Skill development helps them gain confidence, even if those skills are not at expected grade level. They may need help to make better choices (i.e., going to class, getting to school on time, paying attention to instruction, completing class work and homework) and require the necessary supports in order to do so. Every success increases students' academic and emotional stability.

The goal of interventions is to make incremental gains. It is highly improbable that an individual would lose six dress sizes after a week of dieting. It is more realistic to make incremental changes to behavior, and is more motivating to celebrate incremental successes, instead of brooding over failure to reach more ambitious longer-term goals. Losing one pound per week doesn't sound like much success, but losing 52 pounds in a year is a smashing success. Even if the individual only achieved "minimally" adequate results, a half-pound weight loss per week, losing 26 pounds in a year would also be considered a significant success. Same with educational growth. Increasing academic growth incrementally is a cause for celebration. And if the incremental growth is not occurring the team needs to improve its approach, and perhaps intensify its efforts. It should not wait a whole year before deciding its approach is unsuccessful.

Like using a scale or dress size to measure weight loss success, data should be used to make instructional decisions for teaching hard-to-teach students. Instructional strategies must be differentiated when needed, according to formative assessment and outcome measures. In doing so, opportunities will arise to celebrate incremental growth for students who would not otherwise be celebrating their achievements.

As mentioned earlier, one such universal benchmarking tool that has shown repeatedly to be a favorite among practitioners is AIMSweb for its ease of use and practicality (Pearson, 2015). There is up and coming competition to this product, but for years there has been no direct competitor. Do-it-yourself benchmarking and progress monitoring might be on readers' minds. Beware of setting up for failure; D-I-Y documentation and intervention logging is highly labor intensive and fraught with fidelity issues, especially on a large campus. Some teachers just "know" a student has a learning problem but do not have documentation of high-quality interventions or valid data to reflect student response over time. Perhaps those teachers were unable to keep up with the organization and details required to systematically deliver interventions with fidelity and document faithfully. *Fidelity at all levels of the tiered model is of utmost importance.* Lacking quantitative data, school psychologists often find themselves graphing a teacher's qualitative data because the teacher lacks the skill or will to collect quantitative data and input it into graph form to demonstrate trajectory and rate of progress. Throughout the data design, implementation, and collection process, there are many steps to monitor for efficacy. It really takes a team to support teachers with documentation, and it takes the best tools for the job to methodically monitor students. AIMSweb has been an especially convenient managerial tool because the data can be input by teachers systematically and there are local area managers who can monitor which teachers are complying.

Another tool, easyCBM, is a much less expensive alternative, for finding and using grade level fluency probes and fluency levels. The more complicated and labor intensive the tool is, the less likely educators will use it with fidelity, or at all. If your school chooses to forgo an established method of benchmarking and progress monitoring, in lieu of a D-I-Y method, go ahead and try. However, be warned, teams will be faced with pervasive labor and fidelity issues.

Box 3.2

Voice from the Field

When we started a comprehensive multi-tiered support system at my high-risk urban middle school, the needs at my school were extreme. I likened our issues to the weight-loss analogy. Our practices fell within the morbidly obese range. Therefore, our solutions were geared toward more extreme measures. The first thing we decided to do was "weigh" ourselves regularly with quarterly benchmarking and monthly school-wide progress monitoring on our journey of changing instructional practices. Our school principal knew that changing teacher attitude and beliefs would require small steps in the right direction. Just like dieting, we had to have the courage to step on the scale regularly. Even though we were not on a consistent sensible diet at first, we weighed ourselves anyway. The whole school participated, every grade level, every month. The reason we did it that way was because we needed to implement the foundation of our new healthy habits with overcorrection.

When the correct way of doing something is never done, overcorrection is a way of learning and practicing the correct way with multiple repetitions. Learning a new skill requires many steps. It helps to break down the target skill into small parts and practice those small parts before putting it together. Then the skill must be practiced repetitively from start to finish. For example, when teaching a child how to make a bed correctly, overcorrection could be used as a way to have him practice the steps repetitively, practicing each new step after successfully completing the prior steps. Lastly, the bed would be completely unmade and sequentially made to demonstrate he can make the bed correctly. That way, when asked, he will know how to meet the standard of making his bed as a part of successfully cleaning his room.

Benchmarking and progress monitoring at our middle school was taught to teachers in much the same way. Our school decided to use AIMSweb (Pearson, 2015) for benchmarking, progress monitoring, and strategic monitoring of reading, writing, and math fluency. There are fluency measures in grade level reading, writing, math calculation, and math application skills, among other measures. Administration, scoring, and inputting scores is fairly easy to learn. The best part is that the scores are normed for comparisons to average grade level achievement and the data can be accessed remotely by any authorized user. Our school district even generated English Language Learner norms for use within district.

AIMSweb is a tool to assess students on easy-to-administer-and-score fluency measures, compare performance to same-grade peers, and graph data in any number of configurations to help with data analysis. Students' fluency trajectory is graphed over time. Data can be compiled by grade level and subject with repeated measures of the same skill. And growth goals can be established and progress monitored in accordance with the goals. The only limit to its usefulness is the quality and quantity of data input by teachers and the skill of the team who analyzes the information.

Unfortunately, AIMSweb is not free. Many school administrators could argue that their budget does not allow for it. However, it costs much more to educate students with special needs and those with learning gaps than the average student. It would most likely be more cost efficient having a quality indicator helping school teams determine which interventions are most effective with which students, so as not to waste time and resources on practices that are ineffective. Make data collection and reporting easy for teachers. Make it easy to access information to guide instructional decision making. Make it easy for administrators to monitor teacher input. The monetary cost of using an effective online program is more than worth it for the ease of use and value of information it captures. That data can be captured other ways but fidelity issues will suffer. Invest in quality benchmarking and progress monitoring tools in order to provide targeted support to MTSS processes. I have heard arguments about fluency measures not being the best way to measure growth over time, my answer to that is if you can find a quicker, easier, legally defensible way to benchmark students or capture academic strategic progress monitoring data then do it. Still waiting for alternatives that meet the same standard.

Data-Based Decision Making

Some administrators do not have the appetite or constitution for dramatic and intensive changes at their schools, and those administrators may want to implement changes more slowly. Some schools do not need to have such intensive overcorrection because educational practices are currently effective or have a lower risk of student failure due to socioeconomic and community factors. *Overcorrection* is the explicit repeated practice of a desired behavior. In all cases, quarterly grade level benchmarking is an effective way to quickly and easily identify at-risk students and get them into support services as soon as possible. Lower-risk schools may elect not to benchmark the entire school quarterly and may benchmark smaller subpopulations on a quarterly basis: subpopulations such as ELL students, special education students, or students with history of school failure in fundamental/remedial classes.

Higher-risk schools are going to identify far more at-risk students than lower-risk schools, and the process must be ultra-efficient if it is going to be sustainable. More teachers will need to be involved with monitoring students and implementing interventions at higher-risk schools because the number of disadvantaged students is much greater, which is why it makes sense to train and involve all educators in MTSS at a high-risk school. Recommendations in this guide may seem to fall on the more intensive side of intervention, but processes can be scaled back depending on the individual needs of students and number of students who require supports. As with all planning, the MTSS team and school principal take the leadership role in making the best decisions possible.

Universal benchmarking will capture grade level academic fluency of your school population. Progress monitoring and strategic monitoring on instructional level will occur at regular intervals for students identified as needing interventions. Repeated measures of the same skill are absolutely necessary for progress monitoring Tier 2 and Tier 3 intervention outcomes. The trajectory of student performance over time will help teams determine whether or not the intervention is effective, and whether or not each student requires more intensive or less intensive support. AIMSweb has an efficient online system to monitor student growth that uniquely contributes to ease of administration, scoring, input, and remote access of data (Pearson, 2015). The graphs it produces help support instructional decisions in the classroom, as well as provide reliable indicators of student needs. Finally, it can also provide data to support special education eligibility in severe cases of underachievement.

Box 3.3

Voice from the Field

Our school principal decided that putting all of the responsibility of testing on math and English teachers would be hard to sell because average caseload was close to 200 students. Even though AIMSweb is easy to do it would have been time consuming and viewed negatively by teachers having to administer, score, and input benchmarking scores online for all their students across classes. Other factors played into the decision, but the need to benchmark every child on campus quarterly was a big reason we rationed our day with slightly shorter classes allowing for a 21-minute advisory class before first period every day. Almost every teacher on campus was assigned an advisory class which allowed them to develop relationships with students, discuss character development and social-emotional learning, and provided classes time to take tests and have the data managed online. Every teacher had 30 or fewer students to test and manage instead of a handful of teachers testing hundreds of students. Creating an advisory period helped with teacher buy-in, shared responsibility, and reinforcing our data-based decision-making culture.

To ensure that teachers at our middle school could use the AIMSweb program as intended we had to use overcorrection. Our teachers were not benchmarking or progress monitoring academic fluency at all. So, we decided to train them to test for math computation (M-COMP), math application (M-CAP), and reading fluency and comprehension (MAZE). We offered several opportunities for them to be exposed to administering the probes. Teachers were required to attend the first training, which focused on the rationale behind the testing and how often we were asking them to give the tests to students. They practiced reading the directions of each test. They even administered tests on one another to experience the test. Lastly, they were given opportunities to practice scoring the tests and inputting the scores on their class lists in AIMSweb.

Local area managers of the program were trained to support our teachers on campus. During the days of the first benchmarking period, when teachers were required to administer, score, and input their data for the first time, they were required to give up a prep period to be guided with immediate feedback. Teachers went to a room during their prep period and spent time with a local area manager present to answer scoring questions and double check teachers' scoring. Our team wanted to ensure that all teachers had the opportunity to get guided practice scoring the probes correctly. Later that week, they all were required to enter the scores online with supervision in the computer lab.

Because teachers were required to administer, score, and input benchmark and monthly progress monitoring scores, the whole process for our first year of implementation could be considered overcorrection. We practiced each step repetitively with close supervision in the beginning before fading out supports for teachers to implement independently. We went from no fluency data to monthly measures. By the end of the year, even the most stubborn unmotivated-to-want-to-use-it teacher on our campus knew how to use AIMSweb correctly. And by the following school year, we faded the expectation of monthly progress monitoring to only those in Tier 2 interventions, with weekly and biweekly administration of strategic probes at instructional level to those students receiving Tier 3 interventions. A side effect of this type of intensity of school-wide intervention was that a high number of teachers left our school after the first year because they were unable or unwilling to meet the demands of the principal's new expectations. However, we celebrated the fact that we adequately trained every teacher in benchmarking and progress monitoring, and we established the first year of our multi-tiers of support for students.

Our goal was to have a culture that supported training teachers in data-based decision making, and we had improved success with teacher compliance every year after. The teachers that remained on staff the year after implementation of new practices were so thrilled that they did not have to progress monitor all students monthly, they were downright happy to benchmark three times a year. And the teachers who were designated as intervention specialists were very comfortable in progress monitoring and strategic monitoring. By the time we moved to a block schedule, the content level teachers decided to do their own benchmarking for more ownership and oversight of their students' reading and math data. Overcorrection accomplished!

The Voices from the Field box illustrates a win–win situation for teachers and students. The intensive needs of the student populations required a more intensive response. The schools learned to weigh themselves regularly, which allowed them to make adaptations to their intervention plans for students without having to wait until grading period to know if a student failed (or that they had failed a student). It was observed that the teachers who moved on needed to move on because the school culture was changing and they did not want to change with it. There is no "I" in team, remember? But there is an "I" in investment. Invest in your team. Invest in appropriate tools to measure baseline and monitor growth; and invest in high-quality research-based instructional practices, curriculum, and interventions.

As with all tests administered to students throughout the year, students' eyes often glaze over when they hear they have to take another test. Students may not care about testing on a given day for various reasons, and they do not give their best effort. Some school districts are using high-stakes test data as part of teachers' evaluations, and in some cases, school funding processes (Lavy, 2007). Basing teachers' job security and school funding decisions on test data puts a lot of power in students' hands in terms of their maturity and decision making. In reflecting on the developmental levels of average sixth to tenth grade students, who are going through puberty and all the other confusing teen experiences, consistency is often a challenge. Systemically, is it wise for teachers' paychecks to depend on the effort and motivation of young teenagers on any given test day?

With progress monitoring and strategic monitoring, over time and with multiple data points, schools can get a better idea of student growth than a high-stakes, one and done, test score; especially with higher-needs students. This growth model is comprised of rich data points that measure student growth, or lack thereof, over time. The *growth model* is well documented as more effective at determining a student's performance than high-stakes tests in high-risk schools (Freeman, Simonsen, McCoach, Sugai, Lombardi, & Horner, 2016).

Testing is like taking a picture. Even the best students can have "bad hair days," and their yearbook picture is not their best. If an adult has their picture taken right now and they're having a "bad hair moment" that doesn't mean their hair is going to look that way in 20 minutes if they decide to style it with some brushing and gel. But if a teenager does not care what he looks like that morning, leaves the house without brushing his hair, and does not do it when he gets to school, is the teacher responsible for the outcome of the picture? That might be like asking if an adult's hairdresser should be poorly rated on Yelp by whether or not the client styles her hair. Someone might judge how it looked this morning when she woke up late and put no effort into grooming, instead of judging the cut and color received at the salon. Is the client's maturity, effort, and motivation to perform really a fair evaluation of a hairdresser's skills and quality of the salon? Of course not. Is the maturity, effort, and motivation of a student to perform a fair evaluation of a teacher's quality and the quality of a school? The truthful answer is yes, whether that is fair or not is a matter of opinion. Fair or not, we have to lead those horses to water and make them drink. Not all people find tests to be motivating or engaging in any way. How do we get students more motivated to take tests seriously?

One method that has proven successful to increase student buy-in and motivation is the *Three-Pronged Motivation Approach*. The three prongs consist of including students in the data collection and analysis process, increasing student buy-in through teacher motivation, and incentivizing achievement at all levels. These underlying processes are incredibly powerful in increasing the intrinsic motivation of students and increasing the likelihood that they will engage in the learning process willingly and with purposeful intent. The more motivated a student perceives their teacher to be for teaching their given subject matter, the more intrinsically motivated the student will become to learn (Radel, Sarrazin, Legrain, & Wild, 2010).

The following case study is from Palm Middle School where the Three-Pronged Motivation Approach has been implemented successfully and has been effective for nearly a decade. The first prong, *including students in the data collection and analysis process*, is exemplified though the Student Led Informational Conferences (SLIC), where students each manage their own portfolio of work and data. These SLIC nights occur twice a year, separate from teacher conference times and with individual students and their parents or guardians. The first night occurs closely after the first quarter of a school year to discuss baseline assessment information obtained first quarter, and students create their personalized goals. Parent, teacher, and student sign that goal sheet as a contract. Students refer to goals in their portfolios and discuss shorter-term goals periodically throughout the year. The SLIC folders and discussions are managed in advisory class. The second SLIC night occurs in late spring of the school year. In addition to benchmarking data, students are encouraged to gather meaningful projects and writing pieces to share, formative, and summative assessment scores. Student portfolios are reviewed and celebrated by the student's family and the staff. Palm Middle School even has an award-winning mariachi band that performs on those nights, and the school principal often provides picnic-style food. The SLIC nights are in addition to parent-teacher conferences to increase opportunities for positive family engagement, and have a higher turnout rate when paired with other anchor events like a musical performance and science fair.

The second piece of the Three-Pronged Motivation Approach is to *leverage teacher engagement with students* to earn student buy-in for testing efforts. Encouragement and positive relationships go a long way with children, many of whom may not have much positive attention in their worlds. Motivation for learning is contagious. Students who historically may not have valued education, were not invested in their own growth, or thought they could not succeed, can be motivated by their teachers' motivation and excitement for teaching (Radel et al., 2010).

The third part of the Three-Pronged Motivation Approach is based on *incentivizing students* to try their best. Just as teachers seek fiscal rewards for their efforts, so do students. As a result of this realization, the incentive committee at Palm Middle School used their budget for gift cards and prizes not only for students who score highest scores but also for those who made the most growth. Every advisory class has a winner. And the advisory teacher whose students collectively make the most growth also gets gift cards. Bikes, iPads, and sports gear have also been used as end-of-the-year prizes. In addition, students who graduate from needing Tier 2 and Tier 3 interventions get principal recognition resulting in a private congratulation from the school principal, a choice of something in her "treasure box" and/or a gift card. In Palm Middle School, student achievement was celebrated at all levels.

Exercise 3.3

Benchmarking Reflection

Take a few minutes and process how you feel about benchmarking your entire student population. Some things to think about:

- What are the challenges?
- What are your feelings in response to those challenges?
- Are you able to benchmark all students, and if not, which subpopulations might benefit?
- What tool might you use?
- What will you do with benchmark data?
- What do you currently use to monitor student progress in response to interventions?

Research-Based Interventions

Universal benchmarking is a solid way of determining students' academic fluency, which is highly correlated with achievement (Jimerson, Burns, & VanDerHeyden, 2016). Results can be sorted quickly and can be used as a starting point to prioritize which students require more intensive academic supports. A school's MTSS team must consider multiple sources of data when considering students for placement in Tier 2 or Tier 3 intervention classes including grades, attendance, criterion referenced test scores, AIMSweb scores, other standards-based or formative assessments, all progress monitoring data, counselor input, discipline data, teacher observations, parent report, and health records. A health screening including vision and hearing is required for all Tier 2 and Tier 3 students. Students who are below the 25th percentile achievement on grade level benchmark scores are all considered for interventions and receiving Tier 2 supports in addition to the Tier 1 curriculum. For example, on occasion, there are students who work, and read, at a slower pace than expected but they have the content mastered according to other sources. If the time limit for such tests were removed their performance would be no different than on-grade level peers. Teams can triangulate data from multiple data sources and types to find the convergence of information (Creswell, 2008). *Triangulating* data sources for consistency helps teams identify which students need interventions and accommodations versus those who had a "bad hair day" or didn't care when testing. Teams can evaluate whether students have consistent difficulties across data sources and which areas of need are not being met. Interventions can range from intensive supports to a proverbial kick in the pants for motivation.

Once students have been identified as requiring help, what next? That answer depends on how many at-risk students there are in each grade level and what resources are available. The scale of a multi-tiered support system will be smaller on campuses with lower risk factors and will be larger on campuses with higher risk factors. When planning, the tricky part is to have a crystal ball to look into the next school year to predict how many classes will likely be needed at Tier 2 and Tier 3, so that supply meets projected demand. School supports must be planned prior to the school year due to basic logistics and budgeting. Based on successful MTSS programs, it is better to start with a few high-quality intervention classes that are implemented with integrity than to attempt too many remedies at once and have them poorly executed.

An example of a good strategy with poor implementation in practice includes the actual practice of computerized reading programs in secondary schools. There are many good programs, including Edgenuity and Read 180. However, the curriculum is very specific and includes mandatory instruction hours, including direct instruction for certain content components. Computer time is usually highly desirable to students and the lessons are often perceived as higher-interest tasks than typical lectures. Oftentimes, school teams choose to purchase computerized or online guided practice as a supplement to teaching because they allow teachers to differentiate instruction without each student constantly demanding individualized attention from the teacher. When teachers follow curricula as prescribed, and engage students with direct instructional supplementation, they are going to reap the benefits of these tools with achievement gains.

However, when teachers do not follow the curricula as prescribed, these gains are not realized. There is a high rate of abuse and misuse of putting students on computers during core curriculum instruction, not during supplemental instruction times. Some students with academic difficulties are going to present with behavioral problems, due to work avoidance or embarrassment about their lack of skills, which will be disruptive to other students. Teachers with the intent of engaging disruptive students, while being allowed to teach the rest of the class with fewer distractions, tend to over-rely on computerized programs. Sometimes lower performing students are expected to work independently without the required teacher supports or direct instruction, and they get further behind because they miss what is happening during class while they are on the computer. Other times, teachers have limited independent work time for the whole class and they use that "extra 15 minutes at the end of class" to let lower performing students practice skills. But again, the students are typically not on the program for as long as they need to be, or the teacher didn't fully implement the direct instruction piece. In either scenario, the computerized intervention would not be considered implemented with fidelity as prescribed and cannot be considered a valid intervention (Marino & Beecher, 2010).

Computer programs are alluring as a first choice of intervention investment for schools because they are often strong programs backed by research, when used as directed, and they are more likely to be higher interest to students, thus increasing student motivation to work independently (Marino & Beecher, 2010). The reality is that teachers must be highly trained in these programs and must adhere to curriculum as directed, which many do not because of all the competing demands on their time and attention. Lastly, computerized programs are expensive. License purchase prices for these programs have climbed steadily over the past ten years to the point of being cost prohibitive. It is even more cost prohibitive if teachers aren't implementing the program with integrity, and are much less likely to get successful results generalizing to gains of achievement.

The decision to purchase computerized intervention programs is a personal decision by every school administrator. There are pros and cons that must be weighed. The importance of using these tools as directed cannot be emphasized enough, otherwise teams are simply wasting time and money. Time and space will need to be carved out, above and beyond core instruction, as the best chance of implementing these programs correctly is not during core class time. As frequently must be explained and shared with teams, especially those with a principal who is not willing to invest in time or resources for intervention opportunities for at-risk students, there is no such thing as Tier 1 interventions. *Tier 1 is core curriculum.* Intensive instructional opportunities outside of Tier 1 must be implemented systematically and at the student's instructional level (not grade level) for the prescribed amount of time for it to be considered Tier 2 or Tier 3.

A question many secondary school teachers, who may not be accustomed to teaching primary skills, ask is: "What is the difference between Tier 2 and Tier 3 level of interventions?" The simple answer is that Tier 3 students are much further behind than Tier 2 students and require even more individualized supports. Tier 2 students may need a little boost, such as remedial skills practice, to get more out of Tier 1, like improved reading, writing, or math fluency skills.

This increased practice makes learning new material easier for students as they are better able to perform basic skills with automaticity and read with greater prosody (Calet, Gutierrez-Palma, & Defior, 2017; Kuhn & Stahl, 2003). Students in Tier 2 are often referred to as the "bubble kids," and are the students that schools tend to focus on as they are the closest to nearly passing high-stakes standardized tests. Oftentimes, this focus is to the exclusion of lower performing students who are less likely to perform over the threshold for adequate performance on high-stakes tests. Administrators are concerned about the number of students who pass high-stakes tests for a variety of reasons: to maintain funding levels for schools or to reduce punitive damages for underperforming programs (Lewis & Hardy, 2015; Bogin & Nguyen-Hoang, 2014).

Students who are in Tier 3 have a larger learning gap, oftentimes are performing two or more grade levels below expectation, and require intensive remedial instruction and re-teaching of lower level skills. Students in Tier 3 often have a history that supports their learning deficits, such as coming from higher-risk environments, being victims of poverty, or having breaks in their school history including attendance problems, transience, and issues associated with family risk factors. Those students need opportunities to close their achievement gaps with high-quality instruction and evidence-based practices. Bottom line is that nothing replaces direct instruction for low performing students and it is critical that an evidence-based curriculum be available for teachers to use. There are many tools available in different styles, and new tools come along all the time. Like any CEO, administrators should be asking which tools are most effective at the most reasonable cost to target the needs of most students on their campus. *The end of the school year is a perfect time for curriculum and teaching practices to be evaluated and retooled for a fresh start the next school year.*

One example is the case of Wilson Middle School. Wilson Middle School had tried multiple evidence-based curriculum brands over a six-year span in reading, writing, and math subjects. Some curriculum tools were mandated by the school district, some were tried based on popularity in educational circles, some were suggestions made by staff members, and some were random choices to fill a particular need. Some were more effective than others. Why was that? What makes a product pass the test of fit and effectiveness? Keep in mind that curriculum tools alone cannot be deemed effective or ineffective. Implementation factors impact the validity and fidelity of the interventions provided, and some evidence-based curriculum tools and remedial products are better than others. Every student population and staff needs are different, thus will require a differentiated approach. It is up to your administrator and MTSS team to evaluate the quality of a product, monitor the integrity of implementation, and weigh the costs of the programs in terms of opportunity cost of other options and return on investment. Does the brand name program give the greatest bang for the buck? Which programs work best? The answers will vary by school, but can be systematically addressed.

As the saying goes, Rome was not built in a day; MTSS will also take time to grow. The process may take years to get into place and realize positive outcomes. Documenting growth over time is ideal, just remember that teams may not get miraculous results immediately. If teams do see a large leap in growth, they should take it with a grain of salt, because they most likely will not have skyrocketing development every year. There may even be declines the first year, before that aggregate group data moves in the right direction. Disappointment in outcome data can happen. It feels incredibly unfair when a school team goes to heroic efforts to rescue underachievers and its test scores do not reflect its efforts. The issue of aggregate group data that does not correspond to a positive trajectory is especially true at schools with a high student transiency rate. In many urban high-risk schools, there may be a 50 percent transience rate or more, and many of the students starting the school year move away before the high-stakes exams in the spring. In such schools, students who began the school year and received Tier 2 or Tier 3 interventions have since moved and have been replaced by "new" students on high-stakes testing days who have not received such interventions. The "new" students frequently have large numbers of absences, behavior problems on other campuses, and have all the high-risk factors with little history of school support or remediation. If school leadership wants to demonstrate growth outside what the school district requires, especially in schools of high transiency, they may want to consider conducting growth analyses on the students who remained at the school for the entire year to refute any charges that "that school is not making any progress." Regardless of a school's challenges when it comes to outcome data, the important message is to stick with good strategies and replace ineffective practices. The obvious first place to start with effective instruction is Tier 1.

The first thing the school principal and MTSS team should consider when evaluating effective instruction is Tier 1, core curriculum implementation. At-risk students need high-quality Tier 1 instruction as well as opportunities for filling in gaps through remedial instruction. How many students are struggling per grade level, per teacher? The intervention model would depend on how many students are underachieving. Going back to the ideal intervention triangle introduced in Chapter 2, 75 percent of students will ideally be successful with Tier 1 instruction alone. In many urban at-risk schools, both elementary and secondary, the idea of the triangle is a myth.

Many schools have a distribution of Tiers 1, 2, and 3 like an inverted triangle. There are more students struggling in a major way, indicating a need for more Tier 3 supports, than there are students successful at Tier 1. With those kinds of numbers, a gigantic red flag is raised indicating a need to revamp Tier 1 instruction, improve teaching practices, and select the highest-quality curriculum possible. Over time, the distribution of tiered students will more closely resemble a rectangle as the MTSS team pushes more Tier 2 students down to Tier 1 and more Tier 3 students down to Tier 2.

Go where the data takes you. If a whole subject level is floundering it is more effective to address it as a whole, whether that be curriculum, teacher support, or teaching practices, than try to fix things piece by piece. If the curriculum is not working, replace it. If a teacher is not getting results using strong curriculum and tools, look at available teacher supports or teaching practices. If a student isn't achieving in the context of solid curriculum and excellent teaching practices, look to more intensive supports to help that student overcome learning challenges. *Never overlook the importance of Tier 1, in fact, look there first.*

Once a team is confident that Tier 1 is stable and teaching practices are effective, it can begin looking into building up Tier 2 and Tier 3 resources. Teams can start asking themselves, what resources should be used? As long as high-quality teaching practices are occurring, the product brand of the intervention is less important than the fact that it is research-based. Teams may find that certain interventions work better for their population of students over other brands. It is essential to ensure that the teachers are implementing interventions with fidelity and are not picking and choosing the parts of a program they want to implement. When the process of effective implementation becomes cyclical, with constant reflection and refinement, teams will have a continuous improvement cycle with feedback loops to address the trifecta of curriculum quality, teaching practices, and growing resources. The limit to a school's investment in remedial tiers depends on its budget and the creativity and quality of its educators and leaders.

It is not easy to be an educator. Hostile political climate, education budget cuts, and high-stakes testing are a few of the challenges faced. Teachers have all the responsibility for student outcomes with no control over what happens to students outside of class. Getting systems in place to help school leaders support students *and* educators alike will improve educational outcomes. Universal benchmarking and triangulating student data to identify at-risk students is the surest way to effectively target underachievers to be directed into high-quality remedial programming. Ensuring high-quality instruction at Tier 1 is the place to start.

Investing in high-quality benchmarking tools and evidence-based curriculum at all levels is paramount. Paying educators for their overtime and expertise is also critical as they are the mice in the wheel of the school's engine. Validate educators' efforts and grow best practices by rewarding those who help grow the best practices through extra work and effort. Leaders also need to increase socially just practices on campus. One way to do so is by improving school culture and giving students a voice; have them invested in their own learning and teach them to advocate for themselves. Also, make school relevant for all students and provide multiple layers of support to help students achieve their goals in school and beyond. Selecting the highest-quality curriculum and looking for evidence of implementation fidelity in the classroom are key. Evaluate Tier 1 and scale out into Tier 2 and Tier 3 with effective evidence-based practices. Finally, it is essential to engage in continuous improvement cycles using feedback looping and reflection to determine whether practices are working and how to improve.

Exercise 3.4

Review Your Resources

Use the following worksheet to document which programs you are currently using across the tiers. Also list the pros and cons of what you are using and discuss whether the outcomes are going in the right direction. In those same columns, generate a wish list of things you would like to add or programs you would like to learn more about (see Appendix for resources). Encourage team members to research new programs to discuss. Choose a small number of new resources or practices to add to your "intervention bank" of research-based interventions. Examine your school's curriculum quality/teaching practices/growing resources trifecta and refer back to this worksheet at least annually to review and revise.

List the names of programs, tools, and curriculum you currently have along with their pros and cons.

- Tier 1:
    - Reading
    - Mathematics
    - Writing
    - Social-Emotional
    - Positive Behavior Supports
- Tier 2:
    - Reading
    - Mathematics
    - Writing
    - Social-Emotional
    - Positive Behavior Supports
- Tier 3:
    - Reading
    - Mathematics
    - Writing
    - Social-Emotional
    - Positive Behavior Supports

Now list the names of programs, tools, and curriculum you want to incorporate or wish you had at each of the three tiers, and consider ways to work toward obtaining them in terms of budgeting and resource reallocation.

References

Asghar, A., Munawar, S., & Muhammad, R. (2015). The impact of positive and negative attitude of teachers towards corporal punishment on students' achievement in mathematics. *Dialogue, 10*(2), 182–188.

Bogin, A., & Nguyen-Hoang, P. (2014). Property left behind: An unintended consequence of a no child left behind "failing" school designation. *Journal of Regional Science, 54*(5), 788–805.

Calet, N., Gutierrez-Palma, N., & Defior, S. (2017). Effects of fluency training on reading competence in primary school children: The role of prosody. *Learning and Instruction, 52*, 59–68.

Common Core State Standards Initiative (2010). *Common core state standards for mathematics.* Retrieved from www.corestandards.org/wp-content/uploads/Math_Standards1.pdf.

Creswell, J. W. (2008). *Educational research: Planning, conducting, and evaluating quantitative and qualitative research.* Upper Saddle River, NJ: Pearson Education.

Ennis, R. P., Blanton, K., & Katsiyannis, A. (2017). Child Find activities under the Individuals with Disabilities Education Act: Recent case law. *Teaching Exceptional Children, 49*(5), 301–308.

Farmer, L. (2017). How to beat teacher burnout: With more education. *Education Digest, 83*(2), 13–16.

Forman, S. G., & Crystal, C. D. (2015). Systems consultation for multitiered systems of supports (MTSS): Implementation issues. *Journal of Educational and Psychological Consultation, 25,* 276–285.

Foucault, M. (1995). *Discipline and punish: The birth of the prison* (2nd ed.). New York: Random House.

Freeman, J., Simonsen, B., McCoach, D. B., Sugai, G., Lombardi, A., & Horner, R. (2016). Relationship between school-wide positive behavior interventions and supports and academic, attendance, and behavior outcomes in high schools. *Journal of Positive Behavior Interventions, 18*(1), 41–51.

Freeman, M. D. A. (2010). Upholding the dignity and best interests of children: International Law and the corporal punishment of children. *Law & Contemporary Problems, 73*(2), 211–251.

Freeman, R., Miller, D., & Newcomer, L. (2015). Integration of academic and behavioral MTSS at the district level using implementation science. *Learning Disabilities: A Contemporary Journal, 13*(1), 59–72.

Gershoff, E. T. (2010). More harm than good: A summary of scientific research on the intended and unintended effects of corporal punishment on children. *Law & Contemporary Problems, 73,* 31–56.

Gill, B., Borden, B. C., & Hallgren, K. (2014). *Final report: A conceptual framework for data-driven decision making.* Princeton, NJ: Mathematica Policy Research.

Gonser, S. (2016, November). Why Las Vegas is recruiting uncertified teachers. *The Atlantic.* Retrieved from www.theatlantic.com/education/archive/2016/11/are-uncertified-teachers-better-than-substitutes/509099.

Hathorn, T. (2013, November). *The glorification of athletes, not just a media thing.* Retrieved from https://taylorhathorn.wordpress.com/2013/11/04/the-glorification-of-athletes-not-just-a-media-thing.

Jimerson, S. R., Burns, M. K., & VanDerHeyden, A. M. (Eds.) (2016). *The handbook of response to intervention: The science and practice of multi-tiered systems of support.* New York: Springer.

Kuhn, M. R., & Stahl, S. A. (2003). Fluency: A review of developmental and remedial practices. *Journal of Educational Psychology, 95*(1), 3–21.

Ladd, H. F., & Fiske, E. B. (Eds.) (2008). *Handbook of research in education finance and policy.* New York: Routledge.

Lavy, V. (2007). Using performance-based pay to improve the quality of teachers. *The Future of Children, 17*(1), 87–109.

Layton, L. (2015, November). How to build a better teacher: Groups push a 9-point plan called TeachStrong. *Washington Post.* Retrieved from www.washingtonpost.com/local/education/how-to-build-a-better-teacher-groups-push-a-9-point-plan-called-teachstrong/2015/11/08/2b28b824-84c8-11e5-8ba6cec48b74b2a7_story.html?utm_term=.5483e0629e6f.

Lewis, S., & Hardy, I. (2015). Funding, reputation and targets: The discursive logics of high-stakes testing. *Cambridge Journal of Education, 45*(2), 245–264.

Marino, M. T., & Beecher, C. C. (2010). Conceptualizing RTI in 21st-century secondary science classrooms: Video games' potential to provide tiered support and progress monitoring for students with learning disabilities. *Learning Disability Quarterly, 33,* 299–311.

Martin, C., Partelow, L., & Brown, C. (2015). Smart, skilled, and striving: Transforming and elevating the teaching profession. *The Center for American Progress.* Retrieved from www.Americanprogress.org/issues/education/reports/2015/11/03/123747/smart-skilled-and-striving.

Maslow, A. (1943). A theory of human motivation. *Psychological Review, 50,* 370–396.

Mérida-López, S., & Extremera, N. (2017). Emotional intelligence and teacher burnout: A systemic review. *International Journal of Educational Research, 85,* 121–130.

Merz, S. (2017). Who in your class needs help? *Educational Leadership, 75*(4), 12–17.

Meyer, M. M., & Behar-Horenstein, L. S. (2015). When leadership matters: Perspectives from a teacher team implementing response to intervention. *Education and Treatment of Children, 38*(3), 383–402.

National Association of School Psychologists (2010). *Model for comprehensive and integrated school psychological services.* Retrieved from www.nasponline.org/standards-and-certification/nasp-practice-model/nasp-practice-model-implementation-guide/section-i-nasp-practice-model-overview/nasp-practice-model-overview.

National Association of School Psychologists (2017). *Shortages in school psychology: Challenges to meeting the growing needs of U.S. students and schools.* (Research summary). Bethesda, MD: Author.

National Board for Professional Teaching Standards (2016a). *What teachers should know and be able to do.* Arlington, VA: Author.

National Board for Professional Teaching Standards (2016b). *The proven impact of Board-Certified teachers on student impact.* Retrieved from www.nbpts.org/wp-content/uploads/impact_brief_final.pdf.

Nevada Association of School Psychologists (2018). Shortage of school psychologists in Nevada: Challenges in meeting the growing needs of our students' academic, social-emotional, and mental-behavioral health. (Research summary). Las Vegas, NV: Author.

North, C. E. (2006). More than words? Delving in the substantive meaning(s) of "social justice" in education. *Review of Educational Research, 76,* 507–536.

Odden, A. R. (2012). *Improving student learning when budgets are tight.* Thousand Oaks, CA: Corwin.

Odden, A. R., & Picus, L. O. (2014). *School finance: A policy perspective* (5th ed.). New York: McGraw Hill.

Pearson (2015). *AIMSweb software guide version 2.5.10.* Retrieved from https://aimsweb2.pearson.com/aimsweb-frontoffice/helpsupport/help/aimsweb_software_guide2510.pdf.

Pleck, E. (2004). *Domestic tyranny: The making of American social policy against family violence from Colonial times to the present.* Champaign, IL: University of Illinois Press.

Preiss, A. (2015, November). *Release: 40 education organizations unite to launch TeachStrong, a campaign to modernize and elevate the teaching profession.* Retrieved from www.Americanprogress.org/press/release/2015/11/10/125052/release-40-education-organizations-unite-to-launch-teachstrong-a-campaign-to-modernize-and-elevate-the-teaching-profession.

Radel, R., Sarrazin, P., Legrain, P., and Wild, T. C. (2010). Social contagion of motivation between teacher and student: Analyzing underlying processes. *Journal of Educational Psychology, 102*(3), 577–587.

Sawchuk, A. (2015, November). Can a new political campaign to "modernize" teaching succeed? *Ed Week.* Retrieved from http://blogs.edweek.org/edweek/teacherbeat/2015/11/can-new-campaign-to-modernize-teaching-succeed.html.

Shinn, M. R. (2007). Identifying students at risk, monitoring performance, and determining eligibility within RTI: Research on educational need and benefit from academic intervention. *School Psychology Review, 36*(4), 601–617.

Smith, L. R., & Sanderson, J. (2015). I'm going to Instagram it! An analysis of athlete self-presentation on Instagram. *Journal of Broadcasting & Electronic Media, 59*(2), 342–358.

Souers, K. (2017). Responding with care to students facing trauma. *Educational Leadership, 75*(4), 32–36.

Sparks, S. D., & Harwin, A. (2016, August). Students still face paddling in U.S. schools: Punishment rates for Blacks nearly double those for Whites. *Education Week, 36*(1), 1, 16–18.

Straus, M. A. (2010). Prevalence, societal causes, and trends in corporal punishment by parents in world perspective. *Law & Contemporary Problems, 73*(2), 1–30.

Taormina, R. J., & Law, C. M. (2000). Approaches to preventing burnout: The effects of personal stress management and organizational socialization. *Journal of Nursing Management, 8,* 89–99.

Tong, L., Shinohara, R., Sugisawa, Y., Tanaka, E., Watanabe, T., Koeda, T., & Anme, T. (2015). Buffering effect of parental engagement on the relationship between corporal punishment and children's emotional/behavioral problems. *Pediatrics International, 57,* 385–392.

Uversky, V. N., & Dunker, A. K. (2008). Controlled chaos. *Science, 322*(5906), 1340–1341.

Wilson, H. W. (2014). *The reference shelf: Embracing new paradigms in education.* Amenia, NY: Grey House Publishing.

Yaffe, D. (2016). Tackling the teacher shortage: School leaders turn to bonuses, affordable housing, outreach to college students, and other solutions. *Education Digest, 81*(8), 11–15.

Chapter 4

How to Build Your Program

Key Terms

Infrastructure
Physical Capital
Strategic Resource Allocation
Master Schedule
Fidelity
Reliability
Validity
Leadership Fidelity Checks
Unintended Consequences
Positive Class Culture
MTSS Extension Opportunities

Chapter Concepts

In this chapter, readers will learn:

1. The importance of the MTSS program infrastructure.
2. The need for responsible fiscal management and strategic resource allocation.
3. The critical role of the master schedule to MTSS program success.
4. The necessity of leadership fidelity checks to ensure accurate MTSS program implementation.
5. The demand for MTSS extension opportunities: what they are and why they are important.
6. The reason for MTSS team meetings and their role in making timely decisions about students.

You Are Here. Ever look at a map in a large amusement park to try to find how to get to a specific location? The first crucial piece of information the group needs is to figure out where they are. They have to orient themselves to their location on the map if the map is going to be useful. Determining where they are going is obviously the second crucial piece of information needed to get to their destination. People can usually pinpoint their desired destination before knowing their actual location on the map; however, how do they get where they are going if they don't know where they are? They might look for major landmarks like large signs or rides to orient themselves to their location. They can then follow other landmarks to ensure they are going in the right direction.

The same principle could hold true for the direction and movement of a multi-tiered support system and team. Through information provided in the previous chapters, teams now have the necessary supports and skills to begin building their MTSS programs. With guidance and support from administrators, the structure in the MTSS framework has been engineered to empower, motivate, and compensate members for their efforts. They have evaluated their current curriculum and invested in additional researched-based methods to support Tiers 1, 2, and 3. MTSS teams have selected high-quality members to work together to systematically monitor at-risk students on campus to make data-based decisions. Teams have selected a method of universal screening for each domain and trained teachers on its administration to help identify underachievers and cross-referenced data from multiple sources to identify at-risk students. Now, the goal is to orient the team to where they are, and then map where it seeks to go. What are the landmarks that are going to guide the MTSS team? Who is going to lead the way? That all depends on where the team starts and the unique qualities of each team member.

Landmarks that will guide the process of MTSS growth and implementation of MTSS include leadership, human capital, professional compensation, material resources, team building, teacher and staff training, inclusive practices, quality universal instruction and benchmarking, systematic monitoring of student data, intervention implementation and documentation, progress monitoring, data-based decision making, program evaluation through feedback looping and problem solving, and professional communication. Each landmark is an essential element for a school to achieve in order for it to reach the ultimate goal of an MTSS program with a solid foundation poised for sustainability. The following four components will help guide the journey: infrastructure, budgeting, the master schedule, and intervention class scheduling.

Infrastructure

Kevin Costner's character in the motion picture *Field of Dreams* espoused the philosophy "build it and they will come" (Gordon & Robinson, 1989). However, when the masses are already "there" before the infrastructure is adequately built, remodeling can get a little tricky. An MTSS *infrastructure* is the foundational framework that supports data-based decisions about students on campus. It is easier to build school programs and culture from the ground up and to have the requisite infrastructure in place before students ever set foot in class. Like any well-constructed building, it is important to have a solid foundation (Foorman, 2016).

The base of the foundation of effective MTSS is at Tier 1. *Tier 1 must be evaluated for structural integrity before anything else can be reliably built on top of it.* Tier 1 instruction must be effectively delivered using evidence-based practices. Then more intense and more comprehensive tiers of support can grow from a healthy baseline of effective practices. Tiers 2 and 3 have a greater chance of being implemented with fidelity if Tier 1 is solid. It is very difficult to reliably make inferences about Tier 2 and Tier 3 practices, or evaluate outcomes through feedback looping, otherwise. Examination of educational practices, whether starting a new school or reforming an existing one, must begin at Tier 1.

Whether or not Tier 1 is strong, students will require supports at Tier 2 and Tier 3. The quality of additional layers of support will always be correlated to the quality of the bottom layer at the base of the structure. In reality, *all three tiers must grow structurally together.* Tier 1 has to support Tiers 2 and 3, but Tiers 2 and 3 must, in turn, make Tier 1 stronger by supporting all students in an inclusive culture. For schools that are "remodeling" existing structures of educational practices, it is important to examine outcome measures from past years and make changes incrementally every new school year to solidify practices that are working and grow new layers of MTSS infrastructure. The foundational quality of a school's MTSS rests in the construction details. For schools that are "remodeling" existing structures of educational practices, it is important to remember that schools can make changes incrementally to solidify their foundation each school year. The best time to implement new practices in a school setting is always at the beginning of the school year. Sometimes tweaks are necessary throughout the year and a new practice emerges from necessity. However, big picture initiatives must begin implementation at the beginning of the academic year with most of the planning conducted at the end of the prior school year, and through the summer for administrators.

Construction, or reconstruction, of MTSS on a school campus depends on existing structures and where the team is at in the building process. The infrastructure needed for staff and student success should be in place before children ever set foot in a classroom (Odden & Picus, 2014; Sprick, 2013; Shinn & Walker, 2010; Sprick, 2009; Shinn, 2007). Without a clear blueprint, educators find themselves responding to student needs and school problems reactively, rather than proactively, which is time consuming and exhausting to have to constantly reinvent solutions to problems rather than having a problem solving framework already in place. *The importance of a well-constructed MTSS with a solid foundation cannot be overemphasized.* Whether a team is building a new program or remodeling existing structures of educational practice, the school should start conservatively to ensure compliance with, and integrity of, new practices. Additions and improvements can be made incrementally each school year to expand the dimensions of the tiered support system.

Budgeting

Before a comprehensive MTSS program can be implemented, a budget must first be devised. Given the chronic shortage of monies at both the federal and state levels that are allocated for education, a school must adopt a strategic approach to using their funds (Odden, 2012). At the state and district levels, budgetary decisions may be made that impact salary freezes, class size, or decentralizing structures and programming. These decisions will certainly impact individual schools, but each school will need to devise a strategic plan to best use their resources. *Responsible fiscal management and strategic resource allocation is about directly aligning each initiative on campus to the overall school improvement plan to maximize efficiency and enhance student outcomes.* Schools will review the effectiveness of their school improvement plan annually, including their fiscal management and resource allocation strategy, on a formative basis, as well using a structured format, such as through use of a logic model (Forman & Crystal, 2015; Epstein & Klerman, 2013; Mirabella, 2013; Carman, 2010; Frechtling, 2007; Trevisian, 2007; McDavid & Hawthorn, 2006). More about using logic models, program evaluation, and feedback looping will be discussed in Chapter 11.

Teams must know their budget long before the start of the school year. School funding varies depending on numerous student factors including, but not limited to, number of total students as well as those with special education eligibilities, limited language proficiencies, and free or reduced lunch status (Odden & Picus, 2014). Some federal funds are available to states under the Individuals with Disabilities Education Act (IDEA, 2006) to assist states in providing a Free and Appropriate Education (FAPE) to qualified special education students (20 U.S.C. §1411[a][1]). Funds are allocated from two primary funding sources, state education agency and local education agency, and depending on the health of each, a school may be better funded some years over others. School administrators must make a long-term financial commitment to fund physical capital as well as human capital. *Physical capital* includes the tangible tools necessary to implement an MTSS program and includes materials needed to execute the research-based interventions as well as the computerized assessment tools necessary for benchmarking and progress monitoring. *Human capital* includes the competencies, value, and knowledge the professionals on campus bring to the table. These costs are also extended to staffing highly qualified educators, training for highly qualified educators (including substitute teachers and support staff to cover for educators in trainings during school hours, or sending school leaders off campus for training), retaining these accomplished staff members, compensation for MTSS team members who work extra duty, and intervention class offerings.

Strategic resource allocation is part of the school's overall school improvement plan linked to fiscal management, and is a puzzle to be assembled by administrators in school settings. Weighing the benefits and costs of allocating time, money, and manpower for any given initiative is important to the decision-making process (Forman & Crystal, 2015). Ideally, schools prefer to target the greatest number of students with any new initiative to obtain the greatest return on their investment (Jimerson, Burns, & VanDerHeyden, 2016; Sailor, 2015). The more students an initiative targets successfully, the better schools can celebrate those successes and build on what works. Implementation of new systems in school organization takes investment not only in appropriate researched-based methods, but in training staff in how to use those methods (Lane, Carter, Jenkins, Dwiggins, & Germer, 2015). The interaction between the infrastructure and the ability of individuals to act on initiatives is complicated by the bureaucratic structures in which schools must operate, the needs of various stakeholders, and the continuous push for greater accountability and outcomes (Rigby, Woulfin, & Marz, 2016; Robinson, 2015). Building successful and sustainable MTSS infrastructure requires material resources and clearly established procedures, as well as staff buy-in and skill development. The directions of many simultaneously moving parts must be anticipated, accounted for, measured, and corrected within the framework. Getting people to row in the same direction is a leadership skill which is made possible when everyone has the tool(s) they need to paddle and they have received clearly communicated procedures. Teachers must be given a place to practice and use newly adopted methods, and school administration must allocate time for these activities to take place in order for them to be successful. Planning goes back to the basics of who, what, where, when, and how.

Master Schedule

On a secondary campus, the master schedule provides organizational support and the definitive answers to all administrators' questions about what is happening on campus (Forman & Crystal, 2015; Weisz, Ugueto, Cheron, & Herren, 2013). The *master schedule* provides the calendar and timetable to support the hourly, daily, weekly, monthly, and annual activities on a campus and is essential for successful program implementation. By calendaring MTSS activities at the beginning of the school year, team members can plan for meeting times, students will have an intervention block or two built into their school day if needed, and teachers can prepare to teach their intervention classes. As previously mentioned, MTSS has almost no chance of being comprehensively successful for students without the school principal actively supporting the process and leading the direction of infrastructure growth (Marston, Lau, Muyskens, & Wilson, 2016; Muhartono, Supriyono, Muluk, & Tjahjanulin, 2016). *The master schedule is the administrative commitment to providing time and space for MTSS team functions.* The master schedule must reflect several MTSS priorities: the allocation of staff and resources to the MTSS team, scheduled intervention classes with use of evidence-based curriculum, established MTSS team meeting dates and reserved locations, and calendaring of MTSS team functions including scheduled universal benchmarking assessments, assessment reporting dates, and other staff development activities and duties. The master schedule must also have family and community engagement opportunities intertwined with all stakeholders in a child's life; these are critical components to a successful MTSS.

Why does the MTSS team need the master schedule? The answer rests in the very fabric of a school's culture; the MTSS must be woven throughout all aspects of a school and the master schedule is the way to achieve this. The infrastructure and organizational components may look different on each campus, as it is important to customize MTSS according to each school's individual needs, but each piece must be present. As previously mentioned, there are landmarks to the process of implementation: leadership, human capital, professional compensation, material resources, team building, teacher and staff training, inclusive practices, quality universal instruction and benchmarking, systematic monitoring of student data, intervention implementation and documentation, progress monitoring, data-based decision making, program evaluation through feedback looping and problem solving, and professional communication. Decisions regarding these activities and processes impact every educator and child on campus either directly or indirectly.

Creating classes on the master calendar and staffing them with highly effective teachers provides the most reliable way to ensure implementation of interventions using research-based curriculum (Goldharber, 2008). *Using attendance records makes documentation of interventions with large numbers of students simple by using teacher lesson plans as evidence of targeted skills practice without the need for laborious note-taking for individual students on a teacher's part.* Expecting students and teachers to meet as needed, without a required commitment or systematic curriculum to improve academic outcomes, are not interventions that are sustainable, reliable, or valid (Freeman, Miller, & Newcomer, 2015).

Regular meeting times and locations for MTSS team meetings must be in the master schedule to ensure that team meetings are certain to occur. The MTSS meeting schedule will reflect the needs of a school, as higher-risk schools will need to meet more often than lower-risk schools (Taskiran, Mutluer, Tufan, & Semerci, 2017; McKee & Caldarella, 2016; Barrett & Katsiyannis, 2015; Shinn, 2007). However, regularly scheduled sessions to systematically review student data and engage in problem solving for students is mandatory regardless of a school's risk level. These mandatory meetings can occur weekly or twice a month depending on the school's needs. Meeting monthly is not effective for most schools, as the less frequent data analysis schedule is too limited to sensitively respond in a timely manner to difficulties students are experiencing (McKee & Caldarella, 2016; Killeen & Shafft, 2008). Monthly meetings are much less effective in impacting changes to at-risk students' academic, or emotional-behavioral, trajectory in a timely manner. Secondary MTSS teams should meet at the very least twice a month. Teams at higher-risk schools and those with larger campuses need to meet weekly due to the volume of students who require attention. How often the team meets, when, where, and who is required to attend is memorialized in the master schedule to ensure accountability and that all stakeholders have sufficient notice and opportunity to be present (Forman & Crystal, 2015; Freeman et al., 2015; Averill & Rinaldi, 2011; Shinn & Walker, 2010).

Intervention Class Scheduling

Scheduling intervention classes is the most systematic way to hold teachers and students accountable for attending intervention sessions and for tracking outcomes in a secondary setting. Valid interventions will not occur during class "free time," independently at home, or occasionally after school. Expecting students and teachers to voluntarily stay after school on a regular basis is not sustainable or reliable in large school systems, and ultimately will not meet the intervention requirements in the Every Student Succeeds Act (2015) and most state education laws. Intervention outcomes must be systematically monitored by the MTSS team to ensure *fidelity*, or trust in the accuracy and quality of the overall implementation process. The first step is to ensure that the intervention is being delivered *reliably*, or the intervention procedures are being implemented consistently as a treatment each time the classes meet. The second step to measuring outcomes is to systematically evaluate the *validity* of the intervention data; in other words, the MTSS team must determine if the data collected can be used meaningfully to create inferences and make decisions about the students from the scores collected.

The following two scenarios detail cases of reliability and validity. At Summit High School, the MTSS team was concerned when it realized some students on their caseload were not responding adequately to the interventions provided.

However, upon closer inspection, many of those students were not attending intervention classes regularly. In this case, the team was experiencing an issue with reliability of the intervention implemented. The problem solving step for these particular students was to address their poor attendance instead of deeming the intervention unsuccessful. Intervention effectiveness cannot be determined if students are not in class to receive the intensive instruction. If the team had not considered attendance and found it to be the culprit, the team may have recommended other solutions that would not have accurately addressed the underlying problem. Students must reliably receive interventions in order for them to be effective.

In a second scenario, at Lake Middle School, an intervention group was meeting reliably; however, the teacher was lackadaisical in collecting the intervention data, resulting in issues of validity. Due to feedback looping and school *leadership fidelity checks*, this teacher's lack of commitment in collecting intervention data with integrity came to light. Leadership fidelity checks are a review of all aspects of implementation procedures conducted by administration or a member of the leadership team that occur on both a regular or random basis, as needed. These leadership fidelity checks should occur at least twice a year. In this particular case, the teacher was using AIMSweb R-CBM as a strategic monitoring tool to assess basic reading fluency. Administered correctly, this is a valid tool to measure student growth in reading speed and accuracy, which highly correlates with reading achievement and reading comprehension; however, any tool administered incorrectly produces questionable data. Per the administration rules, the students are not allowed to see the teacher's computer screen as he or she is marking off incorrect student responses in real time (Pearson, 2015). If the student is allowed to see their errors as they read, it creates issues of *internal validity* as the data collected will be compromised due to teacher error and participant experience (Creswell, 2008). As a result, a causal relationship between the interventions provided and the outcomes obtained cannot be determined.

Several questions arose from the situation that the MTSS team at Lake Middle School had to consider. Most immediately, was the student truly capable of reading more words per minute fluently? This was an easy problem to address by administering a second, similar probe correctly with the student to get a true snapshot of their current skills, and to begin determining a causal relationship between interventions and outcomes. At a higher level, if the teacher compromised the integrity of the data because of how he or she administered the fluency probe, were the other students' progress monitoring probes being administered incorrectly as well? Had the teacher also been compromising the integrity of the interventions that were provided to the students? This would then require a systemic review of the teacher's performance, and all student data from this particular teacher's intervention group would need to be reexamined for validity.

As a general rule, problem solving is less effective, not to mention a waste of time and resources, if the implementation of interventions is not systematically monitored for reliability and validity. Appropriate scheduling of intervention classes on the master schedule, tracking attendance, and school leadership fidelity checks help to solve issues of reliability and validity.

Which academic content areas do the most students at school struggle in? How many intervention classes, and in which content areas, a school needs depends on the needs of its students. A low-risk school may not require as many intervention classes as a high-risk school. Higher-risk schools will require high-quality Tier 1 instruction with scaffolding and flexibility to allow for targeted re-teaching of gap skills if a majority, or significant number, of students lack those skills. Whether block scheduling, adding additional minutes in the school day or reallocating instructional class time to allow for it, intervention units in content areas must be on the master calendar, with approved instructional lesson plans and curriculum in place, to allow for leadership fidelity checks. Schools will start with as many intervention classes as possible to keep the student-to-teacher ratio low. Certain conditions must accompany the smaller student-to-teacher ratio, such as increasing the intensity of the individualized intervention to remediate skills and the accuracy of the differentiated, targeted instruction (National Center on Response to Intervention, 2013). The greater the duration of data collection, the greater the validity of the data for making data-based decisions for students (Van Norman & Christ, 2016). If a school can only reasonably implement one or two intervention classes per semester without compromising fidelity, start there; if it can go bigger, go for it.

It is not uncommon for schools to offer more English and reading remediation classes than mathematics; even at a 3:1 ratio or higher, depending on the population. Communities with a high population of second language students, or language deprived students, will need a greater number of intervention classes in the areas of reading and vocabulary development than English only communities. This population will also require extended periods of guided language exposure to help fill in missing language and academic learning gaps, in addition to inclusion in school-wide universal learning designs (Sailor, 2015). Populations with students and families living in chronic states of crisis may also require more remedial groups and wrap-around supports. One of the goals of MTSS implementation is to increase supports over time, and schools should only begin with the number of intervention classes they can offer while maintaining integrity of the interventions, while still addressing the critical needs of the students. Schools will need to prioritize their intervention offerings and should strive to establish as many supports as possible while maintaining integrity and accuracy of intervention implementation. Such classes may target mathematics interventions, behavioral interventions, written language interventions, and any other documented area of need at a school.

Scheduling intervention classes to address all areas of need could take years to build up. The sooner teams start building supports in schools, the sooner they will have the requisite number of intervention classes to sufficiently serve the entire school population. For example, at Martinez Middle School, an extra period was added to the end of the day so that instead of going to six different subject class periods per day, students who required intervention supports had seven classes a day. Students who did not require the extra period for interventions due to adequate school performance only had six required classes per day. It was determined that intervention classes would be grade neutral, and each at-risk student was placed in a class that most closely matched his or her *skill level*, not their academic grade level. Over time, intervention classes included several English Language Arts, a few math, and a couple of social-emotional-behavioral classes. Other enrichment opportunities offered after school included clubs, character development, sports, robotics, and music. In addition, numerous teachers were available daily for tutoring or homework club to help any student with homework or review of concepts.

Martinez Middle School continued to grow the number and types of intervention classes it offered for 7th period over the years. Through reflection and data-analysis, the reality of attendance problems was frustrating and data did not look good. Poor student attendance was impacting the success of the 7th period students' growth. More specifically, the eighth-grade students refused to stay for 7th period. Through ongoing analysis and problem solving, the leadership team tried a solution and adjusted the master schedule: they swapped the end-of-the-day intervention class with mid-day fundamental class units for eighth-grade students, which was scheduled in lieu of their elective.

These systemic revisions resulted in improved attendance and improved outcomes, as more students were present for their intervention classes. Throughout the process of adding 7th period and fundamental class periods during the day, considerations had to be made on the front end and concerns were dealt with throughout as unintended consequences were realized. *Unintended consequences* are outcomes that are realized without purposefully working toward them. For example, when adding the additional class period, initial questions were raised regarding who was going to teach it? Were teachers to be provided compensation? If so, how much? The principal at Martinez Middle School elected to pay hourly rate "extra duty" pay for teachers working 7th period and "bought-out" teachers' preparation periods during the day for teaching fundamental classes, so new staff did not need to be hired to cover the additional instructional units in the master schedule. Unintended consequences, such as high student absenteeism from end-of-the-day intervention class scheduling, were addressed by replacing students' elective period with an intervention class during the middle of the school day. However, an unintended consequence of that was lower student engagement in school as the higher interest elective coursework was removed. A positive unintended consequence of adding intervention classes during the day provided more students the opportunity to receive daily double intervention periods, usually in different areas of need, if they also stayed for the 7th period.

Poor attendance for 7th period intervention classes was an unintended consequence of adding a 7th period intervention class. Poor attendance for the class also impacted school attendance counts, which effected the school's annual accountability report. In many states, student attendance counts toward a school's overall achievement rating and also counts toward individual student credit attainment. By reworking the school's master schedule, and adding intervention class units during the school day to increase the probability 8th grade students would attend, improved the outcome measure, attendance rate, for the accountability report. In addition, attendance in general was an obvious area of need for improvement the school had to better target. After years of reviewing, revising, and reviewing again, block scheduling proved to be the best solution to scheduling issues for the following school year. Eight periods scheduled weekly, with A and B days, allow students to maintain an elective and give subject level teachers more accountability and time to work with their own students intensively during scheduled blocks. Leveling students by skill, rather than by grade, for intervention blocks allows flexibility for students changing classrooms during content level blocks, scheduled and executed just like separate intervention classes.

A school can never overestimate how many students on its campus will require interventions, especially on an at-risk campus. Given many of the aforementioned risk factors, such as poverty and language acquisition status, and the high correlation between reading proficiency and long-term student success, many schools elect to start their intervention supports with an emphasis on reading. For any intervention classes, it is important to begin with choosing the evidence-based curriculum that best fits your student population. The ease of use, expense, and training requirements all impact a school's choice of curriculum, but the efficacy of the selected method must be supported by positive and valid research-based outcome measures.

The next step is to select effective teachers to teach the curriculum. The most effective intervention teachers are often the most experienced teachers on your campus, but not always. The most effective intervention teachers will be those who are willing to get to know their students and differentiate their teaching based on student need, not just a student's performance on a test. According to the National Board for Professional Teaching Standards (2016) there are five core tenets, or propositions, that teachers should adhere to and be able to demonstrate in their teaching. Commitment to students and their learning is Proposition One of accomplished teaching (National Board for Professional Teaching Standards, 2016) and getting to know the challenges students face outside the classroom is another way teachers must learn to differentiate instruction based on need, not just performance.

Accomplished teachers are going to inspire students the most, creating a positive class culture of celebrating progress. *Positive class culture* is defined as a learning environment based on trust in which the students are encouraged and empowered to make and learn from mistakes. Once a student has reached their intervention goal and is consistently able to perform at a level typical for their grade, the student is exited from intervention class or advances to the next level. When students are exited from intervention classes, after consistently demonstrating success in accomplishing academic expectations without intense supports, they are publicly recognized with rewards and celebrated. Reflecting back to Martinez Middle School, the MTSS team nominates students for Principal's Recognition after they have achieved their way out of intervention classes and off the MTSS team monitoring list. The honor includes a personal visit with the school principal, a letter of commendation, and choices from the treasure box, which usually contains store gift cards and fast food certificates.

Ultimately, intervention classes need to be memorialized in the master calendar for the entire school year so students can get scheduled in, and out, as necessary. Typically, on a secondary school campus, the school counselors are responsible for making changes to student schedules after the MTSS team recommends the change. Students can graduate from an intervention class and new students can be scheduled in, depending on data analysis across multiple sources of response to instruction documentation. Remember, at-risk student data is reviewed regularly so decisions can be made whether to enter, remain, or graduate a student from intervention class(es). A student who has consistently met their intervention goal, and is to be exited from intervention class, would make that change at the end of the grading quarter. Conversely, students newly identified as needing an intervention class should be placed in it as soon as feasible. Students should have the opportunity to earn credits for intervention classes, especially credit-deficient students. Schools may consider blocking eight periods a day in the master schedule to allow for shorter classes yet more course offerings for intervention and credit retrieval classes during the regular school day, while providing additional electives for the rest of the student population. Longer blocks, scheduled on A and B days, may be preferred.

The bottom line is that students need opportunities to remediate skill deficits in addition to, and outside of, core curriculum classes (Cavendish, Harry, Menda, Espinosa, & Mahotiere, 2016; Forman & Crystal, 2015; Shinn, 2007). Teachers are best able to implement interventions with integrity with scheduled class periods built into the master schedule where they can dedicate time and energy to quality instruction. These interventions classes are essential to closing student gaps between expected progress and actual achievement. The most effective teachers recognize their own value and should be incentivized to teach intervention classes if occurring outside their contract duties. When school administration can celebrate teachers and students for positive outcomes, everyone wins.

How to fit it all in:

- Begin with fewer targeted content areas and build layers
- Establish flexible student scheduling
- Allow flexible teaching groups and student grouping
- Fund after-school tutoring or credit retrieval opportunities
- Provide online resources and supports
- Allow elective flexibility
- Offer supplemental class supports
- Add research-based curriculum designed for Tier 2 and Tier 3 incrementally
- Establish routine program evaluation
- Review, revise, and implement using feedback looping and continuous improvement model

MTSS Team Meetings

Regular MTSS meeting times and locations must be built into the master schedule to ensure that team meetings occur. The MTSS meeting schedule reflects the needs of a school with higher-risk school teams needing to meet more often than lower-risk school teams. Regardless of the frequency of the meeting schedule, they must be held at regular intervals to systematically review student data and engage in problem solving for students. Keep in mind, these meetings can occur once a week or every two weeks, but not as infrequently as monthly. Meeting monthly or less is not effective for most schools because a sporadic meeting schedule is much too limited to respond to the difficulties students may be experiencing. There is a constant need for ongoing revisions to adjust the academic and social-emotional-behavioral trajectories of individual students in a timely manner. Students are not widgets that stay stable over time, and they require vigilant care to address their needs. Many can be put back on track in a timely manner with minor adjustments, and others are going to require routine maintenance. *The key element is that decisions are made in a timely manner.* The highest-needs students, with the most severe behavioral deficits, require teams to discuss them on a more frequent basis than other at-risk students, and they may be selected for further monitoring by other school-based teams, such as the behavioral and mental health team.

MTSS Extension Opportunities

Offering structured learning opportunities outside the school day is an excellent way to expand services to students. MTSS can be extended to individualized supports such as homework clubs, Saturday school programs, and summer school programs with students allowed to earn credit for their participation in intervention programming. The opportunity to earn credit for intervention classes should include MTSS extension opportunities, as students should be able to earn credits for all intervention classes taken throughout the year. *MTSS extension opportunities* are programming options or incentives for students outside of traditional school offerings.

Saturday school and extending the school year throughout summer are options for schools to consider when scheduling additional time and space for interventions within the master calendar. These supports could be offered on a voluntary school-by-school basis or part of a larger, systemic approach to educating students in high-risk schools (Fleming, 2013). Research has long demonstrated that students, especially those from high-risk environments, tend to lose content knowledge after large breaks from structured academic settings (Cooper, 2003; Copple, Kane, Levin & Cohen, 1992). Summer school is one way to remediate this loss and, ideally, would be redesigned as a positive learning opportunity, like camp, rather than a penalty of hard labor for slacking off during the school year.

As a matter of equity, students living in impoverished socioeconomic areas should be funded higher to provide year-round schooling and intervention opportunities for children to thrive in continuity of exposure and practice to academic concepts. Students who are not native English speakers or who are from impoverished backgrounds will require more deliberate practice and support in order to achieve mastery in reading. Mastery of a skill requires extensive and continuous practice over time.

In many high-risk schools, academically underexposed, underachieving students are the majority on campus. *It is important to remember that the Common Core State Standards Initiative (2010a, 2010b) and traditional education structures target the aggregate majority, not the actual majority of students on many campuses.* Summer school helps close the language and academic gaps of students who do not have access to books over the summer or are not motivated to read independently to master reading.

Other opportunities for MTSS extension at the state and local levels is through investments in schools, libraries, and parks to provide free learning experiences for children. These investments could also help support students to get in additional hours of reading, engaging learning activities, and ultimately increasing the probability of becoming master readers. Families with socioeconomic disadvantages are less likely to have access to books to motivate children to read and develop skills throughout their summers off from school, thus getting in less hours of reading compared to their more socioeconomically advantaged peers. More affluent communities would also benefit from summer school programs; however, the fees to attend, hours of operation, and curriculum may differ. Allocating resources for summer school and intervention programs is a matter of equity, not equality, for students who may be victim of social injustices (Francis, Mills, & Lupton, 2017).

Schools are often the first place where students' needs are identified because it is guaranteed that students will bring their problems to school. It is much more effective to have structures and functions in place with prepared school professionals actively monitoring and responding to constantly evolving student difficulties, rather than winging responses haphazardly when problems arise. Reactive practices, rather than proactive practices, lead to multiple missed opportunities to positively impact students. A higher frequency of planned MTSS meetings, carving out time and space for the MTSS team to engage in timely problem solving, is always better than not having enough time to address the needs of students. *Weekly meetings should be the gold standard.* Remember, with the exception of a few members, not all the same team members have to be at every meeting. Scheduling weekly MTSS meetings on the master calendar will weave MTSS tighter into the fabric of the school culture and will help teams to reach MTSS landmarks and their ultimate destination of comprehensive supports by addressing student needs in a timely and efficient manner.

Box 4.1

Connection to Practice

MTSS Planning and Implementation Timetable

Note: this is not meant to be an exhaustive timetable of events and may vary based on the unique needs of the school.

Spring of year before implementation:

- Select MTSS team chairs
- Inquire about which current educators would be a good fit for case managers
- Evaluate current academic curriculum and select evidence-based curriculum and interventions to be used in Tiers 1, 2, and 3
- Evaluate current social-emotional-behavioral learning curriculum and supports, and select evidence-based curriculum and resources to be used in Tiers 1, 2, and 3
- Look at master calendar and schedule MTSS meeting dates, times, and locations
- Administrator must start identifying teaching practices to grow school-wide
- Consider school culture and climate and any changes that could be made
- Build intervention blocks, structure, and processes into the master calendar and teacher resource guides

- Explore community resources to share with staff and families
- Investigate ways to incorporate family engagement throughout the upcoming school year
- Poll families on what type of family engagement opportunities they would like

Summer before implementation:

- Train MTSS chair(s), case managers, and specialists in universal benchmarking and use of progress monitoring tools
- Ensure master calendar reflects MTSS priorities, benchmark windows, intervention classes, meetings etc.
- Ensure all resources are available to support implementation at all three tiers of MTSS for Academic, Behavioral and Mental Health
- Establish school-wide expectations and positive behavioral supports
- Work out any glitches in funding for resources and staff allocations
- Train MTSS team to ensure orientation to framework and responsibilities
- Train at best, or orient at minimal, the entire staff on MTSS framework, procedures, and structure
- Work through any scheduling and meeting logistics
- Contact and establish pathways for community engagement and support
- Establish family engagement opportunities and calendar them to occur at least every other month

Beginning of school year:

- If MTSS team members have not been selected and oriented in summer, do so within the first week of school
- If team members haven't been trained in universal benchmarking and use of progress monitoring tools, do so within the first week of school
- If entire staff has not been oriented to MTSS, do so within the first week of school
- First whole team MTSS meeting should be held as close to the beginning of the year as possible, after which grade level MTSS meetings rotate thereafter
- Team expectations reviewed, master calendar reviewed, meeting etiquette rules reviewed, caseloads disseminated, and problem solving begins
- Entire staff must be trained with guided practice in universal benchmarking and progress monitoring
- Establish and provide training on school-wide expectations and positive behavioral supports
- Fall benchmarking

Throughout school year:

- Follow continuous improvement model
- Follow MTSS Evaluation Frequency and Intensity Framework
- Conduct benchmark assessments during fall, winter, and spring benchmark windows

End of school year:

- Convene leadership team to review, revise, and revamp processes
- Use feedback looping to use data collected as inputs for future planning and decision making
- Consult with outside agencies or partners to bolster any identified gaps in programming
- Determine where advocacy opportunities may lie

References

Averill, O. H., & Rinaldi, C. (2011). Multi-tier systems of support. *District Administration, 9*, 91–94.

Barrett, D. E., & Katsiyannis, A. (2015). Juvenile delinquency recidivism: Are Black and White youth vulnerable to the same risk factors? *Behavioral Disorders, 40*(3), 184–195.

Carman, J. G. (2010). The accountability movement: What's wrong with this theory of change? *Nonprofit and Voluntary Sector Quarterly, 39*(2), 256–274.

Cavendish, W., Harry, B., Menda, A. M., Espinosa, A., & Mahotiere, M. (2016). Implementing response to intervention: Challenges of diversity and system change in a high-stakes environment. *Teachers College Record, 118*, 1–36.

Common Core State Standards Initiative (2010a). *Common core state standards for English language arts and literacy in history/social studies, science, and technical subjects.* Retrieved from www.corestandards.org/wp-content/uploads/ELA_Standards1.pdf.

Common Core State Standards Initiative (2010b). *Common core state standards for mathematics.* Retrieved from www.corestandards.org/wp-content/uploads/Math_Standards1.pdf.

Cooper, H. (2003). Summer learning loss: The problem and some solutions. *ERIC Digest*, 1–7.

Copple, C., Kane, M., Levin, D., & Cohen, S. (1992, April). *The National Education Commission on Time and Learning: Briefing paper* (Issue Brief No. 372–482). Washington, DC: The National Commission on Time and Learning.

Creswell, J. W. (2008). *Educational research: Planning, conducting, and evaluating quantitative and qualitative research.* Upper Saddle River, NJ: Pearson Education.

Epstein, D., & Klerman, J. A. (2013). When is a program ready for rigorous impact evaluation? The role of a falsifiable logic model. *Evaluation Review, 36*(5), 375–401.

Every Student Succeeds Act of 2015, 20 U.S.C. (2015).

Fleming, N. (2013, June). Districts turning summer school into learning labs: Goal is to engage and teach students. *Education Week, 32*(35). Retrieved from www.edweek.org/ew/articles/2013/06/12/35summer.h32.html.

Foorman, B. (2016). Introduction to the special issue: Challenges and solutions to implementing effective reading intervention in schools. In B. Foorman (Ed.), *Challenges to Implementing Effective Reading Intervention in Schools. New Directions for Child and Adolescent Development, 154*, 7–10.

Forman, S. G., & Crystal, C. D. (2015). Systems consultation for multitiered systems of supports (MTSS): Implementation issues. *Journal of Educational and Psychological Consultation, 25*, 276–285.

Francis, B., Mills, M., & Lupton, R. (2017). Toward social justice in education: Contradictions and dilemmas. *Journal of Education Policy, 32*(4), 414–431.

Frechtling, J. A. (2007). *Logic modeling methods in program evaluation.* San Francisco, CA: Wiley, Jossey-Bass.

Freeman, R., Miller, D., & Newcomer, L. (2015). Integration of academic and behavioral MTSS at the district level using implementation science. *Learning Disabilities: A Contemporary Journal, 13*(1), 59–72.

Gladwell, M. (2008). *Outliers: The story of success*. New York: Little, Brown and Company.

Goldharber, D. (2008). The value of teacher quality. In H. F. Ladd & E. B. Fiske (Eds.), *Handbook of research in education finance and policy* (pp. 146–165). New York: Routledge.

Gordon, L. (Producer), & Robinson, P. A. (Director) (1989). *Field of dreams* [Motion picture]. United States: Universal Studios.

Individuals With Disabilities Education Act, 20 U.S.C. § 1400 *et seq.* (2006 & Supp. V. 2011).

Jimerson, S. R., Burns, M. K., & VanDerHeyden, A. M. (Eds.) (2016). *The handbook of response to intervention: The science and practice of multi-tiered systems of support*. New York: Springer.

Killeen, K. M., & Schafft, K. (2008). The organizational and fiscal implications of transient student populations. In H. F. Ladd & E. B. Fiske (Eds.), *Handbook of research in education finance and policy* (pp. 146–165). New York: Routledge.

Lane, K. L., Carter, E. W., Jenkins, A., Dwiggins, L., & Germer, K. (2015). Supporting comprehensive, integrated, three-tiered models of prevention in schools: Administrators' perspectives. *Journal of Positive Behavior Interventions, 17*(4), 209–222.

Marston, D., Lau, M., Muyskens, P., & Wilson, J. (2016). Data-based decision-making, the problem-solving model, and response to intervention in the Minneapolis public schools. In S. Jimerson, M. Burns, & A. VanDerHeyden (Eds.), *The handbook of response to intervention: The science and practice of multi-tiered systems of support* (pp. 677–692). New York: Springer.

McDavid, J. C., & Hawthorn, L. R. L. (2006). *Program evaluation and performance measurement: An introduction to practice*. Thousand Oaks, CA: Sage Publications.

McKee, M. T., & Caldarella, P. (2016). Middle school predictors of high school performance: A case study of dropout risk indicators. *Education, 136*(4), 515–529.

Mirabella, R. M. (2013). Toward a more perfect nonprofit: The performance mindset and the "Gift." *Administrative Theory and Praxis, 35*(1), 81–105.

Muhartono, D. S., Supriyono, B., Muluk, M. R. K., & Tjahjanulin (2016). Implementation of education services in sound governance perspective. *International Journal of Multidisciplinary Approach & Studies, 3*(4), 101–118.

National Board for Professional Teaching Standards (2016). *What teachers should know and be able to do*. Arlington, VA: Author.

National Center on Response to Intervention (2013). *RTI in middle schools: The essential components* (Publication No. 2313-10/12). Retrieved from https://rti4success.org/sites/default/files/RTI%20in%20Middle%20Schools-The%20Essential%20Components.pdf.

Odden, A. R. (2012). *Improving student learning when budgets are tight*. Thousand Oaks, CA: Corwin.

Odden, A. R., & Picus, L. O. (2014). *School finance: A policy perspective* (5th ed.). New York: McGraw Hill.

Pearson (2015). *AIMSweb software guide version 2.5.10*. Retrieved from https://aimsweb2.pearson.com/aimsweb-frontoffice/helpsupport/help/aimsweb_software_guide2510.pdf.

Rigby, J. G., Woulfin, S. L., & Marz, V. (2016). Understanding how structure and agency influence education policy implementation and organizational change. *American Journal of Education, 122*, 295–302.

Robinson, S. (2015). Decentralisation, managerialism and accountability: Professional loss in an Australian education bureaucracy. *Journal of Education Policy, 30*(4), 468–482, doi:10.1080/02680939.2015.1025241.

Sailor, W. (2015). Advances in schoolwide inclusive school reform. *Remedial and Special Education, 36*(2), 94–99.

Schafft, K., & Killeen, K. M. (2008). *Addressing a moving target: Poverty and student transiency in rural upstate New York* (Policy Brief 16). Retrieved from Cornell University Community and Rural Development Institute website: https://cardi.cals.cornell.edu/sites/cardi.cals.cornell.edu/files/shared/documents/ResearchPolicyBriefs/04-2008-RPB.pdf.

Shinn, M. R. (2007). Identifying students at risk, monitoring performance, and determining eligibility within RTI: Research on educational need and benefit from academic intervention. *School Psychology Review, 36*(4), 601–617.

Shinn, M. R., & Walker, H. M. (Eds.) (2010). *Interventions for academic and behavior problems in a three-tier model, including Response-to-Intervention* (3rd ed.). Bethesda, MD: National Association of School Psychologists.

Sprick, R. A. (2009). *CHAMPS: A proactive and positive approach to classroom management* (2nd ed.). Eugene, OR: Pacific Northwest Publishing.

Sprick, R. A. (2013). *Discipline in the secondary classroom: A positive approach to behavior management* (3rd ed.). Hoboken, NJ: John Wiley & Sons.

Taskiran, S., Mutluer, T., Tufan, A. E., & Semerci, B. (2017). Understanding the associations between psychosocial factors and severity of crime in juvenile delinquency: A cross-sectional study. *Neuropsychiatric Disease and Treatment, 13*, 1359–1366.

Trevisian, M. S. (2007). Evaluability assessment from 1986–2006. *American Journal of Evaluation, 28*, 290–303.

Van Norman, E. R., & Christ, T. J. (2016). How accurate are interpretations of curriculum-based measurement progress monitoring data? Visual analysis versus decision rules. *Journal of School Psychology, 58*, 41–55.

Weisz, J. R., Ugueto, A. M., Cheron, D. M., & Herren, J. (2013). Evidence-based youth psychotherapy in the mental health ecosystem. *Journal of Clinical Child & Adolescent Psychopathology, 42*(2), 274–286.

Chapter 5

How an MTSS Team Works Together

Key Terms

Role
Case Manager Model
MTSS Case Manager
MTSS Chairs
Responsive Adaptability
MTSS Student Database
Case Notes
Legitimization
School Counselors
School Psychologists
Specialists

Chapter Concepts

In this chapter, readers will learn:

1. How to incorporate valuable professional roles into one cohesive MTSS team.
2. Who organizes student cases and presents their information at MTSS team meetings.
3. The organization and flow of an MTSS team meeting.
4. The necessity for responsive adaptability in today's education climate.
5. The importance of legitimizing processes into the culture of the MTSS program.
6. The need to uphold certain meeting etiquette from all MTSS team members.

With the infrastructure of a solid MTSS program in place, it is time to train the MTSS team how to support the students on campus. Chapter 5 will delve into how your selected team members work together to form a cohesive unit, and the roles and responsibilities of each member. Specifically, the roles of MTSS case managers, MTSS chairs, school counselors, school psychologists, specialists, and

teachers will be discussed. Leading up to this chapter several foundational supports have been discussed including strong leadership, a budget prioritizing MTSS
funding, and the selection of research-supported Tier 2 and Tier 3 curriculum,
teaching, and intervention materials. Additionally, factors such as scheduled intervention classes, highly qualified teachers working with at-risk students, required
meetings and functions of MTSS memorialized in the master calendar, and the
most effective educators positioned in leadership roles have been reviewed.

Before the start of the school year, MTSS team members should be selected
based on the processes and discussion points from Chapter 2. It is strongly
encouraged to schedule initial training for the MTSS team members prior to the
beginning of the school year because once the students arrive on campus the proverbial train will be in motion and gaining speed as the weeks pass. It is much
more difficult to board a moving train than one docked at the station. If trainings
cannot be scheduled for team members prior to the start of the year, the team
should meet within the first two weeks of school.

On a school campus, the schedule is the axis around which everything rotates.
Team members need a schedule to conduct duties, and organizational timelines
are established from before the first day of the school year through the last day of
the school year (Forman & Crystal, 2015; Freeman, Miller, & Newcomer, 2015;
Averill & Rinaldi, 2011). Organizing MTSS teams, defining roles, and establishing a calendar are no different. *It is important to understand that each role is not bound
to one person or position on the team.* A *role* is a function assumed by a particular
person; it is duty or skill specific, not title specific. When building a solid MTSS
foundation it is essential to define each role clearly before deciding the best
professional on campus to fill that role. A school will typically fill a role based on
a profession. It is important to define the roles in a traditional sense before
making substitutions based on the realities of the campus. School administrators
can then make allowances if necessary to fill the positions based on personnel
available on their campus.

Effective school MTSS teams share the burden of duties and decision making.
Each educator is uniquely qualified to provide a different, but important, perspective that other professional roles cannot fulfill. Role responsibilities can be
shared and may be interchangeable, but each perspective should be considered in
the decision-making model. Relying solely on one or two teachers or specialists
to be the workhorses of the entire team is unrealistic and cannot be sustained
over time. It burns out passionate educators who are trying to make a difference
because others are less willing to contribute to the team's success. Teams will
need to define the responsibilities for the following professionals to ensure quality
control: administrators, school psychologists, teachers, special education teachers,
specialists, school counselors, school nurses, school social workers, and other
licensed professionals. Case managers and MTSS Chair positions will also need to
be defined and responsibilities made explicit.

Each MTSS team member has specific responsibilities that contribute to the
team's success, and these unique roles each complement one another. Every
person on the team contributes a piece to the puzzle of student success, which is
why it is so important to assemble the big picture together. Not every team
member is required to attend every meeting. Indeed, MTSS is structured so that
meetings can proceed whether or not all team members are available, which is

likely to occur due to the many demands and responsibilities of school professionals. With the weekly meeting time established in the master calendar, MTSS teams can plan for certain members to make accommodations to plan their attendance at each weekly meeting.

Team members who should plan to be at every meeting weekly include the designated administrator, MTSS team chairs and co-chairs, school counselors, specialists, school psychologists, and school social workers. The aforementioned group have professional responsibilities to students across grade levels and subject levels. It is unlikely that everyone can attend every meeting every week, but the more who attend, the better the team can function. *This well-rounded panel of professionals expands the breadth of decision making for at-risk students.* The MTSS chair or co-chair must be present to run the weekly meeting and in the absence of the chair, an administrator or administrative liaison must be present to chair the meeting.

The following sections outline the roles and responsibilities of the MTSS case managers and MTSS chairs. In the broadest sense, case managers facilitate the collection of student data, while chairs organize and maintain the digital record of cumulative student data. School counselors, school psychologists, specialists, and teachers will then be discussed regarding the specific value and perspective each brings to the MTSS team.

MTSS Case Managers

The case manager model is an effective way to share responsibility for students with other teachers and school professionals, which provides built-in accountability and expands the network of supports available (Stearns, 2017). The *case manager model* is student-centered and assigns a specific educator to advocate for the students they are assigned to represent. Case managers may be administrators, teachers, school counselors, or other highly trained professionals on campus. An argument for having compensated teachers as case managers is that teachers who feel valued will more likely buy into MTSS for the processes to work most effectively. Educators are more likely to buy into processes that are driven by their peers, that they feel have high efficacy, and that are endorsed by school leadership (Anyon, Nicotera, & Veeh, 2016; Pinkelman, McIntosh, Rasplica, Berg, & Strickland-Cohen, 2015). The strongest teachers should be recruited, and financially rewarded, to be on the MTSS team to help grow better practices schoolwide. Accomplished educators actively supporting the effectiveness of other educators who have challenging students breeds better teaching on campus. Using teachers as case managers increases the "street credibility" of the MTSS process. Other school professionals may be successful in the role, of course, but teachers are mandatory members of a successful MTSS team and optimally in leadership positions. For purposes of discussing this model, teachers are the case managers, even though team roles can be interchangeable among members as long as specialized perspectives are taken into account.

Case managers are responsible for researching and documenting student history, collecting data from multiple sources, presenting data at meetings, communicating changes to student instructional interventions to relevant stakeholders, and getting feedback from student teachers on efficacy of interventions. Student data discussed at MTSS meetings include student grades, standards-based test scores, curriculum-based test scores, formative assessment results, summative assessment results, benchmark and progress monitoring data, behavioral data, discipline data, health information, attendance history, teacher observations, and parent/guardian report to make decisions for students (Sprick, 2013; Dishon, 2011; Shinn & Walker, 2010; Sprick, 2009; Shinn, 2007).

Case managers are often selected to support the grades they teach, and ideally, they represent the grade levels they are reporting on. Thus, at a small low-risk middle school campus, there could be three case managers: one for sixth grade, one for seventh grade, and one for eighth grade. This allows case managers to work with teachers in subject level meetings, and increases the probability that case managers already have working knowledge of the students they are discussing. Larger and higher-risk campuses will require more than one case manager per grade level due to higher numbers of at-risk students to manage. The reason the case manager model works so well in secondary schools is because it creates a focal point in the storm of fast moving information for student data, observations, and recommendations to be gathered, discussed, and disseminated. With large numbers of students on secondary campuses, individual needs may get overlooked due to the sheer volume of information classroom teachers must manage for high numbers of students.

The case manager model allows for the rotation of grade level case managers to be present at MTSS meetings. For example, the sixth-grade case manager is only required to come to the MTSS team meeting when it is rotationally time to present on sixth grade students. This rotation schedule will vary depending on how frequently the MTSS team meets; however, on a typical middle school campus, it will rotate one grade every three (weekly meeting schedule) to six weeks (meeting schedule of once every two weeks): first sixth grade, then seventh grade, and then eighth grade. The time between meetings allows for interventions to be implemented, progress monitoring data to be collected, and case managers to get feedback on individual students from classroom teachers. The grade level case managers must attend their designated week to present student data to the MTSS team, or they must assign another person to represent them at the meeting if they know they are going to be absent.

In summary, case managers' duties include:

- Review records including the following considerations: attendance, summative and formative test scores, report cards, discipline data, behavior data, health status, benchmark and progress monitoring data
- Complete the MTSS Team Referral Form
- Facilitate communication with school nurse, ensure vision and hearing screenings completed, and consider health history
- Correspond with parents/caregivers, as needed, and make attempts to obtain student family and health history forms from caregivers
- Communicate with classroom teachers by requesting feedback and providing feedback
- Organize data in folders; discard old data and ensure current data is available for decision making at MTSS meetings

- Prepare data and present student information to team members at MTSS meetings
- Report issues to chairs and administrators including barriers to implementation, issues of executing team recommendations, teacher compliance with recommendations, or obtaining feedback from teachers on students
- Attend all MTSS meetings pertaining to their caseload.

MTSS Chair and/or Co-Chair

The MTSS chair is the conductor of the MTSS train and ensures that the MTSS meetings stay on track for the duration of the scheduled time. The *chair* communicates MTSS meeting dates, records meeting discussions, leads meetings, problem solves MTSS functions and processes, and liaises with stakeholder groups. Additional responsibilities of the chair can be negotiated, but they should be clearly defined prior to the start of the school year. These duties should then be communicated to administration *before* the first MTSS training to ensure there are no gaps in coverage of responsibilities and to make explicit the understanding of the role by both parties. This shared understanding and recognized value that the educators bring to the team is key in the integrated delivery of intervention services (Rainey & Gifford, 2016). The need for supplementary duties may also arise via iterative feedback throughout the year, especially during the first year of implementation. The chair of the MTSS team is most often an administrator, school counselor, or specialist on a secondary campus. Classroom teachers are discouraged from chairing MTSS due to the amount of work required during the school day, such as follow-up meetings, that could potentially impact their time in the classroom. Teachers with special assignments may be considered to chair or co-chair the MTSS team with preference given to school professionals with the most flexibility during the day to enable timely response to issues that may arise. There are five broad and explicit roles of the MTSS chair:

- Communicate meeting dates and times with the team and reschedule meetings as necessary
- Record meeting discussions and data in the MTSS Student Database
- Lead MTSS team meetings
- Problem solve team functions and processes
- Liaise with stakeholder groups.

The first role of the MTSS chair is that of *communicator* to ensure that messaging of dates and times of grade level MTSS meetings are shared among all school personnel through the master calendar, school-wide memos, and emails or other established communication tools with staff. *Clear and consistent communication is non-negotiable and an essential component to the success of an MTSS team.* The MTSS chair must take full responsibility for communicating and scheduling meetings, and they must hold themselves accountable for sharing meeting dates and times. Any number of school problems may arise that interfere with scheduling; "expect the unexpected" is a healthy mindset for the MTSS chair. There will always be school events, staff responsibilities, and student or school issues that compete with meeting times for team members. The key to success over time is to adapt quickly to interruptions of meeting times and dates to ensure that the meeting(s) are rescheduled as quickly as possible, in any way possible, to guarantee that student needs are addressed in a timely manner.

The MTSS chair will be in charge of effectively communicating and liaising with administrators, teachers, and other stakeholders to find the most reasonable time to reschedule meetings. *Sometimes the MTSS chair has to be creative, and creativity in scheduling on a secondary campus always requires administrative support.* This support may come in the form of finding a suitable location for the meeting or finding coverage for a teacher's duties while attending an off-schedule meeting. Sometimes rescheduling meetings causes more problems than can be compensated for, and meetings simply must be shifted forward a week in the rotation. In such instances, all future meetings are also shifted forward a week. The MTSS chair, with administrative oversight, must balance the pros and cons of rescheduling or postponing meetings that impact MTSS team members and possibly other teachers and staff members.

The specific responsibility of the MTSS chair to ensure meetings consistently take place is a seemingly simple task that can also become the most challenging. Secondary schools are like beehives in that individuals function very systematically. In an actual beehive, bees can organize quickly to address threats to the hive. School systems are not that automated or efficient due to their bureaucratic nature. A bureaucratic system is unlikely to change quickly, but an effective school must be adaptable and make timely changes to respond to community and district requirements. The constantly changing demands in a secondary school environment require responsive adaptability from workers in the system to succeed. *Responsive adaptability* is the ability to quickly and seamlessly adjust to ever-changing environmental demands. Like beehives, sometimes the "worker bees" in schools can be resistant to change and become highly aggressive if order is not followed. Staff members may not be receptive to altering their schedules, or covering for others, on short notice. *A school culture built on responsive adaptability is more likely to succeed in implementing MTSS than schools with rigid cultures and staff members.* All functions of MTSS team members are made easier with active administrative backing and problem solving engagement, starting with administrative support for the MTSS chair. The administrative expectation of responsive adaptability and cooperation among all staff members in supporting functions of MTSS must follow.

The second crucial responsibility of MTSS team chairs is to *record* MTSS team meetings in the digital MTSS Student Database of case notes. The *MTSS Student Database* is the storehouse that archives all data for students who are discussed at MTSS team meetings, and is achieved by creating and maintaining a running record of at-risk student history, interventions implemented, school performance, current needs, and recommendations for school success. *Case notes* are supplemental data that are entered into the MTSS Student Database and that are not otherwise captured in one of the predetermined columns. There are many different formats and styles of documentation and presentation of information team members may prefer. Some teams want more information, some want less. There is a bare minimum of content areas that must be recorded for the team to process together at meetings. Extraneous student information may be included in the MTSS Student Database as long as the information is relevant to student decision making and the information during discussion does not become a distraction, wasting precious time during team meetings.

A visual representation of critical student information should be used to facilitate discussions at meetings. Excel spreadsheets and Google Sheets are an excellent way to summarize large amounts of information on students into one document, boiling down data on numerous students to one or two pages. This is one way to lend legitimization to the MTSS program itself and provides artifacts that serve as a running record of team engagement (Guéguen, Pascual, Silone, & David, 2015). *Legitimization* occurs within an organization when an act or process becomes entrenched in its values and norms. With MTSS programming, handing out copies of the spreadsheet to team members at each meeting formalizes processes and creates an archive of meeting discussions. In doing so, it gives team members documentation of decisions at past meetings and allows them to make personalized notes for their own records. The MTSS chair, or designee, updates team decisions on the spreadsheet at *each meeting* so that there is a dated digital record of recommendations made and who made the recommendations. Note-taking must not be onerous or extensive; however, enough detailed information must be provided so the team does not "go backwards" in recommending efforts that have already been tried. The MTSS Student Database of case notes on every student in the school identified as at-risk academically, socially, emotionally, or behaviorally is one of the most valuable tools professional educators have in keeping track of large numbers of individual student needs and tracking evidence-based outcomes.

The style and format of the MTSS Student Database and case notes can, and should be, personalized for user preferences. The database must be user-friendly, easy to read, and designed to reflect student priorities monitored by the team. Some teams use one data sheet per student, while others use a combined spreadsheet for the grade or school. In paper-free schools, some teams prefer to use technology with SMART Boards, televisions, or computers and projectors during their meetings and do not print out case notes for team members; team members write notes in their own notebooks or take notes on electronic devices. What format of documentation and which style of visual presentation works for a school and its team are fair game. As long as relevant student history, programming, current functioning, and rate of progress over time is captured in the MTSS case notes, any format and style that works for the team is the one that should be used.

The MTSS Student Database should be the gold standard for tracking at-risk students by a multidisciplinary team of educators. With the appropriate credentials and training, almost any member of the MTSS team can be substituted. The information passes on from generation to generation of MTSS team members instead of being lost forever when educators with specific knowledge of students move on. All reports of a student's needs over time have been documented and the next educational professional can pick up where the last educator in that position left off. This ensures that there are paths forward for each student and that they are each supported and monitored by the MTSS team. Likewise, if a student moves or changes schools, case notes could be released to parents and the new school of enrollment. Individual student data should be sent to forwarding schools within the same school district, or out of district, in an attempt to provide students with continued supports at their next school. Parents should be provided this documentation at time of withdrawal so they can advocate for their child's needs at the next school.

Information on each student monitored by the MTSS team and recorded in the MTSS Student Database should include at minimum: name, grade, student identification number, name of school counselor, name of intervention teacher(s), name of intervention class(es), attendance history, pertinent health information, criterion referenced or summative test scores, language proficiency levels (if English is a second language), enrollment history, discipline history, and benchmark scores. A spreadsheet is effective and easy to use, as it can be customized any number of ways to allow for documentation to be completed with checkmarks, dates, and numbers in corresponding boxes and columns, saving time and effort. In addition to student level reporting, aggregate reports can also be run at the grade and school level, with proper spreadsheet formatting.

Some of the information in the MTSS Student Database will remain static while some is constantly evolving. Static information is relevant to decision making and is all but impossible for team members to remember when discussing large numbers of students, for example, student names and student numbers. Some information changes over time and has to be regularly updated, such as attendance or progress monitoring scores. One of the most important columns on the spreadsheet is "Comments and Case Notes" that qualitatively reflects current student issues that cannot be captured by a checkmark or score in a column. The best MTSS Student Databases capture input from team members actively solving problems for students, which leads to next steps.

The third priority for the MTSS chair is to *lead* MTSS team meetings. Predetermined meeting etiquette protocols should be observed to ensure professional and on-topic discussions. All team members should be trained in the established MTSS meeting format, including preparation and presentation of data, at the beginning of the school year so that team meetings will run efficiently (Van Norman & Christ, 2016). If organized and well executed, teams can expect to discuss many more students per hour, situation dependent. If a student's issues are too severe or require more attention than a quick status check allows, the MTSS chair must table further discussion and direct the specific team members needed to get together and problem solve after the meeting. *Overspending meeting time on one student results in less time to discuss the other students on the monitoring list.* Some teams prefer to set a timer for each student up for discussion so they get in the habit of short and focused power conversations to make informed swift decisions. When the timer goes off, decisions are made and documented, and team members agree to discuss the student's case more in-depth outside the MTSS meeting or at a future MTSS meeting date. All side decisions and recommendations are reported back to the MTSS chair for the digital database case notes.

Greater organization on behalf of the case manager results in more efficient discussions and meetings. The more organized case managers are, the faster discussions go. Some students' information can be reviewed more quickly than others because there are no changes or there is an obvious overarching issue, such as attendance. In these instances, the overarching issue must be addressed first. Other times, positive changes are reported to case managers and less discussion time is needed. For example, a student may be demonstrating improved effort and performance in their classes, their grades are improving, or their growth is documented to be promising across sources and class environments. Interventions for students who are making adequate progress in response to the interventions provided are typically short conversations. In such cases, the intervention would be deemed effective, so the decision to continue progress monitoring should be easy with minimal discussion. The MTSS chair provides input to decisions during discussions and keeps the discussions moving when team members get off-topic or get held up on irrelevant gossip about the student, which eats up valuable meeting time.

The fourth priority of the MTSS chair involves *problem solving* with administration. The MTSS chair must take notes of trouble spots in team functions and processes, and communicate any issues with relevant administrators and stakeholders in an effort to get solutions. *Solving problems with MTSS processes relies on collaborative communication with staff members.* The MTSS chair serves as the liaison between the case managers and school administrators regarding efficacy and efficiency of MTSS processes. Case managers may have a hard time getting teachers to provide feedback, even on a Google Form survey that only takes them two minutes to click through and complete. The case managers then report the lack of communication to the MTSS chair, which is monitored by administration. Teachers who consistently shirk their duty to provide case managers with student performance data must ultimately be addressed by administration, and liaising through the case manager is the way to achieve this. Case managers are responsible for getting feedback from teachers to enable the MTSS team to make instructional support decisions. Without the crucial outcome evidence of current performance in the classroom, MTSS team decisions are not guaranteed to be timely or effective. When reasonable efforts have failed to get feedback from a teacher the next step must include administrative supervisors in professional conversations.

As part of the problem solving process, MTSS chairs must build collegial relations with all educators on campus. As an educational leader, it is imperative that the MTSS chair be seen as a critical resource for staff and not as an adversary out to impose discipline. Some educators need a gentle nudge to organize their time and prioritize Student Data Feedback Requests from case managers. Others require more direct administrative directives. Case managers, not classroom teachers, are the ones who look unprepared at MTSS meetings when their colleagues do not do their part in providing classroom performance feedback, and they must let the MTSS chair know when they are having problems getting reports from individual teachers. The MTSS chair communicates with the school administrator in seeking support with the teachers. If direct conversation and offers to assist prove ineffective, electronic communications to the unresponsive teacher is a good way to provide documentation when feedback requests are being made and ignored. The MTSS chair should always copy the direct administrator on the email to improve probability of a response. Administrators supporting success of MTSS must actively promote participation of all staff members in school-wide practices.

Lastly, the MTSS chair is the *liaison* between this important school improvement team and the rest of the staff on behalf of the school's neediest and most vulnerable students. The MTSS chair must be able to work collaboratively, professionally and effectively with all relevant stakeholders in their school. The chair of this committee will need to communicate with others regarding the urgency of intense needs of struggling students that require systematic school-wide supports, as well as monitor the process itself for improvements which can be made to better serve those students. The MTSS chair must be a master of all trades and know when and how to elicit input from administrators, school counselors, school psychologists and other staff to support students and improve educational practices and outcomes for at-risk students.

Investing in personnel, resources, and intervention processes without enforcing best practices is like building an expensive ship and leaving holes in the bottom. Assuming that the school administration has invested in evidence-based practices and supports scheduling, the MTSS chairs can see where holes are in the ship. They do this by monitoring the quality of case manager functioning, teacher engagement and timeliness of feedback, the robustness of progress monitoring data, and administrative backing.

School Counselors

Secondary school counselors are invaluable to supporting struggling students for a variety of academic, social-emotional-behavioral, and personal reasons. *School counselors* provide academic, personal, social, and career support to students (American School Counseling Association, 2017). Besides being a lifeline for students with emotional difficulties, social problems, and life challenges, school counselors are responsible for monitoring credit attainment and whether graduation and/or promotion requirements are being met for the individual students on their caseload. School counselors provide interventions for students regularly and help them plan for the future, facilitate peer mediation, offer focused problem solving, run counseling groups, and advocate for students with parents and teachers. School counselors support students through crises, emotional challenges, and personal issues in addition to academic planning and advocacy with teachers.

School counselors are an essential part of the MTSS team. Some school counselors may want to attend every MTSS team meeting while others attend on a rotational basis to support the grade level(s) they represent. The school counselor should be on the leadership team, possibly as the MTSS chair or supporting the MTSS chair, to actively solve problems with students, offer relevant services, and follow through with outreach and other team recommendations to benefit student growth and development. During the MTSS team meetings, school counselors report on topics such as grades and credit status, lunchroom behavior, and issues with other students. Additionally, they provide important background information that may impact achievement, have insights into student behavior and affect, or offer follow-up counseling services to students which may include incentive planning, checking-in/out, and supporting behavior plans. School social workers, school counselors, and school psychologists should work together to address students' emotional needs that may require counseling services, community resources for basic needs, and referrals for community medical and mental health services.

School Psychologists

School psychologists must be actively involved in the MTSS team on a school campus. They have much to offer this problem solving team when not pigeon-holed into solely testing and qualifying students for special education. *School psychologists* are uniquely trained individuals on a school campus who provide mental and behavioral health supports to students, assist teams with intervention planning, analyze intervention outcomes, and help school administration implement evidence-based policies and programs. It is difficult for school psychologists to be MTSS chairs because of their competing responsibilities, but they are champions of interventions, social-emotional and behavioral supports, and data-based decision making. School psychologists should be involved in leadership decisions in forming the MTSS team, training the MTSS members, and monitoring efficacy and functions of the team with the MTSS chair. According to the National Association of School Psychologists (2014, p.1):

> School psychologists provide direct support and interventions to students; consult with teachers, families, and other school-employed mental health professionals (i.e., school counselors, school social workers) to improve support strategies; work with school administrators to improve school-wide practices and policies; and collaborate with community providers to coordinate needed services.

Integrating the unique perspective of the school psychologist on the MTSS team is a win–win for students, families, staff, and administration. School psychologists should not be perceived as gate-keepers to special education because, in reality, they endeavor to keep the gates open to appropriate instruction for everyone. Having a school psychologist actively participate on the MTSS team makes the framework stronger at a school. It is not a conflict of interest for school psychologists to be on both the MTSS team and the special education multidisciplinary team. It is a conflict of interest when qualified professionals do not support struggling students for artificial reasons. Using a social justice framework, school psychologists strive not only to protect the rights and opportunities for all (Shriberg, Bonner, Sarr, Walker, Hyland, & Chester, 2008), but to create those opportunities as well.

School psychologists are experts in analyzing formative and summative evaluation information, academic functioning, and psychological processes, as well as advocating for students and families in countless ways. School psychologists are teachers in the truest sense, educating adults in children's environments about how to best work with students with unique needs. The skill set of school psychologists is comprehensive and includes not only assessment abilities, but also administrative skills, counseling skills, knowledge of mental health foundations and positive behavioral supports, an understanding of growth and development as it relates to learning and behavior, and an understanding of barriers to organizational changes. *An active school psychologist working on the front end of proactive practices on a secondary campus can only add to the quality of supports in a school dedicated to educating every student.* They must also form relationships with families and community service providers to serve students whose needs exceed the scope of traditional school interventions. Communication with mental health providers and referrals to community services is shared by school psychologists, school counselors, and school social workers.

One important role of school psychologists is the assessment of students for special education eligibility and programming. School psychologists must be diligent in helping school teams implement MTSS (both academic and social-emotional-behavioral), but also following through with MTSS team recommendations when assessment is recommended. When quality control conditions are met with interventions that have been provided reliably and with fidelity, and the MTSS team recommends testing for special education eligibility due to poor rate of progress and inadequate level of performance, the school psychologist must honor the referral. The biggest frustration and disappointment for teachers who follow through with due diligence of intervention implementation and documentation for students suspected of having an educational disability is when the MTSS team referral for special education testing does not result in a completed psycho-educational evaluation. Students who have no clear path forward with general education initiatives and MTSS remediation alone are the students who must be considered for special education eligibility and special programming. The school psychologist must honor quality referrals and respond with good faith in a timely manner to avoid the perception that teachers went through the intervention process for nothing.

As an active participant on the MTSS team, the school psychologist can offer insights and recommendations *along the way*, so as to avoid being the gatekeeper at crucial decision-making points. Even though MTSS functions should support a majority of students coming through interventions *without* needing special education supports, the most severe underachievers or atypically behaved students will require special education. The school psychologist, as part of a multi-disciplinary team, must ensure that students whose functioning meets the criteria of an educational disability get appropriate services as described in the Individuals with Disabilities Education Act (IDEA, 2006). Special education eligibility is never the goal of MTSS, but when there is sufficient evidence to support a suspicion of a disability, it is important for the school psychologist to address the potential special education needs of a student, starting with a timely evaluation for special education eligibility.

It is a matter of fairness, checks and balances that keeps MTSS going. Teachers must believe that the MTSS team actively supports their students. Most teachers are willing to do extra work and go the extra mile to help struggling students. *In a system that supports underachievers, trust is built because all school professionals do their part.* If educators are doing their part on the front end, within the infrastructure administration has provided, then all school professionals must do their part in good faith. After all, good faith is what keeps organizational practices going and allows better practices to emerge. If team members do not do their part, and there is no accountability built in, resentment rears its ugly head and professionals give up before they start because they do not trust the system to respond adequately to the needs of students or staff. In such cases, teachers expect that extra efforts are a waste of time, and their compliance with prescribed best practices is certain to diminish over time.

School psychologists should be a strong resource for counseling and mental health interventions. Depending on the flexibility of their position at their school(s), they may offer parenting classes and family support, train administration and staff on school-wide positive behavioral intervention strategies, and offer a continuum of other staff, student, and community supports. School psychologists may contribute insight to help caregivers and teachers better understand students by conducting short-term support services that involve limited amounts of counseling or testing of academic and social-emotional-behavioral functioning to obtain more information outside of eligibility determination. The purpose of these short-term supports is to gather more individualized information on the student, not necessarily to gather information to use in a special education evaluation.

School psychologists may lead and assist in school-wide social-emotional-behavioral universal screenings, intervention design and implementation, and facilitation of the disbursement and collection of clinical rating scales between physicians, teachers, and families to help physicians make diagnoses and medication recommendations for students. The expertise that school psychologists can offer for suicide prevention, threat assessment and evaluation, crisis response, and community mental health needs should not be overlooked by school teams seeking to provide supports and services to students in a socially just context. School psychologists can be the linchpin for helping to assure that all of students' needs are met. They are particularly effective when given regular opportunities to participate in actively solving problems within smart teams. School psychologists' training, talents, experiences, and analytical skills make them necessary MTSS team participants.

Specialists

Specialists are often teachers on special assignment and are one of the most adaptable resources on campus. They may have the official title of literacy specialist, intervention specialist, or behavior specialist; however, they are jacks of all trades and help fill in teaching gaps for target students. They serve as substitute teachers, quasi-administrators, disciplinarians, and lunch duty supervisors: basically, any role or function that is required to support administrators looking to fulfill miscellaneous responsibilities for students on campus. They often work with special populations of at-risk students as intervention teachers. They also support the functions of educators and other intervention specialists overseeing data collection, providing testing supports for high-stakes testing, and filling in where needed as determined by administration. Specialists should be selected for participation on the MTSS leadership team as they are an excellent source of information. They are often inside classrooms and around campus and are positioned perfectly to have insights into what is working and what is not working for students and staff. Specialists are encouraged to use their unique skill sets to view student problems through different lenses, leading to supports with wider breadth and as supplements to other teachers on campus. In addition to teachers, other specialists who may participate and contribute to the MTSS team are itinerant professionals including school nurses, speech and language pathologists, school social workers, and other related or wrap-around service professionals with specific talents and training who support students. The more people with diverse backgrounds who engage in decision making for students, the better the recommendations and prospects are for struggling children.

Teachers

Grade and content level teachers have an open invitation to sit in on MTSS meetings and participate in discussions regarding students. Some school administrators require classroom teacher participation in meetings to increase ownership of student performance data; however, the MTSS meetings only allow for a very brief report from teachers and are not conducive to detailed discussions regarding specific classroom or curriculum issues with students that could be better addressed at subject level department meetings. *General classroom teachers' primary responsibilities lie in the classroom, using evidence-based practices with integrity, and in providing timely feedback to case managers about student needs and functioning.* Classroom teachers also have the responsibility of responding to case manager requests for students' progress reports prior to MTSS meetings. Special education teachers should also be encouraged to participate. At least one special education teacher should be designated to support the MTSS team to provide advocacy for students with possible special needs. Once again, it is not a conflict of interest to tap all resources on campus to support all students.

Having a special education teacher participate in decision making during MTSS meetings is important because that person can bring another perspective on individual differences to the table. Additionally, the special educator on the team can be considered a case manager for the highest needs Tier 3 students. Because special education teachers already know how to write academic and behavior plans, the special education teacher is a natural fit for writing formalized academic and behavior plans. School counselors can be helpful in writing these plans as well, and in writing less formal incentive plans, but MTSS requires many hands to make the workload lighter.

Special education teachers often appreciate the opportunity to make extra duty pay and to participate in meaningful processes to improve educational outcomes for students with challenges. Plan writing is an opportunity for the professionals with the most knowledge of special needs to work on behalf of at-risk students without identified disabilities; and only a fraction of students monitored by MTSS will even require formalized MTSS academic or behavior plans. Depending on the state or school district, such plans are often legal documents, and in many cases, may become educational records used to build evidence for special education disability criteria, including specific learning disabilities and emotional disturbance. Writing MTSS plans for the highest-needs students who receive the most intensive supports must be completed and implemented with integrity, and special education teachers are highly qualified to support MTSS this way. Of course, professional responsibilities for implementing academic and behavior plans do not end for the team with writing on paper, but also require regular advocacy by case managers, special education teachers and school counselors, in coordination with classroom teachers and students, for best results.

Meeting Etiquette

Participation in MTSS meetings is required of MTSS team members and certain meeting etiquette should be followed. The extent of preparation for each team member depends on position and role. Case managers bear the brunt of preparation for meetings, but MTSS chairs and other meeting participants also need to have their ducks in a row to make MTSS meetings run effectively and within a specific amount of time. As stated earlier, it is crucial for team discussions to be orderly and to remain on-topic. The MTSS chair, or designee, must take leadership of the meetings to guarantee brief, data-based professional discussions ensue. A process for meetings should be established, and all MTSS team members should be trained in meeting rules at the earliest MTSS team training of the school year.

Team accountability is extremely important so that all professionals on the team are doing their part. *Guidelines explaining expectations for preparation and presentation at MTSS meetings should be designed to enable teams to thoroughly discuss large numbers of students in short periods of time.* MTSS chairs are responsible for running meetings, making executive decisions, redirecting team members who have gotten off track, and keeping momentum going during conversations. Information presented at MTSS meetings should follow a general formula with established decision rules to ensure speed and accuracy of student updates and efficient problem solving (Van Norman & Christ, 2016). The MTSS chair may bypass case manager reports on students if they are disorganized or incomplete, which is a natural consequence of poor preparation. Waiting on case managers to rummage through files and work samples to dig up information during meetings wastes valuable meeting time. There are always reasons why case managers are unprepared for one or more student reports to the MTSS team, such as lack of teacher feedback or fluency updates, but the MTSS chair must make executive decisions for the good of the order. Student files that are not prepared to be discussed in an efficient fashion may be postponed until the next regularly scheduled meeting for that grade level, even though current information would have to be provided to the MTSS chair by an arranged time. A student's case should not be postponed more than once as it may be detrimental to the long-term outcomes for a student. Repeated violations of the meeting preparation expectation may be an individual case manager problem, a teacher problem, or it could be an MTSS systems issue. Regardless of the barrier to preparation for case managers, MTSS chairs and school administrators must be dedicated to addressing the weak links so that students have the best opportunities for data-based decisions to be made on their behalf, and they are not inadvertently penalized for their teachers' poor preparation.

The first three rules of meeting etiquette are preparation, preparation, and preparation. Case managers must be prepared to present case notes on each student in a fluid fashion so that multiple students can be discussed thoroughly and recommendations can be made quickly. Case managers need historical information, attendance, grades, teacher feedback on classroom performance and progress, behavior and health updates if any, and current fluency or response to instruction data. Case managers should try to organize individual student folders and stay organized by throwing away old data (much of it is logged in the digital database anyway) and keeping documentation current. Because case managers are the focal points for information on at-risk students, all MTSS team members and classroom teachers are encouraged to keep lines of communication open with them in regards to events and issues that impact students on their caseloads.

School counselors should bring their databases and records to meetings as well, so that information can be easily accessed during meetings and they can answer any questions team members may have. In addition, school counselors are a rich source of qualitative information regarding a student's personal and family history, social life on campus, discipline referrals, counseling referrals, and chronic visits to the school counselor's office or health office. School counselors provide valuable information to which case managers may not have access. Grade level school counselors must be prepared qualitatively and quantitatively to discuss current student performance in context of school problems during the meeting. Other itinerant specialists may also contribute reports and provide them to the school counselor or MTSS chair so their information can be presented to the team if they cannot attend a meeting.

As the MTSS chair leads team meetings, case managers are asked to review student data with the team. All team members should bring pertinent information and documentation regarding student functioning to meetings. After the MTSS chair calls the meeting to begin, case managers immediately take over. It may save time to organize student case folders alphabetically, or in the order they are listed on the MTSS Student Database, to reduce paper shuffling and lost time during meetings. The following presentation example will help case managers most efficiently present information at meetings.

Recommended presentation process at meetings:

1.   State reason for referral
2.   Brief history of pertinent history including, but not limited to: attendance, transience, criterion referenced scores, benchmark history, discipline, health, language proficiency, grades
3.   Baseline progress monitoring score(s)
4.   Present intervention plan(s) and goal(s) if students have them
5.   Review teacher progress reports:
     a.   Updated progress reports are *required* at every meeting. If there is difficulty getting feedback, begin including administrators on communication attempts with teachers
     b.   If there is repeated failure to engage teacher response, then administrative follow up is required
6.   Present *current* graph (throw away old, print or present new)
7.   Review interventions currently in place and discuss suggestions for future steps, such as progress monitoring schedule, add or change interventions, refer to school counselor, or schedule a parent-teacher conference
8.   When possible, plan in advance for any absences by choosing a backup presenter and forward caseload data and folders for the students who are to be presented at the meeting.

If case managers are organized, the above structure provides information needed to make informed decisions with team input. Old information can be reviewed quickly to bring the MTSS team up to speed and provide a background of student needs. New information can be presented succinctly, providing team members with a comprehensive perspective of past and current needs to make decisions. Team members with additional knowledge and documentation who are required to provide input include special education teachers presenting academic or behavioral observations and plans, the school nurse (or designee) reporting health updates, the dean (or designee) reporting discipline problems, and the school psychologist providing leadership, guidance, and feedback. Recommendations for next steps, depending on available resources at school and in the community, are then determined together. The MTSS chair should update new information in the MTSS Student Database and case managers should follow through on any action steps accordingly.

Action steps may include a community-based referral to the student's family for basic needs or counseling. The school social worker or school counselor may volunteer to be the lead person to contact the family. Follow-up by the nurse may be required including rechecking vision status, contacting caregivers about medication schedule, or getting a release of information to talk with student's prescribing doctor or psychiatrist for insights into medical or psychological impact on behavior and performance. A recommendation to the school counselor could be made to change the schedule of a student not currently in intervention classes, to include an intervention class.

The goals of the MTSS team are to identify areas of student need, determine baseline status, systematically provide interventions, revise student interventions based on documented response, and to max out the available resources on campus in order to respond adequately to intensity of student need, resulting in access to community resources if student needs exceed scope of the school. This systematic process to monitor outcomes for students who struggle despite the provision of high-quality instruction will provide more than adequate documentation for prior intervention criteria to fuel special education eligibility team processes, if needed. The decision for a comprehensive evaluation referral for special education programming could be recommended, in which case the school psychologist would bring evidence of student need and response to interventions to the Multidisciplinary Team to address potential identification of an educational disability.

The MTSS team now has a cohesive membership that can work together efficiently and effectively to support student success. Through the diverse roles and contributions of administrators, teachers, specialists, school counselors, school social workers, and school psychologists, the problem-solving process can be maximized.

Box 5.1

Connection to Practice

Case Manager Monitoring Survey

1. Are case managers prepared to present past and current data to provide insight at MTSS meetings?

If yes, go to question 3.

If no, ask:

1a. Is the case manager having problems getting organized and giving enough effort to the task?

If the answer to this question is yes, the problem is with the case manager. Additional trainings, planning periods, and supports are advised. Administrative oversight and directives for case manager is needed if retrainings are not resulting in positive changes. Replacing the case manager with someone more organized and effective is always a last resort.

2. Is there another reason the case manager cannot get information needed to be prepared at the meetings?

If yes, find out where the problem is. For example, if the teachers are not providing timely feedback it is an administrative issue supervisors should address with offending teachers. Another example might be, when records are delayed or communication with students' families or health providers are not forthcoming, the problem lies with outreach efforts and may require a special touch from a school counselor or school social worker. Team problem solving dictates finding someone who can help get information needed.

3. Are there high-quality instructional practices occurring in intervention classes using teaching practices that are research-based?

If yes, go to question 4.

If no, advocate for growing more research-based practices, as described in Chapter 4, and provide further training and supervision for teachers to engage in more effective teaching methods in the classroom, including positive behavioral supports.

4. Are students benchmarked and/or progress monitored regularly for fluency as an indicator of growth over time?

If yes, go to question 5.

If no, advocate for training and support of teachers to comply with expectation of progress monitoring students in interventions using regular fluency measures. Fluency measures do not tell the whole story of academic growth but neither do grades, which can be inflated or subjective depending on the teacher quality. Some intervention teachers need a gentle nudge to get their progress monitoring data to case managers. Or they need administrative support. Another possibility is that the student was not in attendance, in which case attendance interventions would apply.

5. Is school administration actively solving problems and coaching staff to grow MTSS practices?

If yes, the team is fortunate to have the special sauce in the recipe of success for MTSS.

If no, the MTSS chair will have less compliance with best practices thus dilut-
ing the effectiveness of efforts to provide instructional supports for all students. Keep advocating and problem solving as best possible. MTSS chairs
must engage in self-care because chairing MTSS requires much effort and is
just a fraction of their overall responsibilities.

References

American School Counseling Association (2017). *Role of the school counselor.* Retrieved from
www.schoolcounselor.org/administrators/role-of-the-school-counselor.

Anyon, Y., Nicotera, N., & Veeh, C. A. (2016). Contextual influences on the implementation
of a schoolwide intervention to promote students social, emotional, and academic learning.
Children & Schools, 38(2), 81–88.

Averill, O. H., & Rinaldi, C. (2011). Multi-tier systems of support. *District Administration, 9,* 91–94.

Dishon, T. (2011). Promoting academic competence and behavioral health in public schools: A
strategy of systemic concatenation of empirically based intervention principals. *School Psychology Review, 40*(4), 590–597.

Forman, S. G., & Crystal, C. D. (2015). Systems consultation for multitiered systems of supports
(MTSS): Implementation issues. *Journal of Educational and Psychological Consultation, 25,* 276–285.

Freeman, R., Miller, D., & Newcomer, L. (2015). Integration of academic and behavioral
MTSS at the district level using implementation science. *Learning Disabilities: A Contemporary
Journal, 13*(1), 59–72.

Guéguen, N., Pascual, A., Silone, F., & David, M. (2015). When legitimizing a request increases
compliance: The legitimizing object technique. *The Journal of Social Psychology, 155,* 541–544.

Individuals With Disabilities Education Act, 20 U.S.C. §1400 *et seq.* (2006 & Supp. V. 2011).

National Association of School Psychologists (2014). *Who are school psychologists?* Bethesda, MD:
Author.

Pinkelman, S. E., McIntosh, K., Rasplica, C. K., Berg, T., & Strickland-Cohen, M. K. (2015).
Perceived enablers and barriers related to sustainability of school-wide positive behavioral
interventions and supports. *Behavioral Disorders, 40*(3), 171–183.

Rainey, H., & Gifford, E. (2016). Working together: Asset based communities of learning in
Higher Education. *International Journal of Integrated Care, 16*(6), 1–8.

Shinn, M. R. (2007). Identifying students at risk, monitoring performance, and determining eligibility within RTI: Research on educational need and benefit from academic intervention.
School Psychology Review, 36(4), 601–617.

Shinn, M. R., & Walker, H. M. (Eds.) (2010). *Interventions for academic and behavior problems in a
three-tier model, including Response-to-Intervention* (3rd ed.). Bethesda, MD: National Association
of School Psychologists.

Shriberg, D., Bonner, M., Sarr, B. J., Walker, A. M., Hyland, M., & Chester, C. (2008). Social
justice through a school psychology lens: Definition and applications. *School Psychology
Review, 37,* 453–468.

Sprick, R. A. (2009). *CHAMPS: A proactive and positive approach to classroom management* (2nd
ed.). Eugene, OR: Pacific Northwest Publishing.

Sprick, R. A. (2013). *Discipline in the secondary classroom: A positive approach to behavior management*
(3rd ed.). Hoboken, NJ: John Wiley & Sons.

Stearns, E. M. (2017). Effective collaboration between physical therapists and teachers of students with visual impairments who are working with students with multiple disabilities and
visual impairments. *Journal of Visual Impairment and Blindness, 111*(2), 166–169.

Van Norman, E. R., & Christ, T. J. (2016). How accurate are interpretations of curriculum-
based measurement progress monitoring data? Visual analysis versus decision rules. *Journal of
School Psychology, 58,* 41–55.

Chapter 6

It's the Format, Not the Forms

Key Terms

Automatization
Teacher Efficacy
MTSS Student Portfolios
Intervention Plan
Intervention Log
Intervention Graphs
MTSS Meeting Logs

Chapter Concepts

In this chapter, readers will learn:

1. To successfully format and sequence an MTSS program for optimal implementation.
2. To structure automatization and stable procedures into the MTSS organization.
3. The special considerations for behavioral documentation.
4. The responsibilities of the team at each phase of intervention.
5. How to track and maintain records in a student database.
6. How to address common questions with school-based solutions.

The success to building the foundation of MTSS instructional practices and growing effective approaches to positively impact all learners relies on three key elements: fidelity, supports, and oversight. More specifically, teachers must use research-based curriculum with fidelity, teams must implement proactive and positive academic and behavioral supports, and administration must provide oversight to ensure that quality instruction takes place. If the MTSS team is certain that these anchors are in place, documentation can be streamlined because each educational practice will not need to be thoroughly vetted each time a student requires additional supports. MTSS teams will not waste their time chasing forms and documentation and can focus on problem solving for students to close the gap between actual and expected achievement.

While flexibility of documentation is extended to programs built on a solid foundation of MTSS principles, a minimum level of expectation remains for documenting student need and performance. Format of MTSS programming is still key, and the following minimally recommended forms will help teams streamline their paperwork. At the minimum, it is recommended that teams maintain: (1) MTSS Student Database for the school, by each grade level; (2) MTSS Student Portfolio for each student at Tier 2 or Tier 3; and (3) MTSS Meeting Log and sign-in sheet for accountability purposes.

Automation

In general, educators are very attached to forms and checklists on paper. Forms help to track events and provide a level of accountability that something is happening. We rely on forms to communicate professionally with others to ensure all stakeholders do their part and know that others are doing their part. Forms and checklists help busy, creative, driven, fast-paced teachers keep track of important concepts and duties and communicate information to others on the school team. However, separate forms and documentation procedures can also slow down processes resulting in decreased efficiency. Automate as many parts of your MTSS as possible to ensure sustainability of the support tiers in your school (Forman & Crystal, 2015; Freeman, Miller, & Newcomer, 2015; Averill & Rinaldi, 2011). *Automatization* is the result of processes that have been converted from loose implementation to automatic implementation.

There are important processes that depend on documentation, and having an easy to implement format with simple forms to capture time-stamped data is essential. Having systems in place to automate MTSS saves much time and effort. Organization is key to maintain the flow of MTSS implementation and sustainability, and more forms are not the solution. Forms can be one of the most common counterproductive practices in education, and are not the answer to automating MTSS. *Getting organized and staying organized are the secrets to staying on top of MTSS documentation, over-documenting is not.* In secondary schools, teachers who are required to individually document interventions often struggle to do so and are less likely to complete the forms with integrity (Freeman, Sugai, Simonsen, & Everett, 2017; Freeman, Simonsen, McCoach, Sugai, Lombardi, & Horner, 2016). Intense, individual documentation occurs for a very small percentage of students and most likely happens at Tier 3.

Overwhelmed teachers might experience feelings of burnout, and in extreme cases, impairment of emotional capacity and regulation (Mérida-López & Extremera, 2017). Educators affected by Burnout Syndrome may experience the following three symptoms: emotional exhaustion, depersonalization, and a loss of self-confidence or lack of 'Personal Accomplishment' (Maslach & Jackson, 1986). Teachers who are feeling insurmountably helpless to meet the demands of the classroom will be much less likely to document with fidelity or at all. Sometimes, busy, time-pressed teachers deem accurate intervention logs a low priority. Burnout and time management challenges result in inaccurate intervention logs, which lead to less effective MTSS team and program evaluation decisions. Logs are the school's documented guarantee that an evidence-based intervention was implemented as directed on a given day, how long the intervention session lasted, which target skill was addressed, and any relevant outcome notes. Intervention logs are primary artifacts in quality control of MTSS, and may become legal documents when used for special education evaluation and eligibility purposes.

Documentation of valid interventions is often one of the most challenging tasks for teachers who already have too many responsibilities and too little time to fit them all in. When teachers' time–compensation–responsibilities scale does not balance, emotional well-being and professional productivity suffer. Even the most detail-oriented secondary teachers are unable to keep up with individualized documentation for students on a daily basis, and they should not have to. A conservative number of forms and online communication tools can be useful to help teachers and MTSS team members collect, report, and review relevant data sources.

To run a well-oiled MTSS machine, many parts of MTSS need to operate with a high level of automaticity. Investing in evidenced-based curriculum for teachers to use with students in intervention classes takes out all the extra steps teachers typically have to take to vet intervention materials or create themselves. Intervention logs are accountability logs and record that research-based interventions took place and students were in attendance. *Using attendance logs in combination with lesson plans reduces duplicative work and simultaneously automates MTSS intervention logs.* This automation increases efficiency and overall implementation of MTSS structures (Freeman et al., 2017; Freeman et al., 2016; Forman & Crystal, 2015; Freeman, Miller, & Newcomer, 2015; Averill & Rinaldi, 2011).

Leadership plays a critical role in automating school-wide MTSS. When administrators are certain that teachers are implementing curriculum with integrity, as supported by classroom observations and administrative monitoring, these lesson plans and attendance logs can be used as intervention logs in secondary school intervention classes. If the student requires Tier 3 supports, the level of documentation can be more detailed, especially in cases of behavioral interventions, but not necessarily for academic interventions. There is almost never a need to document individually in academic-based intervention classes because teachers need only use lesson plans and attendance history logs, unless the student is engaging in atypical behavior in response to the curriculum or classroom climate. In such cases, the curriculum and teaching practices are not questioned because they have already been evaluated. The limited need for additional documentation would depend on individual characteristics of the student's response to instruction that could not be captured easily on a standard form. For the most part, the number of students requiring additional individualized documentation would be few to none, and would typically be reserved for students with individualized behavior plans.

If patterns of student data from a particular class consistently indicate poor rate of progress across students, then the teaching practices and use of the curriculum with fidelity should be called into question. As a system of quality control, MTSS identifies problems, implements time sensitive solutions, and monitors all aspects of the evidence-based outcomes leading to next steps in a continuous improvement cycle (Bryk, Gomez, Grunow, & LeMahieu, 2016; Freeman et al., 2016). It is up to the MTSS chair and leadership team, after collaboration and discussion, to bring any problems to the administration's attention for trouble-shooting.

Behavioral Documentation

Behavioral interventions are some of the most challenging for school professionals to document succinctly. Sometimes, these behaviors occur naturally in the classroom without a seemingly specific antecedent. Teachers manage student behavior all day long, and there is a wide range of typical behavior in a classroom, which is often predicated on teacher tolerance for noise and movement. From an early age, externalized behaviors and negative student mood within a classroom has been documented to have a negative impact on student learning (Scrimin, Mason, Moscardino, & Altoe, 2015). These externalized behaviors, including conduct problems, attention problems, and hyperactivity, are the most common disruptive behaviors that interfere with teaching and can lead to coercive relationships with teachers (Reinke, Stormont, Herman, Wang, Newcomer, & King, 2014). The most challenging students, with disruptive or defiant behavior, usually end up in the dean's office because teachers often lack the skills or experience to foster positive relationships with students who do not demonstrate appropriate coping skills. These reactive practices will never be as effective as proactive practices. Students with behavioral challenges will require more positive interactions with adults, more opportunities for guided practice in social-emotional learning experiences, and many more opportunities for non-punitive behavioral feedback (Dugas, 2017; Reinke et al., 2014).

In the classroom, there are countless methods to record behavioral data. Different tools can be used across the three tiers and the method selected will depend on the behavior to be monitored (PBIS World, 2017). These collections methods will vary by team and may be digital or manual using pencil and paper. The tool selected will depend on the behavior under investigation as well as the teacher's efficacy in collecting the data (Petty, Good, & Handler, 2016; Tshannen-Moran & Hoy, 2011; Goddard, Hoy, & Hoy, 2010). *Teacher efficacy* is a teacher's perceived level of ability to impact student learning through their instruction, data analysis, motivation, and organization. A common tool that teachers feel comfortable using is a frequency chart, which targets a specific behavior during a specific time period. A frequency chart can also include a place for documenting the intensity and duration of target behaviors and accompanying notes of antecedents or peculiarities describing specific situations. MTSS teams are cautioned to only recommend formal behavior intervention plans in the most severe cases of chronic misbehavior, Tier 3. In most cases, there will not be multiple students with an individualized behavior plan in a single class. If there are, the teacher may require additional supports to implement the plans. Tier 1 classroom management strategies for the whole class are key, and with consistent implementation, can decrease the number of students requiring Tier 2 and Tier 3 supports. Programs such as SLANT (Buffum, Mattos, & Weber, 2012) or CHAMPS (Sprick, 2009) are effective at the Tier 1 level for implementation with whole classes and campuses. Oftentimes, students with challenging behaviors are more rigid in class and let teachers know if discipline is fair. If rewards and consequences are not fairly applied to all students in a class, behavioral strategies will be less effective over time. Personal relationships with students are an educator's first line of defense with misbehaving students requiring a higher level of positive interactions (Dugas, 2017; Reinke et al., 2014). Well executed incentives along with natural consequences, combined with genuine positive regard for students, works with most students. Students whose behavior or circumstances are extreme outliers for expected behavior in a school population should be tracked closely for mental health issues, family systems issues, and emotional disturbance or other educational disabilities.

Student behavioral issues lead to emotional and physical exhaustion for teachers (Mérida-Lopez & Extremera, 2017; Maslach & Jackson, 1986). Upset teachers must be validated. Students who misbehave are challenging and it takes much of a teacher's time and energy to ensure classroom integrity, at best, and personal and student safety, at least. Discussing Tier 3 behavioral problems can chew through regular MTSS team meeting times, which is why an overlapping Behavioral and Mental Health MTSS team, with separate team meeting times, is recommended on secondary campuses to give students' problems the attention, support, and oversight they require for best chances of positive outcomes (see Chapter 10). Teachers are more likely to implement behavioral interventions and document outcomes with integrity if they feel actively supported by administration.

Behavioral documentation need not be time consuming, even in the most severe cases. The dean's database is a gold mine of behavioral history and is a running record of documentation. Assuming that only the most severe behavioral infractions result in discipline referrals to the dean, discipline history through the dean's database is a system already in place that can provide teams with details of all infractions. Chronological data reports of the frequency, intensity, and duration of the most disruptive, or chronic, behavior problems students are experiencing should be made available for regular review by the school staff. There is no need to replicate data captured in a dean's referral database, and the data should be easily accessible to teachers, school-based mental health professionals, and administrators to examine. In doing so, teams are better able to identify individual patterns over time and holistically are able to reflect, revise, and revamp their intervention processes. Referrals to the school counselor's office and health office are often tracked by systems already in place at schools, as well. If not, those incidences can be easily tracked by school counselors and health office staff in simple daily logs with names and dates, which can be accessed by school counselors and nurses to report back to the MTSS team when needed. Brief monthly teacher classroom performance reports are elicited from teachers by case managers to include general behavioral observations recorded regularly for review by MTSS meeting dates. Any additional behavioral idiosyncrasies can be captured in case notes on the MTSS Student Database. Students with the most extreme behavior problems should be monitored by a related, but distinctly different, division of the MTSS team, such as the Behavioral and Mental Health MTSS team.

The goal of academic and behavioral documentation is to make sure that all sources of relevant data are current in real time at MTSS meetings so that teachers, administrators, and MTSS team members can determine the trends of student progress quickly, and informed and timely decisions can be made. Teams that follow a format for data collection and reporting spend significantly less time digging for relevant information, pulling teeth of colleagues who do not respond to requests for documentation, figuring out which solutions have been tried and failed, and searching for outcome data written on sticky notes lost in piles of papers on teachers' desks. Any forms required as tools to accomplish these feats should be brief, condensed, and easy to use. Shared Google Drives and other technology can help simplify processes and create accountability methods for service providers. The format drives what needs to be on the forms, and the forms should never duplicate sources of data that are readily available.

The following examples are forms a team might use, in addition to online databases available to school communities. Such forms for data collection include a classroom performance report used to provide input to case managers, the MTSS Student Database including case notes (managed by the MTSS chair or designee), and other organizational tools that educational professionals want to use to capture reported status on students to assist in decision making.

Current grades, attendance, discipline and behavior problems, medical issues, personal issues, and regularly updated academic progress monitoring scores (including updated graphs) are required to be tracked. Monitoring and updating information becomes more simplified within an established reporting format. Other relevant information captured on the MTSS Student Database can include which intervention(s) the student is receiving (or did receive with dates of implementation and outcomes), any intervention changes made, the name of intervention teachers and counselors, and other formative and summative assessment scores that can be considered to determine whether interventions need to be more intense or less intense for students. The MTSS team must then decide where the problems lie, whether within the student's environmental and family ecosystem, mental health problems, teacher qualities, curriculum and assessment implementation issues, case manager qualities, documentation issues, MTSS chair issues, comprehensive system issues including adequate number of intervention opportunities, or any other number of problems that pop up in team functions.

MTSS Student Portfolios

Case managers compile the most relevant information on student performance and bring MTSS Student Portfolios to all MTSS meetings. *MTSS Student Portfolios* are comprised of the artifacts to present to the MTSS team when making decisions about a student and help support the MTSS Student Database. Even though information in case files is reported in abbreviated fashion on the MTSS Student Database, case managers are encouraged to have copies of important artifacts should questions arise that require checking the information source for accuracy and additional information. Annually, case managers discard outdated information in the MTSS Student Portfolios for every student on their caseload, after first ensuring that the MTSS chair has recorded the data in the MTSS Student Database. Important impressions, observations, or recommendations moving forward should be inputted to the Case Notes section of the MTSS Student Database. Case managers should add the following artifacts in their MTSS Student Portfolios:

- Request for assistance completed by classroom teachers
- Family history and student's health-developmental questionnaire completed by parent
- Cumulative folder review: "Student records typically contain students' attendance, discipline records, health screenings, grades and performance on standardized testing over the years. It can also contain a range of documents

including custody arrangements, legal documents, and school photographs" (Florell, 2014).

- Current vision and hearing screening results
- Current schedule of the student
- Intervention plans (academic and/or behavioral)
- Intervention logs (if not tracked by lesson planning and attendance)
- Intervention graphs (most recent)
- Semester and quarter grades, real-time class grades as of meeting dates
- Current teacher progress report
- Updated discipline history, if relevant

Much of this information can be garnered from school database systems or student enrollment folders held in the registrar's office. The intervention data will be less static and teams will need to be aware of its ever-changing nature. The *Intervention Plan* defines the student's area of difficulty and targets a discreet skill for baseline to enable goal setting. The *Intervention Log* tracks the date, type, and duration of intervention provided. The *Intervention Graph* is the visual representation of scores obtained during progress monitoring data collection cycles. From these data, rate of improvement over time is monitored and instructional supports are intensified as deemed necessary by the team.

MTSS Student Database Structure

As discussed in the previous chapter, the MTSS Student Database is the storehouse that archives all data for students who are discussed at MTSS team meetings. This database is achieved by creating and maintaining a running record of at-risk student history, interventions implemented, school performance, current needs, and recommendations for school success. There are a variety of options for structuring an MTSS Student Database; however, the most common would be the use of a database program such as Google Sheets or Microsoft Excel. Individual data sheets may also be used. It is up to each team to decide what organizational structure will work best for them.

Regardless of the tool used, the following headings should be staples of all MTSS Student Databases:

- Student name
- Student grade
- Student identification number
- Assigned school counselor
- Advisory or lead teacher
- Case manager
- Remediation schedule (e.g., intervention provided during an extended school day intervention class or during the regular school day in a fundamentals class)
- Remediation class subject
- Remediation class teacher's name
- English language placement scores and level of language proficiency (if applicable)

- Attendance or tardiness issues
- Health issues
- Fluency benchmark scores
- Instructional level of fluency
- Most recent progress monitoring or strategic monitoring score
- Case notes

MTSS Meeting Logs

MTSS Meeting Logs are the official dated documentation of the MTSS Student Portfolios and case notes discussed at MTSS Team Meetings are updated during or after each meeting. The MTSS Meeting Logs are recommended to be maintained by the MTSS Chair or designee.

Intervention Documentation

With assured implementation of evidence-based curriculum and teaching practices, intervention documentation is briefly captured in the MTSS Student Database and Case Notes. Intervention plan(s), logs, and graphs are non-negotiables of a strong MTSS program. Beginning and ending date ranges indicating implementation of each type of intervention class can be captured in the column of intervention class subject and teacher, which can be cross referenced with attendance logs. Current fluency graphs, formative and summative assessments, and behavioral tracking through a dean's database or otherwise, count for documentation.

MTSS Team Meeting Decision-Making Model: Questions and Solutions

Does the student have a significant developmental history or have they been identified with a developmental issue?
Students with developmental issues, especially those from low socioeconomic homes, are at a greater risk for school problems (Williams, Landry, Anthony, Swank, & Crawford, 2012). Students with a history of developmental delays (and environmental disadvantages) need more high-quality school and community-based supports, which require closer monitoring of academic growth, social and emotional difficulties, behavioral problems, independent living skills, health issues, and communication skills.

Does the student have a significant family history and/or socioeconomic or ecological factors that influence school attendance or functioning? In what ways does the student's family support the student's education?
School problems tend to run in families as children from the same homes often experience the same social-demographic risk factors and, to some extent, academic risk factors. Individuals who experience multiple forms of adverse childhood experiences, social trauma, and academic failure are the mostly likely to be impacted. In a nationally representative study of 14,736 students, researchers have demonstrated an inverse relationship between the number, not necessarily the severity, of risk factors and academic success (Lucio, Hunt, & Bornovalova,

2012). When students experience 2 or more of these 12 predictors (academic engagement, academic expectations, academic self-efficacy, attendance, school misbehaviors, educational support, grade retention, homework, school mobility, school relevance, school safety, and teacher relationships), they are significantly more likely to suffer from academic failure (Lucio et al., 2012). Further, contact with the juvenile justice system (delinquency) and school expulsions (discipline) are high predictors of negative school outcomes (Robison, Jaggers, Rhodes, Blackmon, & Church, 2016; Henry, Knight, & Thornberry, 2012).

Solutions depend on what the families' needs are. Are the students' and families' basic needs being met? If not, the school social worker or school counselor can often coordinate food and medical assistance as well as referrals to community agencies for shelter, food, clothing, and job assistance to help reduce transience. Are there multiple family members with the same problems, such as mental illness, behavioral problems, drug or alcohol problems, learning problems, and attendance problems? If yes, students should be monitored more closely for school issues and interventions should be implemented accordingly. If the family does not support the child's education, family outreach efforts to provide positive school experiences and relationships between teachers and caregivers/guardians are encouraged. Attendance contracts and incentives may be helpful.

Is the student's primary language English?
Second language acquisition factors should be taken into account when determining the amount or intensity of English learner supports necessary for student success. Students who are newer English speakers, and those with lower language proficiency scores, will require greater vocabulary/language exposure and rehearsal, adapted materials, and adapted grading criteria to ensure an equitable system for their unique language needs.

Does the student have significant environmental trauma or mental health history?
Students with mental health problems and trauma histories have a greater risk for academic and behavioral difficulties and are more likely to engage in delinquent activities (Mallett, 2015). Students demonstrating signs of psychiatric disorders should be monitored closely for school issues and interventions should be implemented accordingly. A family history including incarceration, trauma, and having one or more comorbid psychiatric condition increases instances of criminal engagement (Taskiran, Mutluer, Tufan, & Semerci, 2017; Mallett, 2015). Juvenile youth with Attention Deficit Hyperactivity Disorder and Conduct Disorder were found to be engaged in more severe crimes than those with internalized behaviors, such as anxiety, who engaged in less severe crimes (Taskiran et al., 2017).

Frequency and intensity of problem behaviors in the school setting will need to be tracked and lines of communication between school staff and medical/mental health service providers and caregivers must be open to ensure transparency between home and school. In addition, daily emotional and physical health information should be monitored including hygiene, affect, social living skills, emotional stability, explosive anger, and aggression toward self and others. Students with poor self-regulation may end up in the justice system when laws are broken or injuries occur. The school psychologist, school counselor, school nurse, school social worker, and other behavior mentors on a school campus should be working together, and with the family and community health providers, to actively solve problems and provide supports for these students (Lucio et al., 2012). Students can be paired with a teacher mentor or other supportive adult they already know on campus, and students' teachers should be given positive behavioral strategies to implement (Moore-Partin, Robertson, Maggin, Oliver, & Wehby, 2010). Checking in/out, incentives for students, pressure passes, and formal behavior plans are all options for teams to consider.

Are formative and summative assessment results consistent with other indicators of student success? Do results indicate underachievement?
Does the student have a history of performing on grade level? If no, under-achievement may be a chronically severe problem and more intense interventions should be implemented at the soonest opportunity. If yes, then explore possible reasons for the newly presenting academic difficulties, any lack of consistency in programming and instructional delivery, difficulties at home, and other explanations for where things possibly got off track. This will help to focus solutions on the key problem areas and the associated manifest difficulties. Triangulation of information should be considered from multiple sources including grades, classroom performance reports, environmental or home reports, and current fluency graphs at instructional level.

If performance is not consistent across sources then further discussion at MTSS team meetings must ensue to narrow down to the real issues impacting the student's lack of performance. On occasion, fluency graphs do not capture student performance or growth. For example, some students read at a slow pace but reading comprehension is not negatively impacted. In such cases, grades, other test scores, and classroom performance reports would be better indicators of success. More likely than not, most sources of data for underachievers are consistent across the board. After establishing baseline, students should be put on a strategic or progress monitoring schedule with interventions implemented accordingly.

The most important question to answer at MTSS team meetings is whether the student is responding to treatment or not.
If the student is getting better, according to a preponderance of evidence, then continue the intervention and continue to progress monitor. If there is no change, the team may continue to monitor for another monitoring period, change the intervention, or add another intervention. If a student's problem is getting worse over time, then current interventions are not successful and the team should recommend changing the intervention or implementing a more intensive intervention. If the student is getting maximum levels of Tier 2 and Tier 3 support and demonstrates resistance to instruction over time, across interventions implemented and across data sources, then the student should most likely be referred to the Multidisciplinary Team for a special education evaluation to address the suspicion of disability.

Does the student require an intervention class or a more intensive model of instruction in one or more areas?
The MTSS team should have a menu of supports in Tier 2 and Tier 3 with a continuum of services for struggling students. Teams may devise their own

interventions, or there are several options available to teams to purchase (Macklem, 2011). Schools that have limited seats for intervention classes or those who lack research-based curriculum and opportunities for academic or behavioral remediation, must actively work on growing supports over time for students. If a struggling student is not getting the interventions he or she requires then efforts must be made to remediate deficits. Teams must ensure that students are getting interventions in their area(s) of need and the identified problem area(s) are being monitored systematically for growth over time. Outcome data will dictate whether students continue to require that level of intensive instruction or if supports can be faded with less intensive instruction to maintain success.

How do teams prioritize student problems with complex issues?
Several factors contribute to a student's success on a school campus. Students' basic needs and school attendance must be addressed first before any other school intervention is implemented. Behavior problems also interfere with the success of interventions, so if behavior is a problem, environmental variables and mental health issues must be addressed simultaneously with academic interventions. Sometimes students' maladaptive behavior precludes them from being successful in an academic intervention class and their needs are better addressed, at least initially, in a social-emotional and behavioral learning intervention class. Underperforming students often have multiple layers of deficits. When students have problems in both reading and math, reading is typically addressed first if teams have to choose which area to focus on. In a perfect world, treatment plans for the whole child could be put in place for all areas of need, but in reality, problems must be prioritized and addressed systematically within the limitations of the system. Students may not receive interventions in all areas of need simultaneously, nor do they necessarily demonstrate improvements in all areas simultaneously even if they have comprehensive support.

How often should fluency measures be administered to students?
Intervention teachers should aim for fluency measures either weekly (at most) or once every two weeks (at least). When teachers administer fluency tests weekly, student absences and outlying scores average out. When fluency testing occurs monthly, if the student is absent on the testing day or isn't feeling well, then no data (or skewed data) is recorded and the valuable opportunity for curriculum-based measurement is lost for timely MTSS team decisions. It is the responsibility of the intervention teacher to ensure that at least two monthly data points of current instructional level fluency are accessible to case managers prior to MTSS team meetings.

Does the student struggle in class? Are things going better for the student?
Qualitative teacher progress reports capture information that grades and test scores cannot. Classroom teachers must provide monthly feedback on student academic and behavioral improvements to the MTSS team. Good progress reports measure attitude, effort, participation in class activities and verbal discussions, work quality, organizational skills, work completion rates, and grades. This information is invaluable to team decisions regarding necessity of increasing or decreasing intensity of instructional supports for a student.

Is the student on target for credit attainment for promotion or graduation?
If no, credit retrieval options must be advocated by school counselors and/or other lead teachers. Communications with students, caregivers, and teachers should be required to address reasons for deficiency. Efforts to improve incentives for performance or push opportunities for summer school, online, or weekend programs should be explored. Intervention opportunities may be required.

As MTSS team members habituate themselves to discussing students systematically, the aforementioned questions and answers get reviewed quickly, and appropriate next steps come more easily. The idea of valuing format over forms in documentation of MTSS team functions is that *team processes* become engrained in the school fabric and can then become automated. If the format is in place, abbreviated documentation is possible. Teachers will have less paperwork and more opportunities for direct professional communication with other staff on students' behalf. Status updates can be completed on a Google Doc or Google Sheets in minutes for ease of use and accountability among multiple school professionals. Each educator must do their part.

In a well-run MTSS the outcome data always points to the weakest links.
The weak links may be a lack of intervention opportunities, a lack of funding for evidence-based resources, poor communication between staff members, lack of appropriate progress monitoring processes, a need for greater supports for teachers or itinerant staff, and resistance by stakeholders to MTSS itself. All issues can be addressed systematically by the MTSS team to identify problems and school-based solutions. Ultimately, the school principal is responsible for actively providing solutions to barriers in the implementation of MTSS and reinforcing the desired change. If the school principal's leadership is not strong at a school, and that principal is resistant to change or does not have the skills to reinforce the change, the necessary change will not happen. There is no intervention, short of a new principal, that will fix consistently weak leadership.

Effective systems require many moving parts to work together cohesively. Unfortunately, automation of functions, processes, and professional competencies in a school setting cannot be managed with a disseminated form or checklist. Changing educators' behavior to engage in more effective practices must be shaped. B. F. Skinner (1953), arguably the father of modern behavioral modification techniques, described the concept of shaping using his learning model of operant conditioning, where the association between a new behavior and resulting consequence is learned in repetitive trials. In shaping, new behavior is established through reinforcement of successive approximations toward the desired behavior, and new responses are progressively reinforced until the desired behavior is achieved. Not only must school leaders have a clear vision of MTSS to be able to put all the structures, functions, and processes in place, but they must also be actively involved in shaping the entire staff in better practices and reinforcing those changes; growing and sustaining a culture that nurtures and supports students and educators.

References

Averill, O. H., & Rinaldi, C. (2011). Multi-tier systems of support. *District Administration, 9,* 91–94.

Bryk, A. S., Gomez, L. M., Grunow, A., & LeMahieu, P. G. (2016). *Learning to improve: How America's schools can get better at getting better.* Cambridge, MA: Harvard Education Press.

Buffum, A., Mattos, M., & Weber, C. (2012). *Simplifying response to intervention: Four essential guiding principles.* Bloomington, IN: Solution Tree Press.

Dugas, D. (2017). Group dynamics and individual roles: A differentiated approach to social-emotional learning. *The Clearing House: A Journal of Educational Strategies, Issues and Ideas, 90*(2), 41–47.

Florell, D. (2014, September 28). Right to see student cumulative record. *Richmond Register.* Retrieved from http://mindpsi.net/blog/right-to-see-student-cumulative-record.

Forman, S. G., & Crystal, C. D. (2015). Systems consultation for multitiered systems of supports (MTSS): Implementation issues. *Journal of Educational and Psychological Consultation, 25,* 276–285.

Freeman, F., Sugai, G., Simonsen, B., & Everett, S. (2017). MTSS coaching: Bridging knowing to doing. *Theory Into Practice, 56*(1), 29–37.

Freeman, J., Simonsen, B., McCoach, D. B., Sugai, G., Lombardi, A., & Horner, R. (2016). Relationship between school-wide positive behavior interventions and supports and academic, attendance, and behavior outcomes in high schools. *Journal of Positive Behavior Interventions, 18*(1), 41–51.

Freeman, R., Miller, D., & Newcomer, L. (2015). Integration of academic and behavioral MTSS at the district level using implementation science. *Learning Disabilities: A Contemporary Journal, 13*(1), 59–72.

Goddard, R., Hoy, W. K., & Hoy, A. W. (2010). Collective teacher efficacy: Its meaning, measure, and impact on student achievement. *American Educational Research Journal, 37*(2), 479–507.

Henry, K. L., Knight, K. E., & Thornberry, T. P. (2012). School disengagement as a predictor of dropout, delinquency, and problem substance use during adolescence and early adulthood. *Journal of Youth and Adolescence, 41*(2), 156–166.

Lucio, R., Hunt, E., & Bornovalova, M. (2012). Identifying the necessary and sufficient number of risk factors for predicting academic failure. *Developmental Psychology, 48*(2), 422–428.

Macklem, G. L. (2011). *Evidence-based school mental health services: Affect education, emotion regulation training, and cognitive behavioral therapy.* New York: Springer-Verlag.

Mallett, C. A. (2015). The incarceration of seriously traumatised adolescents in the USA: Limited progress and significant harm. *Criminal Behaviour and Mental Health, 25,* 1–9.

Maslach, C., & Jackson, S. E. (1986). *Maslach burnout inventory manual* (2nd ed.). Palo Alto, CA: Consulting Psychologists Press.

Mérida-Lopez, S., & Extremera, N. (2017). Emotional intelligence and teacher burnout: A systemic review. *International Journal of Educational Research, 85,* 121–130.

Moore-Partin, T. C., Robertson, R. E., Maggin, D. M., Oliver, R. M., & Wehby, J. H. (2010). Using teacher praise and opportunities to respond to promote appropriate student behavior. *Preventing School Failure, 54*(3), 172–178.

PBIS World (2017). *Data tracking.* Retrieved from www.pbisworld.com/data-tracking.

Petty, T. M., Good, A. J., & Handler, L. K. (2016). Impact on student learning: National Board Certified Teachers' perspectives. *Education Policy Analysis Archives, 24*(49), 1–16.

Reinke, W. M., Stormont, M., Herman, K. C., Wang, Z., Newcomer, L., & King, K. (2014). Use of coaching and behavior support planning for students with disruptive behavior within a universal classroom management program. *Journal of Emotional and Behavioral Disorders, 22*(2), 74–82.

Robison, S., Jaggers, J., Rhodes, J., Blackmon, B. J., & Church, W. (2016). Correlates of educational success: Predictors of school dropout and graduation for urban students in the deep south. *Children and Youth Services Review, 73,* 37–46.

Scrimin, S., Mason, L., Moscardino, U., & Altoe, G. (2015). Externalizing behaviors and learning from text in primary school students: The role of mood. *Learning and Individual Differences, 43*, 106–110.

Skinner, B. F. (1953). *Science and human behavior.* New York: The Free Press.

Sprick, R. A. (2009). *CHAMPS: A proactive and positive approach to classroom management* (2nd ed.). Eugene, OR: Pacific Northwest Publishing.

Taskiran, S., Mutluer, T., Tufan, A. E., & Semerci, B. (2017). Understanding the associations between psychosocial factors and severity of crime in juvenile delinquency: A cross-sectional study. *Neuropsychiatric Disease and Treatment, 13*, 1359–1366.

Tshannen-Moran, M., & Hoy, A. W. (2011). Teacher efficacy: Capturing an elusive construct. *Teaching and Teacher Education, 17*, 783–805.

Williams, J. M., Landry, S. H., Anthony, J. L., Swank, P. R., & Crawford, A. D. (2012). An empirically-based statewide system for identifying quality pre-kindergarten programs. *Education Policy Analysis Archives, 20*(17). Retrieved from http://epaa.asu.edu/ojs/article/view/1014.

Chapter 7

Special Education Eligibility and Other Considerations

Key Terms

Discipline
Social-Emotional Regulation
Protective Factors
Implicit Bias
Alingual
Linchpins
Unicorns
Three As

Chapter Concepts

In this chapter, readers will learn:

1. How MTSS and special education intersect and complement each other.
2. To reinforce intervention systems from an asset-based approach.
3. To understand the unique needs of gifted students, language deprived students, and English language learners.
4. How to shift perspectives to think inclusively and to acknowledge that injustices and inequities exist in our schools.
5. How to better understand and support the role of school psychologists and other specialized staff on campus.

Multi-tiered support systems, response to instruction, response to interventions, student study teams, student intervention teams and the like are nothing new in educational circles (Dishon, 2011). Historically, these terms have most often been used to fuel the special education eligibility determination machine at schools. The definition of certain eligibility criteria has required intervention implementation and documentation of outcomes since the 1990s but school communities are still struggling to standardize the intervention process (Ladd & Fiske, 2008). Some schools do very little in terms of differentiated instruction and systematically implementing remedial opportunities, while others are very responsive to the academic and behavioral needs of students (Forman & Crystal, 2015).

The MTSS and Special Education Intersection

School-based intervention plans have been, and continue to be, perceived as stepping stones to special education eligibility in many schools and school districts. While some teachers may perceive it as the route to get their students "into" special education, specialists on campus can help inform on the process to help balance the eligibility scales (Nellis, Sickman, Newman, & Harman, 2014). Beware when eligibility considerations depend more on service providers' judgment than actual data, as it may contribute to the misidentification of students eligible for special education. As general education teachers feel overwhelmed, or underprepared, to handle the needs of at-risk students, these children tend to get pushed out of their classes with the misguided belief that special education is going to be a magical cure.

Any student who does not fit neatly into the general curriculum may not receive the support they need. These students are disciplined more often and more frequently singled out, and kicked out, by teachers "so the students can get the help they need." *Discipline* is the training of adherence to codes or behavior and may include punishments to correct noncompliance. *It is important for educators to keep in mind that students who struggle academically are more likely to act out behaviorally.* At best, when regular education teachers push struggling students out those children become another teacher's responsibility. Hopefully, the educators ending up with the children who require additional supports know how to inclusively cultivate an engaging learning environment and demonstrate mastery of content knowledge and delivery. At worst and more predictably, those children get "managed" somewhere on campus with other struggling students and have the least qualified teachers with the most militaristic supervision.

The management of school children is nothing new. The current education system we have, including its bureaucratic structures, time schedules, grade level divisions, student rankings, and behavioral expectations are rooted in the disciplinary methods of monasteries, armies, and workshops from the seventeenth and eighteenth centuries (Foucault, 1995). A description of such a space in 1762 is described:

> [T]he educational space unfolds; the class becomes homogenous ... "rank" begins to define the great form of distribution of individuals in the educational order: rows or ranks of pupils in the class, corridors, courtyards; rank attributed to each pupil at the end of each task and each examination; the rank he obtains from week to week, month to month, year to year; an alignment of age groups, one after another; ... in this ensemble of compulsory alignments, each pupil, according to his age, his performance, his behavior, occupies sometimes one rank, sometimes another.
>
> (Foucault, 1995, pp. 146–147)

Students who conformed silently and did not require individualized attention were praised as model pupils. Those with individual needs or those with behaviors that fell outside the desired norm, were sent to reformatories, or worse, sent to prison. Thus emerged the very beginnings of the modern school to prison pipeline.

While these ranking and structures of education uniformity have changed little in nearly 300 years, social attitudes toward discipline have. Under the leadership of Le Peletier (1791), radical laws were enacted in eighteenth-century France to ensure that "the punishment fit the crime" for those who violated the laws of society. This was a radical departure from existing discipline structures that predominately included death by hanging, even for trivial crimes. The goal of such disciplinary power was to imprison the offender in an attempt to retrain his behavior and to discourage repeat behavior. However, to rely on a punishment model creates the counterproductive error of expecting different behavioral results without providing an appropriate intervention to teach and reinforce expected behavior. Two hundred years later, behavioral psychologists such as Maslow, Bruner, Piaget, and Skinner began exploring the motivations of human actions and sought to find more positive ways in which to understand and change behavior.

While work still needs to be done to address the school to prison pipeline, society has come a long way in how it treats students with special needs and those who require social-emotional and behavioral interventions. Through an MTSS program, students are able to receive the supports they need, at the level of intensity best needed to address the problem. Successful MTSS programs also consider the unique environmental and cultural influences on students and views these factors through an asset-based, social justice lens and uses restorative practices.

A culturally inclusive MTSS does not push students out, it surrounds students with a proverbial hug of relevant supports and provides them with an opportunity to access general curriculum to the greatest extent. Cultivating positive teacher–student relationships along with student motivation, perseverance, and reward systems can be used to bolster student feelings of belonging at school (Dueck, 2014; Moore-Partin, Robertson, Maggin, Oliver, & Wehby, 2010). A well-integrated MTSS embraces flexibility and responsive supports to groups of students, as well as individual students. This may include groups of students who have like deficits in specific subject areas, or individual students who are not adequately responding to increasingly intensive interventions.

Setting high expectations for all learners is paramount, and students with behavioral difficulties require behavioral instruction as well as academic instruction (Sprick, 2013; Dishon, 2011; Shinn & Walker, 2010; Moore-Partin et al., 2010; Shinn, 2007). In order for all students to reach their personal bests schools must create a culture of safety and inclusiveness that is socially just (Francis, Mills, & Lupton, 2017; Sink, 2016; Shriberg & Clinton, 2016; Shriberg, Song, Miranda, & Radliff, 2013). Ideally, a high-quality education system for students who do not fit standard grade level expectations would include opportunities to obtain specialized supports without having to jump through hoops of special education eligibility first.

Expectations should be high for *all* learners to reach their personal bests. This is especially true for students who receive special education supports and in instances where education laws only specify a "minimal" level of support rather than a maximum level to support comprehensive student learning (Abou-Rjaily

& Stoddard, 2017). Students with behavioral problems require behavioral instruction *and* guided social-emotional learning (SEL) experiences, in addition to high-quality academic instruction. Learning is a braided experience consisting of social, emotional, and academic components (Aspen Institute: National Commission on Social, Emotional, and Academic Development, 2018). Students who are exposed to a SEL curriculum demonstrate long-term benefits. In a recent meta-analysis of 82 studies and nearly 100,000 students, researchers with the Collaborative for Academic, Social and Emotional Learning and partner universities found that "Participants fared significantly better than controls in social-emotional skills, attitudes, and indicators of well-being. Benefits were similar regardless of students' race, socioeconomic back-ground, or school location. Post-intervention social-emotional skill development was the strongest predictor of well-being at follow-up" (Taylor, Oberle, Durlak, & Weissberg, 2017, p. 1). These benefits continued to be realized up to 18 years after being exposed to the SEL curriculum. Additional findings suggest that participants demonstrated long-term benefits of increased empathy and teamwork and decreased rates of conduct problems, emotional distress, and drug use.

Students who struggle with social-emotional regulation and behavior require emotional safety to ask questions they believe everyone else seems to know the answers to, and they need a safe space with a teacher with whom they can form a caring relationship (Schonert-Reichl, 2017). *Social-emotional regulation* is the ability to control and negotiate emotions, thoughts, and behaviors effectively and efficiently. Many of the most problematic students have never had social-emotional regulation modeled or taught to them, have not developed a strong, quality relationship with a caregiver, and lack the protective factors needed to establish emotional trust and stability (Robison, Jaggers, Rhodes, Blackmon, & Church, 2016). "Trust between a child and adult is essential, the foundation on which all other principles rest, the glue that holds teaching and learning together, the beginning point for re-education" (Hobbs, 1982, pp. 22–23).

Protective factors are conditions that positively contribute to student well-being and include factors such as having their basic needs met as well as having resilience skills, strong social connections, and social-emotional skills. Students without sufficient protective factors or who lack a strong, caring relationship with a caregiver often do not believe in themselves, nor do they believe in the adults around them, oftentimes with good reason. The adults in the students' lives have always let them down so they do not believe that a teacher could care about them, let alone help them. It stands to reason that angry, resentful, discarded students are going to try to make teachers feel more miserable than they feel themselves by acting out and disrupting the learning environment. Sometimes, children act out to test the adults at a school to see if and when they are going to be punished or discarded by another adult who says they care; other times students are disruptive simply because it is more fun than remaining confused and feeling incompetent and unsuccessful.

Establishing a continuum of shared governance between families and educators is one way to maximize outcomes for students and reinforce school-family engagement (Garbacz, McIntosh, Eagle, Dowd-Eagle, Hirano, & Ruppert, 2016). This shared responsibility is encouraged and reinforces to students that their teachers and family are working together. Academically and behaviorally deficient students must be able to access opportunities to be retaught basic academic and behavioral skills they are lacking without destroying their fragile egos and sense of self-worth. Schools must step up efforts to make school relevant and unbiased for everyone. For school psychologists, social justice can be promoted by making connections between "promoting best practices in school psychology, conducting culturally fair assessments, and advocating for the rights of children and families" (Shriberg, Wynne, Briggs, Bartucci, & Lombardo, 2011, p. 49).

Special Considerations

Gifted Students

Gifted students are especially prone to unique social-emotional and behavioral challenges due to their giftedness (Peterson, 2006). Many highly gifted students never reach their full potential due to the emotional toll of being smarter than those around them, and not having the social skills or problem solving processes to allow them to adequately work with others or build self-discipline and patience to persevere when things get difficult (Kaplan & Geoffroy, 1993). Gifted students are some of the most undersupported special needs students in the educational system in the United States, and students from culturally, linguistically, and ethnically diverse backgrounds are especially underrepresented (Siegle, Gubbins, O'Rourke, Langley, Mun, Luria, Little, McCoach, & Knupp, 2016; Michael-Chadwell, 2010). Social-emotional learning curricula targeting the needs of this population are strongly encouraged, as are opportunities for additional academic enrichments. Gifted and highly gifted students have unique challenges and differences that should be supported and nurtured. The bottom line is that all students must be given equal opportunities to learn the skills needed to maximize their potential to be successful citizens.

Social Justice

African American students are targets for severe punishment in schools and are significantly more likely to be harshly disciplined than White students or other minority groups for similar offenses, including disproportionately receiving consequences of corporal punishment, out-of-school suspension, and expulsion. According to a recent study, African American students are seven times more likely to experience exclusionary discipline, while Latino and Native American children are two times as likely (Bal, Betters-Bubon, & Fish, 2017). Data does not support that African American children have higher organic rates of anti-social behavior or engage in more deviant behavior than any other child (Gershoff, 2010).

Research on implicit bias indicates a systemic problem in school culture, which disproportionately punishes African American students in comparison to White counterparts (Staats, Capatosto, Wright, & Contractor, 2015). *Implicit bias* are the underlying beliefs, stereotypes, and attitudes that unconsciously impact a person's decision making. This bias, also sometimes referred to as social implicit cognition, is pervasive, is not mutually exclusive to explicit bias, and does not always align with declared beliefs. This is based, in part, on biased stereotypical beliefs that African American students are more aggressive, disruptive, dangerous, less respectful, less honest, and less hard-working than peers from other racial backgrounds (Staats et al., 2015). Negative stereotypes and implicit bias hurt students in school communities by disengaging children from their education, embracing a culture of failure with irrational blame focused on children for matters beyond their control, and creating a school to jail pipeline for children of color. Understanding implicit bias through a cultural lens may be the best way to begin shifting and changing perspectives (Payne & Vuletich, 2017). In this sense, addressing the underlying and explicit social contexts in which our school and communities exist can help decrease the underlying implicit bias. This perspective is essential when working with policy makers and drafting policies that impact society (Payne & Vuletich, 2017).

Problems of injustice in school systems, including disproportionality of punishment for children of color and over-identification of eligibility for special education in minority populations, must be addressed as an issue of social justice. School teams must acknowledge that White privilege exists, listen and learn from others, think and reflect, and finally, take data-based action to rectify the perpetual racial and social injustice that transpires in our schools (Shriberg, 2016). As part of this process, educating school staff and providing cultural sensitivity training in working with students from diverse racial and ethnic backgrounds must take place. In addition to better understanding students from racial and ethnic diverse backgrounds, educators must also be able to attend to the needs of LGBTQ+ youth. This population of students, regardless of their racial or ethnic background, are "at risk for negative mental health outcomes and reduced academic success" (National Association of School Psychologists, 2016b, p. 1).

Underlying Factors

All teachers must consider whether their Tier 1 classroom behavior management skills are effective for regulating behavior in the learning environment and do not penalize or shame students for poor behavioral choices. Developing positive teacher–student relationships is one of the best ways to remedy misunderstandings with students regarding their behavior in the classroom (Moore-Partin et al., 2010). The very same student who struggles behaviorally in one teacher's class may be a perfect citizen in another teacher's class. Schools that embrace the framework of MTSS train their staff to have higher ratios of positive interactions with students and less emotionally charged negative interactions. These positive interactions and relationships support an increased probability of positive outcomes for students (Sprick, 2013, 2009). When misbehavior is punished, without opportunity for remediation or restitution, students are much less likely to learn from their actions, especially when discipline does not seem fairly applied to all (Moore-Partin et al., 2010). In addition, zero tolerance policies need to be reconsidered so that students are not kicked out of school arbitrarily or the policies are not disproportionally applied to racial and ethnic minority students (Verdugo, 2002).

MTSS creates a problem solving culture among school staff, families, and the community, which improves communication and understanding among all stakeholders. The team approach allows a struggling child to have numerous adult advocates on campus to positively impact individual school success and, ultimately, success in life. Too often students are denied remedial opportunities because schools do not fund interventions; however, they do have federal funding for special education (Kincaid & Sullivan, 2017). As a result, there are many cracks in the school's foundation and alternative supports may be overlooked. Instead of evaluating program delivery, teaching competencies, culturally sensitive instructional practices, and positive behavioral supports, schools take shortcuts and over-identify students, frequently minority students, for special education.

Conversely, in many school districts, second language students may fall victim to underidentification of disabilities because of the opposite assumption: that any learning difficulties are due to second language acquisition factors, not an underlying disability (Kincaid & Sullivan, 2017; Sullivan, 2011; Cummins, 2008; Krashen, 1988, 1987). Second language students with unidentified disabilities tend to get passed from grade to grade without receiving the supports they need. This pattern continues until they hit a brick wall in middle school or high school and can get no further in their education due to failure to pass mandated assessments and an inability to earn credits toward graduation.

MTSS teams must have team members who understand second language acquisition theory, including typical rates of development for basic informal communication skills (BICS) and cognitive academic language proficiency (CALP) (Cummins, 2008). It is imperative that the team has at least one team member who can serve as the expert in second language acquisition and inform the team as to whether a student is making adequate progress in relation to their exposure and language history. Factors that go into determining adequate progress include, but are not limited to, student's time of exposure to the second language, proficiency in their native language (BICS and CALP), proficiency in the second language (BICS and CALP), and home language usage. Typically, a student's academic and language proficiencies in English are expected to progress at a commensurate rate, with writing literacy skills to be one of the last skills mastered. If a student's academic proficiency does not progress at a relatively commensurate rate within a specific time frame (relative to length of exposure and the various factors mentioned), this lack of progress could be due to an underlying disability.

Providing interventions early on and monitoring language status is essential, so that teams can target underlying deficits not otherwise explained by language acquisition factors (O'Connor, Bocian, Sanchez, & Beach, 2012). Especially in high-poverty areas, struggling second language students may not adequately develop skills in their primary language, which in turn impacts acquisition of a secondary language. The same holds true for English speaking language deprived students. Students who are in essence *alingual* (not proficient in any language) enter school at a significant disadvantage academically and socially. Students with expressive language deficits at the age of two are predictive of higher rates of anxiety, depression, and withdrawal at the age of three (Carson, Klee, Lee, Williams, & Perry, 1998). Without remediation, these deficits become compounded and lead to further social-emotional difficulties. Beyond language status, socio-economic status also has a significant impact on students' vocabulary and language processing. According to the key research conducted at Stanford University, the language gap between students from high and low socioeconomic families are evident as early as 18 months of age for vocabulary and language processing efficacy (Fernald, Marchman, & Weisleder, 2013). Further, by 24 months of age, this gap widens to 6 months with regard to language processing skills.

Second language and language deprived students are also a group misidentified for speech and language special education services (Pieretti & Roseberry-McKibbin, 2015). The first group because teams oftentimes lack qualified individuals with knowledge of second language acquisition, or they lack a bilingual speech and language pathologist to conduct the communication evaluation and the team chalks any language difficulties up to second language acquisition status. Language deprived students are often underidentified as they tend to be quieter, less confident speaking, or speak using predominately slang and poor grammar, which breeds preconceived and stereotyped beliefs about a student's intelligence. Without a rich vocabulary and semantic knowledge, students often are less likely to verbalize and speak out as much in class as their typical peers. Their deficits often go unidentified because teachers have not heard the student talk enough to suspect the presence of a problem or they suspect lower intellectual skills. The earlier the communication team can provide supports and services for those individuals who qualify, the better the long-term educational outcomes for students. Training and preparing MTSS team members to strategically assess student needs and prioritize relevant interventions at the intensity level students require is paramount to support all types of learners. *Regardless of a student's unique characteristics, special education eligibility should not be the goal of interventions; positive educational outcomes should be.*

Attention School Psychologists

Informal surveys of school principals across a large urban area overwhelmingly indicated that the efficacy and success of a school's MTSS and intervention team processes depend more on the skill level of the school psychologist than any other factor. School psychologists should no longer be thought of as gatekeepers to special education services, but as *linchpins* holding various elements of complicated structures in place to keep students from sliding off into an abyss of school failure. *If students fail and no one is watching, did the students fail or did the system fail the students?* School psychologists have the ability, education, and training to socially engineer positive educational practices in schools for students (National Association of School Psychologists, 2016a). As they are often the most knowledgeable on campus about social-emotional learning, psychology of learning, behavior modification, and special education law, school psychologists can be engaged as leaders who are empowered to contribute to decision making that impacts students directly and indirectly, proactively and reactively.

Schools who maintain school psychologists in a special education testing-only role are missing out on all the benefits of having true psychological services on campus, as well as all the academic benefits. School psychologists are uniquely qualified to lead and participate in selecting and overseeing implementation of Tier 1, 2, and 3 behavioral and social-emotional learning infrastructures at a school in cooperation with school counselors, school social workers, teachers, and administrators (NASP, 2016a). In addition, school psychologists invest in professional development activities and research effective school-wide academic and behavioral practices, as well as evidence-based methods, to remediate target behaviors and academic delays. School psychologists have a wealth of skills and knowledge, and are often underutilized as the goldmine of resources for children that they are. Their time is filled with paperwork, begging individual teachers to try something extra for struggling students, chasing forms and documentation, and appeasing endless parent requests for special education eligibility assessments. Without empowerment to be on the proactive end of instructional practices, school psychologists find themselves reacting to variables in the environment with little control of outcomes for students, like a pinball flying across the game board bouncing off barriers, intermittently scoring, and finding themselves in a dark hole when the game is over.

School psychologists are the unicorns on a school campus. Unicorns are mythological creatures with unique talents and characteristics, and have been critically likened to human rights: imaginary constructs that do not exist (McIntyre, 1984). School psychologists are like unicorns in that they are rarely seen on a school campus yet when they are, or when their impact is felt, it is extraordinary. Whether engaging as a moral advocate on behalf of students or as a political advocate for adhering to state and federal policies, school psychologists, unique and powerful, are indeed real. The power of the unicorn lies in its uniqueness (Botting, 2015). Each school psychologist has unique interests, strengths, and focuses in their individual practices, as well as the skills and knowledge to conduct special education assessments and help guide educational programming. They engage in counseling services for children and families, crisis response, suicide prevention, parenting classes and family wellness, classroom management, positive behavior intervention supports, social-emotional-behavioral learning, program evaluation to improve MTSS practices, advocacy and policy change, among other areas of expertise (National Association of School Psychologists, 2014; Dockweiler, 2016). Many find ways to incorporate their areas of skill and interests into daily and weekly practice while toeing the line for special education. Others get sucked into the monotony of assessment and are used solely to test and place students for special education due to high demand for and low supply of school psychologists. School counselors, school social workers, school nurses, and teachers may share splinter characteristics, skills, and interests with school psychologists, and their professional duties may overlap in some limited ways. *Yet, no other educational professional can replace the background or perspective of the school psychologist when looking at school-wide issues and individual differences.*

School psychologists are among the first to realize when educational practices on a campus are not working. They can be a litmus test for school culture, can assist with getting to the bottom of complex issues quickly, and almost always have an evidence-based contribution on matters large and small. If school psychologists do not have a chair at the decision-making table, then they need to bring their own. However, even before they can bring their own chair, they need to be aware that a meeting is taking place. The Three As are required for having a seat at the decision-making table and participating in making decisions that impact the future. *Awareness, access, and action are all necessary components of inserting the school psychologist's perspective into a school and community's ecosystem.* Input from the school psychologist is invaluable.

It takes psychology science to persuade people to engage in new endeavors and research-based change (Simonton, 2009). School psychologists need to get comfortable with resistance to change and use psychological strategies to help school teams bridge problems with solutions. Children do not typically change their behavior without the adults in their environment changing their behavior toward them, manipulating environmental variables and altering reinforcement schedules. Adult to adult behavioral change is not dissimilar.

School psychologists have little to no leverage over colleagues at work because most are not employed in administrative positions within the school district hierarchy. However, they can use all their psychological tools and skills of persuasion to convince others to empower change within their environments, such as promoting a new research-based remedial program, teaching how to increase the positive reinforcement schedule for a student, and advocating for a comprehensive approach to systematic implementation and monitoring of remedial opportunities. School psychologists have more power than they realize, and not as gatekeepers for special education eligibility determination. They have unique skills and training to persuade school teams to work collaboratively to systematically use best practices in smart groups to solve problems for all students at a school. A well led school will appreciate and utilize these leadership qualities.

School psychologists must *advocate for their duty* to engage in psychological services in school systems. The role of a school psychologist at a school is frequently dictated by the school principal. Some school leaders support and promote the leadership of school psychologists, while others try to micromanage school psychologists to limit their professional activities. The only clearly consistent role school psychologists have across schools is the responsibility to guide special education eligibility assessments and determinations. In schools where no MTSS is in place, and academic and behavioral supports are few and far between, teachers may grudgingly provide "documentation" of interventions and outcomes. This so-called documentation often comes with questionable validity, which may consist of random work samples, incomplete tests, dean's referrals, and failing grades. School psychologists may find themselves continuously reinventing the wheel with each individual student referral and with each individual teacher in an effort to ensure that students receive some sort of remedial opportunity and that teachers are collecting response to instruction data. The repetitious one-on-one consultation is not a productive use of time for the school psychologist or the school, and does not systematically benefit students. When psychologists advocate for universal, systematic processes to address student deficiencies, with outcome measures and continuous improvement practices in place, they are helping *all* students on campus, not just the ones that they ultimately assess.

The more efficiently and flexibly school processes and personnel are able to respond to student needs, the more effective the school psychologist can be at identifying students with severe underachievement and atypical behavior patterns in an effort to obtain appropriate and timely treatment. The nationwide shortage of school psychologists (National Association of School Psychologists, 2016) has resulted in most school psychologists providing services at multiple school sites and to increasingly growing numbers of students. It is not uncommon for one school psychologist to have an assigned caseload of 2,000 to 3,500 students (Nevada Association of School Psychologists, 2018, 2016). There is no way one person alone can manage all the happenings on a large secondary school campus, let alone more than one campus. It is especially difficult for school psychologists to simultaneously manage multiple school sites with multiple school teams, cultures, and systems. Busy school psychologists need super powers because they are responsible for students and school team functions even when they are off campus. Fortunately, effective *MTSS is a collective super power* which all team members benefit from, especially school psychologists, in prioritizing school and student needs and making data-based decisions.

A healthy system of information exchange between MTSS team members increases the probability of a timely response with relevant and helpful feedback from the school psychologist. Staff members can actively support the school psychologist in the following ways:

- Sharing the updated MTSS Student Database and corresponding case notes with the school psychologists after each MTSS team meeting (or provide them access if using a shared Google Folder).
- Supporting case managers to maintain organization and ensure that student deficit areas are matched with appropriate interventions and appropriate outcome measures.
- Keeping the school psychologist in the loop during and after a crisis response; the event could be related to other relevant school safety and student issues. The school psychologist will be able to help mitigate situations through team collaboration, sharing student history, assessing the problem, observing and interviewing the student, de-escalating tense situations, and assisting with intervention design.
- Including the school psychologist in school team meetings and administrative meetings that proactively address academic initiatives, school climate, and student safety.
- Arranging meeting times to work with the school psychologist's schedule as they are often moving between multiple schools.
- Making room at the table for the school psychologist to engage in team problem solving through awareness, access, and action.
- Reimagining school psychologists as more than psychometricians. School districts that have marginalized school psychologists to testing centers or replaced them with psychometricians are missing out on the leadership, inclusiveness, and quality control school psychologists bring to a school culture.
- Providing administrative assistance to help school psychologists with the mounds of paperwork they must complete for compliance purposes. This frees the school psychologist to engage in more specialized activities such as additional problem solving, running student counseling groups, or engaging in positive behavior support planning for students and coaching for staff.

It takes a village to support school psychologists to maximize their effectiveness. School psychologists must advocate for such supports and, in turn, they must make themselves available and accountable to support team functions and follow through with team recommendations.

Multi-tiered systems of support, and the paradigm of three tiers, can be used as a triage model in a school system, which enables MTSS teams to respond to the intensity of student problems with correspondingly intensive interventions. With all MTSS team members doing their part, enormous amounts of information on numerous students can be regularly sifted through and dispersed to relevant stakeholders in a timely manner. Few things are as upsetting to caregivers and school staff as when harm comes to children that is preventable. A combination of well-developed MTSS processes, including conscientious and accountable MTSS team members with strong team communication skills, is the closest thing schools will get to a magic crystal ball that can be used to predict students' futures. If present functioning and behavior are the best predictors of future performance, then fortune telling should be a whole lot easier with several active MTSS team members' eyes on the ball.

When multiple sources of information get disseminated properly and in a timely manner, better decisions can be made for students. Teams must identify students who are at-risk and prioritize their response to minimize negative student outcomes. Getting student information updates to the right ears at the right time is paramount to serve students well. As will be discussed in Chapter 10, MTSS teams who work together effectively and communicate regularly can get ahead of students' emotional and behavioral problems before events happen that cannot be undone, including assault to others, self-harm, and suicide. It is assumed that school psychologists are responsive to student and school crises as part of the crisis response team, perhaps even leading in the efforts. However, like Grandma always said, "an ounce of prevention is worth more than a pound of cure." School psychologists must manage their time to balance the requirement to be proactive with the reality of overwhelming demands that require being reactive to student problems.

Some words for practicing school psychologists whose time is consumed with assessment and eligibility determination:

- Find ways to demonstrate your value to administrators, teachers, school staff, parents and families, and students outside of evaluation duties.
- Be the linchpin for students and connect them to resources to assist in their development and improve opportunities for positive school outcomes.
- Ask the school principal for processes or resources that you would like to see implemented. If the school psychologist does not voice their preferences grounded in evidence-based practices, somebody else may offer something less effective.
- Question established rules if it is in a student's best interest.
- Be mindful of intensity versus volume of student needs and prioritize students who are a danger to themselves or others first, no matter how many other children you have on your referral waiting list. *Student and staff safety always comes first.*
- Listen to caregivers, counselors, and teachers because their accurate and timely reporting increases the school psychologist's ability to synthesize large amounts of data to accurately identify and prioritize student problems, which leads to more effective and timely solutions.
- Nurture the growth of MTSS; school psychologists can positively impact all students and adults in a school community.
- Build relationships with school staff, students, and community members to integrate your unique skills into the fabric of culturally responsive and proactive instructional practices.
- You are a unicorn after all and school communities need the services and input only school psychologists can offer, so advocate for the profession and best practices.

Attention Specialists

A secondary campus has many individuals that fall under the functional category of specialist. Teachers on special assignment, special education teachers, school counselors, school social workers, school nurses, speech and language therapists, school psychologists, and other itinerant professionals all fall under this category and have vested interests in supporting MTSS. Each position and perspective provides an important lens in which to filter student problems through because each specialty has its own criteria for developmental expectations and unique remedies specific to areas of expertise. The school nurse is sensitive to organizing patterns of health symptoms into hypotheses about difficulties students may experience that are health-related. The speech and language pathologist would be particularly sensitive to developmental issues that are impacted by speech and language development in comparison to developmental milestones of communication. School social workers are experts at tracking down information and community resources for families, in addition to directly helping them overcome barriers to access resources. Special education teachers are valuable resources to any school campus because they are the masters of differentiated instruction and working with students who do not learn in typical ways. Each specialist is a necessary and esteemed member of the MTSS team.

As stated earlier, the importance of active participation of specialists in supporting appropriate educational opportunities for struggling learners cannot be overstated. Specialists fill needs that general education classroom teachers cannot. They target specific developmental skills and areas of need that cannot be addressed in the classroom or by any other team member depending on their specialty. Some duties overlap, such as sharing counseling responsibilities between the school counselor, school psychologist, and school social worker, but most MTSS teams carve up team member responsibilities to ensure that the right professional is given the right job responsibilities. Specialists must be especially alert to evidence of students demonstrating low-incidence disabilities, which do not require prior intervention and should be assessed for special education eligibility without delay if there is a suspicion of a disability and a demonstrated need for specialized services. Such eligibilities include, but are not limited to, intellectual disabilities, autism spectrum disorder, and visual impairments.

Classroom teachers work hard to teach curriculum and manage behavior; they are also responsible for differentiating instruction to diverse learners. When they need help from colleagues to support them and their students, they should have easy access without having to go to great lengths for the help. When systems for accessing help become too complicated, or overly dependent on large amounts of pre-referral paperwork, teachers are less likely to request assistance from specialists. MTSS team specialists are encouraged to create formats and brief forms that support documentation of information needed for referrals and for making decisions about students (see Chapter 6). Classroom teachers who believe that MTSS team members follow through with referrals in a timely manner and are responsive to requests for supports are much more likely to fulfill their own MTSS responsibilities.

Specialists doing their part and following through on MTSS team recommendations and referrals in a timely manner should be a given; however, expectations must be made explicit and emphasized. A message to specialists: support school MTSS teams by developing both proactive and reactive systems for supporting students. Develop streamlined procedures of communication with staff and user-friendly documentation from teachers so that you can make timely database decisions and provide direct services to increase student success. The MTSS team requires the expertise of specialists, and students benefit most from specialists who are looking out for student problems proactively. Specialists must step up and speak out on behalf of students, as they are excellent candidates for leadership positions advocating for MTSS on school campuses.

It is remarkable how powerful a fully functional MTSS can be on a school campus, and how many problems it automatically solves for students and school staff alike. Teachers have a community to support struggling students and a recipe to follow when students need access to more help than can be provided within the general education curriculum alone. Students, regardless of their background, can get help when they need it instead of having to fail repeatedly for years to perform "low enough" for special education eligibility and to qualify for special education programming. The MTSS framework supports all students universally and has provisions in place for all types of learners. In a social justice context, special student populations' needs are not only considered but understood through a strengths-based lens and provided for along a continuum of relevant educational services for all. Implicit biases are confronted forthrightly and cognitive behavioral mindsets are checked and readjusted to ensure fair treatment of all students and staff, thus reducing over-identification and under-identification traps. Special education eligibility decisions can be complicated, and all variables must be weighed to make the most informed decisions and to effectively address individualized needs. School psychologists and specialists are uniquely qualified to train and support MTSS team functions, as well as provide a rainbow of alternative service delivery models depending on levels of administrative support, individual interests and areas of expertise, and the demands of caseload assignments and competing responsibilities. Lastly, school psychologists are highly qualified and uniquely talented educators whose talents and abilities to lead and support school changes should not be underestimated.

References

Abou-Rjaily, K., & Stoddard, S. (2017). Response to intervention (RTI) for students presenting with behavioral difficulties: Culturally responsive guiding questions. *International Journal of Multicultural Education, 19*(3), 85–102.

Aspen Institute: National Commission on Social, Emotional, and Academic Development. (2018). *How learning happens: Supporting students' social, emotional, and academic development.* Washington, DC: Author.

Bal, A., Betters-Bubon, J., & Fish, R. E. (2017). A multilevel analysis of statewide disproportionality in exclusionary discipline and the identification of emotional disturbance. *Education and Urban Society.* Retrieved from https://doi.org/10.1177/0013124517716260.

Botting, E. H. (2015). Women's rights may be unicorns, but they can fight wicked witches. *Journal of International Political Theory, 12*(1), 58–66.

Carson, D. K., Klee, T., Lee, S., Williams, K. C., & Perry, C. K. (1998). Children's language proficiency at ages 2 and 3 as predictors of behavior problems, social and cognitive development at age 3. *Communication Disorders Quarterly, 19*(2), 21–30.

Cummins, J. (2008). BICS and CALP: Empirical and theoretical status of the distinction. In B. Street & N. H. Hornberger (Eds.), *Encyclopedia of language and education* (2nd ed., Vol. 2, pp. 71–83). New York: Springer Science + Business Media.

Dishon, T. (2011). Promoting academic competence and behavioral health in public schools: A strategy of systemic concatenation of empirically based intervention principles. *School Psychology Review, 40*(4), 590–597.

Dockweiler, K. A. (2016). State association advocacy: Conversations about conversations. *Communiqué, 44*(7), 1, 32–33.

Dueck, M. (2014). The problem with penalties. *Educational Leadership, 3*, 44–48.

Fernald, A., Marchman, V. A., & Weisleder, A. (2013). SES differences in language processing skill and vocabulary are evident at 18 months. *Developmental Science, 16*(2), 234–248.

Forman, S. G., & Crystal, C. D. (2015). Systems consultation for multitiered systems of supports (MTSS): Implementation issues. *Journal of Educational and Psychological Consultation, 25*, 276–285.

Foucault, M. (1995). *Discipline and punish: The birth of the prison* (2nd ed.). New York: Random House.

Francis, B., Mills, M., & Lupton, R. (2017). Toward social justice in education: Contradictions and dilemmas. *Journal of Education Policy, 32*(4), 414–431.

Garbacz, S. A., McIntosh, K., Eagle, J. W., Dowd-Eagle, S. E., Hirano, K. A., & Ruppert, T. (2016). Family engagement within schoolwide positive behavioral interventions and supports. *Preventing School Failure, 60*(1), 60–69.

Gershoff, E. T. (2010). More harm than good: A summary of scientific research on the intended and unintended effects of corporal punishment on children. *Law and Contemporary Problems, 73*, 31–56.

Hobbs, N. (1982). *The troubled and troubling child*. New York: Jossey-Bass.

Kaplan, L. S., & Geoffroy, K. E. (1993). Copout or burnout? Counseling strategies to reduce stress in gifted students. *The School Counselor, 40*(4), 247–252.

Kincaid, A. P., & Sullivan, A. L. (2017). Parsing the relations of race and socioeconomic status in special education disproportionality. *Remedial and Special Education, 38*(3), 159–170.

Krashen, S. D. (1987). *Principles and practice in second language acquisition*. Upper Saddle River, NJ: Prentice-Hall International.

Krashen, S. D. (1988). *Second language acquisition and second language learning*. Upper Saddle River, NJ: Prentice-Hall International.

Ladd, H. F., & Fiske, E. B. (Eds.) (2008). *Handbook of research in education finance and policy*. New York: Routledge.

Le Peletier, M. (1791). *Report on the draft penal code*. Retrieved from https://criminocorpus.org/en/exhibitions/death-penalty/history-death-penalty-france-1789–1981/debate-national-constituent-assembly.

McIntyre, A. (1984). *After virtue: A study in moral theory* (2nd ed.). Notre Dame, IN: University of Notre Dame Press.

Michael-Chadwell, S. (2010). Examining the underrepresentation of underserved students in gifted program from a transformational leadership vantage point. *Journal for the Education of the Gifted, 34*(1), 99–130.

Moore-Partin, T. C., Robertson, R. E., Maggin, D. M., Oliver, R. M., & Wehby, J. H. (2010). Using teacher praise and opportunities to respond to promote appropriate student behavior. *Preventing School Failure, 54*(3), 172–178.

National Association of School Psychologists (2014). *Who are school psychologists?* Bethesda, MD: Author.

National Association of School Psychologists (2016a). *ESSA and multi-tiered systems of support for school psychologists*. Bethesda, MD: Author.

National Association of School Psychologists (2016b). *Safe and supportive schools for LGBTQ+ students*. Bethesda, MD: Author.

National Association of School Psychologists (2017). *Shortages in school psychology: Challenges to meeting the growing needs of U.S. students and schools* [Research summary]. Bethesda, MD: Author.

Nellis, L. M., Sickman, L. S., Newman, D. S., & Harman, D. R. (2014). Schoolwide collaboration to prevent and address reading difficulties: Opportunities for school psychologists and speech-language pathologists. *Journal of Educational and Psychological Consultation, 24,* 110–127.

Nevada Association of School Psychologists (2016). [Statewide survey for Read by Grade 3]. Unpublished raw data.

Nevada Association of School Psychologists (2018). Notes from a presentation to the Clark County School District Board of Trustees meeting. Nevada Association of School Psychologists, Las Vegas, Nevada.

O'Connor, R. E., Bocian, K. M., Sanchez, V., & Beach, K. D. (2012). Access to a responsiveness to intervention model: Does beginning intervention in kindergarten matter? *Journal of Learning Disabilities, 47*(4), 307–328.

Payne, B. K., & Vuletich, H. A. (2017). Policy insights from advances in implicit bias research. *Policy Insight from the Behavioral and Brain Sciences*, doi:10.1177/2372732217746190.

Peterson, J. S. (2006). Addressing counseling needs of gifted students. *Professional School Counseling, 10*(1), 43–51.

Pieretti, R. A., & Roseberry-McKibbin, C. (2015). Assessment and intervention for English language learners with primary language impairment. *Communication Disorders Quarterly, 37*(2), 117–128.

Robison, S., Jaggers, J., Rhodes, J., Blackmon, B. J., & Church, W. (2016). Correlates of educational success: Predictors of school dropout and graduation for urban students in the Deep South. *Children and Youth Services Review, 73,* 37–46.

Schonert-Reichl, K. A. (2017). Social emotional learning and teachers. *The Future of Children, 27*(1), 137–155.

Shinn, M. R. (2007). Identifying students at risk, monitoring performance, and determining eligibility within RTI: Research on educational need and benefit from academic intervention. *School Psychology Review, 36*(4), 601–617.

Shinn, M. R., & Walker, H. M. (Eds.) (2010). *Interventions academic and behavior problems in a three-tier model, including Response-to-Intervention.* Bethesda, MD: National Association of School Psychologists.

Shriberg, D. (2016). Commentary: School psychologists as advocates for racial justice and social justice: Some proposed steps. *School Psychology Forum, 10*(3), 337–339.

Shriberg, D., & Clinton, A. (2016). The application of social justice principles to global school psychology practice. *School Psychology International, 37*(4), 323–339.

Shriberg, D., Song, S. Y., Miranda, A. H., & Radliff, K. M. (2013). *School psychology and social justice: Conceptual foundations and tools for practice.* New York: Routledge.

Shriberg, D., Wynne, M. E., Briggs, A., Bartucci, G., & Lombardo, A. C. (2011). School psychologists' perspectives on social justice. *School Psychology Forum, 5*(2), 37–53.

Siegle, D., Gubbins, E. J., O'Rourke, P., Langley, S. D., Mun, R. U., Luria, S. R., Little, C. A., McCoach, B., & Knupp, T. (2016). Barriers to underserved students' participation in gifted programs and possible solutions. *Journal for the Education of the Gifted, 39*(2), 103–131.

Simonton, D. K. (2009). Applying the psychology of science to the science of psychology: Can psychologists use psychological science to enhance psychology as a science? *Perspectives on Psychological Science, 4*(1), 2–4.

Sink, C. A. (2016). Incorporating a multi-tiered system of supports into school counselor preparation. *The Professional Counselor, 6*(3), 203–219.

Sprick, R. A. (2009). *CHAMPS: A proactive and positive approach to classroom management* (2nd ed.). Eugene, OR: Pacific Northwest Publishing.

Sprick, R. A. (2013). *Discipline in the secondary classroom: A positive approach to behavior management* (3rd ed.). Hoboken, NJ: John Wiley & Sons.

Staats, C., Capatosto, K., Wright, R. A., & Contractor, D. (2015). *State of the science: Implicit bias review 2015*. Columbus, OH: The Kirwan Institute for the Study of Race and Ethnicity.

Sullivan, A. L. (2011). Disproportionality in special education identification and placement of English language learners. *Exceptional Children, 77*(3), 317–334.

Taylor, R. D., Oberle, E., Durlak, J. A., & Weissberg, R. P. (2017). Promoting positive youth development through school-based social and emotional learning interventions: A meta-analysis of follow-up effects. *Child Development, 88*(4), 1–16.

Verdugo, R. R. (2002). Race-ethnicity, social class, and zero-tolerance policies: The cultural and structural wars. *Education and Urban Society, 35*(1), 50–75.

Chapter 8

High School Recommendations

Key Terms

Teacher–Student Relationships
Intermediate Organizations
LGBTQ+
Decentralized

Chapter Concepts

In this chapter, readers will learn:

1. How to integrate an MTSS framework onto a high school campus.
2. What opportunities exist for the seven most common implementation hurdles.
3. The importance of shifting the mindset and talents of special education staff.
4. How to structure an Academic MTSS team on a high school campus.
5. How to embed social-emotional and behavioral interventions into a Mental and Behavioral Health MTSS.

Multi-tiered systems of support in high school are just as important as they are in elementary school and middle school, only the stakes are different. The goal remains the same even though the student and staff populations are larger: to systematically identify and support students who require academic and behavioral interventions to help them achieve graduation standards. Students who do not graduate have limited options after high school in terms of gainful employment, joining the military, and accessing higher education. Students with a General Education Development or General Equivalency Diploma (GED) are more likely to be employed than high school dropouts without a GED, but have only slightly higher earning potential (Tyler, 2004, 2003). In light of these data, obtaining a high school diploma remains the gold standard of high school success and longer-term earning potential and economic success post-high school. The MTSS framework for high school includes all of the same components as in elementary and middle school, including a multi-tiered intervention model for academics and social-emotional-behavior (SEB), targeted interventions, problem-solving teams, data-driven decision making, positive behavioral interventions, and family-school partnerships (Weist, Garbacz, Lane, & Kincaid, 2017; Freeman, Simonsen, McCoach, Sugai, Lombardi, & Horner, 2016).

Many educational factors contribute to success in high school. If students received pre-kindergarten education, participated in a social-emotional learning curriculum, had strong school-family engagement, or received primary intervention supports, they are more likely to experience success at the secondary level (Project AWARE Ohio, 2017; Williams, Landry, Anthony, Swank, & Crawford, 2012). Beyond high school, students who experience secondary success and graduate high school are more likely to earn more money and generate greater economic productivity within their communities.

Strong and cohesive leadership across all levels, school, district, and state is required for comprehensive support for MTSS structures and functions to ensure optimal high school student outcomes. However, given the limited research on implementation of MTSS in the high school, scant evidence is available to guide efforts (Leko, Handy, & Roberts, 2017). Data does suggest that strong state leadership and district level systems that actively require accountability for administrators in the context of achieving MTSS framework benchmarks have a higher probability that funding, resources, and manpower will go toward evidence-based practices within MTSS. MTSS frameworks must have strong leadership at the district level to increase accountability and implementation fidelity (Freeman, Miller, & Newcomer, 2015).

States and school districts without mandated and defined student improvement frameworks will be less likely to devote human capital, professional development, and investments in systematic processes for problem identification, intervention implementation, and progress monitoring (Morningstar, Allcock, White, Taub, Kurth, Gonsier-Gerdin, Ryndak, Sauer, & Jorgensen, 2016; Masters, 2010). Many high schools opt out of best practices in these matters due to of lack of effective leadership at all levels, lack of allocating resources in an equitable manner, and lack of motivation and understanding about how to build multi-tiers of support.

Seven Opportunities

Seven key obstacles are evident as teams hurdle over the obstacles of implementing MTSS on their high school campuses. With each hurdle comes the opportunity to reflect and revise the implementation process, including perceptions and metrics for measuring success.

I Inclusion

The trend toward more inclusive practices makes tracking or creating more low-level classes a thing of the past, and pushes students upward despite their skill levels. For example, most 8th grade students are placed in either Pre-Algebra or Algebra. This includes special education students and students performing below grade level, which results in teaching more students at their frustration level than at their instructional level (Watt, Watkins, & Abbitt, 2016). This has resulted in students "checking out" of the learning process early on in their educational careers.

Opportunities

Students benefit when they can participate in the general education curriculum expectations successfully. However, there is the law of diminishing returns when the demands of the educational environment exceed the skill level of students, which leads to students giving up on the learning process and increases their likelihood of presenting behavioral issues and academic decline. This is especially true for students who are learning a new language and require additional time to learn the new language. Lack of academic engagement can be predicted from learning and motivational factors, but is rarely considered in the high school setting, especially in urban schools with high Latino populations (Loera, Rueda, & Oh, 2015). Language and other environmental factors must be considered with students who traditionally present as disengaged. Students who fail repeatedly have a lower self-esteem, higher rates of depression, and more social problems (Taylor, Oberle, Durlak, & Weissberg, 2017). The most effective resource in a classroom is the subject level teacher, and it would behoove schools to invest in human capital resources to develop better teaching practices, allow more professional collaborative time, and provide content level information at lower reading levels to supplement students' textbooks. Spiraling, scaffolding, and differentiating instruction to reach students at all levels is a skill, best delivered by individuals with teaching talent and positive regard for students (Vaughn & Fletcher, 2012).

Best teaching practices require good lesson planning. Student engagement in a lesson depends on the "hook" and how prior knowledge is accessed, this is especially true in today's environment of technology and media. Research shows that when students are asked to generate parts of subject matter, through self-explanation or conducting experiments, it leads to greater performance across types of knowledge (Eysink, de Jong, Berthold, Kolloffel, Opfermann, & Wouters, 2009). As any high school student knows, the best teachers are the most engaging, and as any high school student also knows, not all teachers are entertaining, let alone interesting, when teaching. Teachers who do not have the personality skills to carry the curriculum through performance art in teaching must cultivate relationships with students in other ways. Positive *teacher–student relationships* fuel the efforts of students, who can persist despite challenges and are resilient in times of adversity, with the right level of support.

2 State and District Policies

School practices often start at the state level with a policy that gets translated into a procedure at the district level, and then carried out within some sort of program at the school level. At each level of bureaucracy there are many different interpretations and attempts to implement the policy into a meaningful practice that accurately reflects the policy as written. Rarely does a policy get written as was initially intended, there are too many competing influences and agendas. Compounding the policy-making process, potential landmines to negotiate around are the *intermediate organizations* that "operate between policymakers and implementers to affect changes in roles and practices for both parties" (Honig, 2004, 65). These intermediate organizations are typically not comprised of practitioners and their involvement can either impede or facilitate implementation depending on resources and motivations. When their understanding of the structure or subject matter is comprehensive and they have genuine motives for the policy's development, the intermediate organization will mostly likely be a helpful organization. However, if the intermediate organization is looking out for the best interest of their clients, not children or educators, they will most likely be a hindrance; especially if they have a lot of financial backing and social clout. Autonomy of schools to problem solve rigid laws and policies, such as seat time rules, teacher licensure, and graduation requirements, is essential and these intermediaries may be allies to help a school's ability to operate outside the box. They may also be able to assist schools and policy makers in examining unintended consequences that may be detrimental to students and communities.

Opportunities

State and district policies are in place to guide educators in best practices which keeps them working in accordance with laws in terms of curriculum, high-stakes testing, grading, discipline practices, and special education practices to name a few. Most of the time policies make sense, guide educators in best practices, and protect student rights. However, some procedures may be perceived as laborious or overly oppressive because there is little wiggle room for deviation from specific situations. Other times, some policies make little sense to the educators tasked with enforcing them and they seem like barriers to common sense. It is important for school administrators to respect the intent of laws on the books, while looking for ways to grow supports and services that could be supported by other existing policies. Title I schools often have more flexibility in maneuvering through policy to find funding solutions for struggling students (extended school days, Saturday school, summer school, online supports and services). Where there is a will there is a way to help children get an appropriate education. Best practices must be lobbied into state, district, and school policies.

When state, district, and school policies are on target, administrators are able to maneuver deftly to cover student needs with resource allocation, scheduling, and educator training and support, which is the intent of many policies. When policies miss the target, and create insurmountable obstacles to best practices and common sense, unforeseen consequences may arise that negatively impact educators and students alike. These situations can be hard to accept and can create activists out of constituents. Empowered educators and students speaking up for common good such as school safety and inclusiveness, is a byproduct of policies infringing on student rights and the well-being of the school and school personnel. It is not only a right to speak out against misguided state, district, and school policies, but a growing responsibility for affected communities to challenge the status quo of lawmakers to make laws that do not align with research-based practices. Oftentimes these laws are made out of ignorance; however, there are times when laws are passed that primarily benefit special interest groups.

Currently, many districts struggle with how to establish socially just bathroom policies for LGBTQ+ youth. *LGBTQ+* students are those who identify as lesbian, gay, bisexual, transgender, questioning, or gender diverse. While schools and students may be calling for more inclusive policies, parents and religious organizations may be calling for more separatist policies. Through it all,

LGBTQ+ students "remain challenged to navigate marginalization to maintain their well-being" (Asakura, 2016, abstract). Inclusive schools include individuals and subpopulations, who are traditionally marginalized, in the decision making that impacts them, to increase the likelihood of meeting the needs of individuals and the collective. Creating safe spaces on campus for students, forming positive relationships with caring adults, and giving students the opportunity to voice their concerns to advocate for their needs go a long way in establishing trust with students in a school setting.

3 Federal Law

It behooves educators at all levels and professional domains to stay abreast of federal legislation. While this may seem like a daunting task, it must be done because dangerous landmines of special interests get hidden in policy that have devastating impacts on funding and direct services at schools nationwide. Given that students' lives are complex and mostly take place outside the sole context of the school setting, it is also imperative to monitor federal policies outside education to obtain a more comprehensive perspective on what challenges and opportunities influence our students. *Many of our students are not coming to school to thrive, they are coming to school just to survive.*

Despite threats to eliminate significant portions of funding for Education in the President's 2019 budget, along with proposed cuts to several ESSA Title programs, Congress provided additional funding for Education, increasing the 2019 education budget by $2.6 billion to $70.9 billion (Ujifusa, 2018). For example, Title II – Preparing, Training, and Recruiting High Quality Teachers and Principals, Part A was threatened to be eliminated in its entirety at a price tag of $2.1 billion. This cut would have had a dramatic impact on the grants offered to states for collaboration and the professional learning time of teachers. Collaboration and professional learning are key contributors to educators honing and refining their craft (Loughran, 2014). Elimination of these funds had the potential to result in unintended consequences of decreased student performance across the board academically, socially, emotionally, and behaviorally.

Social-emotional-behavioral learning is a significant instructional component that schools should be implementing as part of their Tier 1 instruction; however, the majority of teachers feel ill-prepared to do so. There is an obvious need for continuing staff development in social-emotional-behavioral learning in all schools. Joint collaborative time allows educators to share, reflect, and revise teaching practices to enhance the learning opportunities for students. Often, innovative practices emerge during these professional learning times, as less effective teaching practices are identified and new skills are developed and rehearsed to replace them. The world in which we live is constantly evolving, as are the needs of our students and the teachers who teach them. Educators' practices evolve when regularly structured opportunities are provided for growth of relevant new professional skills in a supportive environment. Cutting collaboration and professional development time cuts off growth opportunities and learning experiences for teachers and students alike, resulting in lower-quality instruction for students and lower educational outcomes.

Looking outside of federal education legislation to legislation emerging from other federal departments is essential to understand the scope of how legislation and policies intimately impact students in schools on a daily basis. For example, student health care and access to health care providers are monumental issues for students, especially those who come from low-income homes. Funding for programs such as Medicaid and CHIP (Children's Health Insurance Program) through the Department of Health and Human Services, Centers for Medicare and Medicaid Services is critical to students obtaining basic health care, as they subsidize access to care so children can qualify for health services, regardless of their parents' financial or insurance status.

Also emerging from the Department of Health and Human Services is H.R. 3770: Community Health Investment, Modernization, and Excellence Act (2017). This bill proposes community-based mental and behavioral health supports and facilitates ease of access. A community-based approach to address the whole child is essential to ensure children's basic needs are being met within all levels of the child, school, and community ecosystems. Common sense would dictate that all high schools are afforded a community-based health center that allows students to access health care and mental health care locally. The fewer barriers for access, including funding and transportation to service providers, the greater probability students and their families will obtain the care they desperately need.

A fairly recent barrier to helping students academically, which impacted the flexibility of administrators in distributing resources justly, was the limited access to some of the most highly trained educators on a campus. Due to changes in the Individuals with Disabilities Education Act (2004) special education teachers could not be the content area teacher for general education students if they did not have their bachelor's degree, were not licensed in that content area, and could not demonstrate subject-matter competency. Most special education teachers carried a generalist degree that supported instruction for special education students, not instruction specific to any one subject such as mathematics.

However, with the Every Student Succeeds Act (2015), these prescriptive highly-qualified definitions and requirements have been removed. Now, "states have sole authority to determine all teacher certification requirements including which teachers are qualified to deliver core content instruction" (Pennsylvania State Education Association, 2016, p. 1). Educators specializing in students with special needs have recently been given more access to struggling students, not less. Elevating the role of special educators on a school campus is a cultural problem as much as a policy problem.

Depending on the school campus, special education teachers are often treated as professionals lower on the totem pole of respect and talent, when the opposite should be considered. Special education teachers bring a wealth of knowledge and expertise to differentiating instruction, managing student behavior, setting individual goals for students, and collecting data to inform instruction. How special educators and related service providers are integrated and how they practice should always be considered in the allocation of school resources. Restrictive policies, such as prescriptive licensing restrictions, do not allow these professionals to serve in the diverse roles in which they are prepared. Unfortunately, many special education teachers in co-taught classes have reportedly been treated as aides by general education teachers, and those in specialized settings may be treated as dumping grounds for students when no one else wants to deal with them. By and by, special education teachers are some of the most talented and resourceful in the profession, and struggling students, regardless of their eligibility status, should have access to powerful resources and interventions to remediate their deficits quickly and without artificial barrier.

Opportunities

Being proactive is the best approach to any policy whether it be at the federal, state, or local levels. Contacting congressional representatives, building relationships with representatives and their staff, and staying abreast of proposed federal policy is ideal. There are even websites such as congress.gov that will track bills and provide subscribers with immediate updates if there are changes to a bill that is of interest. Each state government also has a similar tracking system that interested individuals can sign up for without cost.

Instead of being proactive and staying on top of legislation, school-based teams most often find themselves responding in a reactive manner, especially to federal policy. In such cases, states, districts, and schools must accommodate the new federal policy and build it into their existing budgets, programs, and policies. For example, consider the hurdle schools faced with the shift away from special education teachers being the content area teacher for general education students if they were not licensed in that content area.

Special education teachers are often some of the most dynamic and creative educators in a school. By nature, they understand special needs of students, can differentiate curriculum, have patience for behaviors that interfere with learning, and know special education law better than most teachers and administrators. The perception of special educators still needs work. Perhaps the social stigma of having a disability carries over to special education teachers helping those with disabilities. Regular classroom teachers may not give special education teachers the social status or respect of teaching mastery many deserve, and special education teachers are often perceived as little more than an instrument to remove lower performing students from general education classes. This type of mindset speaks to the general culture and climate of a school and cannot be generalized to all school campuses. With special education teachers being pushed into general curriculum classes more often, regular education must share the teaching duties and spotlight with special educators, who may be just as helpful to non-disabled students as students identified with disabilities.

Empower special educators by putting them in leadership positions to train other teachers. Create opportunities for them to work with students before they are identified with special needs; this is especially helpful at Tier 2 and Tier 3. Pay them extra duty hours to work directly with groups of students, regardless of eligibility, after school hours. Give them a voice and a seat at the table of the MTSS leadership team. Reimburse tuition for college credits as teachers seek to obtain licensures to teach all students, which could boost the profession. This boost supports services for students by finding creative ways for underachieving students to have access to more opportunities and different guided skills practice with highly skilled teachers.

4 Budgets

With budget shortages in districts across the United States, the addition of remediation courses is not only a budgetary issue, but a time constraint issue (Odden & Picus, 2014; Odden, 2012). Given the various demands placed on administrators and their budgets, priority decisions must be made. Typically, remedial and elective classes are the first to be eliminated from the master budget. For example, many districts have had to close down schools leaving those that remain overcrowded and lacking a broad spectrum of resources. High schools have had to eliminate many electives to add core classes with the overflow of student body. Electives are as valuable to student development as core academics; they allow students to explore their creativity and to find success when they are facing failure in their academics. It is common for high schools to use any opening in their master schedule, or to use any additional funding, to find ways to help credit deficient students retrieve credits in order to meet graduation requirements. Many schools have also reduced or eliminated their lower level courses outside of special education, such as lower level sciences and math courses.

Opportunities

Budgets are getting tighter for education dollars, and the allocation of dollars does not always make sense to all schools. As schools' processes are more decentralized, individual schools have greater opportunity to make allocations based on need. *Decentralized* is the transfer of power and decision making from central government to local government. Underfunding remedial supports and credit retrieval programs in high school threatens graduation rates, which has real-life consequences for students and hampers their access and opportunity for success in life. Advocacy for policies and budgets to fund mental health, social-emotional-behavioral programs, and academic services to increase graduation rates is paramount. Like an initial deposit in the bank, those investments earn interest and dividends by increasing student well-being and safety, civilized behavior and problem solving, and independent living skills (Aspen Institute: National Commission on Social, Emotional, and Academic Development, 2018).

5 Standards

Common Core State Standards, proficiency or exit exams and credit requirements for graduation makes it a struggle for teachers to spend their time teaching elementary level reading comprehension skills to their 11th grade students and making sure they are exposed to the curriculum to pass the district's exit exams (Wilson, 2014). Teaching to the test is a common practice schools engage in to improve school ratings and promotion or graduation rates. Teaching to the test, while not promoting utilization of reasoning and processing skills, robs students of important critical thinking skills in their education. While this practice is detrimental to individual students, it often improves the school standing as a whole with accolades for good test takers. The high school student with an elementary reading level will be less likely to learn how to read in school than learn how to take a high-stakes test.

Opportunities

Standards are largely dependent on the political pendulum from conservative to less conservative measures of success. Common Core curriculum-based measures should be a healthy part of assessment and achievement for students, but should not be considered the only measure of success at a school. Unfortunately, this single-measure mentality has been taking place nationwide. Overly emphasizing one indicator of success on a school campus, such as high-stakes test scores or a high school proficiency exam, can be misleading about the quality of the school and the overall knowledge of the student. Educators are blamed and held responsible for factors beyond their control. Students from high-poverty areas are set up for failure by standards that blaringly show them as constant failures unless they measure up to national average individually and as a cohort. In well-intended legislation to leave no child behind, a culture of success and failure based on school test scores has consumed local and national education politics. Compounding the problem is a competing corporate business model impacting educational policy whose marketing strategy is to demonize public schools in media and politics, inciting public fear of privatization (Cooper & Randall, 2008), maximize profit and benefits to private interests, and avoid the same accountability standards they helped create, which ultimately skews the public's perception and destabilizes trust in public schools. This mistrust creates a "need" for more competition in the market from for-profit schools and results in labeling public schools as underperforming in comparison, based on standards that are not evenly applied, nor outcomes measured by the same tools.

Standardized testing for federal and state accountability is a multi-billion-dollar industry whose influence in educational policy should not be underestimated. As a result, knowing that minority, second language students, and students living in poverty will not necessarily achieve on these measures, efforts have been made, with varying levels of success, to grade at-risk schools on the growth model instead of criterion referenced tests using cutoff scores for failure. The opportunity is for stakeholders to publicly advocate for MTSS as the ideal framework designed to elicit and capture growth within a growth model, and with quality control measures in place, accountability standards could be evenly applied. As it stands, demonstrating incremental growth only goes so far in public opinion, and policy is slow to catch up with best practices when it goes against public sentiment. Realistically, high-stakes tests are not going away and students need both test taking skills as well as content knowledge ability, in addition to critical thinking skills. Rather than teach to the test, which has resulted in narrow standards and policies, it is important to grow resilient life-long learners wherever their starting points are. The growth model is embedded in the function of MTSS, which can capture outcomes that inform data-based decision making and implementation feedback looping where high-stakes testing cannot.

6 Unions

Teachers' unions are under attack across the country, and the most influential unions are coming from large urban districts with hard-to-staff schools and less inviting work conditions (Fowles & Cowen, 2014). As teachers' working conditions, health insurance, and other monetary and non-monetary benefits are disintegrating, and private interests are aggressively pushing legislatively to take public monies from public school funding equations, teachers are starting to push back as their livelihoods and professional duties depend on it. Teachers are entitled to a modicum of working conditions, including scheduling that allows for "duty-free" preparation time and time to complete duties that do not involve direct teaching. Successful MTSS implementation requires flexibility in teaching standards but also includes creative scheduling and off-ratio teaching blocks to fit more relevant opportunities in the school day for students to get the remedial instruction they need, while not losing out on required credit-bearing classes. Educators must be compensated for additional work hours, and most will be amenable to schedules that benefit students without infringing on their rights to breaks in the day and duty-free professional time.

Block scheduling additional classes in high school has proved to be one of the most effective ways to provide more scheduling opportunities for students. Schedules that only allow for six traditional periods do not lend flexibility to scheduling for social-emotional and behavioral options or academic credit retrieval or remedial classes. Moving to an eight-period schedule, with shorter class times, or longer class times rotating A and B days with four classes each day, allows students credit retrieval opportunities, remedial classes, and social-emotional and behavioral opportunities in addition to mandated core requirements. Students who do not require remedial or credit retrieval classes can benefit from additional elective courses, enrichment classes, and career enhancement opportunities.

While teachers' unions may be perceived as an obstacle with regard to scheduling, they serve to represent the teachers in this area by ensuring that the teachers are receiving their certain number of minutes a week of duty-free preparation time. This representation has proven to benefit not only the teachers, but student achievement outcomes as well (Vachon & Ma, 2015). Scheduling priorities and demands are a constant struggle on a secondary campus; even with a modified block and extended class periods it does little to reduce the ever-increasing curricular demands.

Opportunities

Teachers' unions and administrative unions have a vested interest in meeting needs of students. The profession of teaching is under siege and entities outside of the education establishment are trying to seize public funding of education and privatize it to maximize profit. The only outcome measure that should be counted is student success. While "success" is a relative and widely debated term, it is still the primary outcome. Unions should focus on the well-being and health of teachers and administrators to nurture and care for children. In the coming technological age where computers can store information, our children need to learn how to process information to understand meaningful relationships, solve problems, and exchange solutions in the context of becoming contributing members of society. Unions need to protect teaching positions with safe working conditions, safe learning conditions, and advocating for funding curriculum supports that meet the needs of all learners and compensates educators fairly.

Teaching may be coming full circle back to the Socratic Method, or cooperative debate, in addition to utilizing technology advancements of our time.

7 Post-Secondary Expectations

Post-secondary expectations spill over to high school and, as a nation, the public education system is producing more students who are not equipped to handle college courses right out of high school (Castellano, Sundell, & Richardson, 2017). College boards and Clearing Houses make the road for those seeking post-secondary education even more difficult. For example, a student on the boys' basketball team who struggles academically, but is a phenomenal athlete, has little room in his schedule for remedial courses, as remedial courses do not meet requirements. To be eligible for an athletic scholarship, the student must follow the twenty-first century course of study and meet Clearing House requirements. Students who do not meet the requirements to receive a high school diploma are limited in their future (McArdle, Paskus, & Boker, 2013). Additionally, the government will not grant them financial aid and they can be turned away from the armed forces.

Opportunities

The transition from high school to college is designed to be a straight path for students but sometimes is a long and circuitous route. Students are finding more barriers than ever to college, and even those who get there often have to take remedial classes to catch up. Across the United States, up to 60 percent of college freshmen are assessed to be unprepared to complete college-level work (Grubb, Boner, Frankel, Parker, Patterson, Gabriner, Hope, Schiorring, Smith, Taylor, Walton, & Wilson, 2011). To prevent this gap at the college level, interventions must be provided during elementary and secondary school.

High school students who require academic interventions will find supports fewer and farther between to meet their needs and schedules. The number of high school student athletes who are going to actually make it onto the college teams, let alone pro leagues, is but a miniscule fraction of students putting their all into high school sports. Academics must be a higher priority than high school sports. Involvement in sports increases student engagement, but also takes away study time and time for late and early bird classes. *A realistic consequence for the high school athlete with academic challenges is for coaches not only to make allowances for intervention classes after school, but to require them as a condition of underperforming athletes staying on the team.* School administration must support this initiative and fully support the coach's decision to enforce remedial and intervention courses. In addition, online learning communities and supplemental programming options will require busy student athletes to structure their own learning time to practice remedial skills with the right tools approved and supported by their schools.

Post-secondary expectations must change as society evolves and artificial intelligence takes over basic tasks and jobs held by less skilled workers in the work force. College is becoming less relevant for more students, on one hand, and continues to be the optimal outcome for high school students, on the other. Education is the best equalizer in society, for people from humble means are able to grow up, learn up, and achieve equality in the work force. College is the ultimate goal for many, but does not fit the needs of all students, especially in light of the ever-increasing costs of college. Teaching all students as if they were all college bound is putting the U.S. educational system at a disadvantage. There must be more options for vocational tracks and careers beyond those that require a college degree. Even highly skilled technological jobs do not necessarily require college to give high school students work experience and work skills that lead to apprenticeships. Many students drawn to the technology field are not necessarily going to fit the traditional model of a college student. With the costs of post-secondary education soaring beyond the reach of even average middle-class students, high school promises of college dreams are not a promising reality for a great number of secondary students. High schools must be more relevant and lead to self-sufficiency and options to afford and attend college as an extension of high school. Loss of home economics courses, replaced by other credit requirements, has also negatively impacted a generation of students' independent living skills out of high school, and should be reconsidered as a required area of instruction for young adults. Learn-to-work opportunities and apprenticeships should be given to everyone, seeding the health of local economies. Students need employable skills most of all. State legislatures are a great place to advocate for dual-enrollment programs and apprenticeship programs, and policies will hopefully catch up with this reality at some point.

MTSS and Structure

MTSS in high school has all the same challenges as implementation in elementary and middle schools, but on a larger scale. Public high school campuses are usually bigger institutions and can have thousands of students, especially in large urban areas. The sheer numbers of students in a high school creates challenges to systematically monitor a large population. Administrative difficulties to enforce best practices with fewer allocated resources for struggling students, and more barriers to getting help, leads to widespread erroneous beliefs that MTSS does not work or is not sustainable in high school. Universal screenings may not seem important for many medium-risk and lower-risk campuses, where credit retrieval often takes precedence over teaching basic skills, even in cases of severe underachievement. Finally, administrators and change agents in high schools have many other school responsibilities and may not feel the need to prioritize regular meetings to address student issues systematically.

Despite all the barriers, major landmarks of MTSS should be implemented in high schools for best outcomes to positively impact the greatest number of learners. High schools can consider a student's middle school performance history to determine their risk factor and possible need for intervention. As students transfer from middle school to high school, their grade point average, grades, attendance, and ACT math scores can all be used to predict students' risk of school failure (McKee & Caldarella, 2016). Students who fall within the at-risk range can then be provided with targeted interventions their first year of high school to support and remediate deficits. Students' response to these interventions can be progress monitored and teams can determine next steps necessary moving forward in subsequent school years.

The best remedy to specific site-based challenges is the development and support of highly trained educators to actively solve problems in smart teams; educators with specialties and subspecialties operationalizing problems, targeting evidence-based supports depending on needs of students and availability of resources at the school and in the community, and monitoring outcomes. Supports can be streamlined or structured uniquely depending on the school, as reflected by team decisions by major stakeholders. As explained in previous chapters, the more students on a campus, the more organized and automated processes have to be for MTSS practices to be effective and sustainable. The more staff members actively engaged in the culture of team collaboration and data-based decision making, the more efficient all processes will be within MTSS.

Lower-risk schools will not have as many referrals for supports, so fewer members of the team are needed to review academic data with counselors. Even though lower-risk schools do not often have the intensity or frequency of issues higher-risk schools have, lower-risk schools still have at-risk and high-risk students to take into consideration and would also benefit from sticking to the MTSS recipe on a smaller scale. It is a mistake to view team selection, team development, and regular meetings as unnecessary in lower-risk and smaller schools because systematic team processes catch the students who may not make it through school otherwise. Once automated, reviewing student data as a team and making data-based decisions for students takes less planning and preparation because the master schedule allocates time and space for team functions, including intervention classes that ease documentation requirements for teachers and spreads efforts across team members.

MTSS and Academics

Academic MTSS looks somewhat different in high school than middle school. Usually, school teams are smaller and options more limited in high school, even though the opposite should be the case. One person may make the bulk of MTSS decisions pertaining to individual students for scheduling, or intensifying supports, such as a counselor or special education specialist. As long as Tier 2 and Tier 3 student data is reviewed regularly, albeit in smaller groups, and there are adequate supports to help struggling students, fewer team members can be effective. MTSS processes must also be automatized in schools with smaller teams because there are fewer eyes on student data. The more efficient the system, the more likely information can be adequately synthesized by fewer team members. Limiting MTSS team size to one member, the chair, especially in a large school, will be a daunting and unsustainable process for the educator unlucky enough to be pushing that giant boulder up the steep mountain. Most schools, and especially higher-risk high schools, would benefit from sticking more closely to the MTSS recipe to positively impact the greatest number of students: implementing universal benchmarking, using the case manager model, triangulating data for problem identification, growing a network of evidence-based interventions taught with fidelity by highly effective teachers, putting regularly scheduled meetings in the master schedule, conducting regular, highly structured team meetings with data-based decision making, and ensuring reliable, reciprocal communication within and without professional learning communities and with families.

Roles and responsibilities of staff may be shifted among MTSS team positions at the high school level. In addition to referrals through the use of screeners, counselors take on an even greater importance in making referrals, and reporting academic data along with credit monitoring. Though, in higher-needs schools with greater numbers of at-risk students, a team of grade level and/or subject level teachers and learning strategists can be assigned as case managers to support school counselors to ensure that low achieving students do not escape notice in the systematic review of student data.

One tool to screen and identify students early is the Early Warning System High School Tool (Therriault, O'Cummings, Heppen, Yerhot, & Scala, 2013) developed by the National High School Center at the American Institutes for Research, in collaboration with Matrix Knowledge Group. This tool was created to assist high school counselors and MTSS teams in identifying students with high indicators of dropping out of school including attendance issues, behavior problems, poor grades, past history of school failure, and other relevant target areas for school dropout prevention efforts to help teams to identify, prioritize, and intervene. High schools are fast-paced environments and school cultures do not necessarily support having yet another school team with scheduled duties and meetings. MTSS meetings must occur regularly, so cutting those meetings are not actually a short-cut and will undermine all the other processes in place.

Universal benchmarking and progress monitoring fluency in high school is a valid method to identify underachievers in high school despite a significantly lower rate of implementation of benchmarking than middle or elementary schools. The most reliable areas to measure in high school for fluency benchmarking and progress monitoring include those from AIMSweb: MAZE, Math Concepts and Application, Math Computation, and Writing Samples (Pearson, 2015), as well as vocabulary matching (Lembke, Allen, Cohen, Hubbuch, Landon, Bess, & Bruns, 2017). Identifying at-risk and high-risk students, evaluating your school's needs and building your team, investing in resources, building and training your team, and growing units to support students with skills deficits can all follow the same formula for MTSS as middle school.

High schools who are starting the process of MTSS, or recommitting to the idea, can start by focusing on 9th grade with universal benchmarking and systematic intervention delivery, with the intent of growing systematic supports and services into higher grades as a phased rollout. Ninth grade is perceived as a make or break year and success in 9th grade correlates highly with high school graduation rates (McCallumore & Sparapani, 2010). Educators on high school campuses need to make timely decisions for students to intensify instructional opportunities when required. High school administrators must ensure that targeted and intensive academic and behavioral supports are in place for students to support educators in implementation of effective instruction. Implementation of PBIS and SEB experiences in terms of the three tiers is important from kindergarten through 12th grade.

Growing team MTSS processes, starting with a focus on 9th graders, to identify, intervene, and monitor at-risk students may assist large campuses in not getting overwhelmed too quickly in ambitious intricacies of school-wide MTSS. Processes delineated in previous chapters can be used to guide team decisions and bolster team member functions. High school administrators and teams can decide where to start and how big to start depending on their current resources and commitment to growing additional resources to improve outcomes for all students. MTSS is conducive to a phased roll-out across years and grades if done with intentionality, follow through, and fidelity.

Exercise 8.1

- What are the barriers to implementation of MTSS at your high school campus?
- Which MTSS mileposts seem easiest to address?
- Which MTSS mileposts seem the most difficult?
- Order mileposts from least to most difficult:
    - Universal benchmarking

    - Using the case manager model

    - Triangulating data for problem identification

    - Growing a network of evidence-based interventions taught with fidelity by highly effective teachers

    - Putting regularly scheduled meetings in the master schedule

    - Conducting regular, highly structured team meetings

    - Using data-based decision making

    - Ensuring reliable, reciprocal communication within and without professional learning communities and with families.
- Which mileposts can be addressed most easily?
- What steps can be taken to get mileposts in motion?

Some references for effective high school practices and mindset include the books *Visible Learning* (Hattie, 2009), *Excellence Through Equity* (Blankstein & Noguera, 2016), *The Five Dysfunctions of a Team* (Lencioni, 2002), *Focus: Elevating the Essentials to Radically Improve Student Learning* (Schmoker, 2011), *Transforming Brockton High School* (Szachowicz, 2013), and the websites Research for Better Teaching: Empowering Sustainable School Improvement (2016) and the Education Trust (2018).

MTSS and Mental and Behavioral Health

Mental and behavioral health supports for high school students must be a priority. Building Behavioral and Mental Health MTSS should be required in all state level, district level, and school level policies and practices in middle schools and high schools. Having a highly qualified team of educators monitoring students and intervening can literally be the difference between life and death for students. High school students must have additional opportunities to learn appropriate behavior and coping skills through targeted instruction. Social-emotional and behavioral opportunities must exist in Tiers 1, 2, and 3 at the high school level. In high schools, the tiered model becomes a triage system for the most emotionally and behaviorally traumatized children. Universal social-emotional-behavioral screeners are well worth the investment, and some are free, to help identify students requiring immediate treatment which ultimately saves lives, especially those with internalizing problems. The students with externalizing problems usually come to the attention of administration through discipline procedures, unlike students with internalizing problems. Students with internalized problems, such as depression and anxiety, often go unidentified without the screenings, which can lead to associated risks including drug and alcohol use, unsafe sex, and suicidal ideation (Substance Abuse and Mental Health Services Administration, 2017; Taylor et al., 2017).

Regular communication between school staff members regarding student mental health needs improves outcomes for students by increasing access to community resources and timely provision of mental health supports in and out of schools. If high schools have the ability to improve school safety, student safety, and increase the capacity of the school system to support emotionally and behaviorally at-risk students, they must do so. High schools should screen for suicidal students and those engaging in high-risk behaviors, including expressing the intent to harm others, so that necessary services and supports for students can be prioritized and implemented. Regular mental-behavioral health and academic MTSS team meetings to address high priority students must take place so that actions can be set in motion to improve services to increase educational outcomes and, ultimately, health of students.

References

Asakura, K. (2016). Extraordinary acts to "show up": Conceptualizing resilience to LGBTQ youth. *Youth & Society*. Retrieved from https://doi.org/10.1177/0044118X16671430.

Blankstein, A. M., & Noguera, P. (2016). *Excellence through equity: Five principles of courageous leadership to guide achievement for every student.* Alexandria, VA: Association for Supervision and Curriculum Development.

Castellano, M., Sundell, K. E., & Richardson, G. B. (2017). Achievement outcomes among high school graduates in college and career readiness programs of study. *Peabody Journal of Education, 92*(2), 254–274.

Community Health Investment, Modernization, and Excellence Act of 2017, H.R. 3770, 115 Cong. (2017).

Cooper, B. S., & Randall, V. (2008). Fear and privatization. *Educational Policy, 22*(1), 204–227.

Every Student Succeeds Act of 2015, 20 U.S.C. (2015).

Eysink, T. H., de Jong, T., Berthold, K., Kolloffel, B., Opfermann, M., & Wouters, P. (2009). Learner performance in multimedia learning arrangements: An analysis across instructional approaches. *American Educational Research Journal, 46*(4), 1107–1149.

Fowles, J., & Cowen, J. (2014). In the union now: Understanding public sector union membership. *Administration & Society, 47*(5), 574–595.

Freeman, J., Simonsen, B., McCoach, D. B., Sugai, G., Lombardi, A., & Horner, R. (2016). Relationship between school-wide positive behavior interventions and supports and academic, attendance, and behavior outcomes in high schools. *Journal of Positive Behavior Interventions, 18*(1), 41–51.

Freeman, R., Miller, D., & Newcomer, L. (2015). Integration of academic and behavioral MTSS at the district level using implementation science. *Learning Disabilities: A Contemporary Journal, 13*(1), 59–72.

Grubb, W., Boner, E., Frankel, K., Parker, L., Patterson, D., Gabriner, R., Hope, L., Schiorring, E., Smith, B., Taylor, R., Walton, I., & Wilson, S. (2011). Understanding the "crisis" in basic skills: Framing the issues in community colleges. Basis skills instruction in California community colleges. *Policy Analysis for California Education*. Retrieved from https://edpolicy-inca.org/sites/default/files/2011_WP_GRUBB_NO1.pdf.

Hattie, J. (2009). *Visible learning: A synthesis of over 800 meta-analyses relating to achievement*. New York: Routledge.

Honig, M. I. (2004). The new middle management: Intermediary organizations in education policy implementation. *Educational Evaluation and Policy Analysis, 26*(1), 65–87.

Individuals with Disabilities Education Act, 20 U.S.C. § 1400 (2004).

Leko, M. M., Handy, T., & Roberts, C. A. (2017). Examining secondary special education teachers' literacy instructional practices. *Exceptionality, 25*(1), 26–39.

Lembke, E. S., Allen, A., Cohen, D., Hubbuch, C., Landon, D., Bess, J., & Bruns, H. (2017). Progress monitoring in social studies using vocabulary matching curriculum-based measurement. *Learning Disabilities Research & Practice, 32*(2), 112–120.

Lencioni, P. (2002). *The five dysfunctions of a team: A leadership fable*. San Francisco, CA: Jossey-Bass.

Loera, G., Rueda, R., & Oh, Y. J. (2015). Learning and motivational characteristics of urban Latino high school youth. *Urban Education*. Retrieved from https://doi.org/10.1177/0042085915602536.

Loughran, J. (2014). Professionally developing as a teacher educator. *Journal of Teacher Education, 65*(4), 271–283.

Masters, G. N. (2010). Teaching and learning school improvement framework. *Australian Council for Educational Research*. Retrieved from https://research.acer.edu.au/monitoring_learning/16.

McArdle, J. J., Paskus, T. S., & Boker, S. M. (2013). A multilevel multivariate analysis of academic performances in college based on NCAA student-athletes. *Multivariate Behavioral Research, 48*(1), 57–95.

McCallumore, K. M., & Sparapani, E. F. (2010). The importance of the ninth grade on high school graduation rates and student success. *Education Digest, 76*(2), 60–64.

McKee, M. T., & Caldarella, P. (2016). Middle school predictors of high school performance: A case study of dropout risk indicators. *Education, 136*(4), 515–529.

Morningstar, M. E., Allcock, H. C., White, J. M., Taub, D., Kurth, J. A., Gonsier-Gerdin, J., Ryndak, D. L, Sauer, J., & Jorgensen, C. M. (2016). Inclusive education national research advocacy agenda: A call to action. *Research and Practice for Persons with Severe Disabilities, 41*(3), 209–215.

Odden, A. R. (2012). *Improving student learning when budgets are tight*. Thousand Oaks, CA: Corwin.

Odden, A. R., & Picus, L. O. (2014). *School finance: A policy perspective* (5th ed.). New York: McGraw Hill.

Pearson (2015). *AIMSweb software guide version 2.5.10*. Retrieved from https://aimsweb2.pearson.com/aimsweb-frontoffice/helpsupport/help/aimsweb_software_guide2510.pdf.

Pennsylvania State Education Association (2016, March). The Every Student Succeeds Act: "Highly Qualified" teacher requirements. *Professional Learning Exchange*. Retrieved from www.psea.org/globalassets/for-members/psea-advisories/advisory-essa-highlyqualified teacherreqs.pdf.

Project AWARE (2017). *Family engagement: Building school-family partnerships for behavioral and mental health*. Columbus, OH: Project AWARE Ohio.

Research for Better Teaching: Empowering Sustainable School Improvement (2016). *Research for better teaching: Empowering sustainable school improvement*. Retrieved from www.rbteach.com.

Schmoker, M. (2011). *Focus: Elevating the essentials to radically improve student learning*. Alexandria, VA: Association for Supervision and Curriculum Development.

Substance Abuse and Mental Health Services Administration (2017). *Issue brief: Mental health and academic achievement*. Rockville, MD: Author.

Szachowicz, S. (2013). *Transforming Brockton High School: High standards, high expectations, no excuses*. Rexford, NY: International Center for Leadership in Education.

Taylor, R. D., Oberle, E., Durlak, J. A., & Weissberg, R. P. (2017). Promoting positive youth development through school-based social and emotional learning interventions: A meta-analysis of follow-up effects. *Child Development, 88*(4), 1–16.

The Aspen Institute: National Commission on Social, Emotional, and Academic Development (2018). *How learning happens: Supporting students' social, emotional, and academic development.* Washington, DC: Author.

The Education Trust (2018). *The education trust.* Retrieved from https://edtrust.org.

Therriault, S. B., O'Cummings, M., Heppen, J., Yerhot, L., & Scala, J. (2013). *High School Early Warning Intervention Monitoring System Implementation Guide: For use with the National High School Center's Early Warning System High School Tool.* Washington, DC: National High School Center at the American Institutes for Research.

Tyler, J. H. (2003). Economic benefits of the GED: Lessons from recent research. *Review of Educational Research, 73*(3), 369–403.

Tyler, J. H. (2004). Does G.E.D. improve earnings? Estimates from a sample of both successful and unsuccessful G.E.D. candidates. *ILR Review, 57*(4), 579–598.

Ujifusa, A. (2018, March 23). *President Trump signs spending bill that includes billions more for education.* Retrieved from http://blogs.edweek.org/edweek/campaign-k-12/2018/03/president_trump_signs_spending_bill_increases_education_money_billions.html.

Vachon, T. E., & Ma, J. K. (2015). Bargaining for success: Examining the relationship between teacher unions and student achievement. *Sociological Forum, 30*(2), 391–414.

Vaughn, S., & Fletcher, J. M. (2012). Response to intervention with secondary school students with reading difficulties. *Journal of Learning Disabilities, 45*(3), 244–256.

Watt, S. J., Watkins, J. R., & Abbitt, J. (2016). Teaching algebra to students with learning disabilities: Where have we come and where should we go? *Journal of Learning Disabilities, 49*(4), 437–474.

Weist, M. D., Garbacz, S. A., Lane, K. L., & Kincaid, D. (2017). *Aligning and integrating family engagement in positive behavioral interventions and supports (PBIS): Concepts and strategies for families and schools in key contexts.* Center for Positive Behavioral Interventions and Supports (funded by the Office of Special Education Programs, U.S. Department of Education. Eugene, OR: University of Oregon Press.

Williams, J. M., Landry, S. H., Anthony, J. L., Swank, P. R., & Crawford, A. D. (2012). An empirically-based statewide system for identifying quality pre-kindergarten programs. *Education Policy Analysis Archives, 20*(17), 1–36.

Wilson, H. W. (2014). *The reference shelf: Embracing new paradigms in education.* Amenia, NY: Grey House Publishing, Inc.

Chapter 9

Family Engagement

Key Terms

Gerrymander
Cultural Brokering
Ethnic Match
Schoolcentric
Communitycentric
Student Led Information Conferences

Chapter Concepts

In this chapter, readers will learn:

1. The roles of schools as safe harbors and service centers.
2. To be purposeful and inclusive in their definition of family engagement.
3. To use culture as an asset to negotiate healthy school and family connections.
4. How to value family input and participation instead of simply expecting it.
5. How to empower students to be leaders in their own learning.
6. Effective tools to promote family wellness and engagement.

Schools are community centers for social and cultural activities, as well as learning institutions. Family and community members are drawn to schools not only because that is where their children are, but where the future possibilities of their children are housed. Broadly speaking, public education in the United States is a vehicle to equalize inequities in society, and those with the highest levels of educational attainment often experience the greatest benefits such as longevity, earning power, and social status (Freiman, 2016; Walsemann, Gee, & Ro, 2013; Marina & Holmes, 2009). Public schools aim to provide daily shelter, sustenance and mind-expanding experiences for all children regardless of race, religion, social class, gender, or background. Schools are supposed to be neutral ground where children leave their circumstances behind, and enter a world of knowledge and cognition dedicated to improving their life skills and to prepare them to successfully function in, and contribute to, society. All students deserve and require a safe environment that teaches self-discipline and provides opportunities for growth regardless of income level, social status, or individual abilities and disabilities. Public schools should be the islands of stability in the stormy seas of public division, class wars, and poverty.

School and Student Realities

Children bring their families with them to school, whether other family members are physically present or not. Students come to school with a variety of experiences, values, and traumas that shape who they are, how they think, how they act and, ultimately, how they are going to interact with others on any given day. Students bring their family values and experiences to school without understanding that others have also brought their family values and experiences to school, which can lead to conflict within the school environment and without.

Some communities have gone to great lengths to minimize cultural and socioeconomic diversity to avoid the compromises that conflict creates. In the United States, many school districts have become, or remain, segregated because of racial districting that pushes out minority-based majorities into substandard school districts and segregated charter schools. Elite stakeholders are profiting from substandard charter schools with limited accountability (Hurst, 2017), and high-stakes testing has become a racially biased practice that disserves minority students (Au, 2015).

Lines are drawn on maps so that preferred students and communities are kept in, while non-preferred students and communities are kept out. Gerrymandered political regions have created haves and have-nots in the lottery of producing and supporting good schools and "exacerbates segregation" (Richards, 2014, p. 1119). *Gerrymandering* is when the geographic boundaries are manipulated to benefit one political party over another. Regardless of politics and quality of school, the neighborhood school is often considered the safest place for children to be, where children overcome their challenges and prepare for advancement in life.

Historically in the United States, children have worked with the civic belief that their industriousness served to prevent idleness and ending up in the poorhouse (Abbott, 1908). Such jobs entailed spinning yarn, carrying water, feeding chickens, and running errands. Immediately following the Civil War, freed slaves' children and child immigrants were employed as apprentices for training purposes and were basically re-enslaved by former slave masters or patrons until laws challenging this practice were introduced during the Reconstruction period (Schuman, 2017).

The Industrial Revolution brought machinery that increased the capacity and output working children could produce. From the time of the Industrial Revolution to the passing of the Fair Labor Standards Act in 1938, that regulated employment of children, the belief that children in the United States were expected to work continued. The mentality was that child labor kept children from being lazy and out of trouble, with the added bonus of substantial contributions to family income. These exploited child labor practices occurred across professions and several industrial sites including mills, mines, and factories (Schuman, 2017).

In addition to the Fair Labor Standards Act, another contributing factor to the decrease in child labor was the increase in mandatory schooling, or compulsory education (Tyack, 1974). Common schools in the United States were conceptualized with a variety of motives, chief among them was to instill honest civic beliefs and individual moral character within the newly formed Republics (Tyack, James, & Benavot, 1987). Students were to be taught moral character; however, over time, these values were overshadowed by gross inequities with respect to non-Whites and immigrants with prejudices that persist to the present. A democratic education was just not possible given the realities of social injustice. As one educator (as cited in Tyack, 1974) wrote about the conditions of education at the turn of the twentieth century: "As long as Negroes [sic] are the victims of lynching, police brutality, disfranchisement, residential covenant, higher rents, segregation, unsanitary living conditions, meager recreational opportunities, and other forms of discrimination, the social-civic aim of education is defeated" (p. 218). This painful history cannot be changed, but must be acknowledged, just as implicit biases must be acknowledged because they persist to this day. In our quest to devise one singular "best" system for educating our youth, we have created a system that ineffectively serves our poorest students *systematically* (Tyack, 1974). This deliberate and systematic exclusion of the unique characteristics of students and communities is damaging to individual children and society as a whole.

In addition to the ongoing evolution of a democratic education system, new changes are also taking place. With the rise of technology and artificial intelligence, some educators prognosticate that school buildings will become a thing of the past. Physical learning spaces are expected to be obsolete because students will be able to access technology and learning opportunities online or in ways not yet conceived. A compelling argument against this future for public schools lies in the fact that schools are already irreplaceable as a location for childcare, and are becoming more so in times of uncertainty for family cohesiveness and public assistance.

Many schools have already transformed into community health centers, community food and clothing banks, and community social hubs. Schools are slowly taking over more roles and responsibilities for children than ever before, including providing basic needs and surrogate parenting. When other social safety nets fail, schools are expected to support and nurture children, and by proxy their families, regardless of what needs they have. Public schools are being overtaken by the charter school movement as the fast-food chain model of education service delivery, which reduces the health and funding of public schools. Defenders of public education must advertise their advocacy efforts and highlight their value to the public so that elected officials will hear loud and clear from constituents not to take away funding from public schools, funding that is necessary to reduce inequitable opportunities for already oppressed communities. Educational policy must preserve free appropriate public education and put the same accountability standards on charter schools as on public schools.

Perhaps becoming safe harbors of society is not such a bad role for the school system. In times of alternative facts and civil discord, schools can safeguard civilization with social responsibility, emphasizing social reciprocity, community tolerance, and a sense of belonging for all community members. Schools are already the heart of many communities and are the glue of civilized society, bringing elements together for the good citizenship of children. Future generations will probably be competing for jobs with robots, so education must be humanistic. The best schools are run like families, with the efficiency of factories.

Exercise 9.1

- List challenges that families at your school are struggling with most.
- List the strengths that families at your school report enjoying and benefitting from.
- List the main reasons parents and families come to your school.
- Develop and integrate family engagement opportunities that incorporate the strengths of each list.

What is Family Engagement?

Family engagement encompasses much more than parent–teacher conferences. The use of "family" engagement versus "parental" engagement is intentional and aligns with the realities of families in communities. A majority of families are not comprised of biological parents at the helm, but of blended families with an infinite number of configurations. Children are being raised by relatives, neighbors, and extended family even when parents are in the picture. Families are under more pressure than ever before to meet their basic needs. These basic needs, compounded by economic factors, mental illnesses and addictions, and less understood family systems, all undermine students' success at school. The need for family engagement is not limited to at-risk neighborhoods and many of the same challenges in getting families to support their children's education permeate all socioeconomic backgrounds. Families with higher socioeconomic status often excel over their lower socioeconomic counterparts in relation to advocacy and engagement as they often have access to, and knowledge about, how to maneuver effectively. Comparatively, families from lower socioeconomic backgrounds often lack those same advocacy skills and maneuvering (Van Velsor & Orozco, 2007).

Systemic transformation and *cultural brokering* are needed to bridge socioeconomic and cultural barriers to family–school engagement (Ishimaru, Torres, Salvador, Lott, Cameron-Williams, & Tran, 2016). In doing so, culture can be used as an asset and can be used to positively influence and bridge family and school relationships. Differences in language, social class, and ethnicity all require consideration through the inclusive lens of the LIQUID Model. School providers must be proactive in addressing implicit bias educators may have about families' commitment to support their children in school, as well as to bridge the divide from dominant culture's expectations to inclusive practices. Effective school outreach provides opportunities to validate families and invite participation in a nonthreatening and welcoming manner to the minority cultures.

Ethnic match is one such barrier to school and family engagement. *Ethnic match* occurs when a student's teacher and family both identify with the same ethnic background. Latinos have a lower rate of family engagement than other minority groups; however, when there is an ethnic match between the family and the teacher, family engagement increases considerably (Mundt, Gregory, Melzi, & McWayne, 2015). Special considerations must be given to immigrant families with primary languages other than English as they may be intimidated by the bureaucracy of a school system due to communication barriers and fear of authority. Other families may fear the deportation of some, or all, of its family members depending on immigration status.

Teachers tend to hold *schoolcentric* views of family involvement (Lawson, 2003). However, instead of framing the narrative around how families can help schools to promote student education, the conversation should be *communitycentric*, in the sense that a broader community influences and promotes student success (Van Veslor & Orozco, 2007; Lawson, 2003). This communitycentric perspective shifts the predominant narrative and can be used to increase family engagement with schools. Reframing teacher attitudes and improving school climate to reflect a more inclusive view of *family* engagement must be part of this shift. Six communitycentric strategies to increase family involvement are: learn about the families of the children in the school; learn about the community where the students live; provide on-site services for caregivers; help caregivers address community concerns; offer in-service training for school personnel; and utilize family cultural capital (Van Veslor & Orozco, 2007).

Communication with families must transition from a "school knows best" perspective to valuing and inviting the contributions and knowledge of families. The traditional hierarchical model of educators telling families what to do is not effective and promotes distrust and distance between families and schools (Weist, Garbacz, Lane, & Kincaid, 2017). Emerging is a partnership model of family engagement, which is much more effective. This model invites families' feedback on topics such as when convenient times to meet are and what engagement opportunities families would like to see transpire; instead of schools telling them when the engagement will take place and what it will look like. Traditionally, activities happen during the school and work day when caregivers are working. These caregivers are then shamed for not attending during these restricted hours. Caregivers must work to meet the basic needs of their children and while they want to engage with educators, many cannot do it during school hours. Compensating teachers for meeting after school or on flexible hours is one way around this barrier. Other ways in which schools can foster a partnership paradigm of family engagement is by valuing family voice, their cultural strengths, and shifting the language used when describing the engagement of families from "including" families to "partnering" with families (Weist, Garbacz, Lane, & Kincaid, 2017).

Schools need to provide a welcoming and inclusive environment for students' families because there is a high correlation between family involvement and positive educational outcomes for students. The family system is arguably the true Tier 1 of instruction for a child. Bronfenbrenner (1979) placed the child at the center of his bioecological model of development to explain how interactions between the child and the environment help shape and influence how a child will grow. While the child is the microsystem, the family and school are the next immediate ring of influence at the mesosystem. According to this theoretical construct, individual and basic needs of a child must be addressed first and then further enhanced and supported by the school and family. In accordance with this model and integral to iterative evaluation cycles, obtaining student feedback that can be used as input for future planning is essential. See Exercise 9.2 for a sample Student Data Feedback Request Form. Such a form can be comprised of open-ended, Likert scale, or combined type questions. Regardless of the specific information gathered, obtaining student voice provides incredible insight toward the overall function, effectiveness, and perception of MTSS.

Exercise 9.2

Student Data Feedback Request Form

- Do you like school?
- If you do not like school, what don't you like about it?
- What are you good at?
- What is the most difficult subject area for you?
- Do you have a teacher or teachers you really like?
- How well do you handle stress?
- What would make things easier for you at school?

Basic needs are part of that Tier 1 foundation critical to a student's success, and a sense of belonging could be Maslow's (1943) most underrated and under-appreciated basic need. Providing avenues for supporting parents and family leaders, helping them to construct and use their voices, and encouraging them to participate in learning experiences and celebrations creates a culture of responsiveness. Positively engaging families in a friendly, culturally respectful, and nurturing manner increases good will and collaboration. Therefore, earning trust of families and finding pathways for them to participate in their children's education are paramount to understanding students' needs and helping them to overcome difficulties (Dotterer & Wehrspann, 2016).

Opportunities to Increase Engagement

Frameworks exist to build, enhance and sustain relationships with families to promote academic and behavioral health between home and educational settings. Motivating family leaders to support academic and behavioral learning at home, as well as participate in school-based activities, indisputably increases student success at school. The intent of engagement and sustainability extends to the national level, and the U.S. Department of Education has recently appointed its first Family Ambassador. This Family Ambassador serves to promote the voice of families to liaise between families and stakeholders, including the U.S. Department of Education. To support this engagement and capacity, the U.S. Department of Education (2018) offers a framework for schools, families, and communities to follow. The Centers for Disease Control and Prevention (2012) also provides a framework that can be used to increase family engagement in school health: Parent Engagement Strategies for Involving Parents in School Health. This framework serves to connect caregivers with schools to support student learning and health, it engages caregivers in opportunities to be involved with school and student activities, and it sustains engagement by overcoming barriers to building and maintaining relationships with families.

At the school level, frameworks also exist to support students, families, and teachers. Teachers are understandably natural liaisons between home and school, but as their responsibilities grow along with their class sizes, they are less able to shoulder the burden of all duties, and they may not have the tools to effectively engage families, let alone sustain relationships individually. Inclusive MTSS practices automate some systems and processes to promote positive interactions between school staff and families while providing a blueprint of a welcoming school environment for all.

Barriers to effective family–school engagement practices include parent and family factors, child factors, family–teacher interaction factors, and societal factors (Hornby & Lafaele, 2011). Using an additive view of family engagement, caregivers become involved due to their perceptions and constructs surrounding their role in educating their child, their sense of efficacy for helping their child, and the general engagement opportunities that exist at their child's school (Hoover-Dempsey & Sandler, 1997). Parents who feel that their involvement is as much valued as required at school, and that family–school partnering increases the well-being of their children, are more likely to be involved at school. Otherwise, family leaders will not prioritize school involvement as an effective use of family time or perceive school involvement as a resource to healthy child and family development. Even with a multitude of opportunities to engage, without improved parental perceptions of their role and increased efficacy for their level of support, family engagement will continue to suffer (Hoover-Dempsey & Sandler, 1997).

Child factors that may influence family involvement at school include individual differences, abilities and disabilities, and behavior problems (Hornby & Lafaele, 2011). For example, children who demonstrate behavioral difficulties at school often demonstrate the same at home, and parents may feel defensive, embarrassed, and unprepared to share their feelings with school professionals or seek input. On the other hand, parents may be very vocal about difficulties and circumstances surrounding variables that contribute to or maintain maladaptive child behaviors but are not willing, or able, to change their own behavior to reinforce new variables in the environment that support change. Individual student strengths and challenges also pose unique circumstances for educators and families. Every child's needs are different, as are every family's ability to cope, and depending on the resources available in each school and district, what a school or teacher is able to provide may vary greatly.

Family–teacher factors may be influenced by perceived accessibility to one another. If families do not feel like they can communicate effectively with teachers or solicit advice without harsh judgment, they are less likely to request feedback. Alternatively, if teachers cannot reach families or do not feel supported by them with homework or consequences for misbehavior, teachers are less likely to make efforts to invite parental or caregiver input. Whatever the barriers may be, schools and educators need to do a better job partnering with parents and families in the school community. Oftentimes, it is as simple as *valuing* the input and participation of families, instead of expecting it.

The importance of positive relationships between school staff and families is indisputable and should focus upon several key objectives. School campuses should focus on the primary family engagement tools of: increasing communication between home and school; building positive home–school relationships; building reciprocal structures for support; increasing trust between community and school; encouraging parents to motivate children; and valuing family culture and participation (Dotterer & Wehrspann, 2016; Cattanach, 2013; Neuman, 2013). Above all these goals is the overall ambition of providing caregivers with the tools to guide, support, and encourage their children. Not only do families need to have regular opportunities to participate and be involved in their children's school lives, they also need to feel that their contributions are of value. Parent or caregiver sessions focusing on family wellness activities and providing a forum for addressing community concerns are avenues to build working relationships with families. Multiple opportunities for families to obtain basic services (e.g., health services, clothing and food giveaways), attend open houses, enjoy celebrations, and participate in parent-teacher organization meetings attract families to get involved.

Methods to involve families come in all flavors and styles. Providing a comfortable experience for families is strongly recommended. Higher-risk schools often have trouble attracting families to academic nights and events due to caregiver work schedules, child-care for younger siblings, and difficulty organizing family functions with multiple family members. In all communities, food, giveaways, and entertainment are a winning combination to bring families in to events at school. Breaking bread, sharing a meal or snack, creates goodwill and brings in families with limited means. In general, food should be available at all family events, and accessibility to other community resources can be offered. Home visits by administrators, positive phone calls from teachers, and follow-up from caring specialists in a helping capacity (e.g., school social workers, counselors, psychologists) goes a long way to earn trust and cooperation from parents (Tunison, 2013).

There are systematic functions in place in most schools that automatically invite families into the school to participate in activities and celebrations of students. Open houses, parent–teacher conferences, band performances, and sports events are some of the opportunities in place at most schools for family involvement. Open house usually occurs in the first week or two of a school year where administrators and teachers make positive overtures for relationships with family leaders, showcase the upcoming curriculum, explain classroom and school expectations, and promote school pride.

Musical and theater performances, school club events, and sports practice and games compel families to campus like no other draw because the students are vested in performing and families are motivated to watch their children perform. Learning new skills, practicing new skills, achieving mastery of skills, and successfully applying learned skills is never better celebrated than at school performances and sporting events. If all learning activities could be similarly supported and celebrated by families and the school community, students might be much more excited and motivated to succeed academically. Educators can aim to capture the excitement and inclusionary spirit of school performances in other opportunities for families to support students.

Exercise 9.3

- What opportunities do parents and families currently have on your campus to be involved and excited about their students' learning and performance?
- What, in particular, about these events do families and students most enjoy?
- Which above elements can your school leadership incorporate into academic functions and other family participation opportunities?
- What are ideas your school leadership can initiate to increase family outreach (e.g., phone calls, post cards, home visits) amongst educators and other staff members?

Ideas to expand inclusive opportunities for family engagement and parent participation on campus should be explored at least annually in the context of MTSS. Some choices are simply administrative decisions, like Student Led Informational Conferences, but other ideas are best addressed using a team approach to improve parent participation, including creation of a parent or family center at school, developing trainings to give hands-on modeling and guided practice in effective family leadership, and informal meet-and-greets with administrators to give caregivers a voice and an opportunity to air difficulties outside of discipline procedures.

Student Led Informational Conferences

Student Led Informational Conferences (SLIC) are a powerful evidence-based method to encourage students to take responsibility for their own learning (Conderman, Ikan, & Hatcher, 2000; Hackman, 1996). Conferences require self-reflection, identification of strengths and needs, goal setting, and self-monitoring, as well as organizational practice and communication skills. Such meetings are also powerful opportunities for parents to have structured academic-based conversations with their children a few times a year, in addition to report cards and other traditional methods of communication between caregivers and the school. SLIC helps students be more accountable for their efforts and output, and starts a conversation at home about empowering students to achieve academic goals.

The school principal must be committed to SLIC by the beginning of a school year, as the conference dates are memorialized in the master calendar, so that teachers have the time and training to prepare their students. Student led meetings are not part of the traditional parent–teacher conference cycle, which has a separate date and place. SLIC meetings occur twice a year, once in the first semester and again in the second semester, paired with main events like a school performance or a science fair to increase attendance. Teachers train their students in the process as they collect artifacts for their SLIC portfolios, and students are required to reflect on their performance along the way.

The first SLIC portfolio presentation, held no earlier than end of first quarter but no later than end of second quarter, includes: baseline information (selected work samples from across subject levels, tests and test scores, benchmarking scores or instructional level fluency levels, or any other relevant assessment data); goals selected by the student; anticipated steps required to achieve their goals; and personal reflections about effort and time management. Students are guided by teachers in practicing presentation skills to explain their SLIC portfolios to their parents or guardians. The student and their parents or guardians meet at a scheduled time with a lead teacher observing and discussing current levels of academic functioning, as showcased by their assignments and assessments. Students explain their strengths and weaknesses to their parents and the goals they set for themselves, all under the tutelage of one of their teachers. Teachers may be able to monitor several meetings occurring simultaneously, so as to be a resource to assist in conversations on the periphery, but not necessarily participate directly. The second SLIC portfolio presentation, held during the fourth quarter, includes: reviewing work samples across academic domains; formative and summative assessments; progress monitoring graphs, if any, determining whether they met their goals; and personal reflections. SLICs have high validity for increasing student motivation and achievement (Conderman et al., 2000; Hackman, 1996). Combining "SLIC Nights" with student musical performances and cultural foods and festivities improves community outreach, and ultimately increases participation, in a highly effective educational practice.

SLICs take administrative planning, direct instruction in preparations, and reminders for each milestone. Teachers must have calendars to follow in terms of daily and weekly preparation for upcoming SLIC meetings. Having clearly delineated procedures with a timeline will help make SLIC events most effective. Information required includes: how SLIC works; established worksheets students can use to record information; parent communication forms regarding scheduling; and checklists to improve organization and execution of steps and responsibilities will make SLIC nights the most productive.

Building positive relationships with the local business community is essential, and including them in school functions and celebrations will increase their generosity toward school families as they provide economic and social supports. Cultural celebrations can help cultivate relationships with local businesses investing in community health through local schools. In turn, businesses appreciate being publicly honored for community service, and students and families can patronize businesses which provide services and supports for them. Win-win for all.

Exercise 9.4

- What cultural celebrations does your school currently practice?
- Are there ways to grow culturally inclusive school celebrations at your school? If so, how?
- Which businesses in the community might support school celebrations and relationships that could be cultivated?

Family Center and Wellness Opportunities

Family wellness and parenting classes are popular opportunities for families to positively engage with school staff and share positive interactions with other parents. An actual location on school campus where families can be present in a structured manner gives them a sense of value and belonging to the school community. Resources to support basic needs, incorporating Community in Schools (where available), monthly family wellness classes, opportunities for enrichment and communication, and collaboration with community partners can be offered. For safety reasons, at most schools it is not feasible or allowed to have families walking around campus unsupervised by a staff member. The Family Center can be staffed by any number or combination of individuals including community liaisons, community family services workers, school social workers or other safe schools professional, school psychologist, school counselor, health teacher or coach, support staff or any educator fluent in the dominant language of the families, such as Spanish. Community and school partnerships provide students and their families with basic needs' support including food, clothing, and health care.

A family center provides a comfortable location for parent trainings and parent outreach functions including welcoming community partnerships with organizations, such as Boys Town, and providing regular community education and enrichment. Some schools offer a business center for parents who do not have access to computers, fax and copy machines, and supplies at home. A welcoming environment could include a children's corner with books, toys, and activities for young children to enjoy while their caregiver is involved in family center activities. Comforts may also include couches, tables, chairs, water dispenser, coffee, snacks, and a refrigerator. Community resource information can be clearly posted and available for parents to take copies.

Caregivers and families should also have universal access to research-based curriculum in learning and practicing healthy parenting and family relationship practices. Monthly family connection meetings can be utilized to educate family leaders in more effective proactive positive parenting and less punitive and punishing practices. One particularly effective model can be taught in English, Spanish, and presented in English and Spanish concurrently. Survival Skills for Healthy Families (Creighton, Doub, & Scott, 1999), now in its fifth edition, "teaches, encourages and supports families, and those who work with them, to promote healthy communities. Practical skills are taught based on proven principles that strengthen, support and empower families" (p. 1). While Survival Skills for Healthy Families has proven effective, it is just one of many programs that are available for school teams to consider.

Goals of family connection meetings include increasing partnerships between families and schools, to support caregivers with engagement in student academic life, to provide families access to enrichment opportunities to improve family health, and to bridge the gap between parents and community resources. Other goals may include providing English classes for parents or caregivers who are not native English speakers and would like to learn the language, inviting community guest speakers, offering business or budgeting classes, offering small group parenting classes, or hosting social opportunities, such as family dances.

Box 9.1

Connection to Practice

Practicing Survival Skills for Healthy Families (Creighton, Doub, & Scott, 1999, p. 1), supported by practicing family wellness curriculum, includes the following goals:

- To improve student behavior at home and at school
- To increase communication between home and school
- To build trust between community and school
- To validate cultural values and caregiver contributions
- To build on home-school relationships
- To gives parents tools to guide, support, and encourage their children
- To help parents make rules and learn how to stay in charge in relation to school and home responsibilities
- To give parents alternatives to physical discipline
- To give hands on modeling and guided practice in effective parenting
- To encourage parents to motivate children to improve efforts at school with reinforcement at home
- To give parents a voice to air difficulties outside of discipline procedures
- To role play, coach, and group activities to show family members how to be unified, promote learning from each other, and expand the support network for families
- To use ethnic matching to engage in culturally responsive practices and to fit the needs of the community in their native language and ethnicity
- To provide a road map to health for families

Quality family wellness or parenting programs, such as Survival Skills for Healthy Families (Creighton et al., 1999) or Strengthening Multi-Ethnic Families and Communities (Steele, Marigna, Tello, & Johnson, 1999), are designed to prevent child abuse, the mistreatment of children, and longer-term maladaptive generational family issues that stem from behavioral patterns passed along from parents to their children and to their children's children. Teaching family wellness and engaging in parent level counseling interventions must be taught under a framework that includes both values and concepts (Prilleltensky & Nelson, 2000) and can be structured and allocated in the same way as all resources in MTSS.

Universal instruction is designed to provide opportunities for the entire school–parent community to learn communication and discipline practices consistent with effective parenting, highlighting family values and rehearsal of more functional parent–child interactions. Selective, targeted instruction and guided practice opportunities in smaller groups could be available for families with greater dysfunction and child behavior problems. The highest tier of support would likely align with court ordered interventions and out-of-home placement for child safety while children get individualized counseling and parents get rehabilitation services. Review of data on effective parenting (McKinney, Morse, & Pastuszak, 2014) has found that the benefits included improved parental empowerment and competency, increased positive parenting practices, increased social connection, improved child behavior, improved parent–child interactions, improved parental mental health and well-being, and decreased use of corporal punishment and risk of child abuse. Using parents as mentors, making cultural adaptations and actively engaging parents was also recommended.

Box 9.2

Voice from the Field

In my school, parent connection meetings are held monthly and presented by the school psychologist and bilingual health teacher. Survival Skills for Healthy Families (Creighton, Doub, & Scott, 1999) is relevant for families of students of all ages (from pre-school through high school), though our program discussions are geared toward middle school age issues. Materials are provided in both English and Spanish, and all activities and discussions are also presented in both English and Spanish. Parents and caregivers are given multiple opportunities to reflect and discuss their personal parenting struggles with other parents, ultimately getting answers to their questions in the context of age-appropriate and developmentally relevant feedback from instructors. Family wellness is a well-established family education and family enrichment model for teaching skills, enhancing healthy family interactions, and connecting family members to each other and their community.

In addition, parents are offered opportunities to socialize with our school principal, other parents and selected staff members each semester at our Principal's Potluck. Our principal sponsors a luncheon for parents, and we encourage parents to bring a dish to share but it is not required to attend. The principal fosters discussions in a relaxed setting with parents providing a comfortable format to hear about challenges in the community from parents' perspectives. The Principal's Potluck allows parents a low-pressure opportunity to interact by breaking bread with the school principal at a family meal.

A common logistical challenge for any family wellness program is getting caregivers to attend meetings. Some solutions to work around this issue include scheduling meetings in the evening to accommodate working parents, scheduling later in the morning to allow caregivers to take younger siblings to school first, and videoing sessions that can be live-streamed by caregivers or available for online viewing. Other outreach efforts include advanced notifications of upcoming meetings, personalized calls to families in their native language to encourage attendance the week of the meeting, parking lot campaigns to give families meeting information while they drop off and pick up their children, providing delicious breakfasts and snacks at all family connection meetings, offering gift card drawings at the end of meetings, combining food giveaway opportunities on same day as meetings, and allowing opportunities for parents or caregivers to discuss personal problems individually with instructors after meetings.

Depending on the demographics, industry, and social factors of a community, some caregivers may be more apt to attend during the day or the evening. At one school, it was more difficult to get parents to attend in the evening than during the school day, but at other schools communities may find that evening and weekend meetings work best. Ideally, older students are able to attend skills sessions with their families as well because they benefit from learning strategies to develop individually and how to get along better with others, including better communication with parents and how to ask for and respect boundaries. Taking students out of class to attend meetings with their families is always a challenge because students might miss important class content. Evening meetings allow children to attend meetings with their families without interruption to class. Student schedules, teacher lesson plans, and student behavior all impact whether students are able to attend sessions held during the school day.

Lastly, a major challenge is freeing up personnel from other duties to engage with families before and after school. Meetings that occur during school hours require planning to cover the teacher's classes during sessions, scheduling other important meetings around Family Connection meetings, and effectively communicating with staff and students about the importance of family engagement. Aligning with the culture of compensating staff for the extra work that they do, the school principal can also provide extra-duty pay to cover educators' prep buy-out and planning times. This is a great incentive for staff to be involved above and beyond school duties. By prioritizing the teaching of positive parenting practices by highly qualified, and personally invested, site-based educators sends a clear message to the community about the importance of school–family engagement and relationship building, which increases the probability of sustainability of reciprocal support. Schools can also outsource their family wellness trainings to have parenting skills taught on campus by persons from outside agencies. However, parenting services presented by providers outside of school staff may turn into missed opportunities, and could potentially miss the point of building and sustaining school–family relationships, which cannot be outsourced. If the outside organization is framed as an opportunity to build school–community–family partnerships, this can be a positive experience for all parties involved.

Box 9.3

Connection to Practice

Who Is Involved In The Planning, Implementation, and Evaluation of the Practice?

It is optimal if the teacher, counselor, social worker, school psychologist, or administrator planning to implement a family wellness curriculum is adequately trained in the parenting practices they are teaching, if not holding advanced certification. Like effective teaching, training parents and families in best practices requires a highly qualified instructor. At one school, the school psychologist was also a certified family wellness instructor and led family engagement sessions. Planning and implementation of Survival Skills for Healthy Families was led by the school psychologist and supported by a co-presenter, the bilingual health teacher. The co-presenter translates English to Spanish and Spanish back to English, as well as engages in role plays, facilitates discussions, and brings her own wealth of knowledge and experience to the training. Supporting school staff members involved in trainings, and events included involvement of the safe schools professional, Community in Schools staff member, learning strategist, Title I specialist, school counselors, school nurse and first aid safety assistant, office manager and secretaries, and school dean. The school principal also attended meetings and supervised all functions. Parents were given surveys at the end of each session to evaluate topics and presenters.

How Is This Practice Funded?

Family center and family connection meetings, community and school partnerships, and Survival Skills for Healthy Families trainings are funded by Title I, state dedicated funding streams, and Strategic or Flexible Spending budget.

How Does the Practice Link to Student Outcomes?

- To improve student behavior at home and at school
- To increase communication between home and school
- To build trust between community and school
- To build on home–school relationships
- To give parents tools to guide, support, and encourage their children
- To increase student and staff pride through music and culture

How Is This Practice Evaluated? What Has Been Learned From This Evaluation?

The family center connection meetings, presenting Survival Skills for Healthy Families, are evaluated by parents after every session. In one school, these meetings have occurred monthly for the past four school years and parent feedback has been 100 percent positive. Parent responses on Title I evaluation forms are reviewed after every session. In addition, the school principal, her supervisor, and other school district administrators have also attended meetings and given positive feedback. The school has learned that its family wellness trainings have been very worthwhile. Parents love the practical advice and family problem solving model. Administrators and teachers love the high energy of meetings and relevant discussions with parents in a culturally sensitive and safe environment.

What Advice Would You Offer to Someone Wanting to Implement the Practice?

All schools would benefit from hosting a parent–family center and parent connection meetings using Survival Skills for Healthy Families curriculum or other evidence-based curriculum. Investing in a comfortable and welcoming place for parents on a school campus says a lot about a school's culture. Engaging with parents in a friendly, nurturing manner increases good will, a sense of pride, and collaboration with families. It also demonstrates the value schools and teachers believe that caregivers bring to the table. This shift toward a communitycentric, versus schoolcentric, dynamic is essential to achieve positive family engagement. Parents want to do better, and presenting family leadership skills in a fun way increases the chance that caregivers will try strategies at home.

Listening to parents talk about their needs allows school personnel to address small problems before they become big problems. Organization and preplanning are key to any new program in terms of who does what, when and how. The outstanding professionalism of staff members working together collaboratively to proactively engage with parents increases opportunities for parents to feel con-nected to our school and staff members. Parents are educators' best allies in fos-tering academic and emotional growth in students. Literally teaming up with parents gives educators the best odds of meeting the needs of all our students.

References

Abbott, E. (1908). A study of the early history of child labor in America. *American Journal of Sociology, 14*(1), 15–37.

Au, W. (2015). Meritocracy 2.0: High-stakes, standardized testing as a racial project of neolib-eral multiculturalism. *Educational Policy, 30*(1), 39–62.

Bronfenbrenner, U. (1979). *Ecology of human development: Experiments by nature and design.* Cam-bridge, MA: Harvard University Press.

Cattanach, J. (2013, March). Support parents to improve student learning. *Phi Delta Kappan,* 19–25.

Centers for Disease Control and Prevention (2102). *Parent engagement: Strategies for involving parents in school health.* Retrieved from www.cdc.gov/healthyyouth/protective/pdf/parent_engagement_strategies.pdf.

Conderman, G., Ikan, P. A., & Hatcher, R. E. (2000). Student-led conferences in inclusive set-tings. *Intervention in School and Clinic, 36*(1), 22–26.

Creighton, F. P., Doub, G. T., & Scott, V. M. (1999). *Survival skills for healthy families* (2nd ed.). Holly Springs, NC: Family Wellness Associates.

Dotterer, A. M., & Wehrspann, E. (2016). Parent involvement and academic outcomes among urban adolescents: examining the role of school engagement. *Educational Psychology, 36*(4), 812–830.

Freiman, C. (2016). Poverty, partiality, and the purchase of expensive education. *Politics, Philo-sophy & Economics, 16*(1), 25–46.

Hackman, D. G. (1996). Student-led conferences at the middle level: promoting student responsibility. *NASSP Bulletin, 80*(578), 31–36.

Hoover-Dempsey, K. V., & Sandler, H. M. (1997). Why do parents become involved in their children's education? *Review of Educational Research, 67*(1), 3–42.

Hornby, G., & Lafaele, R. (2011). Barriers to parent involvement in education: An explanatory model. *Educational Review, 63*(1), 37–52.

Hurst, D. (2017). The end of public schools? The corporate reform agenda to privatize educa-tion. *Policy Futures in Education, 15*(3), 389–399.

Ishimaru, A. M., Torres, K. E., Salvador, J. E., Lott, J., Cameron-Williams, D. M., & Tran, C. (2016). Reinforcing deficit, journeying toward equity: Cultural brokering in family engage-ment initiatives. *American Education Research Journal, 53*(4), 850–882.

Lawson, M. A. (2003). School-family relations in context: Parent and teacher perceptions of parent involvement. *Urban Education, 38*(1), 77–133.

Marina, B. L., & Holmes, N. D. (2009). Education is the great equalizer: Or is it? *About Campus, 14*(3), 29–32.

Maslow, A. (1943). A theory of human motivation. *Psychological Review, 50,* 370–396.

McKinney, C., Morse, M., & Pastuszak, J. (2014). Effective and ineffective parenting: Associ-ations with psychological adjustment in emerging adults. *Journal of Family Issues, 37*(9), 1203–1225.

Mundt, K., Gregory, A., Melzi, G., & McWayne, C. M. (2015). The influence of ethnic match on Latino school-based family engagement. *Hispanic Journal of Behavioral Sciences, 37*(2), 170–185.

Neuman, S. B. (2013, May). The American dream: Slipping away. *Educational Leadership*, 18–22.

Prilleltensky, I., & Nelson, G. (2000). Promoting child and family wellness: Priorities for psychological and social interactions. *Journal of Community & Applied Social Psychology, 10*, 85–105.

Richards, M. P. (2014). The gerrymandering of school attendance zones and the segregation of public schools: A geospatial analysis. *American Educational Research Journal, 51*(6), 1119–1157.

Schuman, M. (2017). History of child labor in the United States – Part 1: Little children working. *Monthly Labor Review*. Retrieved from www.bls.gov/opub/mlr/2017/article/history-of-child-labor-in-the-united-states-part-1.htm.

Steele, M. L., Maringa, M. K., Tello, J., & Johnson, R. F. (1999). *Strengthening multi-ethnic families and communities: A violence prevention parent training program* [Facilitator manual, parent manual and materials, workshop manual]. Los Angeles, CA: Consulting and Clinical Services.

Tunison, S. (2013). The Wicehtowak Partnership: Improving student learning by formalizing the family-community-school partnership. *American Journal of Education, 119*(4), 565–590.

Tyack, D. B. (1974). *The one best system: A history of American urban education.* Cambridge, MA: Harvard University Press.

Tyack, D. B., James, T., & Benavot, A. (1987). *Law and the shaping of public education, 1785–1954.* Madison, WI: University of Wisconsin Press.

U.S. Department of Education (2018). *Family and community engagement.* Retrieved from www.ed.gov/parent-and-family-engagement.

Van Veslor, P., & Orozco, G. L. (2007). Involving low-income parents in the schools: Communitycentric strategies for school counselors. *Professional School Counseling, 11*(1), 17–24.

Walsemann, K. M., Gee, G. C., & Ro, A. (2013). Educational attainment in the context of social inequity: New directions for research on education and health. *American Behavioral Scientist, 57*(8), 1082–1104.

Weist, M. D., Garbacz, S. A., Lane, K. L., & Kincaid, D. (2017). *Aligning and integrating family engagement in positive behavioral interventions and supports (PBIS): Concepts and strategies for families and schools in key contexts.* Center for Positive Behavioral Interventions and Supports (funded by the Office of Special Education Programs, U.S. Department of Education. Eugene, OR: University of Oregon Press.

Chapter 10

Behavioral and Mental Health MTSS

Key Terms

Trauma-Informed Care
Behavioral and Mental Health MTSS
Social-Emotional and Behavioral (SEB)
Contagion Effect
Change Agents

Chapter Concepts

In this chapter, readers will learn:

1. The importance of providing comprehensive SEB programming.
2. The underlying role adverse childhood experiences have on all aspects of a child's life and the importance of trauma-informed care.
3. How a Behavioral and Mental Health MTSS team functions and what roles the key members have.
4. What SEB intervention looks like at each tier.
5. When to screen students and how to monitor their response to SEB interventions.
6. Red flags for students on path to attack.
7. LIQUID Model in Behavioral and Mental Health MTSS.
8. Introduction to Healthy Minds, Safe Schools: An integrated SEB MTSS Mental Health Model for schools in action.

Behavioral and mental health services are increasingly becoming a necessary function of school systems. Schools are the defacto mental health hospitals for children just as prisons are the defacto mental health hospitals for adults. School shootings, school violence, student killings, extreme bullying, student suicide, and harsh discipline procedures against minority students have been blasted across the social consciousness in an alarmingly increasing number of incidences (Mazer, Thompson, Cherry, Russell, Payne, Kirby, & Pfohl, 2015). Educators help to keep students safe every day despite the challenges of managing hundreds to thousands of students with individual personalities and problems on one school campus. Some students are more challenging to manage than others, and as is often the case, the small percentage of students with the most severe emotional and behavioral problems can cause the most mayhem in an educational setting.

Consequences for social-emotional and behavioral issues can be very punitive and applied inequitably in schools, especially for, but not limited to, at-risk minority youth. Such students are often viewed through a school's discipline lens to control crime; these at-risk students face greater consequences of exclusion and harsher punishment than their less at-risk peers (Hirschfield, 2008). Three factors appear to contribute to the bureaucratic default of the discipline lens to crime control in higher-risk schools: "a troubled domestic economy, the mass unemployment and incarceration of disadvantaged minorities, and resulting fiscal crises in urban education" (Hirschfield, 2008, p. 79). Severe punishment of children from communities experiencing economic disadvantages, negative cultural bias, and a high risk of incarceration further exacerbates the poverty cycle and school to prison pipeline. The need for inclusive proactive practices in all schools and communities has never been more evident.

Students are faced with numerous adverse childhood experiences (ACEs) and traumas that permeate all aspects of their lives throughout development. Examples of ACEs include physical abuse and neglect, sexual abuse, emotional abuse and neglect, parental violence, substance abuse in the home, mental illness in the home, caregiver divorce, and caregiver incarceration (Substance Abuse and Mental Health Services Administration (SAMHSA), 2017a). Students tend to experience ACEs in clusters, with more than 50 percent of children experiencing at least one ACE, nearly 40 percent experiencing two or more ACEs, and 12.5 percent experiencing four or more ACEs (Felitti, Anda, Nordenberg, Williamson, Spitz, Edward, Koss, & Marks, 1998). Research suggests that it is not the severity of any one ACE that a child experiences, it is the *number* of ACEs a child experiences that has the greatest impact on their functioning (SAMHSA, 2017a, 2017b). Knowledge of students and relationship building between school staff and students and their families is essential to understanding and addressing the underlying basic needs of students.

Supporting students with ACEs and trauma is an expanding responsibility for educators. There are core strengths which children need to be healthy socially-emotionally and behaviorally, including attachment, self-regulation, affiliation, awareness, tolerance, and respect, which lead to student resourcefulness and resilience in the face of adversity (Perry, 2002). The Neurosequential Model of Therapeutics (Perry & Hambrick, 2008) is an example of an evidence-based practice to train educators and build school capacity to provide safe learning experiences in a compassionate way by working sequentially to systematically nurture and heal regions of the brain impacted by trauma, in precise order, from the lowest level at the brain stem, to the diencephalon, to the limbic system, to the highest level at the frontal cortex. The Neurosequential Model of Therapeutics emphasizes that the best biological interventions for students with behavior problems are a safe environment, human interactions that do not re-traumatize the brain, and positive relationships with others, which reorganize and heal trauma-related brain impairment over time. Focusing treatment on brain health, and targeting treatment on the correct part of the brain, in the correct sequence, will have a direct and positive impact on behavior. Creating an atmosphere of physical and emotional student safety and relationship building are the primary roles for all educators in the social-emotional-behavioral health of students and in providing trauma-informed care (Cavanaugh, 2016). *Trauma-informed care*, broadly, is an organizational framework that can be used to guide responsiveness to various types of trauma.

When intervening on behalf of students who have experienced some form of trauma, care must be given to understanding the role of the limbic system that guides internal organization and neuronal connections of the brain (Braak, Braak, Yilmazer, & Bohl, 1996). It is important to note that prefrontal cortex interventions that involve thinking and reasoning, like listening and talking coherently with a teacher or dean, do not work well when hyper-vigilant students interpret events as threatening because their brains easily downshift into their limbic systems, engaging their fight or flight responses. This tug-o-war between the limbic system and the prefrontal cortex interferes with human choice making in the present at the potential expense of future consequences (Schüll & Zaloom, 2011). Cortex functioning is impaired when the limbic system takes over. When students are upset or angry, no matter the cause, one of two *involuntary* limbic system responses are activated including flight (i.e., withdrawal, putting head down, hoodie over eyes, hiding under desk, leaving class) or fight (i.e., verbal altercations with other students and teacher, throwing objects, shoving or assaulting people, destroying school property, and other explosive combative behaviors). Whether a threat is physical or psychological, the limbic system limits decision making to fight or flight. Emotionally and behaviorally dysregulated children tend to get the adults around them to act *just like them* because adults get upset in response to student behavior and downshift into *their* limbic systems. The only chance educators have to keep a step ahead is to remain in their own cortexes by planning ahead and remaining calm, which neurologically allows them to have the capacity to be strategic in choosing which variables to reinforce in anticipation of students' behavior.

In order to overcome limbic system havoc, repeated rehearsal of expected behavior is critical for the student as well as the teacher. Both must be retaught behavior and learned responses in order for the intervention to be effective, and for the student and teacher to attain successful outcomes. A limbic system intervention gives a student time and space to recoup without additional prefrontal cortex demands that may be further interpreted as threatening, which, as an unintended consequence, may keep the child in limbic system mode. Taking a break, going to a designated quiet area in the classroom, deep breathing, using relaxation techniques or visual imagery for self-calming gives the brain time to feel safe again which must happen before any thinking, reasoning, or learning can take place. If the student is able to rehearse these coping skills in advance, including a secret signal between teacher and student when the teacher suspects that an upcoming event may trigger the behavior, the student can exhibit the desired practiced behavior on cue, based on trust and safety, which decreases the probability of limbic system responses and seemingly impulsive aggressive behavior. When students have overactive limbic systems they are not making bad choices, they are making the only choices their brains will allow them to make, fight or flight; giving students a sense of safety and trust is the best offense and defense for educators working with hyper-aggression in students.

Social-Emotional and Behavioral Practices

Despite the current political appetite to fix or destroy the Patient Protection Affordable Care Act of 2010 (PPACA, 2010), the PPACA promotes school-based health center programs and cites that addressing students' mental health outcomes in a school setting has become a priority. It is also noted in PPACA language that evidence-based programs and evidence-based interventions are frequently under-implemented in school settings. More than one in six students experience mental health issues, with those in the foster care system experiencing even greater rates, yet only approximately one in ten of these students receive treatment (Maag & Katsiyannis, 2010). Given easier access to highly lethal weapons, more mentally and emotionally unstable students and adults are targeting schools and children specifically to cause massive harm on a large scale (Bonanno & Levenson, 2014). Alarmingly, threats to schools are increasing. Only a coordinated and systematic approach to social-emotional and behavioral supports in schools, in conjunction with family outreach, community health services and law enforcement efforts, can effectively address the challenges of preventing school violence and mitigating effects of the aftermath.

Schools are traditionally safe places for children; however, in recent years, high-profile acts of school violence have been sharply on the rise. Preventative and administrative measures are needed to decrease this violence and the resultant discipline issues in our schools (Whitford, Katsiyannis, & Counts, 2016). At the school level, a behavioral threat assessment and management model (BTAM) can be used to reduce or block imminent threats to others and "to connect a student of concern (and potential victims) to continually available resources" (Reeves & Brock, 2017, p. 1). At the student level, communication is key in prevention and crisis response. Teachers and parents can use certain techniques when speaking to children to help them understand and work through the aftermath of threats or acts of violence. This includes reassuring children of their safety, making time to talk to them about what happened, keeping explanations developmentally appropriate, limiting exposure and time on social media, observing their emotional state immediately following and after a traumatic event, reviewing safety procedures, and keeping up with normal routines (National Association of School Psychologists, 2017b).

A school's academic MTSS team can support students with social-emotional and behavioral issues much of the time, as can IEP (individualized education program) teams supporting and monitoring students with educational disabilities. A *Behavioral and Mental Health MTSS* team is comprised of highly trained individuals tasked with school safety, student behavioral health, and emotional well-being of students in a school and community setting. The Behavioral and Mental Health MTSS framework must follow the same tiered support system as the academic intervention framework. It is critical to emphasize that evidence-based behavioral practices in a school setting need to start at Tier 1 before Tier 2 and Tier 3 can be effectively implemented and evaluated, as is the case in academic tiers of support. Building capacity for training and supports at Tier 3 only is a thinking error many school teams make, focusing interventions solely at the highest-risk offenders. However, implementing social-emotional and behavioral instructional opportunities beginning in earlier grades at Tier 1 and Tier 2 would alleviate the need for expensive and effort-intensive Tier 3 interventions much of the time. As any secondary classroom teacher can attest, individualized behavior plans for high numbers of misbehaving students in classes are difficult to implement, at best, and highly disregarded, at worst, because of the complexity of implementation and documentation requirements. Regular education teachers are not typically prepared to manage multiple students with individualized behavior plans in one class and typically should not have to.

In general, the behavioral health of students in a classroom is largely dependent on the skill of the teacher. Educators who teach behavioral expectations and strategically pay more attention to students when they act civilly rather than uncivilly, are most likely to have students who behave within classroom expectations (Sprick, 2009, 2013). These strategic reinforcements are brief, preplanned corrections that follow the expectations established by the teacher at the beginning of the year. Proactive classroom management is considered Tier 1 behavioral instruction, as are explicit teaching methods of school-wide expectations through positive behavioral instructional supports (Sprick, 2009, 2013). Environments where expectations have been clearly taught by caring educators who strive for positive relationships with students and who reinforce, or manipulate, the right variables in the classroom and throughout the school, trump individualized behavior plans for most students most of the time.

Universal Tier 1 instruction in *social-emotional and behavioral (SEB)* functioning, from pre-kindergarten through high school, should be as valued in school as academic rigor. Intervention programs that specifically target behavioral interventions (the *B* in SEB) have been correlated to a decrease in anti-social behavior and an increase in prosocial behaviors, while programs that focused on social-emotional learning (without the B in SEB) demonstrated less impact and less rigorous investigations into behavioral variables (Sabey, Charlton, Pyle, Lignugaris-Kraft, & Ross, 2017). Even with the significant impact SEB intervention has, SEB screening only occurs in approximately 2 percent of schools (Harrison, Vannest, & Reynolds, 2017). Children need to be taught behaviors that are conducive toward living socially and emotionally healthy lives. Learning prosocial behavior is dependent on learning in the home environment through family values and social structures into the community, but should not be depended upon as the sole source of instruction in civil behavior.

As evidenced by the increasing numbers of students who do not have good role models of proper civil behavior at home, and who do not demonstrate appropriate social behavior at school, school-based solutions are needed. While many at-risk students exhibit poor coping skills and problem solving in the face of frustration in increasing numbers, they are not the only ones, and *all* students would benefit from research-based SEB learning experiences in school curriculum. Ideally, SEB instruction should be mandated from kindergarten through 12th grade, like academic content for subject levels. SEB curriculum that is implemented with fidelity will hold educators more accountable for providing valid behavioral interventions and enforcing discipline fairly, which is socially just. Students who perceive that discipline is fairly distributed by teachers who care about them are more likely to accept natural consequences, which may increase their cooperation with efforts to replace behaviors that are maladaptive with more functional behaviors to meet their needs.

Critical thinking skills and cognitive behavioral strategies must be nurtured in students, as well as cultural sensitivities and tolerance. Likewise, educators must be cognizant of their own implicit bias and mindset when handling diverse students' issues competently to reinforce resiliency and to ensure equity in discipline and corrective behavioral practices (Brooks, Brooks, & Goldstein, 2012). Changing implicit bias is easier achieved through changing social contexts rather than trying to change peoples' beliefs (Payne & Vuletich, 2017). In this framework, improving the school climate and culture go a long way toward reducing educators' own implicit biases with consistent implementation of proactive practices toward all students. Systematically teaching SEB strategies increases the probability that students will feel more connected to others, become more resilient, and lead more meaningful social lives (Aspen Institute: National Commission on Social, Emotional, and Academic Development, 2018). Research suggests that childhood resilience is linked to long-term outcomes, and "clinicians should begin to focus on the development of resilience or protective factors for the most vulnerable youth" (Naglieri, Goldstein, & LeBuffe, 2010, p. 354).

The danger of not having frequent guided socialization opportunities from early childhood on, with explicit and appropriate modeling, is that children who do not know how to play well with others grow into big kids and adults who do not play well with others. In some elementary schools, recess in kindergarten and beyond is all but a thing of the past due to mandatory academic seat time and test preparation with skills drills, which robs students of social skills development and social problem solving opportunities that unstructured play allows. In some states, SEB instruction and achievement of SEB benchmarks are mandatory in kindergarten; however, after that, success in school is only monitored and defined in academic terms. If students have not learned appropriate classroom behavior after first grade, intensity of punitive measures increases as grade levels rise without guarantee of targeted learning experiences to address underlying skills deficits. Students who should be "old enough" to know how to act right, but clearly do not behave within expected norms, must have repeated exposure to appropriate modeling and rehearsal with reinforcement of new behaviors to improve coping skills, anger management skills, or social skills deficits. Instead of punishing students with skills deficits, students need to be retaught and given enough time and reinforcement to acquire, rehearse, and sustain new behaviors. Many students will respond to direct behavioral instruction for all, some will require targeted skills practice in smaller groups, and a small percentage will require intensive instruction and individualized support.

Explicit SEB Instruction and Intervention

Regardless of age, all students, especially those with social, emotional, and behavioral deficits, should be given SEB learning opportunities in a school setting. Lack of adequate screening procedures and classrooms full of students with SEB problems are some of the leading causes of teacher burnout and job dissatisfaction (McCarthy, Lambert, Lineback, Fitchett, & Baddouh, 2016; Benner, Kutash, Nelson, & Fisher, 2013). Teachers who feel unprepared to adequately manage students in the classroom are at the highest risk of leaving the profession (Charner-Laird, Kirkpatrick, Szczesiul, Watson, & Gordon, 2016;

Brezicha, Bergmark, & Mitra, 2015). The need for investing in teacher skill development and competencies to support students behaviorally in the classroom cannot be overemphasized. Educators must have interdisciplinary skills, be experts in content areas and masters of their own cognitive behavior in choosing which variables to reinforce in the environment for students, regardless of personal experiences, feelings, or opinions. Ideally, educators are perfect role models for students, remaining calm and collected through all situations; realistically, they are people with personal experiences, feelings, and opinions.

Teachers should be mindful not to accidentally reinforce inappropriate behaviors, thus increasing the likelihood of those undesirable behaviors occurring in the future. For example, giving too much attention and power to disruptive students or sending them to the office for misbehavior which the students know will allow them to avoid un-preferred tasks can be a negative behavior-consequence cycle. When student behavior crosses the threshold from off-task to atypically disruptive, behavior problems can impact academic growth of self and others. When students misbehave, their attention is diverted from instruction and often diverts other students' attention from instruction resulting in a contagion effect when other students become off-task and disruptive. *Contagion effect* refers to a replication of a particular behavior by others, due to proximity or social media exposure. Relationship skills, positive interactions with students, and improving teacher classroom management skills to reinforce and increase on-task behavior are some of the most important and effective strategies to positively impact student learning in the long term.

Students must be given more opportunities to learn social-emotional regulation skills if they do not learn them naturally or from positive and negative consequences in the general environment. At Tier 2, interventions for behavioral and emotional regulation must provide a more targeted approach, including exposure to appropriate behavioral modeling and rehearsal of new behaviors with guided feedback. Tier 2 students are typically progress monitored weekly. Check in-check out programs, evidence-based social skills curriculum, and anger management programs taught by school social workers, counselors, or other trained educators to small groups of students can be very effective for targeted instruction (Ross & Sabey, 2014). In secondary schools with MTSS, an early bird class, or 7th period class after school, specifically identified in students' class schedules, could target SEB remediation, including communication with classroom teachers, to ensure valid implementation and generalization of Tier 2 and Tier 3 SEB interventions. Block schedules can also allow for SEB instructional periods as long as those instructional periods are reserved specifically for implementing the SEB curriculum, and instruction occurs consistently as scheduled during that time. One example of such research-based curriculum is PREPARE: A Prosocial Curriculum for Aggressive Youth (Goldstein, 1999), targeting interpersonal skills, anger control, empathy training, social perception, and anxiety management, among other areas for learning and sustaining appropriate social skills. Whatever curriculum is used, there must be repeated opportunities to practice new skills with guided feedback. Accommodations including limbic system interventions, pressure passes (allowing students to leave stressful situations for a predetermined safe place), extended processing time, and alternative work locations, if warranted, can all be part of Tier 2 behavioral supports leading up in intensity to Tier 3 level supports, if required regularly and specifically.

As found in earlier chapters of this text, scheduled Tier 2 and Tier 3 level SEB intervention classes, like scheduled academic intervention classes, provide the added bonus of simplified documentation of interventions with lesson plans and attendance logs. Block scheduling allows for creative "blocking" of intervention times and allocates specific time within the master schedule to provide evidence-based interventions that can be monitored by administrators for fidelity. It is important to note that learning a new habit or behavior requires daily rehearsal for long enough to become part of one's behavioral repertoire. The formation of new behaviors takes an average of 66 days, or 9–10 weeks (Lally, van Jaarsveld, Potts, & Wardle, 2010) or more for students who do not rehearse the desired behavior on the weekends.

In a perfect world, funding for SEB intervention programs would be budgeted for the target students' entire school year, but school budgets are tight. At the very least, SEB intervention programs should be funded for at least one full semester for students who are functioning at a Tier 2 and Tier 3 level. The positive outcomes of building community partnerships, allowing students apprenticeships and relationship opportunities through development of life and work skills outside of school, should not be underestimated either. School districts should pay now for culturally competent teaching practices and adequate SEB supports in schools, or society will pay later for building more prisons for all the children the system will fail generationally. All students must be given ample opportunity to learn successful SEB skills.

A small percentage of students will demonstrate behavior that is atypical, maladaptive, and resistant to proactive management strategies over prolonged periods of time across settings so as to provide evidence for suspicion of a lower incidence disability (i.e., emotional disturbance) under IDEIA. These students may require an individualized education program (IEP) with a behavior intervention plan, or a 504 plan if deficits can be addressed with accommodations alone. SEB intervention classes must provide the requisite documentation of prior interventions and response needed for IDEIA services. This documentation includes student participation through teacher lesson plans, behavioral notations and progress reports, attendance logs, discipline history through dean's chronology, counselors' notes, and any other anecdotal documentation by teachers or other educators in regards to frequency, intensity, and duration of behavioral episodes.

Behavior plans are considered Tier 3 territory, as are IEPs, reoccurring direct school counseling services, individualized incentive planning and behavioral charting, and supports that are intensive in the community including psychological and counseling supports, psychiatric supports, medical supports, and mandatory court interventions for students with history of problems with law enforcement. Students receiving Tier 3 SEB supports require that behavioral performance is monitored daily. Many schools already have MTSS teams, behavior teams, and individualized education planning teams to support these functions. General referrals to MTSS for behavior, and social or emotional problems, can often be managed by grade level case managers with MTSS team supports in coordination with parents, classroom teachers, and school counselors. Some students requiring Tier 3 may qualify for special education services and have IEPs with detailed behavior plans.

A very small percentage of the most acute students requiring Tier 3 intensity supports, whether they have an IEP or not, will require active case management by a school team that specializes in overseeing the treatment plans of the most severe Tier 3 caseload. This particular smart team includes individuals with highly concentrated talent working in coordination with other related or overlapping teams of highly concentrated talent, communicating systematically to work together efficiently in identifying, assessing, and managing potential threats and intervening early. In this light, a school's Behavioral and Mental Health MTSS team is positioned to be incredibly smart.

The Tier 3 Behavioral and Mental Health MTSS team is considered the most intensive SEB support team, comprised of all school personnel licensed to conduct suicide protocols and threat assessments and all administrators on campus, to actively manage the most dangerous students, as in a triage model. This team engages in proactive treatment efforts for this specific population as well as reactive problem solving. Administratively, it is wise to remember that if a student is *suspected* of having an educational disability that student has the same legal protections and rights as the students who have already been identified with the disability, including disciplinary protections against expulsion as a consequence of behaviors that appear to be a manifestation of the suspected disability.

Exercise 10.1

- *List Tier 1 behavioral supports or any initiatives currently in place at your school to teach behavioral expectations to all students.*
- Team exercise: Research curriculum options and brainstorm possible SEB learning opportunities that could be incorporated into current curriculum.
- *List Tier 2 behavioral supports or any initiatives currently in place at your school to teach behavioral expectations to a selected number of students requiring more intensive re-teaching.*
- Team exercise: Research curriculum options and brainstorm possible SEB learning opportunities that could be incorporated into current curriculum.
- *List Tier 3 behavioral supports or any initiatives currently in place at your school, or in the community, to teach behavioral expectations to high-risk and special needs students.*
- Team exercise: Research curriculum options and brainstorm possible SEB learning opportunities that could be incorporated into current curriculum.

Behavioral and Mental Health MTSS

Ready or not, educators will have students whose behavior and affect range from the norm to highly atypical and dysfunctional. Teachers who do not have positive proactive classroom management skills are going to struggle with even the most benign behaving students in otherwise structured settings. Teachers with higher student referrals to the dean should be provided mandatory skill development opportunities, both formal and informal, to improve classroom management skills, and, ideally, get individually coached by a colleague trained in accomplished teaching with at-risk populations (Cannata, McCrory, Sykes, Anagnostopoulos, & Frank, 2010). When a student is not succeeding in a classroom environment sometimes the problem lies in a lack of understanding, compassion, or skill on the part of the student, teacher, or both.

Teachers with highly effective management skills, who do not respond to student behavior emotionally, are always the best choice for students with special behavioral needs. Administrators should be mindful that the most effective teachers often get tapped out quickly with extra duties on campus, in addition to managing the most difficult students on campus, which leads to burnout. Some students are unstable, unpredictable, disruptive, and highly explosive no matter who is teaching. Of course, not all students who make threats or act threatening are actual threats to student safety; just as not all students who are actual threats to student safety make threats or behave volatilely. It is important to have systems in place for observation, communication, and problem solving, especially on secondary campuses, to quickly identify and support students who are at risk of engaging in behaviors that lead to dangerous situations for themselves, other students, school staff, and those in the community.

Where to Start?

Some schools and school districts use universal SEB screenings to help identify emotionally fragile students and those in need of more immediate and intensive interventions for signs of depression and signs of suicide. For example, schools within Boston Public Schools use universal screening methods to ask straightforward questions about students' thoughts and feelings about their behavioral and mental health (Boston Public Schools, 2017). Universal screenings cast a wide net and allow educators to systematically sift through student responses to focus attention on students who fall within the at-risk range for internalized and/or externalized behaviors. Follow-up interviews by school mental health care providers are required to further address students with significant indicators. For example, students who are identified as having significant internalizing problems may be asked if they have had thoughts of suicide and self-harm, and if they are engaging in high-risk behavior or behaviors that put others at-risk of harm. Staff members must be trained to perform screenings to competently identify students with internalizing and externalizing problems, leading to quicker identification of those with moderate to imminent risk of suicide, self-harm, and harming others, as well as those who would benefit from follow-up with less urgent, but very serious, needs requiring mental health and community supports. These schoolwide SEB benchmark screenings are recommended to occur at least twice a year; ideally, they would correspond to academic benchmark or assessment periods three times a year. There are several free tools available to schools, in addition to programs for purchase.

Schools conducting universal SEB screenings can use results to examine Tier 1, identify students for Tier 2 and Tier 3 programming opportunities, and as mid- and post-screenings to measure SEB functioning and perceptions over time. Larger schools may be reticent about implementing SEB screenings due to fears that the screenings automatically lead to a tremendous spike in the number suicide protocols, and other types of threat assessment, which could overwhelm school-based mental health supports and referrals to community medical and mental health care facilities. Rather, the screenings should be viewed as a temperature check on students' SEB status which helps inform and guide the MTSS team in their formation of Tier 2 groups and Tier 3 individualized interventions. Large secondary schools may not feel they have the resources to conduct full-scale SEB screenings; however, many screenings can be administered and scored electronically, and schools often find that the proactive value of identifying at-risk students and increasing opportunities to intervene early outweighs the upfront inconveniences of scheduling and manpower it takes to conduct the screenings. Using a phased roll-out, starting with smaller subpopulations, (i.e., 9th graders) and growing over time, may seem more manageable to implement, as a team compromise to address barriers to universal SEB screenings.

The administration of most screenings takes very little effort for students and teachers; however, following up with higher-risk students will require the attention and expertise of school-based mental health service providers to the exclusion of performing other duties during that time period. The perception at the school level is that schools do not have the capacity to support the potentially high number of students identified with moderate to high-risk factors. Identifying students who are at-risk for depression and self-harm without having anywhere or anyone to send them to in the community for treatment could leave school districts and states open to liability issues for not properly responding to students with identified risk factors. This is why it is important for teams to have intervention supports in place at all tiers and to have established wrap-around services readily available in which to refer at-risk students. Without these supports, sole responsibilities then fall on parents and families to closely monitor emotionally unstable children, requiring constant adult supervision and locking up medications, guns, chemicals, knives, tools, and anything that can be used as a weapon to ensure they do not have access to potentially harmful elements.

Lack of capacity of mental health supports in schools and in the community is a public hazard, and a perceived barrier in the administration of universal SEB screeners in secondary schools. Nonetheless, SEB universal screenings are one of the most powerful tools schools can use to quickly and accurately identify vulnerable secondary students who require mental health supports most acutely. In addition, how teachers feel about their comfort, commitment, and culture of supports in administering and using these measures has a significant impact on their success (Brackett, Reyes, Rivers, Elbertson, & Salovey, 2011).

Effective proactive and reactive practices can be ingrained in school culture, ultimately protecting student rights, improving school safety, and saving lives. Highly charged emotional and behavioral situations can be minimized, or negative outcomes mitigated, if handled effectively; likewise, unfortunate and permanent damage can result if such situations escalate despite, or as a result of, actions taken to intervene. Advanced training in de-escalation techniques is critical for school staff members to know how to decode student behavior, identify the function of behavior, determine the skill deficit, and apply the right intervention, such as described in the research-based curriculum of Life Space Crisis Intervention (Long, Wood, & Fecser, 2001). Sometimes the escalation of student behavioral issues can be more gradual over time and likely outcomes predicted. Long-term damage to students on the wrong path may be reduced, if not prevented, when one caring adult is paying attention and has the power to actively make changes to the student's probable trajectory by building a trusting relationship. When adults are trained to actively promote treatment within the school setting and out in the community, students' support networks increase. Students with behavioral and mental health issues can be especially exhausting for teachers to manage long-term, which is why a network of support in the school setting is so critical. Even a tenacious, well-intentioned staff member may not get too far in garnering support for advocating for a student's mental health care alone, as there can be a maze of steps to get services.

Connecting with students and helping them with access to resources they need is extremely time consuming. Finding quality community mental health service providers who have openings in their schedule and take caregivers' insurance takes time. Insurance issues, lack of ability to provide co-pay to providers, lack of transportation, parent denial of severity of issues, and a host of other factors can be barriers to students getting timely treatment, which requires educators' patience, encouragement, and finesse to gently push families into community sector supports when student mental health needs exceed the scope of school interventions. Teachers, administrators, and support staff are probably not going to have the time or ability to help students this way.

There truly is power in team work, sharing strengths and shouldering burdens together. Mental health providers in schools, including school psychologists, school counselors, school nurses, and school social workers, are needed in every school so they can prioritize risks for students and assist families by making connections with appropriate resources in the community. Unfortunately, most school districts do not have near enough school psychologists, school counselors, school nurses, or school social workers, who are critical to bridging supports and services between school, home, and community. Whether or not local education agencies or states prioritize mental health supports for students in schools, the need is there and overworked, underpaid educators are left carrying the burden of supporting all students with mental and behavioral health problems, and their families by proxy.

What Now?

Addressing student behavior and mental health needs in smart teams on secondary campuses will improve informed decision making, which will result in more equitable decisions for students. There has to be a clear process in place to address concerns about students' SEB stability so that mental health supports can be provided in a timely manner. An obstacle for preventing some student suicides, or other preplanned violence, is when adults and students who have valid concerns about erratic behavior and emotionality of other students do not know who to tell or how to tell others about what they know ahead of time, let alone know how to ask for help for themselves. An inhibition to report is especially likely when an adolescent who suspects a pending act of violence has been a victim of violence themselves or has previously witnessed violence (Zaykowski, 2012). Schools that have clearly defined procedures on how to report, and respond to, SEB concerns will be more sensitive to those reports and more accountable for acting on potential threats. They will also be better prepared to deal with the contagion effect that often follows suicide completions. Mandated educational policies have emerged after tragedy to provide clear procedures previously lacking, which school staff must follow to keep students safe.

For example, in Nevada, a middle school student named Hailee Lamberth died by suicide in 2013 after a series of severe bullying incidences went unaddressed over a prolonged period of time. Hailee's parents had no idea that bullying was taking place, even though evidence indicated that complaints of Hailee's bullying had been reported to a teacher and on the school district's website allowing for anonymous reporting. Her parents were never notified about the bullying until reading Hailee's suicide note. After the student's death, her family sued the school district and won. In 2015, Nevada became the twentieth state in the union to pass anti-bullying legislation with Senate Bill 504. Anti-bullying policies were determined, providing a host of supports and procedures for school districts. Mandates were put in place for bullying complaints to quickly travel up the chain of command. School staff must immediately report any complaints of bullying to a school administrator, in which case the school principal is required to immediately stop the bullying and ensure the safety of victims. Principals must formally respond to the complaint by the end of that day or the next school day, with required phone calls to all parents of students involved in the bullying. In addition, principals must maintain written documentation of incidences. Failure to follow procedure could result in immediate termination for school staff members. In Nevada, Senate Bill 504 (2015) is referred to as Hailee's Law.

Policies such as Hailee's Law could be generalized to include reported acts of violence and mandating administrative accountability for following up on threats of pending acts of violence. Keeping students emotionally and physically safe is a reality for educators in all schools. Barriers should be low for students to be referred for behavioral and emotional supports, and barriers should be even lower for reporting safety concerns to school staff with the expectation that the threat will be assessed and addressed in a reasonable amount of time. School safety measures are replicable and should be required to have uniform components applied at all schools. Procedures and processes can be standardized so students have a basic understanding of how to get help no matter which school they attend. When school procedures for identifying and acting on potential threats are established and followed, the next challenge is accountability for coordinated community resources with parent/caregiver follow-through.

School safety is a multifaceted problem that requires many moving parts to work well together. The physical security of a school site must be addressed in terms of school site layout, limited entry points, limited access to students, and school safety drills; however, what keeps children most safe inside schools is relationships with educators resulting in student connections to staff and other students. The effects of increasing security measures in schools are not clear, and some efforts, like metal detectors, may decrease students' feelings of safety (NASP, 2018). Schools with positive cultures of supports for all students, such as those with PBIS and MTSS in place, systematically evaluate school incident data and make data-based decisions to make schools safer in smart teams.

Schools can prioritize mental health and student safety by empowering a Behavioral and Mental Health MTSS team to identify, monitor, and support students with the most severe Tier 3 SEB needs on a secondary campus. Behavioral and Mental Health MTSS enables a team of highly specialized educators to systematically evaluate student behavioral data and monitor the social-emotional and behavioral functioning of the highest-risk students on campus. Sources of information include dean's database, teacher report, parent report, student report, school counselor report, school nurse report, school social worker report, school psychologist report, and administrator report. Regular meetings guarantee all parties regularly share pertinent student information, allowing the team to work together cohesively to address student SEB issues head-on by sharing responsibilities and actively promoting appropriate supports and services for students within and out of the school setting.

Referrals for Tier 2 and Tier 3 behavioral supports can come through staff recommendation or through the regular MTSS team's triangulation of data sources, including student SEB screener scores. Schools with universal SEB screenings can get ahead of the ball by identifying and tracking students with the most severe externalizing and internalizing behavioral and emotional issues quickly. Schools that do not use universal SEB screeners are at a disadvantage because responses to behavioral and mental health issues are going to be more reactive and less proactive. Students who act out or have extreme externalizing problems usually come to the attention of school administration on their own. Others are brought to the attention of school counselors through teacher report, parent report, peer report, and self-report. The goal of a school-based Behavioral and Mental Health MTSS team is to engage in active problem solving to minimize the impact of mental illness, behavioral disorders, and maladaptive behavioral functioning, which is often compounded by family, social, and socio-economic stressors; and to use a coordinated approach to connect the most socially-emotionally and behaviorally unhealthy students to the supports and services they require. Anyone can refer a student to the Behavioral and Mental Health MTSS team, but typically school counselors on a secondary campus are in the best position to know whether students require Tier 3 level management beyond typical Tier 3 accommodations, interventions, and special education supports. Students requiring case management by this team are selected because they are deemed a high risk of threat to self and/or others. Whether students are managed by the Behavioral and Mental Health MTSS team or not is a team decision based on data, experience with the student, and professional judgment.

The Behavioral and Mental Health MTSS team monitors all of the most severe SEB problems and high-risk students on campus, regardless if a student is already receiving special education support. The majority of students monitored by the Behavioral and Mental Health MTSS team may never be referred for special education evaluations because of a variety of situational and environmental factors, severe attendance issues, or high transience. Bottom line is that emotionally fragile students can break with pressure if not adequately supported. The question is not whether potentially dangerous students are on secondary school campuses, the question is whether these students are going to cause significant damage to self or others before they get help, or if they can be identified and provided services prior to unfortunate, yet potentially predictable, events, including assaults on students and others, self-harm, and threats to do the same. Children are vulnerable to to inconceivable horrors, such as abuse, neglect, sexual assault, sex trafficking, drug addictions, bullying, gang violence, and horrifying family situations. Many parents struggle to survive with their own issues and have no idea how to protect their children, let alone successfully navigate the challenges of raising children with severe mental and behavioral health problems. Systematically watching out for traumatized, behaviorally and emotionally unstable students, and actively solving problems for them at school could be a matter of life and death, and is a necessary component of safe schools.

Who Now?

Secondary classroom teachers and school counselors are the most likely school professionals to directly monitor students' performance and behavior on a secondary campus. They often communicate and collaborate together about how best to address student concerns. In large schools and school systems the sheer number of students can be difficult to keep track of when teachers and counselors have hundreds of students to monitor. Usually the students with the most inappropriate, aggressive, or disruptive behavior already come to the attention of the dean's office and school administrators. Discipline by itself does not usually correct chronic behavior problems which are better addressed in the long term with comprehensive positive behavioral instructional supports. School discipline reform is much needed, which is a nuanced function of technical tasks such as resource utilization, normative processes such as conflict resolution, and political maneuvering to shift power (Wiley, Anyon, Yang, Pauline, Rosch, Valladares, Downing, & Pisciotta, 2018). Teachers are required to do their progressive discipline procedures, school administrators are required to do their progressive discipline procedures, and school counselors are stuck in the middle with no control over outcomes. School counselors, trying to support students by providing social-emotional learning experiences and helping support families with referrals to community agencies, may also feel pressed into being a part of the progressive discipline plan. Most school counselors probably prefer to be associated more positively and proactively with students than as a necessary part of the negative reinforcement cycle of discipline procedures.

The school dean, or administrator in charge of discipline, usually knows every child with a behavioral challenge on campus by name and knows their caregivers' phone numbers by heart. The school dean has as much, if not more, pertinent information on students with social-emotional and behavioral challenges than any other school staff member. Communication between the school deans and school counselors seems like a natural relationship, as counselors help students with getting through emotional and social crises, as well as communicating with caregivers, monitoring credit attainment, and attending parent–teacher conferences. However, relationships between discipline and counseling are sometimes strained, with two opposing desired outcomes. Discipline depends on consequences, and harsh consequences are sometimes warranted. Mediation, understanding, social skill development, character building, and second chances may also be warranted. Whose decision is it to give a student more chances, more counseling, harsher discipline, or even consideration of eligibility for special education services when facing students with severe and chronic emotional and behavioral problems? Are second chances applied fairly? Are harsh punishments applied equitably?

Oftentimes, such decisions are made unilaterally by a single person, often the teacher, the dean, or the principal. Who ensures that discipline practices are applied equitably? How much more equitable could student outcomes be if a team of mental health-based school professionals worked together regularly to actively manage students with wrap-around services within the school and extended out to home and community?

Having a Behavioral and Mental Health MTSS team in place on a secondary school campus is necessary to systematically monitor students who are severely struggling emotionally and behaviorally; which in turn positively impacts student outcomes and increases school safety. The Behavioral and Mental Health MTSS team's structures and functions will provide the backbone to systematic procedures to increase interventions and monitoring in the lives of students with the most severe emotional-behavioral issues. Each role on the Behavioral and Mental Health MTSS team has unique and overlapping responsibilities. Members of the Behavioral and Mental Health MTSS team often include many of the individuals who can help facilitate change on campus. Required team members include: all school administrators, all school counselors, the school psychologist, the school nurse, the school social worker, community and school advocates, and any other behavior mentor who has a close relationship with target students.

Roles of Behavioral and Mental Health MTSS Members

Pinpointing types of services provided by team members, and wrap-around resources provided by the school, will improve the automaticity, sustainability, and effectiveness of Behavioral and Mental Health MTSS (National Resource Center for Mental Health Promotion & Youth Violence Prevention, 2017). Building effective relationships within the school environment and among community agencies will increase the probability that students in need will receive appropriate and timely services, thus increasing student and campus safety. The Behavioral and Mental Health MTSS team operates at the highest level of student confidentiality, and though confidential information can be shared freely with team members, it is important to safeguard student confidentiality, as would be expected in any mental health or educational setting, unless students intend to hurt themselves or someone else.

Administrators

School administrators must actively lead and support Behavioral and Mental Health MTSS, just as they must actively lead and support a culture of MTSS. All of the school administrators on campus are automatically part of the Behavioral and Mental Health MTSS team, whether or not they attend meetings. As in the beginning of any new initiative on a school campus, the school principal is strongly urged to take an active interest in the performance of Behavioral and Mental Health MTSS. *When the principal visibly supports this team, the message to other administrators and staff members is that Behavioral and Mental Health MTSS is a school priority, and working to support students with behavioral and mental health issues is a school priority.* The principal's regular attendance at Behavioral and Mental

Health MTSS meetings, at least initially, commands professional behavioral standards at the meetings. Assistant principals and deans will be required to communicate with school counselors, and other Behavioral and Mental Health MTSS members, on matters relating to discipline issues, administrative actions, and teacher directives pertaining to interactions with students and caregivers, which may be relevant in team decision making. At some point, the school principal can nominate one administrator to attend Behavioral and Mental Health MTSS meetings to speak on behalf of the school administration so that not all administrators have to attend all meetings. Ideally, the administrator representing all the school's administrators at meetings will be able to contribute information and provide support to the team with the understanding of teachers' needs, the knowledge and experience of the dean in student discipline issues, and the voice of the principal in decision making. At least one school administrator is required to attend every Behavioral and Mental Health MTSS meeting but all have an open invitation to discuss students of concern at any meeting. Administrators are required to communicate with counselors about students chronically coming to dean's office for discipline, communicating with special education department if a student has an IEP to ensure disciplinary suspensions do not exceed limits before compensatory time is owed, tracking student behavior requiring being taken out of normal routine, reporting SEB incidences regarding target students to the team, communicating with parents about concerns and team discussions, providing insights into the function of student behavior, as well as making executive decisions for student and staff safety, when necessary, and ensuring discipline is applied equitably. School administrators will be called upon to support school mental health care providers' decision making in times of crisis. Each state has different laws and procedures; however, districts do have policies in place for their school administrators to legally have students hospitalized for observation and treatment without parent presence or consent in the most extreme cases.

School Counselors

School counselors are an integral part of a school's behavioral and mental health supports. Counselors help students through issues large and small; giving students second chances and avenues to make their way back when they have gotten off track. School counselors are often aware of students' credit attainment, personal histories, adverse childhood experiences, successes and failures in social circles, family issues, and many other facts about students that few others may collectively know. *All school counselors on campus are required to be on the Behavioral and Mental Health MTSS team and attend all meetings.* In most schools, school counselors interact with all age levels of students throughout the day during campus supervision before and after school, lunch duty, and other responsibilities that bring them in direct contact with all grade levels. Counselors have their frequent flyers and usually know the frequent flyers to the dean's and nurse's offices, as well. They communicate with numerous students on a personal level throughout the day and hear all kinds of reports from students about what is happening on campus. School counselors have skilled eyes and ears to process and prioritize social-emotional-behavioral information from various sources. School counselors often handle significant student issues independently, sometimes administratively, and occasionally with other mental health professionals. Some students have problems that are more chronic and more severe than a typical student going through hard times.

Students whose mental and behavioral health issues exceed the supports offered at Tier 1, Tier 2, and Tier 3 may get referred to the Behavioral and Mental Health MTSS team. School counselors are responsible for student counseling duties, but at Tier 2 and Tier 3 also: incentive planning with students and spearheading behavioral planning in partnership with the special education teacher designated to support the regular MTSS team; helping keep track of frequency of students out of class for SEB issues; reporting SEB incidences regarding target students to the team; monitoring student data and credit attainment; and changing schedule of students if recommended. *Depending on the school district, shared responsibilities between school counselor, school psychologist, school social worker, and school nurse include*: providing counseling services; assisting with behavioral planning; consulting with teachers on strategies to work with students with SEB issues; providing insights into the function of student behavior; communicating with parents about concerns and team discussions, threat assessment and crisis management; helping provide mental health follow-up within the school setting and in the community, including getting release of information and communicating directly with mental health services providers. School mental health providers also communicate with school police officers when necessary, and assist with having students committed to community mental health treatment centers as needed.

School Psychologists

School psychologists are natural leaders and participants on this committee. Their advanced level training in normal and atypical development, school psychology, counseling, assessment, and educational research puts them at the top of the human capital food chain at a school in terms of skills requisites for participating on the Behavioral and Mental Health MTSS team. They are very qualified to chair the team, provide training for other team members, lead team discussions, make recommendations, and record significant case notes on individual students for the team. *School psychologists are sensitive to psychological issues that impact students and staff, and have relevant background knowledge to weigh in on prioritizing student needs and assisting in obtaining relevant services for students at school and in the community.* They are often experts at narrowing issues quickly and generating probable hypotheses by reviewing criteria of known mental illness and educational disability criteria. As stated previously, special education eligibility is never the goal of MTSS, nor is it the goal of Behavioral and Mental Health MTSS. However, Behavioral and Mental Health MTSS will lay the groundwork for adequately documenting problem behaviors and response to interventions, which will more than cover legal requirements for evidence-based interventions and documentation of outcomes needed for special education eligibility determination, if warranted. In addition to the previously mentioned overlapping responsibilities with other school mental health professionals, other responsibilities for school psychologists on this team involve: consulting with parents about target concerns, strategies and treatment options; monitoring intervention implementation and frequency/intensity data; bringing referrals to multidisciplinary team for special education evaluation; conducting comprehensive or short-term psychoeducational assessments and communicating with special educators; and providing support and counseling for school staff when debriefing after traumatic incidences. Other supports psychologists might provide include trauma-informed counseling, consultation in behavior modification, staff development, family engagement/parenting sessions, and sharing assessment information and recommendations with community service providers. The school psychologist is required to attend all meetings.

School Nurse

The school nurse is the local medical expert on campus. He or she has access to the medical information of all students including health histories, medical diagnoses, and physician contact information. *They are natural liaisons between home and school regarding students' health.* School nurses have an understanding of side effects of medication that could impact behavior or school performance. In addition to overlapping responsibilities with other team members, they are responsible for sharing pertinent student medical information with the Behavioral and Mental Health MTSS team, contacting parents to discuss medication issues and recommendations for physician follow-up, monitoring students for acute signs of mental illnesses, hygiene problems, and/or substance abuse requiring immediate medical attention, helping keep track of frequency of students in the nurse's office for somatic issues, and reporting SEB incidences regarding target students to the team. Nurses are often able to help parents get reduced cost or insurance covered medical referrals, free or reduced cost medicines, state Medicaid applications, free glasses and dental services, and other health-related community services. The nurse is required to attend all meetings.

Social Workers and Other Licensed Service Providers

Other helpful participants on the Behavioral and Mental Health MTSS team include the school social worker, community partner advocates (available in many urban areas), or any other mentor on school campus including teachers on special assignment with knowledge of a student. Mentors and teachers, including school police, can attend parts of meetings pertaining to discussions about students they have working knowledge of but should be excused after they have participated so as not to violate FERPA/HIPPA for students' records they should not know about. *As mental health providers, social workers can engage in counseling services directly with students and can support the student's family as an extension.* The school social workers often have the most flexibility in scheduling and can allocate a bigger percentage of time to engage in community outreach compared to school counselors, the school psychologist, and the school nurse. Creating relationships with parents, providing referrals for community resources, making home visits, problem solving with families, finding ways for students to get medical care and mental health care regardless of lack of insurance and transportation barriers, resource mapping the most relevant and responsive service providers, and developing working relationships with those service providers are critical to the team's functions. In addition, school social workers share many overlapping skills and responsibilities with school counselors, school psychologists, and school nurses, as much as their licenses allow. If the school is located in an at-risk neighborhood, school social workers might work closely with community partner representatives who bring fresh fruits and vegetables, free food giveaways, a community closet, basic toiletries, and other information and services to connect families to resources. Social workers are required to attend all meetings.

Community partners are critical and complement school-based mental health supports, providing qualified and caring coordinators who serve as stabilizing factors by offering nurturing relationships with students and assistance with basic needs (Villarreal & Castro-Villarreal, 2016). The more adults at a school who strive for positive relationships with students and families, increase positive ratio of interactions with troubled students specifically, and are good role models within and out in the school community, the better the outcomes for students.

Exercise 10.2

- Who are your Behavioral and Mental Health MTSS Team members?
- What are their individual strengths and weaknesses?
- What are their collective strengths and weaknesses?
- Identify areas of training that could benefit team member decision making.

Essential Behavioral and Mental Health MTSS Team Functions

Engaging in resource mapping of school and community resources and assessing the needs of a school are proactive ways to support all students' behavioral needs (National Resource Center for Mental Health Promotion & Youth Violence Prevention, 2017; Sprick, Booher, & Garrison, 2009). It is important to define basic services, establish consent and release policies, agree on basic roles and expectations, participate in community partner meetings, and identify agencies who support students in terms of mental health crises, health issues, social work support, counseling, and wrap-around services. It is also helpful for site-based Behavioral and Mental health MTSS teams to have an emergency list of reliable professionals and support staff who can help de-escalate students within the school using evidence-based practices, such as Life Space Crisis Intervention (Long et al., 2001). Enlisting collaboration with community agencies and growing relationships with outside service providers will ensure a more fluid response to student mental health crises, during and after extreme behavioral episodes. Resource mapping will require constant updating to reflect needs of school, skills of staff members, and qualitative experiences with community service providers to establish a preferred list of responsive and effective services for students and their families in the community. School teams must aim to increase student access to quality treatment options in the community for the most mentally, emotionally, and behaviorally unhealthy students.

Making the Change

According to the National Implementation Research Network (2017) there are three main categories that effect implementation: organizational issues (resources and procedures); leadership practices (budgeting and staff motivation); and competency issues (staff training and development). Successful implementation of MTSS is affected by each of these categories. Academic interventions may be perceived as easier to implement with fidelity than behavioral interventions because teachers feel more prepared to address the former over the latter. However, the very systems of universal screening, systematic monitoring of students' data, growing intervention opportunities, data-based decision making, and streamlining documentation into manageable procedures for teachers and other educators can be amended for students' behavioral and mental health needs from the regular MTSS model.

Systematically monitoring and proactively intervening with the highest-risk students on secondary campuses increases school and student safety (Benner et al., 2013). Secondary school teams who effectively implement a data-based decision-making model for academics will have a much easier time adapting to Behavioral and Mental Health MTSS roles and functions because the processes overlap in many ways. The organizational issues are exactly the same in terms of procedures: scheduling time and space in the master calendar for regular meetings and locations; ensuring meetings take place and are conducted professionally; having a chair lead team discussions and document case notes; all team members being prepared to present data to the team at meetings; and data-based decisions being made and communicated to those who need to know. The Behavioral and Mental Health MTSS team meetings mirror the format of regular MTSS team meetings except for different required team members and sources of data discussed.

Data sources, referral procedures, and team members' functions differ somewhat from regular MTSS processes, but the format is almost identical. Students selected to be managed by this team demonstrate social-emotional and behavioral needs that exceed what can be provided through universal Tier 1, targeted Tier 2, and the most intensive Tier 3 supports. Only students with the most severe SEB difficulties, usually a small percentage of students requiring Tier 3 level supports, will be actively managed by this team; students who have been identified in the highest-risk category of potential harm to self and/or others. Regular meetings are necessary (twice a month or weekly) to draft, review, and revise treatment plans, present new information, document behavioral status, and add or terminate services and resources. The regular meeting schedule for Behavioral and Mental Health MTSS is preferably every other week, because it allows a cushion for meetings to get moved back a week in cases of having to cancel or reschedule without sacrificing bi-monthly team attention to emotionally and behaviorally fragile students. In larger secondary schools, teams may find that they need to meet weekly to address all students requiring the most intensive of Tier 3 interventions, support, and monitoring. Larger teams, such as those with six or more school counselors on staff, may consider splitting caseloads into two different meeting groups (i.e., with half the counselors meeting with the team one week and the other half meeting with the team the next week on a rotational basis). Larger schools have more students and have to meet more often to address the volume of students' needs. Meetings should not typically go over an hour and 15 minutes in duration because longer meetings compete with other essential professional responsibilities of team members. School teams must ultimately choose the best Behavioral and Mental Health MTSS team meeting schedule, taking into account school realities and student populations, while supporting regular meetings to ensure the success and sustainability of team functions and communication.

Change Agents

As implementation science can verify, getting people to change their practices in a professional setting is easier said than done (Bryk, Gomez, Grunow, & LeMahieu, 2016). This framework for implementation describes the content, procedures, and empirical nature of interventions in relation to the individuals implementing program practices, known as change agents. *Change agents* influence innovation and make decisions that align with the central mission of an organization. They are external experts who engage within the system to help diffuse innovative practices and processes (Hall & Hord, 2006). Ideally, change agents in schools are school administrators, but that is not always the case. Often, school psychologists, counselors, and teachers take leadership roles in MTSS to move current practices to new practices with better outcomes. It cannot be stated enough, if the school principal does not actively support school leaders in leadership roles, school staff will be much less likely to respond or comply with new practices. The principal depends on networks of many individuals to support the school's overall MTSS framework, including a unique team to support Behavioral and Mental Health MTSS. By administratively supporting the change agents on campus, desired initiatives have a better chance of succeeding. Change agents must be empowered to act on school improvement measures and deliver the message of expected professional duties within the structures and functions of MTSS.

Exercise 10.3

- Who are your current natural leaders and change agents on your school staff?
- How are change agents empowered to actively grow school community participation in best practices and new practices?
- What ways can be implemented to improve the reinforcement, power, and effectiveness of change agents?

There are several barriers to overcome in development of a behavioral and mental health model in schools. Potential barriers to changing mental health support structures in secondary schools include:

- Too many students and not enough time to get to know each individually.
- Too few people trained in mental health supports in schools: shortages of school psychologists, school counselors, school social workers, school nurses, special education teachers, and culturally competent role models.

- Lack of communication between staff members.
- Different agendas of staff members (i.e., discipline vs. treatment).
- Lack of staff commitment and follow through in response to safety issues
- Resistance to cultural change. Team approach to mental and behavioral health issues feels like one more responsibility to team members who may not appreciate more meetings or responsibilities.
- Lack of adequate training. Teachers and staff must be trained to recognize warning signs of student instability and know how to report concerns and observations of poor student hygiene, bizarre student perceptions, and risky behavior.
- Inconsistent expectations and implementation of procedures. Oftentimes students and staff are aware of which students are struggling emotionally and behaviorally, but they do not know how to get help. Who to tell? Where to go? How to do it? School staff can be accountable for following clear procedures.
- Lack of adequate screening and data triangulation procedures. Depressed students are under-identified without universal screenings, externalizing factors, or peer reporting.
- Over-use of zero tolerance policies. Most hyper-aggressive students get suspended or expelled before help happens.

Barriers to behavioral and mental health programming and supports in school can and must be addressed. There will always be barriers at both the micro- and macro-levels; however, with adequate time, planning, and partnering, these barriers can be overcome.

Exercise 10.4

- What are barriers to behavioral and mental health supports at your school?
- What are some solutions to barriers at your school?
- What additional supports or resources are needed?

Red Flags

There are red flags in student behaviors that require immediate attention. Aside from average hyper-aggressive students making impulsive threats that can often be quickly assessed and ameliorated, there are patterns of behavior that can arguably be predictive of which students will initiate school violence and possibly school shootings. As researched by the U.S. Secret Service and the U.S. Department of Education (Fein, Vossekuil, Pollack, Borum, Modzeleski, & Reddy, 2004) there were consistencies between perpetrators of mass school violence and warning signs that should be monitored, communicated, and acted upon. The Behavioral and Mental Health MTSS team is tasked with evaluating the threat level of students, intervening accordingly, and closely monitoring outcomes. There is no valid profile of a school shooter; however, such individuals share commonalities, including history of mental health difficulties, engaging in social isolation, perceptions of having experienced a catastrophic loss, and having access to weapons (Bonanno & Levenson, 2014). Using the threat assessment approach, as would be used by Behavioral and Mental Health MTSS teams, teams must consider previous interactions with a potential attacker and history of stressful events, the current situation, and any identified target or targets (Fein et al., 2004). Key findings reported in two U. S. Secret Service and U. S. Department of Education (Vossekuil, Fein, Reddy, Borum, & Modzeleski, 2004; Fein et al., 2004) reports indicate the following about those who have engaged in school attacks:

- Incidents of targeted violence at school are rarely sudden, impulsive acts.
- Prior to most incidents, other people knew about the attacker's idea and/or plan to attack.
- Most attackers did not threaten their targets directly prior to advancing the attack.
- There is no accurate or useful "profile" of students who engage in targeted school violence.
- Most attackers engaged in noticeable behavior that caused concern, or indicated a need for help, prior to the attack.
- Most attackers were known to have difficulty coping with significant losses or personal failures. Many had considered or attempted suicide.
- Many attackers felt bullied, persecuted, or injured by others prior to the attack.
- Most attackers had access to and had used weapons prior to the attack.
- In many cases, other students were involved in some capacity.
- Despite prompt law enforcement responses, most shooting incidents were stopped by means other than law enforcement intervention.

(Fein et al., 2004, p. 17)

Warning signs that a student is on a "path toward an attack," which requires immediate investigation, threat assessment, and interventions initiated and monitored by the Behavioral and Mental Health MTSS team include:

- ideas or plans about injuring him/herself or attacking a school or persons at school;
- communications or writings that suggest that the student has an unusual or worrisome interest in school attacks;
- comments that express or imply the student is considering mounting an attack at school;
- recent weapon-seeking behavior, especially if weapon-seeking is linked to ideas about an attack or expressions about interest in an attack;
- communications or writings suggesting the student condones or is considering violence to redress a grievance or solve a problem; and
- rehearsals of attacks or ambushes.

(Fein et al., 2004, p. 50)

Students who display violent behavior verbally, imaginatively, and overtly must be evaluated by threat assessments to determine if they have plans and access to weapons, or means, to carry out acts of destruction. According to studies, individuals with a history of a previous suicide attempt are four times more likely than first time attempters to successfully complete a later attempt (Christiansen & Jensen, 2007). Recent major losses and/or pending major losses often tip the scales in favor of students acting rashly, especially when it is perceived there is no other way to solve the problem or end their suffering. Such emotions are not restricted to any one gender, race, or ethnicity. However, these feelings of hopelessness and the corresponding suicide attempts and lethality rate are higher for Black Americans than for White Americans (Durant, Mercy, Kresnow, Simon, Potter, & Hammond, 2006). Teams must be especially alert to students who have actively been seeking weapons and rehearsing attacks. It is important to ensure that barriers are low to report behavioral concerns to school staff by students, parents, and community. Threat assessment, crisis response, and monitoring follow-up are important functions of the Behavioral and Mental Health MTSS team to prevent school violence, respond to crises, and increase school safety. The PREPaRE training curriculum (NASP, 2017a) is one such crisis response model. A more preventative approach is the comprehensive Framework for Safe and Successful Schools that outlines the various tiers of intervention as part of an MTSS system and has been developed in partnership with, and vetted by, several national organizations: National Association of School Psychologists, American School Counselors Association, School Social Work Association of American, National Association of School Resource Officers, National Association of Elementary School Principals, and the National Association of Secondary Schools Principals (Cowan, Vaillancourt, Rossen, & Pollitt, 2013).

In July 2018, the U.S. Secret Service National Threat Assessment Center released an operational guide for preventing school violence, *Enhancing School Safety Using a Threat Assessment Model: An Operational Guide for Preventing Targeted School Violence*. The call for a "comprehensive targeted violence prevention plan" (p. 2) is comprised of eight steps that directly align with building and sustaining systematic SEB MTSS teams and functions in every school:

Step 1: Require each school to form a multidisciplinary threat assessment team, which meets on a regular basis, includes team members from a variety of disciplines, has a specifically designated leader, and has clearly established protocol, roles, and procedures.

Step 2: Define prohibited and concerning behaviors, which includes understanding the continuum of concerning behaviors, a low threshold for access to interventions, and assessing concerning statements and actions.

Step 3: Create a central reporting mechanism.

Step 4: Determine the threshold for law enforcement intervention.

Step 5: Establish assessment procedures.

Step 6: Develop risk management options.

Step 7: Create and promote safe school climates, with teachers actively building trusting relationships with students and helping students feel connected to one another and the school.

Step 8: Conduct training for all stakeholders.

These steps are accounted for in a school with functional implementation of multi-tiered systems of support.

All evidence supports Behavioral and Mental Health MTSS teams' structure, functions, and processes in a school setting. It is clear that MTSS is the ideal framework in which comprehensive targeted violence prevention plans may come to fruition. The Behavioral and Mental Health MTSS team outlined in this book more than meets the minimum standard for a multidisciplinary threat assessment team as described in the U.S. Department of Homeland Security and the United States Secret Service report, and should become the gold standard in both secondary and elementary schools.

Behavioral and Mental Health MTSS Meetings

Once structures, functions, and processes are in place to identify and prioritize the highest-risk students, the real work begins with interventions and progress monitoring. The school administration has made the mental and behavioral health of students a school priority, with vision and action. Like regular MTSS, the master calendar has been considered, team meeting dates and locations are memorialized, and intervention classes with research-based SEB curriculum are scheduled. Behavioral and Mental Health MTSS team members have been trained in roles and functions, the team chair selected, and school staff have been trained to spot and report potential red flags and been instructed on the importance of student-centered relationship building skills, communication, and team problem solving. Given the comprehensive nature of this framework, the planning and training of Behavioral and Mental Health MTSS usually begins prior to the school year in which it is to be implemented.

Behavioral and Mental Health MTSS team members will lay the groundwork for resource mapping within the school and out in the community: empowering change agents, creating safe spaces on campus, teaching students how to access supports, and growing relationships with community service providers and neighborhood community leaders. Family engagement efforts to encourage communication and collaboration between home and school are underway. Everything and everyone is in place to identify high-risk students and support them.

A universal school-wide SEB screener will detect indicators of internalizing and externalizing factors proactively, leading to scheduling SEB interventions and supports for Tier 2 and Tier 3 students, monitored by the regular MTSS team. If students with severe SEB issues are not getting the maximum Tier 3 supports on campus, they should be implemented immediately. As previously mentioned, the Behavioral and Mental Health MTSS team's caseload is selected by school counselors in collaboration with teachers, administration, and other mental health service providers on campus. Triangulation of data sources ensures that students do not slip through the cracks or receive unnecessary interventions for having a bad week or two. Some students who do not have a history of severe behavioral or mental health issues are in the midst of situational stressors that would adjust perceptions of SEB outbursts as falling within the range of normal response, such as homelessness or death of a family member, which would require patience and care to get through the difficult time period. Some socially-emotionally and behaviorally unstable students do not demonstrate academic delay or have overarching issues such as attendance problems, which might preclude them from rapid identification to be monitored by the regular MTSS team. High-risk SEB-involved students sometimes come up before the regular MTSS team, sometimes not. When students with Tier 3 mental health and behavioral needs exceed the resourcefulness of the regular MTSS and/or IEP teams, those students may go on to be monitored by the more intensive team, the Behavioral and Mental Health MTSS team. In doing so, students would still have access to resources allocated through regular MTSS, including: academic and behavior supports; progress monitoring; and behavioral plans written in partnership and supported by the consulting special education teacher, with school administration and staff coordinated in supporting teachers in implementation of behavior plans, and convenience of documentation of interventions through lesson plans and attendance logs. Many processes are virtually identical to regular MTSS, though it must be noted that academic and behavior functions performed by the regular MTSS team will not be replicated by this team.

The Behavioral and Mental Health MTSS Student Database includes brief documentation of pertinent history, SEB benchmark screener scores, academic benchmark scores, current behavioral performance and events, actions taken, next steps, and identified team members' responsibilities to follow-up. A Microsoft Excel spreadsheet or Google Sheet can be used. Columns may include student name, grade, identification number, assigned counselor, homeroom/advisory teacher, intervention classes or teachers currently on student's schedule, number of referrals to dean (current, and past years' when warranted) including types of referrals (i.e., assault vs. insubordination), scores on SEB benchmark screeners, academic benchmark scores, medical diagnoses and medication (if any), and dated case notes. The team chair, or designee, records and updates relevant case notes in real time for the team and distributes electronically or otherwise prior to the following meeting. All of the same historical factors as regular MTSS are reviewed for significance, including enrollments, attendance, grades, health, and discipline history. Data sources indicating functional levels across multiple settings, in addition to students' family ecology and home environment, are also considered.

Once the Behavioral and Mental Health MTSS Student Database is up to date, team members can refer to the Google Sheet or Microsoft Excel spreadsheet for review prior to and during participation at meetings. The team chair need not verbalize comprehensive student case notes but may briefly review presenting problems, review action steps recommended from previous meetings, check in with team members tasked with follow-up as designated, and open discussion to updates of how well things are going. These decisions are evidenced by data sources including current discipline events through dean's database, documented response to Tier 2 and Tier 3 interventions, medical updates, parent–teacher conferences, teacher reports, counselor reports, special education updates, law enforcement actions, and other information relevant to decision making.

Team members are focal points of student information, like regular MTSS case managers, gathering subjective and objective reports from school personnel, caregivers, and community service providers who have pertinent student information that may impact team decisions. For example, the school psychologist is a natural liaison with regular MTSS and special education teams regarding students identified with educational disabilities or suspected of such. Sharing team recommendations with interventionists and special educators in implementation of Tier 3 supports needed will allow school staff to effectively coordinate efforts. School counselors are natural liaisons to teachers who are likely to report experiences of abnormal student interactions to them. Likewise, school counselors are responsible for communicating with teachers regarding recommendations from the team that will impact students in the classroom. They may also take the lead in parent–teacher conferences or directly share plans with caregivers. Each Behavioral and Mental Health MTSS Team member may be assigned follow-up responsibilities that are specific and overlap. Typically, the Behavioral and Mental Health MTSS Team Chair will ask for volunteers or assign responsibilities based on presenting variables that match strengths, schedules, as well as roles, of team members.

School-based mental health providers will share burdens and take on tasks as team players, rather than only supporting the team with one specific duty or function. These dynamics will vary campus to campus depending on the relationships of school service providers and their ability or availability on any given day. Collegial support and leaving personal egos out of problem-solving processes is required, which builds trust and improves effective communication among team members. Reflective practices and feedback looping will inform whether practices are working as intended or revisions are required for implementation. Effective collaboration between Behavioral and Mental Health MTSS team members and school staff help teachers feel supported by administration in efforts to help students with the most severe SEB difficulties and, as a byproduct, creates a culture of team problem solving, professional collaboration, and trust. Students and schools are safer when all professionals on a campus are systematically looking out for at-risk students, actively attempting to solve problems with them including outreach and growth of support networks, providing case management and care, and closely monitoring outcomes.

Box 10.1

Connection to Practice

The LIQUID Model to Behavioral and Mental Health in Schools

Leadership

Effective school leaders provide ongoing opportunities for students, staff, and families to build competence and relationships to achieve personal and community social-emotional and behavioral health. Key components of Leadership to SEB health in schools:

- Prioritizes emotional health and well-being, proactive, listens to staff and community members' concerns, effectively addresses issues, and dedicates the right level of support
- Fully committed to funding Tier 1 social-emotional and behavioral learning opportunities and building Tier 2 and Tier 3 supports
- Sets performance goals, e.g., lowering expulsions, lowering student-to-student violence

- Treats staff, students, and parents with dignity giving voice, giving comfort
- Supports community resource networking
- Values competencies, visibly supports and empowers MTSS and Behavioral and Mental Health MTSS team members and functions
- Has an administrative presence and support at Behavioral and Mental Health MTSS team meetings
- Requires and reinforces SEB benchmark screenings throughout the year to help identify and track student behaviors
- Supervises SEB instruction to ensure fidelity of implementation

Inclusiveness

Making school relevant using culturally competent practices is a priority. Prevention, family outreach, community-based services, and lowering barriers to treatment improve access to supports and services. Key components of Inclusiveness to SEB health in schools:

- Universal, high-quality SEB learning experiences from K-12
- Explicitly taught community and social skills
- Implementation of valid behavioral interventions improves equity
- Higher accountability for educators enforcing discipline fairly
- Implicit bias must be addressed openly and directly
- Nurture critical thinking using cognitive behavioral strategies, increase cultural tolerance, and improve sensitivity and empathy
- Culturally competent teaching practices

Quality Control

Standardized processes and procedures are implemented to automate required components (scheduling, intervention class curriculum, documentation of data within tiered supports), and teams have confidence in the system and the quality of the interventions provided. Students get the help they need when they need it, with functional systems to provide timely services, and with reflective and corrective practices in place. Key components of Quality Control to SEB health in schools:

- Universal, high-quality SEB learning experiences from K-12 implemented with fidelity
- Evidence-based Tier 2 and Tier 3 SEB learning opportunities are accessible and implemented with fidelity
- Leaders conduct random fidelity checks of SEB curriculum and activities
- The quality control experts are school leadership and the school-based mental health providers (in accordance with evidence-based practices).
- All school administrators, school psychologist, school counselor, school nurse, school social worker, additional specialists and mentors meet regularly to discuss mental and behavioral health school-wide issues, identify and monitor the management of the highest-risk Tier 3 students, liaise with off-site stakeholders
- Regular communication between team and staff in the care of and planning for students *requiring intensive Tier 3 supports and services* is well coordinated
- Responsive to teachers and families who have students with SEB challenges

- Engage in crisis-response planning, implementation and debriefing
- Follow a continuous improvement model with feedback looping
- Build and grow supports, solve problems oftentimes with limited resources
- Keep barriers low for accessing SEB services

Universality

School-wide access to Tier I SEB instruction, with targeted and intensive supports available as needed. All students have access to intensity of instruction they require. Regardless of the severity of the academic or behavioral issue, each student is receiving quality support at their individual level. Every student has their SEB temperature checked at regular intervals to determine if follow-up services may be required. Continuous care and monitoring for those who need it, supports and functions are in place to allow opportunity for *all* students to access instruction. Key components of Universality to SEB health in schools:

- All students have access to early problem identification and intensified supports as needed in Tier 2 and Tier 3.
- All students participate in the universal SEB benchmark screenings, whether they have past history of problems or not.
- All students have access to supports and services if they have a demonstrated need.
- Social-emotional and behavioral skills are taught to all students using evidence-based practices at corresponding developmental age levels at Tier I. For example, all students receive social-emotional learning opportunities and they learn positive behavioral expectations across all areas on campus (classroom and school-wide).
- Tier I practices must meet standard criteria to align with evidence-based practices and teaching competencies. Tier I, Tier 2, and Tier 3 practices must meet standard criteria to align with evidence-based practices and teaching competencies.

Implementation and Feedback Looping

Schools must have structures, functions, and processes in place to support student SEB development and remediation. The MTSS and Behavioral and Mental Health MTSS teams work together to provide case management and actively solve problems for students demonstrating the need for additional SEB support through data sources. Staff and school community member input is valued and all are encouraged to freely contribute to the feedback loop of how responsive systems are to the needs of the school community. Program evaluation cycles allow for examining practices resulting in improved service delivery. It is imperative for teams to stay on top of resource mapping and create a referral database of the most current reliable and effective resources available to support student SEB health. Key components of Implementation and Feedback Looping to SEB health in schools:

- Put structures and functions in place to support all students behaviorally and develop social-emotional learning opportunities at Tiers I, 2, and 3.
- Select evidence-based SEB learning curricula and schedule delivery times in the master calendar.

- Support MTSS school functions by providing continual learning opportunities for teachers in classroom management and relationship building with students.
- SEL and PBIS (SEB) health is integrated and embedded in school culture to improve socially just practices.
- Build and support a mandatory site-based Behavioral and Mental Health MTSS team who share responsibilities for managing high-risk students. This team serves as the quality control panel for site-based problem solving and resource networking as it pertains to student behavioral and mental health, specifically, and student and school safety, in general. Team is responsible for examining and improving practices.
- Feedback looping cycles, both single-loop and double-loop, to inform on routine daily implementation and long-term program sustainability (see Chapter 11).

Data-Based Decision Making

Using a variety of data sources to make informed decisions about students, the efficacy of implementation of the MTSS framework, school culture, and staff procedures and processes helps teams prioritize and implement adequate supports to the needs of their unique schools. Data leads the discussions of whether practices are effective or not based on data trends, and fidelity of implementation must be ensured before accurate data-based decision making can occur. If trends indicate that systems or treatments are ineffective, then new solutions must be tried and closely monitored for quantitative and qualitative outcome data.

Key components of Data-Based Decision Making to SEB health in schools:

- Students are screened at least twice a year at regular benchmark intervals to strategically monitor their SEB performance levels.
- Students are systematically monitored for a number of indicators across data sources. When triangulated data suggests that interventions are required or new treatment is warranted, help happens and changes are made to address student deficits.
- Specialized, highly confidential, data used by the Behavioral and Mental Health MTSS team in solving problems for students with SEB issues may include behavioral, health, and developmental histories; scores on SEB benchmark screeners, counselor documentation and impressions; history or reports of trauma; psychological and psychoeducational evaluation reports; police history; medical/psychiatric report and records; parent report; student reports to teachers and staff; nurse's report; school psychologist report; discipline report; response to behavior plans/supports and progress monitoring data; teacher report and anecdotes; and reports of current events or problems on and off campus.
- Team meets at least every other week to discuss the entire caseload, new developments, and new directions for supports and services. They communicate regularly on *all* irregular student activities, major losses and disruptions, or events that may impact behavioral and mental health.
- Behavioral and Mental Health MTSS team members are responsible for communicating with parents, guardians, and outside agencies (with proper releases signed); and for actively contributing to feedback looping by mapping

and evaluating the usefulness of resources based on how well the services and service providers respond to needs of students referred to them.
- Barriers are addressed to improve access of care for students with SEB issues.
- Data-based decision making for SEB occurs according to the MTSS Evaluation Frequency and Intensity Framework (see Chapter 11).

Box 10.2

Voice from the Field

Healthy Minds, Safe Schools

Healthy Minds, Safe Schools is an example of putting initiative into action using the LIQUID Model, which is adaptable to the unique characteristics of individual school environments and aligns with the recommendations of the Framework for Safe and Successful Schools (Cowan et al., 2013). Healthy Minds, Safe Schools began in select urban schools as a comprehensive model to systematically implement social-emotional learning (SEL) *and* positive behavioral interventions (PBIS) in high-need schools (Dockweiler & Clark, 2018).

Healthy Minds, Safe Schools is a trademark of
Dockweiler & Clark, 2018.

The marrying of SEL and PBIS tenets into a combined social-emotional-behavioral (SEB) framework is a novel approach supported by research as one of the most impactful ways to improve student mental and behavioral well-being (Cook, Frye, Slemrod, Lyon, Renshaw, & Zhang, 2015). While SEL and PBIS alone result in impactful outcomes, combining the two has an impressive effect size that exceeds 1.0 and far outperforms the implementation of either group individually (Cook et al., 2015). The SEB approach of Healthy Minds, Safe Schools methodically addresses internalized and externalized behaviors on both elementary and secondary campuses, and is conducive to a phased rollout. It is a flexible model for schools to customize based on the unique needs of their campuses from a selection of various programming and curricular options.

Healthy Minds, Safe Schools seeks to increase students' protective factors, resilience, problem-solving skills, emotional regulation, and behavioral performance; to reduce office referrals; and to reduce student-to-student violence (Dockweiler & Clark, 2018). It aligns with esteemed and well-known evidence-based practices of the Collaborative for Academic, Social, and Emotional Learning (Aspen Institute, 2018), positive behavior intervention supports (Sprick, 2009), and provides SEB instructional support to teachers with coaching through the Principles of

Accomplished Teaching (National Board for Professional Teaching Standards, 2016). Community support and family engagement are critical pieces of the framework that provide an additional layer of protective supports for students and staff.

Case Studies

Middle School A began implementing Healthy Minds, Safe Schools due to an overwhelming increase in the number of students thinking about, threatening, and attempting suicide. The school team could no longer afford to use short-term fixes to solve their students' social-emotional and behavioral problems. A comprehensive, long-term solution was called for; school teams knew *what* the problem was and *why* addressing it was important. What they did not have was the *how*. Healthy Minds, Safe Schools was birthed from evidence-based practices as the how.

Middle School A is an urban Title I school with a population of approximately 1,350 students. The student population is 96 percent free-reduced lunch and 95 percent limited English proficient; 84 percent Hispanic and 11 percent Black (Nevada Report Card, 2018). The transiency rate has been near 50 percent for the past ten years. Middle School A already had a healthy culture for Academic MTSS, so when the waves of students in crisis peaked, the Behavioral and Mental Health MTSS grew to respond to intensity and volume of student need. Tier 1 and Tier 2 included evidence-based curriculum delivered during home-room universally and during scheduled Tier 2 SEB classes. Tier 3 supports were layered incrementally to individually address student needs, in addition to increasing outreach to community resources.

The Behavioral and Mental Health MTSS team met regularly to discuss and actively manage the highest-risk students. Over the next two years, student-to-student violence decreased 28 percent with the implementation of Healthy Minds, Safe Schools (Dockweiler & Clark, 2018). To put this 28 percent decrease in perspective, nearly half of all discipline incidences statewide fell under the category of Violence to Other Students. This number of incidences has remained virtually unchanged (decreased 0.81 percent) in the last decade (Nevada Report Card, 2018). For Middle School A to decrease their student-to-student violence rate by 28 percent in two years is quite significant and has become a sought-after model to scale.

Elementary School B began implementing Healthy Minds, Safe Schools with a two-year phased roll-out. Four months into the two-year roll-out, the school had already decreased their office behavioral referrals by 33.7 percent (Dockweiler & Clark, 2018). Elementary School B is a Title I school with approximately 950 students, with 55 percent being free-reduced lunch and 11 percent limited English proficient; 24 percent Hispanic, 24 percent Caucasian, 22 percent Asian, and 17 percent Black (Nevada Report Card, 2018). Data collection efforts are underway targeting internalized as well as externalized behaviors, teacher efficacy, school culture and leadership, and how behaviors are linked to student academic achievement.

Healthy Minds, Safe Schools is currently being scaled out at both the elementary and secondary levels, and is receiving praise for its comprehensive and customizable approach to addressing students' social-emotional-behavioral needs on campus. This proactive approach, based on the MTSS framework, is showing great success in the reduction of externalized behaviors and is promising in the early identification and remediation of internalized behaviors.

References

Aspen Institute: National Commission on Social, Emotional, and Academic Development (2018). *How learning happens: Supporting students' social, emotional, and academic development.* Washington, DC: Author.

Benner, G. J., Kutash, K., Nelson, J. R., & Fisher, M. B. (2013). Closing the achievement gap of youth with emotional and behavioral disorders through multi-tiered systems of support. *Education and Treatment of Children, 36*(3), 15–29.

Bonanno, C. M., & Levenson, R. L. (2014). School shooters: History, current theoretical and empirical findings, and strategies for prevention. *Sage Open, 4*(1). Retrieved from https://doi.org/10.1177/2158244014525425.

Boston Public Schools (2017). *What is CBHM?* Retrieved from http://cbhmboston.com/what-is-cbhm.

Braak, H., Braak, E., Yilmazer, D., & Bohl, J. (1996). Topical review: Functional anatomy of human hippocampal formation and related structures. *Journal of Child Neurology, 11*(4), 265–275.

Brackett, M. A., Reyes, M. R., Rivers, S. E., Elbertson, N. A., & Salovey, P. (2011). Assessing teachers' beliefs about social and emotional learning. *Journal of Psychoeducational Assessment, 30*(3), 219–236.

Brezicha, K., Bergmark, U., & Mitra, D. L. (2015). One size does *not* fit all: Differentiating leadership support to support teachers in school reform. *Educational Administration Quarterly, 51*(1), 96–132.

Brooks, R., Brooks, S., & Goldstein, S. (2012). The power of mindsets: Nurturing student engagement, motivation, and resilience in students. In S. L. Christenson, A. L. Reschly, & C. Wylie. *Handbook of research on student engagement* (pp. 541–562). New York: Springer.

Bryk, A. S., Gomez, L. M., Grunow, A., & LeMahieu, P. G. (2016). *Learning to improve: How America's schools can get better at getting better.* Cambridge, MA: Harvard Education Press.

Cannata, M., McCrory, R., Sykes, G., Anagnostopoulos, D., & Frank, K. A. (2010). Exploring the influence of National Board certified teaching in their schools and beyond. *Education Administration Quarterly, 46*(4), 463–490.

Cavanaugh, B. (2016). Trauma-informed classrooms and schools. *Beyond Behavior, 25*(2), 41–46.

Charner-Laird, M., Kirkpatrick, C. L., Szczesiul, S., Watson, D., & Gordon, P. (2016). From collegial support to critical dialogue: Including new teachers; voices in collaborative work. *Professional Educator, 40*(20), 1–17.

Christiansen, E., & Jensen, B. F. (2007). Risk of repetition of suicide attempt, suicide or all deaths after an episode of suicide: A register-based survival analysis. *Australian & New Zealand Journal of Psychiatry, 41*(3), 257–265.

Cook, C. R., Frye, M., Slemrod, T., Lyon, A. R., Renshaw, T. L., & Zhang, Y. (2015). An integrated approach to universal prevention: Independent and combined effects of PBIS and SEL on youths' mental health. *School Psychology Quarterly, 30*(2), 166–183.

Cowan, K. C., Vaillancourt, K., Rossen, E., & Pollitt, K. (2013). *A framework for safe and successful schools.* Bethesda, MD: National Association of School Psychologists.

Dockweiler, K. A., & Clark, A. G. (2018, April). *Multi-tiered systems of support: Behavioral and mental health in schools.* Paper session presented at the Nevada Department of Education Mega Conference, Las Vegas, Nevada.

Durant, T., Mercy, J., Kresnow, M., Simon, T., Potter, L., & Hammond, W. R. (2006). Racial differences in hopelessness as a risk factor for a nearly lethal suicide attempt. *Journal of Black Psychology, 32*(3), 285–302.

Fein, R. A., Vossekuil, B., Pollack, W. S., Borum, R., Modzeleski, W., & Reddy, M. (2004). *Threat assessment in schools: A guide to managing threatening situations and to creating safe school climates.* Retrieved from U.S. Department of Education website: www2.ed.gov/admins/lead/safety/threatassessmentguide.pdf.

Felitti, V. J., Anda, R. F., Nordenberg, D., Williamson, D. F., Spitz, A. M., Edward, V., Koss, M. P., & Marks, J. S. (1998). Relationship of childhood abuse and household dysfunction to many of the leading causes of death in adults: The adverse childhood experiences (ACE) study. *American Journal of Preventative Medicine, 14*(4), 245–258.

Goldstein, A. (1999). *PREPARE: A prosocial curriculum for aggressive youth.* Champagne, IL: Research Press.

Hall, G. E., & Hord, S. M. (2006). *Implementing change: Patterns, principles, and potholes* (2nd ed.). Boston, MA: Pearson Education.

Harrison, J. R., Vannest, K. J., & Reynolds, C. R. (2017). Social acceptability of five screening instruments for social, emotional, and behavioral challenges. *Behavioral Disorders, 38*(3), 171–189.

Hirschield, P. J. (2008). Preparing for prison? The criminalization of school discipline in the USA. *Theoretical Criminology, 12*(1), 79–101.

Lally, P., van Jaarsveld, C. H. M., Potts, H. W. W., & Wardle, J. (2010). How are habits formed: Modelling habit formation in the real world. *European Journal of Social Psychology, 40*(6), 998–1009.

Long, N. J., Wood, M. M., & Fecser, F. A. (2001). *Life space crisis intervention: Talking with students in conflict* (2nd ed.). Charlottesville, VA: Pro-Ed.

Maag, J. W., & Katsiyannis, A. (2010). School-based mental health services: Funding options and issues. *Journal of Disability Studies, 21*(3), 173–180.

Mazer, J. P., Thompson, B., Cherry, J., Russell, M., Payne, H. J., Kirby, E. G., & Pfohl, W. (2015). Communication in the face of a school crisis: Examining the volume and content of social media mentions during active shooter incidents. *Computers in Human Behavior, 53*, 238–248.

McCarthy, C. J., Lambert, R. G., Lineback, S., Fitchett, P., & Baddouh, P. G. (2016). Assessing teacher appraisals and stress in the classroom: Review of the classroom appraisal of resources and demands. *Education Psychology Review, 28*, 577–603.

Naglieri, J. A., Goldstein, S, & LeBuffe, P. (2010). Resilience and impairment: An exploratory study of resilience factors and situational impairment. *Journal of Psychoeducational Assessment, 28*(4), 349–356.

National Association of School Psychologists (2017a). *PREPaRE training curriculum.* Retrieved from www.nasponline.org/professional-development/prepare-training-curriculum/about-prepare.

National Association of School Psychologists (2017b). *Talking to children about violence: Tips for parents and educators.* Retrieved from www.nasponline.org/resources-and-publications/resources/school-safety-and-crisis/talking-to-children-about-violence-tips-for-parents-and-teachers.

National Association of School Psychologists (2018). *School security measures and their impact on students* [Research summary]. Bethesda, MD: Author.

National Board for Professional Teaching Standards (2016). *What teachers should know and be able to do.* Arlington, VA: Author.

National Implementation Research Network (2017, August 8). Retrieved from http://nirn.fpg.unc.edu.

National Resource Center for Mental Health Promotion and Youth Violence Prevention (2017, August 8). Retrieved from www.healthysafechildren.org/sites.

Nevada Report Card (2018). Retrieved from http://nevadareportcard.com/di.

Patient Protection Affordable Care Act of 2010, 42 U.S.C. §18001 *et seq* (2010).

Payne, B. K., & Vuletich, H. A. (2017). Policy insights from advances in implicit bias research. *Policy Insight from the Behavioral and Brain Sciences, 5*(1), 49–56.

Perry, B. D. (2002). *Training series 2: Six core strengths for healthy child development.* Houston, TX: The Child Trauma Academy.

Perry, B. D., & Hambrick, E. P. (2008). The neurosequential model of therapeutics. *Reclaiming Children and Youth, 17*(3), 38–43.

Reeves, M. A. L., & Brock, S. E. (2017). School behavioral threat assessment and management. *Contemporary School Psychology*. Retrieved from https://doi.org/10.1007/s40688-017-0158-6.

Ross, S. W., & Sabey, C. V. (2014). Check-in check-out + social skills: Enhancing the effects of check-in check-out for students with social skill deficits. *Remedial and Special Education, 36*(4), 246–257.

Sabey, C. V., Charlton, C. T., Pyle, D., Lignugaris-Kraft, B., & Ross, S. W. (2017). A review of classwide or universal social, emotional, behavioral program for students in kindergarten. *Review of Educational Research, 87*(3), 512–543.

Schüll, N. D., & Zaloom, C. (2011). The shortsighted brain: Neuroeconomics and the governance of choice in time. *Social Studies of Science, 41*(4), 515–538.

Senate Bill 504, Nevada (2015).

Sprick, R. A. (2009). *CHAMPS: A proactive and positive approach to classroom management* (2nd ed.). Eugene, OR: Pacific Northwest Publishing.

Sprick, R. A. (2013). *Discipline in the secondary classroom: A positive approach to behavior management* (3rd ed.). Hoboken, NJ: John Wiley & Sons.

Sprick, R., Booher, M., & Garrison, M. (2009). *Behavioral response to intervention*. Eugene, OR: Pacific Northwest Publishing.

Substance Abuse and Mental Health Services Administration (2017a). *Adverse childhood experiences*. Retrieved from www.samhsa.gov/capt/practicing-effective-prevention/prevention-behavioral-health/adverse-childhood-experiences.

Substance Abuse and Mental Health Services Administration (2017b). *Risk and protective factors*. Retrieved from www.samhsa.gov/capt/practicing-effective-prevention/prevention-behavioral-health/risk-protective-factors.

U.S. Secret Service National Threat Assessment Center. (2018). *Enhancing school safety using a threat assessment model: An operational guide for preventing targeted school violence*. Retrieved from www.dhs.gov/sites/default/files/publications/18_0711_USSS_NTAC-Enhancing-School-Safety-Guide.pdf.

Villarreal, V., & Castro-Villarreal, F. (2016). Collaboration with community mental health service providers: A necessity in contemporary schools. *Intervention in School and Clinic, 52*(2), 108–114.

Vossekuil, B., Fein, R. A., Reddy, M., Borum, R., & Modzeleski, W. (2004). *The final report and findings of the Safe Schools Initiative: Implications for the prevention of school attacks in the United States*. Retrieved from U.S. Department of Education website: www2.ed.gov/admins/lead/safety/preventingattacksreport.pdf.

Watkins, A. M., & Maume, M. O. (2011). School victims and crime reporting. *Youth Violence and Juvenile Justice, 9*(4), 333–351.

Whitford, D. K., Katsiyannis, A., & Counts, J. (2016). Discriminatory discipline: Trends and issues. *NASSP Bulletin, 100*(2), 117–135.

Wiley, K. E., Anyon, Y., Yang, J. L., Pauline, M. E., Rosch, A., Valladares, G., Downing, B. J., & Pisciotta, L. (2018). Looking back, moving forward: Technical, normative, and political dimensions of school discipline. *Education Administration Quarterly, 54*(2), 275–302.

Zaykowski, H. (2012). Reporting physical assault: How experiences with violence influence adolescents' response to victimization. *Youth Violence and Juvenile Justice, 11*(1), 44–59.

Chapter 11

Program Evaluation and Feedback Looping

Key Terms

Iterative
MTSS Evaluation Frequency and Intensity Framework
Outside Evaluator
Feedback Looping
Logic Model

Chapter Concepts

In this chapter, readers will learn:

1. How to integrate a program evaluation schedule into their implementation efforts.
2. How to analyze data from the evaluation cycles to inform continuous improvement to the model.
3. How to use an MTSS Evaluation Frequency and Intensity Framework to guide evaluation cycles.
4. The importance of feedback looping and iterative evaluation mechanisms.
5. How the conditions of LIQUID are met through program evaluation and feedback looping.

A program is only as successful as its evaluation, reflection, and revision. No program can remain nimble and continue to meet the needs of those it serves without the capacity for refinement. New programs require courage and innovation to work things differently, and refinement processes occur simultaneously with implementation through lessons learned on the way. It is always recommended to re-evaluate practices comprehensively at the end of each school year, but the school year need not be over to reflect and revise. Established programs require tenacity to sustain successful systems and processes while replacing ineffective practices with targeted solutions. In this Chapter, readers will learn the importance of integrating a program evaluation schedule into the implementation of their MTSS. These regular evaluation cycles will serve to inform on the effectiveness of the program and ensure that no time or energy is spent needlessly (Yuen, Terao, & Schmidt, 2009).

Program Evaluation

Unintended consequences, poor treatment effect, and negative trends are all possible outcomes in program implementation, but these are risks teams must be willing to take and are not permanent conditions in a system of continuous improvement. Productive reflective processes strengthen organizations and professional relationships with collective experiences designed to strengthen the organization and professional relationships. When analyzing data trends for decision making, relationship skills with team members may become complicated. Some team members may have differing agendas or be attached to certain outcomes, or they may come to different conclusions about causes and effects. Counterproductive behaviors and attitudes, such as finger pointing and blaming, may also occur.

When data demonstrates students' growth and improvement, joy and celebration occurs. When the data demonstrates students' lack of growth or academic or behavioral decline, educators may feel discouraged or entrenched in faulty assumptions and thinking patterns. They may try to "fix" problems without adequately evaluating all the components of program and service delivery before making targeted changes. Effective instruction relies on a multitude of variables and methods for measuring those variables, which impact outcomes. School problem solving teams must have confidence that they understand those variables, have the ability to influence those variables, and are using the right outcome measures to inform practices. Determining which changes to make, and how to make them, requires interpersonal skills to negotiate team discussions resulting in decisions that can be supported by all within the organization. A respectful, collaborative professional environment allows for delivery and support of corrective actions in regard to implementation fidelity of high-quality curriculum. Instruments selected for feedback looping, including both qualitative and quantitative measures, may be used for different purposes. Some will be used as a broad measure to evaluate total outcomes, while some will be selected due to their sensitivity in identifying and detecting changes in the trajectory of discrete skill development, cultural attitudes, and systems which support those discrete skills.

A program implemented without constant reflection and evaluation will not last, nor will it be successful while it is in operation. Implementing a program, or a framework, without an established evaluation cycle results in entropy, much like letting small children run loose on a playground: some will branch off and play alone, some will run in circles, one might climb the fence and run away, and others may play in groups, collaboratively or combatively, with no clear organization or goal. Without regular check-ins, structured evaluative and problem solving systems with timeframes in which to regroup, a program can run amok quickly.

Program evaluation begins before the program even starts. Key members of the program evaluation team include the school administration, representation from the MTSS team who has an interest or expertise in program implementation or data collection, and the school psychologist. The program evaluation team may select a planning measure, such as the Hexagon Tool (Blase, Kiser, & Van Dyke,

2013), to evaluate the implementation readiness of their program before rolling it out. The Hexagon Tool investigates six components: needs, fit, resource availability, evidence, readiness for replication, and capacity to implement. If a team is lacking any of these critical components, then they have an opportunity to bolster their weak areas before the school year starts to see that their MTSS program is a success once it is introduced to staff in the fall. It is recommended that members of the program evaluation team be assigned one or more of the six components, collect relevant data, and report back to the team (Blase et al., 2013). The team then completes the corresponding Hexagon Tool rubric to determine their score, or level of readiness, in each of the six categories. Whether or not a team selects a specific planning measure, it is important to consider the fundamental questions of which needs will be targeted, how the targeted needs will be supported systematically, what resources are needed, which outcome measure(s) will be monitored, and whether evidence supports continuing or revising practices over time.

MTSS Evaluation Frequency and Intensity

There are several components of an MTSS program that must be evaluated on an iterative cycle. *Iterative* refers to a repeated process that occurs at regular intervals with the purpose of achieving an established goal. Comparing actual rate of improvement to expected rate of improvement at consistent intervals over time will guide teams in their decision making with regards to maintaining or replacing current practices. *Programs must regularly be refined to maximize efficacy and effectiveness.* In an effort to find solutions with substantial and immediate outcomes, educators often throw the baby out with the bath water when instead they should give the baby some time to grow with proper nutrition and care. Oftentimes, a program is deemed ineffective, when in reality, if it had undergone another round or two of iterative feedback, it would have been successful (Epstein & Klerman, 2013). Program evaluation can be accomplished in MTSS through the use of an MTSS Evaluation Frequency and Intensity Framework (see Figure 11.1). Under the *MTSS Evaluation Frequency and Intensity Framework*, some practices must be evaluated universally, or on a regular basis, largely through formative assessment measures. Others must be evaluated on a targeted basis, for example during benchmark windows; while some will require intensive, in-depth, and thorough investigation, such as an annual report of the program.

Data must be collected and evaluated on an iterative basis to effectively inform on the MTSS program and to enhance service-delivery at all levels of intensity: student, staff, and school. At the core, efforts must be made to collect information from the micro- to the macro-levels, and at various frequencies, throughout the school year. Data collected at each of the three intensities can be analyzed in isolation, as well as how they contribute to the larger MTSS program, depending on what outcomes the team is looking to reflect upon. Some practices must be evaluated universally, on a regular or daily basis, largely through formative assessment measures. Some practices must be evaluated on a more intensive, targeted basis, such as at benchmark periods; while others will require intensive, in-depth and comprehensive investigation, such as an annual report of the program.

Working backwards from the macro-level, the intensive investigation may include an end-of-the-year program summary that can summarize the program's

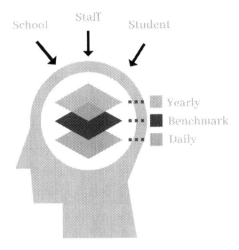

Figure 11.1 MTSS Evaluation Frequency and Intensity Framework.

goals and the school's progress toward meeting those goals. This document is a compilation of multiple data collection cycles and sources and can be used for planning purposes and to share with stakeholders, including state departments of education, individual school districts, or community interest groups. If the MTSS work is being conducted under a grant, or receives funds as part of larger grant project, this type of intensive reporting is typically conducted and reported by an outside evaluator. This *outside evaluator* is an impartial person hired to collect data and report out on the program's progress toward their stated goals; the report may include information about resource utilization, efficiency, effectiveness, and fiscal allocations. If the work is not being conducted under a grant, as outside funding is not necessary to restructure and repurpose the existing resources on a campus, it is still best-practice to have an annual meeting to review the MTSS goals, progress, barriers, and opportunities.

Targeted program evaluation would occur at regular intervals such as quarterly or at benchmark cycles, depending on how the school or district is calendared. This information would be collected to inform upon student progress, teacher efficacy, or program targets. For example, at the student level, regular benchmark data can be collected to determine student progress in the key content areas or any academic domain of concern. At the staff level, if the school is implementing a new math intervention curriculum, pre-, mid-, and post-surveys can be given to determine the teacher's efficacy in implementing the new intervention program to give school leaders an idea of where training opportunities may lie or where they may need to direct their efforts. At the school level, regular bench-marking can be used to monitor the roll-out of MTSS components. For example, if a school decides to implement a Behavior and Mental Health MTSS program but does not have the resources to implement all three tiers with fidelity, or if they do not have sufficient planning time to build the entire program before the school year starts, establishing a roll-out calendar with pre-set benchmarks and targets will help keep the school team on track as stages of implementation develop. For example, targeting 6th graders in a middle school for universal SEB benchmarking and instruction, and then adding 7th grade screening and supports in addition to 6th grade the following year, and so on. There may be unanticipated barriers that can threaten the implementation schedule, which requires stakeholders to review and revise the roll-out schedule. Comparing actual progress to desired progress at regular intervals will help keep a program's overall implementation schedule on track. Active problem solving by the leadership team, with a sense of urgency to stay on schedule, can often be the tipping point for successful incremental growth and sustainability.

Universal program evaluation must occur at the micro-level on a regular basis to ensure that universal instruction is being provided, that interventions are being implemented, and that progress monitoring probes are being executed with fidelity. *The universal level of an MTSS program is its foundation and without proper implementation, the structure falls apart.* Each member on campus must hold themselves accountable to implement universal learning opportunities with fidelity on a daily basis, and if they are not sure how to implement a piece of the curriculum or program, they must have the confidence to ask through an established pathway in which to seek advice.

Checks and balances can be used to reinforce this daily fidelity. In the classroom, this includes randomized observations and drop-ins from school leaders. Administrative and mentor observations can inform on the general instructional techniques and content delivery of the staff. It can also serve to inform on the classroom management, or lack of management, style in the classroom. This can be an opportunity for peer coaching if there is a specific piece of the universal foundation that is missing from a teacher's repertoire.

Frequent checks should also be made during intervention and progress monitoring sessions. If the intervention probes are not being conducted according to the standardized procedures, then the data collected becomes questionable and cannot be deemed valid for making decisions about students. For example, when delivering AIMSweb R-CBM probes, the student should be positioned in such a way that they cannot see the examiner's paper or computer screen. There have been cases where the teacher sat the child down next to them and had them read the passage from their computer screen. As the student misread a word, the teacher clicked on it and marked it wrong. This violates the standardized procedures of the assessment and has a negative impact on the student's psyche. Such an instance must be reported to the school administrator who needs to address this issue with the teacher and offer opportunities for training. If practices are not upheld with fidelity, the entire integrity of the program suffers, and quality control diminishes.

Evaluation Tools

There are several tools available to evaluate programs depending on the unit under investigation. For example, if a school is implementing a program to reduce students' problematic behaviors, the School Wide Positive Behavior Intervention Support (Algozzine, Barrett, Eber, George, Horner, Lewis, Putnam, Swain-Bradway, McIntosh, & Sugai, 2014) evaluation tool can be used to determine the effect of the program school-wide. For social-emotional status, regular screeners can be used to determine the trajectory of reported internalized and externalized maladaptive behaviors over time. For academic evaluation, schools often determine the success of their intervention program by an increase in student performance on high-stakes tests. However, these measures may not be sensitive enough to pick up on positive student growth, and other tools are recommended to celebrate incremental gains and progress. If the school has a particularly high transiency rate, the team will want to take this information into account and may want to consider comparing the progress of only the students who have been in attendance at that school since the very beginning of the school year and have had the full benefits of MTSS supports.

Feedback looping is integral to any type of evaluation and is a prevalent tool used by institutional organizations, which includes the bureaucratic field of education (DiMaggio & Powell, 1991). *Feedback looping* is when the outputs of a reflection or outcome are used as inputs to inform and improve upon the next phase of the cycle. Feedback looping can be either single loop or double loop; each serves a specific purpose (Hanson, 2001, 2003). Single looping is feedback on the updating of routine and repetitive aspects of a program (Argyris, 1999; Hanson, 2001). In the school setting, this may be likened to the universal, micro-level components such as instruction, program delivery, and daily check-ins. Double looping involves acquiring new knowledge to promulgate the long-term success of an organization or program in an ever-changing environment (Argyris, 1999; Hanson, 2001). This may include annual review of cumulative evaluative measures, benchmark trends, and staff efficacy reports. In this vein:

> Smart organizations are also cognizant that all acquired knowledge is not equal when it comes to organizational learning for problem-solving. With single-loop learning, the acquired knowledge is for the short term and intended to facilitate routine day-to-day problem-solving. Double-loop learning, on the other hand, is intended to ensure the long-term future of the organization by analyzing core issues and making policy judgments.
>
> (Hanson, 2001, p. 658)

Before the school year starts, the school's leadership team should determine what evaluation tools to use, how often to use them, who will be responsible for their execution, what feedback loops exist and what new ones may need to be created, who will be responsible for the data, and how the data will be used. It is helpful to calendar these evaluative meetings before the school year starts so that other priorities do not get in the way. If a school establishes quarterly benchmark assessments to monitor student progress (academic, social-emotional-behavioral), it is recommended that the leadership team meet at a similar interval. That way, after the students are benchmarked, the team can sit down, review all the data, and make decisions about the program and students.

At the macro-level, the team can determine if the procedures and programmatic tools are aligning with the pre-established program benchmarks. Any major issues can be discussed and through feedback looping, be used as inputs for improvement moving into the next quarter of MTSS implementation. At a less aggregate level, grade level or classroom data can be reviewed to determine if there are any significant irregularities. For example, if 6th and 8th graders are showing progress with their basic reading skills, but 7th graders are not, perhaps there is an underlying issue with the 7th grade teachers that the MTSS team will need to identify and remediate. At the micro-level, the team can determine which students are making progress, who can be exited from programming, and who may need an intervention change.

All data collected can be used to inform program decisions and assist in making causal inferences by way of a logic model (Epstein & Klerman, 2013). A *logic model* can be used as an effectiveness framework to ensure inputs are leading to desired outputs in the short and long term. There are a variety of models available for teams to adopt, and they can be customized depending on the needs, inputs, and outputs a team deems necessary. The MTSS team will want to assign one or two people to the duties of collecting data that can be used to inform the logic model. This information can be collected during each of the evaluation meetings that follow the regular benchmarking periods. They may also engage researchers from local colleges and universities to assist with the data collection and analysis. The better the school is able to understand data and translate that data into meaningful interventions for students, the greater the opportunities and outcomes are for students.

School leadership may identify improving the capacity of the school leadership team to make data-driven decisions with efficacy as an area to monitor, while increasing intervention opportunities and outcomes for students. In this the case, a pre- and post-test Data-Driven Decision-Making Efficacy and Anxiety Inventory (3D-MEA) (Dunn, Airola, Lo, & Garrison, 2013) may be used. Depending on the resources of the team, including any researchers or research institution partners, success can be measured using the 3D-MEA as well as any subsequent analysis of variance investigations or content analysis of open-ended teacher reports.

At the teacher level, an evaluation tool can be selected to determine the teachers' efficacy in implementing a program. For example, if a school is implementing a school-wide social-emotional learning program, the Social and Emotional Learning Beliefs Scale (Brackett, Reyes, Rivers, Elbertson, & Salovey, 2012), can be used. In conducting a pre- and post-test, the Social and Emotional Learning Beliefs Scale can be used to determine teacher comfort (sense of confidence), commitment (desire to participate), and culture (school-wide support) for implementing social-emotional learning in their classrooms. Based on feedback from the scale, teams can make decisions about what professional learning opportunities may need to be offered, how committed their teachers are to the social-emotional learning program, and what additional supports may be needed that will ultimately increase outcomes for students.

Regardless of the tool used to measure program progress and performance, several constants must be present:

- A planning assessment must be conducted to determine if the program can feasibly be rolled-out.
- Iterative feedback looping must transpire at regular intervals to hone and improve the program once it has been rolled-out.
- The MTSS Frequency and Intensity Framework must be followed.

- The team must decide what programmatic goals it would like to measure and select corresponding data collection tools.
- Regular meetings must occur to analyze, record data and progress, and make improvements.
- Team relationship building opportunities must be supported annually or more often as warranted. This may be in the form of maintenance workshops, effective teamwork activities, or team problem solving retreats.

As part of the program evaluation and iterative feedback cycle, all components of the LIQUID Model are constantly in a state of analysis. Leadership, inclusiveness, quality control, universality, implementation and feedback looping, and data-based decision making do not function independently, rather, they are all part of each other at various points of implementation. With regard to the second "I," implementation and feedback looping, this must be integral within each of the other components. Reflection on the overall implementation of MTSS and using feedback as inputs to drive future decision making are critical to leadership. Using these data, the school principal can make decisions based on evidence and can steer the MTSS team in the necessary direction. Inclusiveness based on feedback looping is a key goal of MTSS practices, and can be used to build a more socially just system. Without cultural competence embedded in teaching practices and school culture, the effectiveness of instruction will be significantly attenuated. Implementation and feedback looping are also critical to quality control; without it, the MTSS recipe would fall short and the cake would be flat. Universality addresses all students' needs with quality learning experiences and screens them for possible deficits allowing for early intervention. These educational practices are monitored by feedback looping for implementation fidelity. Data-based decision making permeates all ingredients of the MTSS recipe and goes hand in hand with implementation and feedback looping. MTSS requires constant evaluation, reflection, and revision to ensure that elements are the right proportion to make school equitable and relevant for each and every student.

References

Algozzine, B., Barrett, S., Eber, L., George, H., Horner, R., Lewis, T., Putnam, B., Swain-Bradway, J., McIntosh, K., & Sugai, G. (2014). *School-wide PBIS Tiered Fidelity Inventory.* OSEP Technical Assistance Center on Positive Behavioral Interventions and Supports. Retrieved from www.pbis.org.

Argyris, C. (1999). *On organizational learning* (2nd ed.). Malden, MA: Blackwell.

Blase, K., Kiser, L., & Van Dyke, M. (2013). *The Hexagon Tool: Exploring context.* Chapel Hill, NC: National Implementation Research Network, FPG Child Development Institute, University of North Carolina at Chapel Hill.

Brackett, M. A., Reyes, M. R., Rivers, S. E., Elbertson, N. A., & Salovey, P. (2012). Assessing teachers' beliefs about social and emotional learning. *Journal of Psychoeducational Assessment, 30*(3), 219–236.

DiMaggio, P. J., & Powell, W. W. (1991). The iron cage revisited: Institutional isomorphism and collective rationality in organizational fields. In P. J. DiMaggio & W. W. Powell (Eds.), *The new institutionalism in organizational analysis* (pp. 63–82). Chicago, IL: University of Chicago Press.

Dunn, K. E., Airola, D. T., Lo, W., & Garrison, M. (2013). What teachers think about what they can do with data: Development and validation of the data driven decision-making efficacy and anxiety inventory. *Contemporary Educational Psychology, 38*, 87–98.

Epstein, D., & Klerman, J. A. (2013). When is a program ready for rigorous impact evaluation? The role of a falsifiable logic model. *Evaluation Review, 36*(5), 375–401.

Hanson, M. (2001). Institutional theory and educational change. *Educational Administration Quarterly, 37*(5), 637–661.

Hanson, M. (2003). *Educational administration and organizational behavior.* Boston, MA: Allyn & Bacon.

Yuen, F. K. O., Terao, K. L., & Schmidt, A. M. (2009). *Effective grant writing and program evaluation: For human service professionals.* Hoboken, NJ: John Wiley & Sons.

Chapter 12

Advocacy and Policy Making

Key Terms

Stakeholder Networks
Connector
The Why
The Ask
Unfunded Mandate
Braided Funding
Formula Funding
Discretionary Grant Funding
Base Funding
Categorical Funding
Dedicated Funding

Chapter Concepts

In this chapter, readers will learn:

1. Where to begin their advocacy efforts and with whom.
2. How advocacy efforts differ at various levels of government.
3. The importance of identifying and integrating the why of others.
4. How to allow the initiative to evolve and grow by starting advocacy efforts early.
5. The importance of relationship building and maintenance.
6. What funding sources are available and why some options are better than others depending on the initiative.

Quality programming for students, along with structures and supports for staff, are not divorced from advocacy and policy making. As experts in their fields, education leaders have a duty to share evidence-based practices and research with others. If data and evidence are not driving the conversation, something else will. Pet projects, emotionally driven practices, and "that's just the way we do things" are all too common, and can be replaced by better policies and practices when educators advocate for, and demand, change.

This chapter delves into promoting best practice at the state and district levels, and advocating for policies that reflect these practices. Once a team's MTSS are up and running smoothly, how can it ensure that funding will remain available to support the program (Odden & Picus, 2014)? How can teams partner with stakeholder groups to advocate and promote MTSS programs; what examples currently exist (Dockweiler, 2016)? Who in a team's stakeholder network can elevate MTSS awareness and who in the network may be detrimental to its success and should be avoided like the plague? Understanding the perspectives, needs, and "whys" of stakeholder groups will help teams better navigate the complicated political arena and leverage existing relationships (Rigby, Woulfin, & Marz, 2016; Robinson, 2015). Advocating for, and legislating, evidence-based programs may not sound like a key piece of the recipe for MTSS success; however, it is critical for long-term student success.

Where to Begin?

Different advocacy is required depending on the level of government. MTSS advocacy is not only a federal or state policy issue; it is also relevant at the district and school levels (Morningstar, Allcock, White, Taub, Kurth, Gonsier-Gerdin, Ryndak, Sauer, & Jorgensen, 2016). At the district or school level, it might be as simple as presenting the MTSS concept to the school principal and gauging their level of buy-in. Similarly, at the district level, it might be as simple as presenting the notion to the local School Board or Superintendent. Stakeholder networks are vital to the success of initiatives. *Stakeholder networks* "are based on a common understanding and extend beyond a single stakeholder group, which can lead to greater impact in times of need" (Dockweiler, 2018, p. 26). They are a web of stakeholders who share similar interests and who can reach out within, and across, their own networks to spread news and help build support for an initiative.

In general, the further up the advocacy chain, the more stakeholders and community support will be needed. If the advocacy is at the school level, the stakeholders may include other respected educators, the school leadership team, or parent group(s). At the district level, stakeholders may include the local teachers' union, local administrators' union, non-profit organizations, and county associations. At the state level, stakeholder groups are going to include those with members state-wide; for example, the state administrators', teachers', and support staff's unions; state professional organizations (school boards, superintendents, school psychologists, speech and language pathologists, school nurses, school social workers, school counselors, etc.), state non-profit organizations, and state-level for-profit businesses. When advocating at the federal level, having local voice with a coalition of other state organizations, is going to be beneficial. The local voice will be beneficial to the specific congressional representative that covers that constituent base, whereas the coalition is going to lend strength to the breadth and depth of an issue. *A general rule of thumb: the higher the level of government or bureaucracy, the greater quantity and diversity of representation is going to be beneficial to push an agenda item through.*

Wherever the level of advocacy, whether it be school, district, state, or federal, the first thing an education leader must do is identify what the desired initiative is and what structures need to be put in place. From there, a map can be developed consisting of what's missing, or preventing (either inadvertently or blatantly), in the initiative and devise a plan. *Barrier identification is key because each barrier is going to need a unique and specific plan of attack to bring that barrier down.* Some strategies may be similar or linked, but until each barrier is identified, the problem cannot be comprehensively addressed or solved. As part of the strategy building, stakeholders and other individuals or professionals who are experiencing similar barriers can be brought in to strengthen the efforts and build a coalition. There are five key steps that need to take place on the front end before any advocacy work can even begin:

- Identify the desired initiative
- Identify the necessary level of advocacy
- Identify the barriers
- Identify the strategies to eliminate barriers
- Begin coalition building

These steps may take place organically, or they may take a more structured format. Often, one or two key individuals will recognize a problem, and will walk through these five steps without even knowing they are doing it. Other times, a group of leaders or associations may get together and may require guidance as to how best begin their efforts. The organic or structured format does not always correlate to level of advocacy. Great state-level advocacy efforts have been born from one person saying, "This isn't right."

Central to advocacy, coalition building, and demonstrating value is credibility. As professional educators, practitioners have the actual boots-to-ground experience of being "in the field" with the ability to accurately report on what they see happening daily from their credible perspectives in schools. While experience can build credibility, poor behavior and presentation can strip it away. Be mindful of not only what you say, but who you say it to, and in what manner. Written (email, Twitter, Facebook, other social media), verbal (formal and informal conversations), and nonverbal (body language and personal presentation) communication must always be respectful, professional, and tactful. Any transgressions can immediately erase an educator's credibility and result in the death of an educator's advocacy efforts or being blacklisted. Messaging is critical and finding ways to get a point across without being confrontational or accusatory can take time, but is essential to advocacy and coalition building.

How to Offer Value

Once the barriers and strategies have been identified and the coalition has been built, the individual(s) or group(s) must immediately begin formulating and offering solutions. It is not enough to simply say, "We want an MTSS program in our district," the group must show value and be a resource to stakeholders. Whoever is spearheading the efforts must offer viable solutions to remediating specific problems; while pathway A may be the preferred course to get to MTSS, also offer pathways B, C, and D as options because you never know what may resonate with those in decision-making positions and that may align with other initiatives that may currently be underway.

A word of advice for those educators whom advocacy and diplomacy do not come naturally: don't do what *you* would do, do what you believe someone in *your position* should do. This may feel a bit like acting at first, and will be very uncomfortable, as it is out of most people's typical scope of work; however, it is absolutely necessary. Whether you are a parent who disagrees with a particular law or practice at your child's school, or an educator who sees the unintended consequences of a policy day in and day out, it is your duty to stand up for your children. If you won't, who will? The old cliché is true, if it were easy, everyone would do it. *However, if it is uncomfortable, you are learning and growing, which will only serve to benefit your cause and children.*

Educators cannot be experts in all things. Bring in those with experience and expertise that differs from the norm who can offer unique perspectives. If funding is a major issue for an initiative, seek out an accountant, banker, lobbyist, or anyone else who is familiar with funding and funding streams. If you have a legal question, seek out a lawyer. Chances are, within your coalition, someone has a friend, or has a friend of a friend, or is related to someone who knows someone. *Leverage existing relationships to maximize the reach and strength of the collective group.* In education, the initiatives being proposed are (hopefully) in the best interest of children. Most people do not mind donating a few hours of their time to lend their professional expertise to an initiative that will benefit students. Sometimes what groups need is a *connector* in their organization or coalition, someone with high social capital who can put the group in touch with other like-minded individuals or with individuals who have a specific skill set that can benefit the initiative.

Consider solutions from many angles and from many perspectives. The group of education leaders who want to implement academic MTSS may have a different "why" than their principal, the superintendent, or the school board. The *why* is the individual's purpose or motivations behind their actions. The teachers' *why* may be: "We have students who are failing and we need to help them." The principal's *why* may be: "Students are struggling and bringing down the overall ratings of my school." The school psychologist's *why* may be: "Few of the referrals for special education testing are appropriate because no interventions have been put in place or have been documented." The parents' *why* may be: "My child is frustrated with school and doesn't want to go." While this is an oversimplified example of considering the whys, motivations, or purposes, of various stakeholders, if a solution, or ask, can be presented that positively addresses each stakeholders' concerns, it is a win-win for everyone. The *ask* is a specific request made from one individual or group to another. In this particular case, the ask would be a systematic manner in which to identify gaps in learning, provide interventions, and monitor student progress, in other words, an MTSS infrastructure with multiple levels of high-quality universal and targeted learning experiences. This particular ask may be made by educator leaders to the school principal, district representatives, or state representatives, depending on what level they are advocating for.

Typically, the whys of groups are often complicated and may be kept close to the vest, at least the *true* why behind what they are trying to achieve. Stakeholders are not necessarily duplicitous on purpose, but the messaging of their why may change depending on their audience. This is true for education leaders as well.

For example, knowing that the why of the principal is overall school performance, when teacher leaders approach the principal with their ask, they can frame the conversation around their why of noticing student failure and they can also incorporate the why of the principal into the dialogue. In doing so, the teacher leaders have demonstrated their value and have essentially solved a problem for the principal. If they can take it one step further and discuss solutions to funding, staff training, and scheduling, their value and resourcefulness will be even further amplified.

Advocate Early

Just as district and school level planning for the next school year begins before the current year ends, so does state legislation. If a group of leaders thinks it can begin building relationships with legislators during the legislative session and request that bills be filed, they are sadly mistaken. Leaders are cautioned to be mindful of bill draft timelines and to plan accordingly. For example, if state legislators can begin putting in bill drafts December 1, they will be looking for ideas and having conversations with organizations and individuals during the spring and summer prior, if not sooner. This allows them time to research the initiatives and bring together stakeholders that share similar concerns so there are not multiple bills being proposed that say nearly the same thing. It also gives them time to keep an eye out for competing initiatives. If a group has the ear of a legislator, continue to maintain a relationship with them and demonstrate value in and out of legislative sessions.

Ideally, relationships will be maintained so that new relationships will not need to be forged each session. *Relationship building is essential and time consuming, and it is easier to maintain a relationship than build a new one.* However, depending on the state or district, term limits may impact the length of time someone stays in office, such as on the local school board or state legislature. There are pros and cons to term limits and election cycles, with revolving-door relationship building certainly being one of the biggest downsides. Once a group has built a relationship with a legislator, school board member, or key decision maker, they are more likely to have their ear when issues arise. The key is to build relationships early, and outside times of crisis or necessity, so organizations or individuals can access that relationship in times of need. This access goes both ways and allows elected officials and other stakeholder groups to reach out to educator leaders when questions or concerns arise. Relationships must be maintained and sending informational emails updating the elected official as to what a group is doing is one quick and easy way to keep a presence.

Never take "no" for an answer. Sometimes "no" is simply "not yet," "not in this form," or "not with these people." Advocating early allows groups time and space to strengthen their efforts, gather more information, or take their initiative to someone else who sees the vision in the work. Oftentimes, initiatives arise out of a need to counter an existing proposal or practice. It can be a full-bodied response that screams: "We cannot do this to our children!" and, as a result, a counter practice, program, or policy is initiated. Be mindful that most policy is not devised from people with foresight sitting around a conference table thinking about all the good that can be done. More often, policy arises to fill a need or a gap in existing practice that wasn't even evident until something less than desirable happened. For example, many states and districts do not have mandated social-emotional-behavioral programming in place. These programs have been used infrequently by some schools in the form of social-emotional learning or positive behavior intervention supports, but were not brought to the front of America's consciousness until the recent years' school shootings, such as Parkland, Florida, and Santa Fe, Texas. Now parents, educators, and communities are screaming for increased mental-behavioral health supports and school safety policies. Behavioral and Mental Health MTSS (Chapter 10) is a great way to systematically address the social-emotional-behavioral needs of students and is a critical infrastructure for school leaders to advocate for at all levels of bureaucracy.

Having a window of opportunity to advocate for a particular initiative due to a recent crisis or a sudden public awareness benefits the advocacy process. Kingdon (1984) refers to this phenomenon as policy building through multiple streams, with the three streams being the problem, the solution, and the political will. Political change cannot happen without an initiative reaching the political agenda. Kindgon argues that these three streams must converge at a given point in time in order for this change to happen. If a problem has been identified and the perfect solution has been found, it will not make it into the public's consciousness without the political will. Until a legislator can be found to champion the cause, a bill draft will never be submitted let alone heard before a committee. And one legislator is not enough. Many legislators from both political parties must be on board and must be prepared to push the initiative through multiple committees, including finance, in order for a bill to pass out of the legislature successfully and to be signed by the Governor. Ultimately, if the Governor is not on board, a bill will not become law, even with legislative support.

Funding

Depending on the level and type of programming, various funding streams may be available and may vary significantly state by state. At the school level, certain programming options can be written into the school's budget. As long as the costs are not too exorbitant, school-level programming options can typically be funded, especially if the planning is done during the prior school year so priority can be given to the new program or initiative.

District level initiatives are costlier and are better received by individual schools, administrators, and staff if they are adequately funded. *Unfunded mandates* are statutory requirements or regulations imposed without funds provided to carry out the directive. These unfunded mandates, or underfunded mandates, are seen at the federal level with requirements put on state education agencies, and they are also seen at the state level with requirements put on the local education agencies. Unfunded mandates are some of the most difficult for schools to implement as they are often expected to do more with less. Again, planning is key, as districts and school board representatives can prepare, budget, and plan for new initiatives if they see them coming. Reactionary measures are taken when they are caught off guard, lose lawsuits, or are forced to make drastic cuts. Arbitration decisions with local unions also make a difference in what districts are required to pay, which in turn, impact the amount of money they have in their budgets for initiatives. Staff are a school's greatest asset and compensating them for their time, education, and expertise is essential. Local teachers' unions have been holding walkouts in states such as West Virginia, Kentucky, Oklahoma, Arizona, and Colorado in protest of low educator pay, and this has resulted in many educators receiving higher compensation. This compensation must come from somewhere, and if money is pulled from a district's budget to (rightfully) increase educator pay, something else in the budget must be decreased.

At the state level, a variety of funding sources are available from the federal budget, to supplement the state budget, for programs and human capital. *Braided funding* is the weaving of funds from multiple sources and is useful in maximizing impact without relying too heavily on any one funding source. The multiple sources can include the various funding levels of federal, state, or local and may include private and public funds. State education agencies can use federal funds and grant monies to offset and supplement local education agencies costs. The majority of states, 90 percent, use formula funding to cover education costs (Tilsley, 2017). In a very broad sense, *formula funding* is the dollar amount assigned from the state to each district based on various computed factors. To ensure equity and transparency of dollars spent, the majority of states:

> use data-driven, cost-based education funding formulas to meet these goals. Most of these formulas use accurate student data, account for differences among school districts, direct funding to address those differences, and do so with a goal of ensuring all students have adequate funding to meet state standards.
>
> (Klehr, Presson, Schaeffer, & Zelno, 2013, p. 1)

Discretionary grant funding are monies that are awarded through a competitive application process. Such grants are typically available at the federal level and have specific stipulations about who can apply, the amount of funds available, and what the funds can be allocated toward. In addition to federal public grant monies, state grant monies and private grant monies may also be available for qualifying organizations. Oftentimes, when applying for grant monies, in addition to the actual application, a budget must also be submitted that outlines where each dollar requested will be spent. Formula funding may be better for long-term planning of initiatives due to the temporary nature of grant funds. If a state receives federal grant funds for a particular program or initiative, after the grant expires, the funds are no longer available. If possible, it is ideal to get funding for a new statewide initiative into the Governor's budget as this ensures that monies will already be allocated to support it. As a result, when the bill is heard before the legislature, the likelihood of it passing increases as decisions about whether to fund a bill or not are less of an issue.

Looking at the Behavioral and Mental Health MTSS discussed in Chapter 10, several different funding scenarios may be present at the state level. First, a bill may be introduced into the legislature that requires each school in the state to implement a Behavioral and Mental Health MTSS model. Even if the model presented is data-driven and evidence-based, who is going to pay for its creation and implementation in the schools? Staff training would be required and materials would need to be purchased; there are many different ways in which schools would benefit from financial support to implement the initiative. If a bill does not pass out of committee, it will die. If a bill passes out of the introducing committee it could still die in the finance committee without the motivation of the committee chair and committee members to allocate monies to support it. If the bill does manage to pass through all the necessary committees without funds attached to it to support its implementation, and the Governor signs the bill into law, then districts could be faced with an unfunded mandate.

Looking at another scenario with the same Behavioral and Mental Health MTSS bill, the bill could also pass into law, but could come with funding provided by the state. If the Governor of a state knows when he or she is designing their budget that X is going to be a priority, specific funding amounts can be earmarked. Similarly, state legislatures can pass funding and budgeting requests, and the process for doing so will vary state by state. Various funding streams may be available to support education initiatives, such as base, categorical, and dedicated. *Base funding* is the amount of money a state sets aside to cover the basic costs of education. *Categorical funding* is reserved for a very specific program or purpose: "with categorical funds, priorities are set by the state to enact what state officials view as the most desirable programs. By its nature, categorical funding is narrowly directed, and as such, district flexibility is limited" (Smith, Gasparian, Perry, & Capinpin, 2013, p. 1). In the example of the implementation of a Behavioral and Mental Health MTSS program, categorical funds set aside for this could not be used by districts on other types of programs. Common uses for categorical funding may also include special education, gifted and talented education, and class-size reduction. *Dedicated funding* in a broad sense is somewhat similar except the monies are dedicated for a specific purpose, such as teacher salaries, through a dedicated funding source, such as specific tax revenues. Both have a practical use and it just depends on the initiative as to which is more appropriate.

A third, and optimal, scenario for the Behavioral and Mental Health MTSS legislation example is that the Governor of a state recognizes the initiative as an upcoming priority and puts money aside in their budget, *and* the state uses federal funds to back the initiative. In the case of mental-behavioral health and school safety, there are three suggested federal funding sources to investigate. First is Title I of the Every Student Succeeds Act (ESSA, 2015). This is a formula fund that passes monies from the state education agencies to the local education agencies. Monies from this funding source can go toward implementing school-wide programs, such as Behavioral and Mental Health MTSS, and to fund counseling and school-based mental health supports (National Association of School Psychologists (NASP), 2018). Title II of ESSA is also a formula fund for states to pass down to local education agencies and funds can be used for professional development on a variety of topics surrounding student well-being and safety. Title IV-A of ESSA is another formula fund for state education agencies to pass down to local education agencies surrounding the implementation of trauma-informed practices, comprehensive mental and behavioral health systems, violence prevention programs; the training of intervention and prevention programs for students at risk; and the development of restorative justice and positive discipline strategies versus exclusionary and punitive discipline (NASP, 2018). These various federal formula funds are also relevant to investigate for other related initiatives, not just those related to Behavioral and Mental Health MTSS.

Federal grants that support behavioral and mental health are also a good source of additional funds and worth exploring. Additionally, if a state currently does not have existing pathways for their school psychologists and other school-based mental health professionals to bill for Medicaid services, it would behoove the state to look into establishing this avenue as a funding source (Ekland, von der Embse, & Minke, 2015).

Moving Forward

If given the opportunity to assist in the writing of legislation, opt to use policy language that is written in the form of a commissive, not a directive. In doing so, effectiveness and impact of policies can better be determined (Dockweiler, Putney, & Jordan, 2015) and can lend information for iterative, data-based decision making. Also, in writing state policies with commissive statements, state level accountability will be easier to determine. Many state education policies are written in the form of a *directive*, which tells the local education agencies what to do, rather than a *commissive*, that commits itself to action (Dockweiler et al., 2015; Dockweiler, 2012). Policies that are written in the form of a directive make implementation fidelity difficult to determine; however, when policies are written in the form of a commissive, it is easier to determine if the intended actions have indeed been carried out (Dockweiler et al., 2015; Dockweiler, 2012). Typically, state legislative council bureaus, lawmakers, or non-educators write state education policies. Being involved in the policy writing process is a great opportunity for educational leaders to advocate for policies that are written using commissive statements and have state level accountability measures built in.

Box 12.1

Voice from the Field

It was the day after the 2016 presidential election. Ten weeks earlier, our Title I middle school staff, students, and families had been informed that our school could be forced into a newly formed Achievement School District (ASD) by the end of the year due to persistently low high-stakes test scores. Most of our students were English language learners, living well below the poverty line, and our school had a transiency rate that hovered around 50 percent. Unbeknownst to us, there was a hidden time-bomb tucked into the law established during the previous legislative session, which would force all public-school district employees out of selected schools, while the school building, computers, and all equipment inside the school would be turned over to a selected for-profit charter organization, to turn around school achievement for select schools in the state. The criteria for qualifying for the ASD included the bottom 5 percent state-wide of school performers on the annual high-stakes test, Smarter Balanced Assessment Consortium (SBAC), and our school fell within this range.

All neighborhood children would be forced to attend the charter school unless they could get their own transportation to attend the next closest public school. The school principal, teachers, support staff, students, and neighborhood families were stunned that our community school could be forcibly taken over, and an out-of-state charter school with no vested interest in the neighborhood or community would be given all the power to do with our children whatever they wanted or needed to do. Research on charter schools in places such as New Orleans, North Carolina, Arizona, Rhode Island, and Chicago does not indicate empirically better outcomes, and indicate a confluence of intermediaries and financial variables that contribute to charter school operations (DeBray, Scott, Lubienski, & Jubbar, 2014; Chingos & West, 2015; Paino, Renzulli, Boylan, & Bradley, 2013; Teresa & Good, 2017; Wronowski, 2017). The extracurricular activities and clubs that students depended on for enrichment and engagement would no longer be offered. None of the supports and services helping our families and children, including assistance with basic needs, disabilities, and behavioral-mental health problems would be guaranteed for students the following year. Our whole community was horrified and turned otherwise benign constituents into activists.

A minimum of six schools from across the state were to be selected to forcibly participate in the ASD. A long list of schools put forth by the state Department of Education turned into a short list of schools to be considered. All the schools identified for take-over in the state happened to be located within a 20-mile radius of the poorest section of the largest county in the state, with the highest number of minority and second language students. Local schools were pitted against neighboring local schools in the fight to get off the list. Led by our tenacious school principal, staff, students, and parents testified at the State Board of Education meetings to have our school removed from the list of potential ASD schools. Our students and staff went on a letter writing campaign. We were in the newspapers and on television, speaking out at every opportunity against the flawed concept of bringing in an unknown out-of-state charter school vendor to turn our neighborhood school into nothing more than what we imagined would be prison style experiences.

The "Save our School" rally was one of the most extraordinary experiences in my career. Our families and parent center team worked with students and teachers to make signs, which were plastered all over the front of the school and carried by every single person. Our orchestra set up on the sidewalk and played. Our cheerleaders cheered up and down the sidewalks. Our teachers, students and parents walked arm and arm, chanting to save our school. We had at least 75 people at our school rally, and then the media showed up. More people came. Local politicians spoke out on our behalf. We were televised live on all three major television news stations and Telemundo broadcast across the country. News helicopters filmed us from overhead, as it was the largest local school rally to date. The news world heard our voices. Our state Department of Education heard our voices. The legislature heard the combined voices of our school. Shortly after the world witnessed our continuing dedication to our community and our school with a successful rally, we were taken off the list for consideration of the ASD. I am still in awe of that day. Everything went perfectly in terms of safety, organization, and teamwork. We could never have planned the media's response and the compassionate light they shined on us. I will never forget the power harnessed by our community that day, like harnessing lightening.

In the end, selection of the six schools was put on hold due to contentious community backlash when the disreputable behavior of the charter organization chosen by the state Department of Education was revealed, as evidenced by an FBI raid charging fraud, fiscal mismanagement, and misuse of public monies meant for school children. Efforts to have a bill sponsored to repeal the ASD were successful but ultimately died, and the original ASD law (2015) stands, with implementation currently being recrafted. Our staff and school community learned the hard way that education policy will impact a school community directly, intimately, and invasively. If it can happen to us, it can happen to any school, when community and staff members in the field are not working together to lead discussions to develop better solutions. If educators are not leading the charge, then other people with agendas of their own will drive decisions in their best interests that do not necessarily align with evidence-based practices or student and community well-being. That school year we all learned the importance of advocacy and policy making as a required part of educator responsibilities in school practices.

References

Chingos, M. M., & West, M. R. (2015). The uneven performance of Arizona's charter schools. *Educational Evaluation and Policy Analysis, 37*(1), 120–134.

DeBray, E., Scott, J., Lubienski, C., & Jabbar, H. (2014). Intermediary organizations in charter school policy coalitions: Evidence from New Orleans. *Educational Policy, 28*(2), 175–206.

Dockweiler, K. A. (2012). *Language of instruction policies: Discourse and power.* University of Nevada, Las Vegas University Libraries. (ISBN 9781267755230).

Dockweiler, K. A. (2016). State association advocacy: Conversations about conversations. *Communiqué, 44*(7), 1, 32–33.

Dockweiler, K. A. (2018). Responding to tragedy through stakeholder communication networks. *Communiqué, 46*(7), 26.

Dockweiler, K. A., Putney, L. G., & Jordan, T. S. (2015). Enhancing the policy analysis process: Case studies using the Layers of Analysis Framework. *Journal of Ethnographic and Qualitative Research, 10*(4), 87–103.

Ekland, K., von der Embse, N., & Minke, K. (2015). School psychologists and school-based Medicaid reimbursement. *National Register of Health Service Psychologists.* Retrieved from www.nationalregister.org/pub/the-national-register-report-pub/the-register-report-fall-2015/school-psychologists-and-school-based-medicaid-reimbursement.

Every Student Succeeds Act of 2015, 20 U.S.C. (2015).

Kingdon, J. W. (1984). *Agendas, alternatives, and public policies.* Colchester, UK: The Book Service.

Klehr, D., Presson, E., Schaeffer, B., & Zelno, S. (2013). *Funding, formulas, and fairness: What Pennsylvania can learn from other states' education funding formulas.* Retrieved from the Education Law Center website: www.elc-pa.org/wp-content/uploads/2013/02/ELC_schoolfunding report.2013.pdf.

Morningstar, M. E., Allcock, H. C., White, J. M., Taub, D., Kurth, J. A., Gonsier-Gerdin, J., Ryndak, D. L., Sauer, J., & Jorgensen, C. M. (2016). Inclusive education national research advocacy agenda: A call to action. *Research and Practice for Persons with Severe Disabilities, 41*(3), 209–215.

National Association of School Psychologists (2018). *Framework for safe and successful schools: Considerations for action steps* [Brief]. Bethesda, MD: Author.

Odden, A. R., & Picus, L. O. (2014). *School finance: A policy perspective* (5th ed.). New York: McGraw Hill.

Paino, M., Renzulli, L. A., Boylan, R. L., & Bradley, C. L. (2013). For grades or money? Charter school failure in North Carolina. *Educational Administration Quarterly, 50*(3), 500–536.

Phillips, A. M., & Elmahrek, A. (2017, March 6). Inside Celerity charter school network, questionable spending and potential conflicts of interest abound. *Los Angeles Times*. Retrieved from www.latimes.com/local/education/la-me-edu-celerity-beginnings-20170306-story.html#.

Rigby, J. G., Woulfin, S. L., & Marz, V. (2016). Understanding how structure and agency influence education policy implementation and organizational change. *American Journal of Education, 122*, 295–302.

Robinson, S. (2015). Decentralisation, managerialism and accountability: Professional loss in an Australian education bureaucracy. *Journal of Education Policy, 30*(4), 468–482, doi:10.1080/02 680939.2015.1025241.

Smith, J., Gasparian, H., Perry, N., & Capinpin, F. (2013). *Categorical funds: The intersection of school finance and governance*. Retrieved from Center for American Progress website: www. Americanprogress.org/wp-content/uploads/2013/11/CategoricalSpending1-brief-4.pdf.

Teresa, B. F., & Good, R. M. (2017). Speculative charter school growth in the case of UNO chart school network in Chicago. *Urban Affairs Review*. Retrieved from https://doi.org/10.1177/1078087417703487.

Tilsley, A. (2017). *How do school funding formulas work?* Retrieved from Urban Institute website: https://apps.urban.org/features/funding-formulas.

Wronowski, M. L. (2017). Beacon charter school needs a school: A case of capital outlay of charters in a public district. *Journal of Cases in Educational Leadership, 20*(3), 56–64.

Chapter 13

Trouble Shooting Guide

There are many obstacles to effectively implement MTSS on a school campus. Some remedies are easily identified, while other solutions seem elusive and out of reach. It is important to identify barriers to implementation and barriers to change on your school campus (Forman & Crystal, 2015). As mentioned in Chapter 5, if the school principal is not actively solving problems in this process, your success of systematic implementation of supports is in serious jeopardy. If the principal is passively allowing MTSS at your school, other issues will arise (Averill & Rinaldi, 2011). Obstacles to organizational change in bureaucratic institutions are all but assured, and the key to success in building and sustaining best practices is responsive adaptability. Nurturing team functions and supporting team decisions are the responsibility of all stakeholders and each educator must fill a role. This chapter introduces the most common barriers to implementing and sustaining MTSS, as well as solutions for teams to help identify, and troubleshoot past, the obstacles.

Eighteen Common Barriers to Implementation of MTSS

I The School Does Not Have a Principal Who is on Board With Supporting MTSS

This situation is the worst-case scenario for effective implementation of MTSS. Ideally state and district level leadership is not only backing MTSS efforts, but leading efforts with advancing the framework that includes accountability standards built into performance goals for school leaders. School principals are the key to laying foundational supports for scaling MTSS and maintaining the system once it is started. There are several critical incidences that are associated with positive change in practice and the principal is associated with each: "multidisciplinary leadership, access to professional development, consistent language and/or practices, consultation with external partners, and a focus on student outcomes in evaluation and planning" (Charlton, Sabey, Dawson, Pyle, Lund, & Ross, 2018, abstract). Additionally, teachers reported wishing that they had greater access to individuals who had more expert knowledge and training surrounding MTSS and had more effective interventions available to them (Charlton et al., 2018).

Outside active high-level leadership, including state or district level mandates directing the school principal to build tiers of support, the responsibility to convince the school principal to allow MTSS usually falls to the school psychologist or other motivated educator leader. Most school principals understand that major eligibility criteria for special education is dependent on prior interventions, and many can agree that intervention implementation and making data-based decisions to determine students' response to instruction makes sense, at some level. What many are not willing to commit to is investment in evidence-based practices, supports to structure intensified instruction, assistance in organizing or training teachers in implementing interventions or team development, and providing assessment tools to measure outcomes consistently across teachers and grade levels (Anyon, Nicotera, & Veeh, 2016; Cavendish, Harry, Menda, Espinoza, & Mahotiere, 2016; Averill & Rinaldi, 2011).

Getting agreement in principle with the principal about the MTSS framework is always the first goal of building MTSS, as it is instrumental in determining the success of new practices (Printy & Williams, 2014). If that fails, the next step is to attempt to obtain support for one part of MTSS, such as Academic MTSS. Success may be had with principals' support for small-scale or part of Academic MTSS, such as a pilot study, using curriculum-based measures to measure progress of Tier 2 and Tier 3 readers. Staff buy-in and implementation goals may need to be incremental, and small successes can help to get a foothold in the school for teachers to build upon.

If efforts to obtain principal buy-in are not effective, then the task becomes enticing teachers and support positions to work intervention magic on a small scale; with individualized teacher(s) implementing and documenting interventions and outcomes within their class(es). In large schools, small-scale individualized efforts are rarely sustainable. Small-scale efforts that grow because of popularity, effectiveness, and relationship building with stakeholders, other than the school principal, may lead to a leadership crisis for the school principal who must either publicly back the initiatives, or more likely, crush outward practices that threaten leadership priorities or self-image. When this happens, intervention implementation and documentation go underground, and experienced teachers who have concern for suspected special needs students will continue to collect response to intervention data quietly to support students and to build evidence for eligibility. This can create a hostile school climate and good teachers will eventually leave the school in search of a more supportive administrator (Boyd, Grossman, Lankford, Loeb, & Wyckoff, 2011). School psychologists, special education teachers, counselors, speech therapists, learning strategists, and other supporters can advocate, educate, and demonstrate the benefits of MTSS as often as possible at all leadership levels.

2 The School Does Not Have a Principal Who Actively Leads MTSS on Campus

The disorganized and disengaged principal is worse than it sounds, and is almost as difficult a scenario as the principal not backing MTSS at all. Like a teacher with students, the school principal sets priorities for the staff and reinforces desired teaching practices, or not. When it comes to classroom management, teachers who are comfortable with chaos are the most difficult to help motivate to change their own behavior in how and when they reinforce variables in the classroom environment. Students in such teachers' classes basically do whatever they want, whenever they want, and sometimes the teacher gets upset for no clear reason because expectations are never clear. Teachers who are comfortable with chaos are extremely unlikely to be successfully coached by peers or administrators in positive behavioral supports. For the school psychologist who seeks to assist in helping teachers change their selective attention and behavior strategically to positively impact students, successful coaching of comfortable-with-chaos teachers is nearly impossible. Such teachers are not bothered enough, or motivated enough, to become self-disciplined and make the effort to change themselves.

When teachers are *uncomfortable* with classroom chaos they are often willing to make substantial effort to reinforce the correct variables to increase the probability of positively impacting student behavior, which in turn improves classroom climate and productivity. Increasing rate of positive reinforcement of students and using preplanned unemotional responses to address misbehavior are cognitive behavioral tasks for the adults managing them. Improving teaching practices, like learning and rehearsing anything new, takes sustained mental effort; and if the goals are not perceived to be worth the effort, then the quality of effort will suffer. Like teachers, comfortable-with-chaos administrators will struggle with the efforts required to build and actively manage MTSS. Changing staff beliefs and behaviors toward the structures and practices of MTSS are among the greatest barriers to implementation (Anyon et al., 2016).

Principals who are comfortable with chaos also lack leadership, so others will not follow, resulting in teachers basically doing whatever they want, whenever they want, because performance expectations are never clear. The outcome of leadership chaos is a leadership vacuum that attracts someone else to the top of the heap to create "order," much as in the book, *Lord of the Flies* (Golding, 1954). When your school campus is run by Lord of the Flies, school culture suffers and educators find themselves trying to please all or none. Welcome to Bolman and Deal's (2017) jungle. Building and sustaining relationships with the "quasi" administrators to influence cultural attitudes toward better practices is required for stakeholders wishing to improve student outcomes through generating useful, evidence-based solutions to school problems. Fortunately, school psychologists and other leaders on staff are adaptable, and convincing self-appointed tyrants to try things differently is all part of the job.

Some very laid-back principals can still clearly be in charge. Under a distributed leadership model, administrative responsibilities may get shifted to assistant principals, deans, and quasi-administrative positions. With proper implementation, distributed leadership is correlated to teachers' positive feelings about their school and their desire to remain and be a part of the organization (Ross, Lutfi, & Hope, 2016). Under this type of model, collaboration and decision making usually transpires within the leadership team on executive resolutions that impact MTSS.

The administrator in charge may be part of this decision-making team or they might make decisions unilaterally. It is important to get agreement in principle of the MTSS framework with both the principal and the administrator overseeing MTSS (if they are not the same person). If accomplished, then the school psychologist and MTSS team would work with the appointed administrator in the same capacity as the principal. If the principal and administrative appointee do not agree in principle to the MTSS framework, the need to educate, demonstrate, and advocate would apply to build consensus. As long as the principal agrees in theory and supports funding efforts, all possibilities for MTSS implementation are on the table. Administrators must see MTSS as an embodiment of the school, not something separate from the school or an add-on (Averill & Rinaldi, 2011). This becomes a matter of relationship building with stakeholders within the school and not compromising who, what, where, when, and how supports are implemented. Starting MTSS processes is not the most difficult part; growing and sustaining effective practices through teamwork from stakeholders and adapting responsively to address challenges, is the ultimate accomplishment of successful MTSS.

3 The School Lacks Research-Based Curriculum or Interventions

School principals get much of the heat for not implementing best practices, when as often, if not more often, state-level decision-making bodies, school boards, and school districts sabotage efforts of MTSS intentionally and inadvertently. Policy makers jump on bandwagons without looking at implications of research-based outcomes from the national level to the state level. When disregard for evidence-based practices in school settings is evident throughout the country, it is no wonder that school principals have a difficult time weighing cost-to-value ratio of instructional practices. Principals and school teachers do not like wasting time with practices that do not work. Sometimes ineffective practices are mandated by school districts and school boards for political reasons, and there is little principals can do except supplement teachers with additional tools to fill in gaps that the curriculum does not touch.

MTSS advocates can build support for teachers in the classroom with teaching supplements, online resources, and documentation or charting tools that produce and capture measurable outcomes, many of which are free. Lack of effective intervention material is cited by teachers as a challenge that, ideally, could be remedied in their schools (Charlton et al., 2018). There are also grant opportunities that can fund supplements and supports, which cost the school little to nothing. Success is a motivating factor for students and teachers alike, and successes create a stronger appetite for investment in interventions that work. Working small scale with individual teachers willing to try something new is progress no matter how small, and those efforts often lead to other teachers becoming interested or taking initiative in implementing helpful and easy to use processes.

Growing best practices one teacher at a time is a virtue, especially when the school principal(s) does not make MTSS processes a priority and turn their backs on supervision and visible support. Schools with similar populations often look to each other to find promising solutions to similar issues. Educators leading and learning with other educators, despite lack of coordinated leadership efforts, is challenging but can lead to successes on a smaller scale. Feedback looping, unfortunately, will not be possible to evaluate intervention implementation until the issues of systematic service delivery are ironed out. Otherwise, each teacher is recreating intervention magic on an individual basis, which mostly relies on professional judgment in program evaluation to cover for reliability and validity issues.

Picking a target skill, choosing a research-based method to address the skill deficit, recording the amount of time the student is getting the intervention, and progress monitoring outcomes can be accomplished by a classroom teacher, and is most often the case without systematic supports. Obviously, when systems are in place for teachers, at-risk students are quickly identified and teachers are more likely to provide earlier intensive instructional supports that are implemented with integrity. They can do this because they are not scrambling to find time to squeeze interventions in the instructional day, find lower level materials, maintain intervention logs for each student, or measure outcomes with alternative assessments. Teachers who have to create remedial opportunities for their students on an individualized basis have to go to many extra efforts to put it all together, which is a barrier to implementation and results in fewer students getting help when they need it. The more teachers and other educators advocate for systems in their schools to address student needs, the more open school leaders may be to provide supports in a systemic fashion. Educating, demonstrating, and advocating the benefits of evidence-based practices school-wide, district-wide, and state-wide is required.

4 The School Has Teachers Who Are Resistant to MTSS Despite Training Efforts

The teachers who are resistant to MTSS may not be convinced that the promised outcomes justify the efforts, or may not have received sufficient training to carry out the initiative. When educational fads come and go, teaching practices change with the direction of the wind, and the only constant thing is change, teachers lose heart in the "next best thing." Teacher buy-in is a crucial milestone to successfully implementing MTSS, and teachers belong in leadership positions to make decisions that impact their daily teaching practices (Brezicha, Bergmark, & Mitra, 2015). It is difficult to argue with the need for evidence-based practices, but there is hardly consensus on how to best choose or implement evidence-based teaching practices. Guidelines to supporting implementation of best practices include following a research-based framework, selecting practices with sufficient data to support effectiveness, and using data to guide decision making (Mazzotti, Rowe, & Test, 2012).

As discussed at length, teachers have amazing skills and must be masters of curriculum and behavior management to survive teaching successfully. Effective teaching requires purposeful intent and sustained effort. Requiring educators to do more with less is one thing, but asking them to do differently with more supports is another. When given a choice to do more work without administrative support, additional compensation, or celebration, why would teachers choose more work? Because the majority of teachers honestly want to help their students, which is why they got into education. Most teachers would be happy simply to have current textbooks for students and enough classroom supplies without spending their own money. But of course, celebration and compensation of educators to engage in best practices, which lead to best outcomes, should be the gold standard.

If school leaders provide the tools and structures to implement MTSS practices to grow extraordinary learning opportunities for all students, and teachers let those opportunities go to waste because of lack of skill or motivation, then the solution is to provide greater training or supervision. One possibility could be to include the resistant teachers on the problem solving team to help them understand the needs of others and allow *them* to find solutions that work for everyone. Complainers can turn those frowns upside down by being a part of the solution, and actively working with the school team to address the issues. Things change constantly in education and change is hard for people sometimes. When changes are unpalatable, allowing others to simply have a seat at the table can be part of the solution.

Administrative guidance is the best remedy to resistant teachers. Compliance with effective teaching practices is often reflected in teachers' annual evaluations, which should determine corrective actions and, in extreme cases, possible professional discipline. Barring administrative oversight, teachers are influenced by other teachers' success with students, participating in a distributed leadership model, and making extra duty pay. Administrators who reward change agents publicly and provide plenty of opportunity for staff collaboration and development, will see the greatest movement of resistant teachers toward best practices. In schools that have a well-run MTSS, life gets easier for everyone because the staff has what they need to get the job done, and the students get what they need when they need it.

5 Interventions Are Not Being Implemented With Fidelity

Supervision of teaching methods falls squarely on the school principal and school administration. When teachers are not implementing interventions with fidelity, it is up to the school administration to provide leadership as to how the interventions should be implemented through re-teaching, modeling, or guided practice. Lack of intervention fidelity may include not using research-based curriculum, providing interventions consistently for the recommended amount of instructional time, or not using the curriculum as prescribed.

Tier 1 must always be occurring with fidelity first before evaluating Tier 2 and Tier 3 practices. The selection of intervention tools and methods at Tier 2 and Tier 3 is a function of MTSS administrative team with professional learning community feedback or goodness of fit (Cheney & Yong, 2014). If teachers are not adequately trained in the prescribed teaching methods, then they need more opportunity for skills development in instructional strategies, and doing so will also increase likelihood of teacher retention and decrease of attrition from the teaching field (McCarthy, Lambert, Lineback, Fitchett, & Baddouh, 2016). If teachers do not have enough time to use the methods as validated, then more time must be carved out of the students' day to be exposed to the interventions.

Supplementing research-based tools without using the method with fidelity cannot be counted on for positive results, nor can the results be blamed due to the efficacy of the method because it was not implemented as directed. Physicians have the same problems with patients who do not take their prescriptions as directed. When the antibiotics did not cure the infection, doctors cannot blame the treatment because the patient did not take all the doses for the amount of time that is statistically needed to remedy the problem. Educators cannot blame the curriculum if they did not follow the prescribed method with the length of exposure to materials statistically needed to remedy the problem. Not using intervention tools as directed is simply a waste of time and money, and no reliable inferences can be made whether the method works or if a student is responding adequately to it. School administrators must ensure integrity with teaching practices through supervision, monitoring, and professional feedback and guidance.

6 Interventions Are Not Being Documented Adequately

Documentation for large numbers of students is laborious at best and impossible at worst. If large numbers of students are not responding to instruction and require interventions, the effectiveness of Tier 1 instruction must be addressed. Teachers who find that school structures do not support systems of interventions, such as scheduled intervention classes, and have to find "free time" to remediate student skills' deficits, have a bigger problem than just documentation. Students who receive interventions through an intervention-based scheduling design out-perform their peers who receive interventions ad hoc or not at all (Dallas, 2017). Getting hold of research-based interventions and scheduling ample time for implementation are the true challenges. If the intervention method is preselected as meeting criteria for evidence-based, and intervention blocks are scheduled and adhered to, attendance logs suffice along with lesson plans as documentation of having participated in the session. When teachers have to cobble together their own intervention plans, find their own tools for interventions and progress monitoring, and write notes about what they're working on sporadically, with ten minutes here, ten minutes there, intervention logs are much less reliable. In such cases, documenting the interventions is as much of a challenge as implementing the interventions regularly with fidelity. The solution to one problem solves the other.

7 The School Staff Perceives MTSS as a Function of Special Education Eligibility Outcome, Not as a Path to Solutions for Student Difficulties in and of Itself

You have to start somewhere. If the principal's and teachers' initial buy-in to MTSS is for special education eligibility purposes, start there. Squeezing in evidence-based practices for one student improves accessibility to evidence-based practices for all others as a byproduct. A common mistake that occurs on campuses solely collecting response to intervention data for special education eligibility purposes is that curriculum-based measurement (CBM) data is collected repeatedly over time, yet the instructional opportunities are rarely intensified during that time period and/or interventions are not valid or implemented with fidelity. For example, a student's math computation fluency graph is flat for a whole year, yet no interventions were documented. MTSS teams and school psychologists can build on that. Teachers are already dedicating time and effort to progress monitoring, yet that effort is wasted because documented interventions to intensify instruction did not occur along the way to determine if anything more intensive worked. Adding intervention opportunities in classrooms already utilizing CBM is a small leap compared to the initial step of implementing regular

CBM assessment. This staff is half-way there. Educate, advocate, and demonstrate benefits of evidence-based practices and MTSS processes to more productive outcomes.

8 The School Does Not Have Sufficient Funding to Address MTSS Adequately in Terms of Personnel and Resources

Like having a baby, you're never really 100 percent sure if you're ready. The underlying insecurity is whether there will be enough resources (money, time, energy) to support the baby. Babies are expensive and a lot of work. MTSS is also a lot of work and requires significant investment. Unlike the unpredictability of raising children, MTSS can be grown in incremental manageable steps. Low-cost practices that depend more on staff buy-in and effort can be implemented to begin the mindset needed for change that will ultimately lead to better practices. Secondary schools can start by scheduling advisory periods in the master schedule, or 0 period (additional minutes added to 1st period), to carve out time and space for evidence-based practices school-wide, across grade and subject levels, to possibly include student benchmarking, SLIC portfolio guidance, character development, and social-emotional-behavioral experiences. Team building can begin in the context of solving site-based issues with existing resources. Not all evidence-based interventions are expensive, many free or low-cost supports can be found online. Some such examples include intervention.org, rtiforsuccess.org, interventioncentral.org, xtramath.org, Interventions for Math Difficulties, easycbm.org, Florida Center for Reading Research, Reading A-Z, What Works Clearinghouse, PBIS.org, National Center on Intensive Interventions, and PBIS World. Some fee-based online interventions also allow free trials or limited-use trials.

Schools starting MTSS from scratch have many things to consider. They should begin with the following six items: (1) picking a universal screener or determining how to identify at-risk students; (2) scheduling at least one intervention class or block with intensified curriculum; (3) ensuring implementation fidelity of evidence-based practices; (4) selecting which progress monitoring tool to use; (5) identifying who is going to monitor outcomes; and (6) identify who is going to make data-based decisions on behalf of students with support of classroom teachers. Leaner teams can operate efficiently until they need more hands on deck based on the number of referrals. The average case manager can typically actively manage up to 15 students at a time keeping track of student data and portfolios of interventions, but the goal is to have 10 or less. If the case manager model cannot be funded, counselors and learning strategists not bound to classrooms can act as case managers with the understanding that comp time and other professional perks can be built in to compensate extra duties at some point until dedicated funding can be established. Start lean and grow.

9 The School Does Not Engage in Universal Benchmarking, nor Are Progress Monitoring Tools Being Used Consistently for Data-Based Decision Making

This is a fairly common situation and a thinking error on part of many school leadership teams. School administrators may be unaware of its necessity, or they may want to save money and time. However, investing in the cost of human capital resources and tools to implement universal screenings to root out under-performing students actually saves time and money because benchmarking quickly identifies students who may not come to the attention of teachers as requiring remediation until much later in the school year, if at all. Old-fashioned methods rely on parent or teacher referral requests, which often occur after prolonged aca-demic failure, and may be compounded by the amount of time it takes to track down and sort through student data by cross-referencing sources. Only the most persistent educators track down student records from previous schools. Schools without universal benchmarking are going to be on the reactive end supporting underachievers rather than at the proactive end, where they are able to quickly identify at-risk learners and target and remediate skill deficits. The reactive approach does not align with research and best practice, and often violates states' laws requiring the use of screening measures to identify and remediate student deficits early in their academic careers (Salinger, 2016). The toll of wasting instructional opportunities resulting in prolonged school failure is much higher than the initial deposit of money and human capital it takes to be proactive using universal benchmarking to identify at-risk kids and invest in evidence-based interventions, progress monitoring tools and human capital to professionally monitor and manage outcomes.

10 The Teachers Are Overwhelmed, Cannot Take on New Responsibilities, and Do Not Have Time to Engage in Professional Development Activities Pertaining to MTSS

MTSS is a framework that allocates school resources in a proactive manner and as a triage model. State level and school district level protocol for adhering to evidence-based practices should guide implementation at the school level, but sometimes required practices at the school level prove to be labor intensive with no clear benefits. Continuing to pile on responsibilities to teachers' workloads, including mandating new duties, more paperwork, and time intensive activities, only serves to be counterproductive. Giving teachers more work without taking anything away from their job responsibilities leads to less compliance with all job duties. There are only so many hours in a day and job requirements can tap teachers' reserves only so much, as generations of teachers can attest. Obviously, compensating teachers with financial and non-financial benefits for their extra time and efforts is a certain moti-vating factor and well earned. The rest lies in common sense. Educators must pri-oritize which tasks require immediate attention and those that can wait, tasks that have the most impact to students and those that have less impact, and tasks that make most sense and those that make less sense.

MTSS is a framework designed to address the needs of all students. The frame-work requires evidence-based Tier 1 instructional practices first and foremost, which impacts everyone. The MTSS framework also provides the path for actionable steps to follow in times of academic and behavioral difficulty for stu-dents requiring Tier 2 and Tier 3 supports. By shifting perceptions from MTSS as "more" work to "more effective" work, school teams will realize practices actu-ally become *less* labor intensive with automaticity as it becomes embedded in the schools' culture of functions and processes to support all students.

The first-time practices are changed universally on a school campus may be shocking to the community as some people can be resistant to change. Time passes and new practices become established practices. Like money in the bank, investing in teacher and educator development, supports, and services earns interest like no other down payment. Leaders must evaluate school priorities, eliminate unnecessary or duplicative processes and paperwork for teachers, and foster a culture of shared responsibility for problem solving by automating as much of the process as possible embedded within school culture. Barriers should be low for teachers to advocate for help of students, and intervention efforts should be celebrated and compensated. *A little love and support for educators goes a long way toward helping them help their students.*

11 The School Psychologist Does Not Honor Teachers' Intervention Implementation or Documentation, Which Makes Referral for Special Education Evaluation, and Ultimate Eligibility Determination, Almost Impossible

School psychologists are in the unenviable position of being perceived as *gate-keepers* to special education. If the school psychologist does not conduct an evaluation, the target student is definitely not going to be eligible for any additional services; thus, "letting students in" or "keeping them out" of special education, like a gate. Closer to reality, the challenges school psychologists face include the often-unavoidable position of unilaterally evaluating MTSS practices in schools with no control over intensifying supports for students without pursuing special education eligibility. Nationally, there is a shortage of school psychologists practicing in the field, as well as professors and higher education training programs (National Association of School Psychologists (NASP), 2016). If shortages of school psychologists could be addressed, there could be enough school psychologists to work proactively, guiding teamwork in the development of layers of supports and networks within the tiers of academics, social-emotional and behavioral functioning, family engagement, special education, mental health, and resource networking. A reasonable school psychologist caseload, that aligns with the nationally recommended 1:500–700 ratio (NASP, 2016) would allow school psychologists to engage in these essential prevention and intervention services (Bocanegra, Grapin, Nellis, & Rossen, 2017).

School psychologists may not be able to get to all referrals immediately and must prioritize their referral list based on intensity or need, which is why supports and services should not be dependent on one person as a gate-keeper. The time and expertise of the school psychologist is a valuable human capital resource, and more should be invested in school psychological services. The school psychologist can sort through large amounts of student data to generate hypotheses about student functioning and variables that maintain dysfunction, which leads to highly educated recommendations for solutions. Proactively prioritizing student need and providing supports within MTSS not only benefits individual students, it also aligns with the Every Student Succeeds Act, as it can improve school climate and safety and it benefits *all* students on a school campus (NASP, 2017). When MTSS systems are automated, everyone does their part because structures are in place to allow each professional to do their part; and active problem-solving processes are in place so that everyone can figure out how to do their part despite obstacles and unexpected situations.

When school psychologists have to literally run down teachers to plead for MTSS documentation, it is never an efficient use of limited time. When interventions are on the master schedule, when data can be accessed remotely by all stakeholders, and when meetings occur regularly to engage in problem solving for students over time, then teams can run efficiently. These systematic processes can be relied on and prevent school psychologists from the untenable task of tracking down or squabbling over unreliable documentation and making judgment calls. Systematic processes help protect teachers, school psychologists, and students and help ensure that everyone's time is used wisely and efficiently.

The question ultimately is whether the student demonstrates lack of adequate progress and performance over time in response to highly intensive instruction with severe enough underachievement to warrant eligibility. The difference between MTSS being in place or not for the student referred for eligibility is that, in the end, students who do not meet criteria for special education eligibility will *still* get assistance at the level they need because the school offers other levels of support within the functions of MTSS. Whereas in schools without MTSS, special education eligibility is the only way for underperforming students to get differentiated instruction to meet their needs. The worst thing for the school psychologist–teacher relationship is when the school year is over and the student is even more behind, the teacher blames the school psychologist for the child not getting more help, and the school psychologist blames the teacher for not having the acceptable documentation to meet legal criteria for eligibility to adequately address suspicion of disability in terms of prior interventions.

Practices need to change, and one shift that can occur is for school psychologists to be more flexible in working with teachers to negotiate and problem solve intervention practices that meet criteria for eligibility determination. Got to give a little to get a little. When the school psychologist is an active and participating member of the MTSS team, issues of documentation tend to be eliminated as the school psychologist has been guiding and supporting intervention processes every step of the way.

12 The Parents or Guardians Do Not Want Interventions, They Want Special Education Eligibility Determination

Rarely is this the case. The most common thread in parental requests for assistance is that they want help for their child(ren) in the school setting and beyond. Oftentimes, when parents or family leaders make a request "for an IEP" for their child, they do not know what they are asking for, what the process is to be found eligible, or what eligibility even means in the long run. Families who need help for their children can and should be persistent in requesting supports, services, and documentation of outcomes. Parents who write a letter requesting a psychoeducational evaluation or an IEP, including third-party requests from counselors, lawyers, parent advocate groups, and physicians (often in the form of prescriptions) are simply proxy parent requests asking for help from the school psychologist and teachers for the child's benefit.

Occasionally, parents seeking financial public assistance consider special education eligibility as an income generating proposition, but only a tiny fraction are out for Social Security Income. In reality, what they are unknowingly seeking is an advocate in the system to promote for best practices to ensure the welfare of their child in a school setting. If students can get help they need with an added intervention class or a layer of support without eligibility, and without waiting periods, most parents are on board. Help the students when and where they need it. Educating parents and families about MTSS may be time consuming on the front end, but pays off in the long run. Strong family–school partnerships will also will lower barriers for families when they are seeking help as they will feel more comfortable going directly to the school rather than through a third party. In rare cases when special education evaluation *is* warranted and the team is delaying the evaluation, then parents have the right to ask for a timely assessment in writing with a response provided by the school within ten days.

13 The Behavioral Supports Are Too Complicated to Implement Systematically or They Do Not Exist At All

One of the biggest mistakes school systems make is providing behavioral supports only at Tier 3, often in the form of in-house suspension. Systemic behavior supports at Tiers 1 and 2 have been shown to have significant positive impact not only on students' behavior, but also on students' academic performance; especially for those students with emotional-behavioral disorders (Lewis, McIntosh, Simonsen, Mitchell, & Hatton, 2017). Beginning at Tier 1 means everyone has exposure to learning experiences and everyone has equal opportunity to earn rewards and positive reinforcement. Classroom management gets the biggest bang for its buck on a school campus, closely followed by school-wide positive behavior intervention support (PBIS) practices. There are many variables to consider in PBIS, and it can be overwhelming to manage too many new initiatives at once.

Start with a solid foundation, like Tier 1 social-emotional-behavioral opportunities, and build in Tier 2 and Tier 3 intervention classes slowly as capacity grows. Get good at the first layer before building on the next layer too heavily. Growing practices incrementally is far more sustainable than revamping and rebuilding constantly, which is ineffective and leads to fatigue and burnout. Layers of support are very likely occurring at Tier 2 and Tier 3 on your campus but are not being captured systematically with data and monitoring. Schools often operate as a system of teams; through better identification and understanding of the underlying motivations, school leadership can better predict successful system performance and processes (Rico, Hinsz, Burke, & Salas, 2016). Look around campus and find out what is happening in terms of counselors, coaches, mentors, and teachers putting in time to build relationships, building skills to offset academic frustrations, and teaching critical thinking and problem solving to students. Every little bit counts. Tweaking current practices to add evidence-based methods is a smaller leap than starting from scratch. New initiatives must be weighed by the MTSS team to make the best decisions for a particular campus.

14 The High-Needs Students Are Frequently Absent or Do Not Attend Classes

Students who experience school failure are less likely to want to participate in school, which is often the source of their suffering and failure. It goes back to school being relevant for everyone. A student who is required to trade her elective during the day for a fundamental class, because she refuses to stay for 7th period after school, may lose enthusiasm for coming to school because she is less engaged. Taking away electives is a gamble because the student either values the elective enough to put effort into not losing it, or they give up even more so. How to make school relevant is the million-dollar question and teachers who know their students will be more successful than those who don't. Especially when students face a multitude of barriers to success outside of school. One hook to securing students' attention in school is to provide interesting and engaging instructional experiences.

Students ultimately need employable skills and remaining in school increases their chances for success. Individually, "dropouts are significantly disadvantaged compared to high school graduates with respect to employment, earnings, avoiding crime and incarceration, avoiding teenage childbearing, parenting children within wedlock, having good health, civic engagement, well-being, and intergenerational upward mobility" (Hoffer, 2015, p. 81). In addition to the individual consequences, there are also economic and social consequences of dropping out, including "reduced economic activity from unemployment and reduced tax revenues from foregone higher earnings associated with high school completion; and higher costs to society of increased crime, increased welfare use, and increased use of public health insurance" (Hoffer, 2015, p. 81).

To gain employable skills students need work experience, apprenticeships, volunteerism, club involvement, and extracurricular opportunities in school and the community. Community opportunities could be contingent on school attendance and grades, as could be the ability to obtain drivers' licenses in some states; though this could penalize students who already face multiple barriers, especially when schools are not responsive in providing remediation and opportunities. Family outreach and supporting families to help their children get to school with free bus passes, attendance contracts and incentives, and enabling relationships with families so that they allow their children to participate in extracurricular and community learning opportunities to increase engagement. Considerations should also be made by the team to identify, and support, students who may be homeless as their educational access and self-advocacy may be compromised (Ausikaitis, Wynne, Persaud, Pitt, Hosek, Reker, Turner, Flores, & Flores, 2014).

15 Tier 1 Instructional Practices Are Not as Effective As They Should Be and Getting Tier 3 Supports for Students Takes Too Long

This is the most common framework error, party foul, and saboteur of success at other tiers. How can a building withstand weight and gravity without a proper foundation? Tier 1 systems of a school should be the theoretical blueprint with sufficient tons of iron re-bar and cement underground to hold up a skyscraper. If the base of the building is unstable then nothing built on top is going to be stable either. Tier 3 solutions do not fix problems at Tier 1, but Tier 1 solutions can resolve and prevent issues at Tier 2 and Tier 3. Scheduling, building layers of support, providing access to supports based on need, decision-making models, growing data sources and tools, universal benchmarking, teaching behavioral expectations proactively, providing a school culture of achievement and shared responsibility all impact the success of Tier 3. Hopefully, through these strategies, processes, and practices schools can keep students out of Tier 3 because they are engaged in Tier 1 and are receiving remediation in Tier 2.

Family engagement and parents' or guardians' voices are often louder than educators' voices within a system and can advocate for Tier 1, 2, and 3 supports more effectively than all other advocates. Family advocacy groups are important contributors to schools and are most successful when there is a collaborative and proactive rapport with staff and school leadership (Matthews, Georgiades, & Smith, 2011). Nationwide parent advisory councils are gaining decision-making powers at school organizational levels, and parents and guardians must be educated about best practices so they can advocate for those practices locally and nationally.

16 The Administrator Has Decided That Additional Intervention Classes Cannot Be Scheduled and That Interventions Should Be Taught by Subject Level Teachers

These schools may also have an administrator who believes the case manager model is unnecessary because teachers should take ownership of identifying underachievers and implementing solutions in the classroom. Teachers *should* take ownership of student outcomes in the classroom. By all means, classroom teachers should know their students' instructional and performance levels and should be making data-based decisions. Problem solving and team meetings can be grade level or subject level and be run in much the same manner as the case manager model, as long as the lead subject or grade level teacher for that child takes over the responsibilities of the case manager. At-risk students require a focal point of advocacy on large campuses, and classroom subject level math and English teachers would bear the brunt of the caseload.

Expecting the English and math teachers in a middle school or high school to be responsible for benchmarking and progress monitoring all students in their classes may feel unrealistic. With block scheduling and having a reading or English language arts block every day, this can approach 200–300 students per teacher in a large urban secondary school. The argument against adding some additional minutes to the beginning of the day for an advisory period would be that the teachers testing the students do not necessarily work with the students in that subject area. Frankly, it doesn't matter, as long as the screening is administered as directed. The testing is the snapshot taken at regular intervals. It won't matter who takes the snapshot, but the English and math teachers would be required to look at the snapshots and take ownership to make instructional decisions. In the first scenario, the teachers are responsible for benchmarking, progress monitoring, and advocating for low performers for 200–300 students. In the second scenario, all teachers across campus testing their 0 period or 1st period class and share the load by testing 30–50 students each and uploading the scores in a shared database; subject level teachers are still responsible for decisions to intensify instruction, they just have help getting the data from shared responsibility. The math and English teachers may prefer to get the data themselves in case the band or art teachers might not be invested in the screening process; school culture and leadership team decisions will dictate how shared responsibilities are divided.

Target students can be monitored by subject level teachers, and those teachers could be responsible for problem solving at grade level and subject level collaborative team meetings, just like case managers. Block scheduling can work well if the interventions are scheduled into the block to ensure enough class time for using the evidence-based curriculum with fidelity. Breaking up intervention blocks this way works just like scheduling intervention periods and supervision can occur to monitor implementation, which always increases compliance. A drawback is that, if not paced adequately, time can be wasted during block scheduled classes. For example, in a double English language arts class that approaches a two-hour block, if pace of instruction wanes or students are socializing or otherwise off-task, the teacher can experience time management issues that interfere with curriculum delivery. If the first part of the blocked period was for Tier 1, then Tier 2, Tier 3, or enrichment instruction can be scheduled the second half of the period as if it were a separate period. Then students successful in Tier 1 can engage in independent study while Tier 2, Tier 3, and high performing students receive enrichment or evidence-based intensified instruction with a specific curriculum during the second half of the period. Block scheduling makes more sense than having an extra period after school or early bird classes in terms of attendance issues because all students are required to attend the extended day. The key to successfully implementing Tier 3 in a general education environment on a secondary campus would be to break the block period into parts to assist with time management, which is a substantial barrier to implementation fidelity when large numbers of students are involved.

17 The School Has Found a Better Way to Deliver Instruction Than Described in This Field Guide to MTSS

By all means, this guide is intended to inspire and generate conversations among stakeholders regarding how to allocate resources and problem solve most efficiently and effectively on a school campus. If a school's MTSS team has figured out how to improve, expand, modify, tweak, or build upon the foundations of MTSS to meet the needs of Tier 1, 2, and 3 then bravo, all roads lead to Rome.

18 The Principal Has Left the School, Will Any of the MTSS Infrastructure That Was Created Last?

The truth is that it depends. With personal vision and priorities, new building principals choose to do things differently. Hopefully they will evaluate existing programs and improve on what works. Sometimes when school administrators move on from a school, large numbers of staff also leave with them or move on themselves. When the educators with the MTSS leadership skill set leave a campus, new training opportunities must be established for new staff if the system has any chance of sustainability within school culture. A principal who has experience and success with MTSS is much more likely to be open minded to keeping systems in place and to improve upon those systems than an incoming principal who does not. It is almost guaranteed that a new building principal will change some systems and processes. MTSS is non-transferable principal to principal unless the incoming administrator already buys into it and has the skills to be responsively adaptive and actively support staff leadership positions and team problem-solving activities. MTSS is replicable, yet it rarely is replicated exactly. Finding functional and sustainable MTSS in a secondary school is rare indeed, but does not have to be.

References

Anyon, Y., Nicotera, N., & Veeh, C. A. (2016). Contextual influences on the implementation of a schoolwide intervention to promote students' social, emotional, and academic learning. *Children & Schools, 38*(2), 81–88.

Ausikaitis, A. E., Wynne, M. E., Persaud, S., Pitt, R., Hosek, A., Reker, K., Turner, C., Flores, S., & Flores, S. (2014). Staying in school: The efficacy of the McKinney-Vento Act for homeless youth. *Youth and Society, 47*(5), 707–726.

Averill, O. H., & Rinaldi, C. (2011). Multi-tier systems of support. *District Administration, 9,* 91–94.

Bocanegra, J. O., Grapin, S. L., Nellis, L. M., & Rossen, E. (2017). A resource guide to remediating the school psychology shortages crisis. *Communiqué, 45*(6). Retrieved from www. nasponline.org/publications/periodicals/communique/issues/volume-45-issue-6/a-resource-guide-to-remediating-the-school-psychology-shortages-crisis.

Bolman, L. G., & Deal, T. E. (2017). *Reframing organizations: Artistry, choice, and leadership* (6th ed.). San Francisco, CA: Jossey Bass.

Boyd, D., Grossman, P., Lankford, M. I. H., Loeb, S., & Wyckoff, J. (2011). The influence of school administrators on teacher retention decisions. *American Educational Research Journal, 48*(2), 303–333.

Brezicha, K., Bergmark, U., & Mitra, D. L. (2015). One size does *not* fit all: Differentiating leadership to support teachers in school reform. *Educational Administration Quarterly, 51*(1), 96–132.

Cavendish, W., Harry, B., Menda, A. M., Espinosa, A., & Mahotiere, M. (2016). Implementing response to intervention: Challenges of diversity and system change in a high-stakes environment. *Teachers College Record, 118,* 1–36.

Charlton, C. T., Sabey, C. V., Dawson, M. R., Pyle, D., Lund, E. M., & Ross, S. W. (2018). Critical incidences in the scale-up of state multitiered systems of supports. *Journal of Positive Behavior Interventions.* Abstract retrieved from https://doi.org/10.1177/1098300718770804.

Cheney, D. A., & Yong, M. (2014). RE-AIM checklist for integrating and sustaining Tier 2 social-behavioral interventions. *Intervention in School and Clinic, 50*(1), 39–44.

Dallas, W. P. (2017). Systemic sustainability in RtI using intervention-based scheduling methodologies. *Learning Disability Quarterly, 40*(2), 105–113.

Forman, S. G., & Crystal, C. D. (2015). Systems consultation for multitiered systems of supports (MTSS): Implementation issues. *Journal of Educational and Psychological Consultation, 25,* 276–285.

Golding, W. (1954). *Lord of the flies.* London: Faber and Faber.

Hoffer, T. B. (2015). Dropping out: Why students drop out of high school and what can be done about it. *Contemporary Sociology: A Journal of Reviews, 45*(1), 80–82.

Lewis, T. J., McIntosh, K., Simonsen, B., Mitchell, B. S., & Hatton, H. L. (2017). Schoolwide systems of positive behavior support: Implications for students at risk and with emotional/behavioral disorders. *AERA Open, 3*(2). Retrieved from https://doi.org/10.1177/2332858 417711428.

Matthews, M. S., Georgiades, S. D., & Smith, L. F. (2011). How we formed a parent advocacy group and what we've learned in the process. *Gifted Child Today, 34*(4), 28–34.

Mazzotti, V. L., Rowe, D. R., & Test, D. W. (2012). Navigating the evidence-based practice maze: Resources for teachers of secondary students with disabilities. *Intervention in School and Clinic, 48*(3), 159–166.

McCarthy, C. J., Lambert, R. G., Lineback, S., Fitchett, P., & Baddouh, P. G. (2016). Assessing teacher appraisals and stress in the classroom: Review of the classroom appraisal of resources and demands. *Education Psychology Review, 28*, 577–603.

National Association of School Psychologists (2016). *Addressing shortages in school psychology: Resource guide.* Bethesda, MD: Author. Retrieved from www.nasponline.org/resources-and-publications/resources/school-psychology/shortages-in-school-psychology-resource-guide.

National Association of School Psychologists (2017). *ESSA and multitiered systems of support for school psychologists.* Bethesda, MD: Author. Retrieved from www.nasponline.org/research-and-policy/current-law-and-policy-priorities/policy-priorities/the-every-student-succeeds-act/essa-implementation-resources/essa-and-mtss-for-school-psychologists.

Printy, S. M., & Williams, S. M. (2014). Principals' decisions: Implementing response to intervention. *Educational Policy, 29*(1), 179–205.

Rico, R., Hinsz, V. B., Burke, S., & Salas, E. (2016). A multilevel model of multiteam motivation and performance. *Organizational Psychology Review, 7*(3), 197–226.

Ross, L., Lutfi, G. A., & Hope, W. C. (2016). Distributed leadership and teachers' affective commitment. *NASSP Bulletin, 10*(3), 159–169.

Salinger, R. L. (2016). Selecting universal screening measures to identify students at risk academically. *Intervention in School and Clinic, 52*(2), 77–84.

Chapter 14

Moving Forward Together

MTSS is a living garden that requires constant attention and care, and in return, provides the manna to build and sustain nutrition of all students, staff, and school community. MTSS gardens can be ignored and starved, which leads to mangled educational practices with no solid root system. MTSS practices that only provide sunlight to the top of the tiers may also get root rot and die. Schools that neglect Tier 1, the root system, will never have rich enough soil or strong enough seeds to grow sustainable best practices to support all students. Only school systems that commit to growth will survive changes in weather and be healthy enough to meet community needs into the future. The ingredients of LIQUID support MTSS growth and sustenance just as plants need water to grow and survive. Good educational outcomes are the result of good educational practices. Good educational practices are the result of strong Leadership; Inclusive practices; Quality control through supervision, educator development, and team empowerment; Universal practices; Implementation of evidence-based curriculum valid for academic and social-emotional-behavioral instruction at Tiers 1, 2, and 3 with engagement in feedback looping; and Data-based decision making.

Leadership

Viewed through the Leadership lens, every decision made on a school campus reflects the vision and quality of the school principal and administrative team to carry out school level initiatives in compliance with federal, state, and district guidelines. MTSS requires high competence in leadership qualities of organization and supervision in order to put structures, functions, and procedures in place, as well as maximize human capital and most effectively budget to allocate scarce resources. Restructuring existing roles, responsibilities, and resources to enable highly specialized collaborative communities to flourish improves school culture, increases effectiveness of communication and personal responsibility, and helps with budgeting. Principals with strong organizational management skills who can inspire, motivate, and reward educators are more likely to reach school-wide goals (Grissom & Loeb, 2011; Stetler, Ritchie, Rycroft-Malone, & Charns, 2014). Investing in human capital, evidence-based curriculum, and having a clear blueprint for building and sustaining best practices are all required for effective leadership. School leaders are required to actively solve problems to ensure barriers to implementation of MTSS are successfully overcome. Leaders must continually review and revise all practices to keep on course with evolving student and staff needs and realities of circumstances. When leadership makes MTSS a school priority, then it shall be a guiding framework on a school campus.

Inclusiveness

When decisions on a school campus are viewed through the Inclusiveness lens, leaders and staff members must take into account how existing and proposed educational practices impact all individuals with differing ethnicities, languages, cultures, religions, backgrounds, and beliefs. If a current practice is not universally implemented nor equitably applied, groups of students, families, staff, and community members could be alienated by not having equal access to supports or having legal protections equitably applied to all. When the rights of one are institutionally violated, the rights of all are violated, with risk of disintegration of all said rights. Procedures must align with best practices to expect them to work as intended. Cultural competence is required to provide a respectful and adaptively responsive learning environment to the needs of diverse populations. School leaders support inclusive practices by continually challenging educators to challenge their own implicit biases, effectively building relationships with people from different backgrounds, and creating learning opportunities to grow more inclusive practices through staff development and community outreach. Restorative justice is a perfect example of an inclusive practice which provides an effective alternative to ineffective discipline procedures with zero tolerance. School psychologists are poised to positively consult and contribute to these efforts on school campuses (Song & Swearer, 2016). Increasing cultural competence and using restorative justice practices benefits all stakeholders.

Quality Control

Quality control is the overarching construct for maintaining fidelity of implementation of any program or practice on a school campus. Ensuring that practices are evidence-based, and that teachers are implementing instruction with fidelity is paramount. Every day, educators are faced with more responsibilities, more requirements, and more seemingly pointless roles. Educators want to work smarter, not harder. With every new practice in a school, a competing less effective practice should dissipate for educators in order for them to have the time and energy to comply with new expectations. Yet, rarely is that the case. It makes no sense to add more criteria to what teachers are required to do without addressing the obstacles to policies with unintended consequences that make teachers' work less meaningful. Evaluating current practices, through measureable outcomes, is required to shed ineffective practices; however, selling educators on new roles and responsibilities is not a simple task. *Quality control of resources is much simpler than quality control of human capital.* Nonetheless, data-based decision making is at the crux of quality control of effective systems in schools. The way to initiate and sustain quality control measures relies on the continuous improvement model of implement-review-revise (Bryk, Gomez, Grunow, & LeMahieu, 2016). Leadership must be constantly supervising practices for fidelity to ensure quality control because directives that are not enforced through active supervision are never sustained. Most teachers simply do not have enough time, resources, or administrative support to build or sustain new complex systems without states, school districts, and school administrators actively solving problems at the point of service delivery. Research-based practices are grown when there is room to grow, and the way to make room for new practices should include reducing unnecessary paperwork, reducing unnecessary meeting times, reducing the unreasonably high levels of pressure of teaching to the test, and reducing busy work required of administrators and educators for high-stakes testing.

Universality

Universal is best described as "all means all." Every student counts and every student should have a place in a high-quality school. Giving equal opportunity and equal access is the foundation of social justice in education. Beyond that, individualizing educational supports for students is required for many to be successful presently and is the wave of the future in education. Providing evidence-based instruction with fidelity for all students should be the goal of every school. Educational practices that have the biggest impact at a school are those that all students benefit from. For example, students benefit from practices that are aligned with MTSS, and there is a level of support for all students who have a range of needs. Students are screened universally to help identify those at-risk proactively, which saves instructional time for them when they are given opportunities and remedial interventions as quickly as possible in their educational careers. All students require low barriers to access to the level of support they need to be successful in school.

Implementation and Feedback Looping

The Implementation and Feedback Looping lens of educational practices magnifies the nuts and bolts of the what, when, why, where, and how educational practices are rolled out. Oftentimes the idea behind an educational practice is noble, but the implementation of it is a disaster. When this is the case, the product or outcome does not meet the hype of promised results and administrators may become discouraged. When results are not as desired, school leaders may have the inclination to throw the baby, or the educational practice, out with the bathwater, without having evaluated implementation integrity. It goes back to best teaching principles and using evidence-based instructional practices to maintain quality control in terms of supervision fidelity. Staff motivation and positive reinforcement of positive practices and outcomes is at the heart of the implementation lens. Feedback looping must occur constantly to determine efficacy of practices, which is tied to quality control. The only way to grow best practices is to give a voice to those implementing those practices to review and revise the practices as necessary to adjust and adapt or stay on course. Once again, success breeds more success, as does empowering and rewarding educators who deliver the what, when, why, where, and how.

Data-Based Decision Making

Data-based decision making is the engine of MTSS. Data should drive instruction, and most other decisions on campus. The data lens is the tool for hyper focus on outcomes, indicators, trends, trajectories, and systematic feedback. Multiple sources of information and observational opportunities must be triangulated to get the whole picture of instructional quality. Instructional decisions based on one source or one type of assessment may drive assumptions that are faulty or misleading. If the curriculum is of high quality, if teachers are implementing with integrity, if the data collection methods are sound, then the outcome data should be reliable. To gain a clearer picture of practices at a school, or in the classroom, a variety of instruments should be used, both formative and summative. Relying on one measure, such as high-stakes testing, may not give an accurate reflection of whether instructional practices and educators are effective or not. Systems must be designed to manage the rich sources of data available to continually renew and update in real time, so that timely decisions for students may occur. Practices not supported by positive impact of achievement data should be re-evaluated for fidelity of implementation before being abandoned completely. The quality controls of MTSS depend as much on quality data as stringent supervision of implementation fidelity.

The Basics

Administrative accountability is inevitable. School principals, school district administration and associate superintendents, and school boards must be accountable to the public for providing adequate supports to their schools' multi-tiered support systems. The days of optional evidence-based services in the field of education should be as frowned upon as instances of physicians not washing their hands before conducting surgical procedures. Best practices should be supervised for accountability because they will never otherwise be adequately built or sustained. As evaluation standards for teachers and other licensed educators are beginning to align with national teaching and other professional standards, administrative job performance evaluations for principals, as well as school district administration, associate superintendents, and school boards should also be aligned and measured by more transparent standards, especially in failing schools and districts.

High-stakes tests often fail to measure true gains of high-risk, high-poverty populations. Including benchmarks and goals in the growth model on administrators' annual evaluations will allow district superintendents and state superintendents to hold administrators, as well as teachers, accountable for student growth. The politics should be taken out of schools, and fair evaluation standards should apply. Any school taking any amount of public school dollars for students should be held to the same standards. School principals should have MTSS criteria on their evaluation rubrics to ensure that such practices are taking place. When the school principal refuses to provide, or inadequately provides, supports for all, they are not serving their students or the community justly. Nearly everything can be broken down to a leadership issue in education. School principals who value professional development and training in evidence-based practices can take steps to implement MTSS and create a better school culture that produces greater opportunity for all students. Change takes time, and children are usually the least resistant to change in comparison to the adults supporting them.

Teacher motivation and compensation are huge factors in the success of MTSS. Expecting more of educators without taking away other burdens is not a long-term solution. Taking advantage of salaried workers only goes so far before quality of service suffers. Educators need a comfortable salary and health benefits so they do not have to work two and three jobs, as has been indicated by teacher walkouts from West Virginia and Kentucky to Oklahoma and Arizona in the past year. Professional compensation and valuing educators' specialized skills that lead to positive educational outcomes for all students is the best way to get high-quality efforts from the educational workforce. Extra work should come along with extra pay. Extra duty compensation, additional pay from longer school days or school years, and comp time are only fair.

Administrators are forced to make hard decisions, such as cutting budgets and staffing positions, because many states do not fund education as fully as they should. However, until the day that highly trained educators working directly with students are treated like the venerable developmental experts they are and compensated accordingly, schools will continue to face issues of staff attrition and quality. It is time to restructure the way schools are funded and the way educator pay is allocated. In the meantime, MTSS can grow incrementally if it is a priority. Once the new practices take root in a school, automaticity dramatically increases the likelihood of sustainability. MTSS practices built from scratch can be sustained, as long as best practices are supervised for implementation fidelity and positively reinforced.

A motivated and well-trained school staff can accomplish the impossible with students. Whether children have disabilities or high giftedness, building and sustaining relationships with teachers as positive role models increases students' critical thinking and prosocial skills. Healthy children need adults as leaders and as models (Creighton, Doub, & Scott, 1999), and today's children especially need guidance in a safe space so they can make judgment errors in a confusing world without lasting repercussions. With social media and instant publishing of personal images and private moments, children are growing up in a very unforgiving world. Information on the internet lasts forever. Schools have become less forgiving as well, if they ever were at all. Kicking children out of school, through expulsion, takes away their rightful opportunity to receive guided practice in a forgiving environment. Mistakes are guaranteed in life, especially in childhood, which is why zero tolerance discipline policies are so unfair to so many students.

Situations get out of hand quickly in emotionally charged moments, and training educators, support staff, and school police to de-escalate, rather than escalate, with students is key. Using these conflict situations as teachable moments for empathy and social skills problem solving should be a national priority. Research suggests that authenticity and empathy are expected of both students and teachers, yet these skills are not explicitly taught or actualized by both parties at the same time (Bialystok & Kukar, 2017). Further, this can create competing demands and tensions that undermine social justice in education. The less students understand themselves and each another in childhood, the less understanding there will be in adulthood. Children with a history of trauma, emotional and environmental instability, mixed with gaps in school attendance, severe underachievement, and poor impulse control or understanding of social expectations have little hope for positive outcomes in a system that prepares disadvantaged children for prison instead of remediating the problems through humanistic treatment and culturally competent teaching.

Some solutions are very expensive, unfortunately. Mental and behavioral health services in the community cost a fortune, Medicaid and insurance will cover less and less, and service providers are limited in how many low-cost patients they can support. Many of the most talented psychiatrists, psychologists, and mental health providers in the private sector accept cash only for treatment because insurance coverage is constantly changing and billing is problematic. Another barrier to treatment, in addition to cost for services, is transportation. It is becoming more apparent that schools with community health centers are a necessity. Behavioral health, psychiatric services, and therapeutic counseling for children and families at school sites could solidify schools' role as the safe harbors in society and should be funded as the pillars of the community that they are. Helping parents and family leaders with advocacy for behavioral and mental health treatment is key for schools to succeed in interventions for mentally and behaviorally unhealthy students who grow to be mentally and behaviorally unhealthy adults otherwise.

Where to Start?

The place to start, of course, is wherever you are. Evaluate your resources. Determine what you have and what you should keep in place when the data supports that it is working. All school administrators should strive to improve Tier 1 instructional practices. Many realize that the needs of Tier 3 easily overwhelm resources on campus and may need to start with a major investment there and grow out Tiers 1 and 2 as byproducts of necessity. Bottom line is that better practices can lead to better practices in both directions, though growing from the foundations of strong leadership and effective Tier 1 is healthier and more sustainable.

With established MTSS, solid Tier 1 can ensure that less students require Tier 2 and Tier 3 instruction. However, Tier 3 cannot fix problems with Tier 1. Poor instruction or intervention, in combination with apathy and other risk factors, can create lifelong learning problems in students. Realistically, not all educators at any one school are exceptional, and they are not all bad either. Most schools have a mix of many accomplished and less accomplished teachers. Administrators are tasked with increasing the skills of less accomplished educators, nurturing the talents of teacher leaders, and improving delivery of evidence-based practices across all educators. No matter the etiology of student delays, evidence-based skills curriculum, spiraled throughout K-12 with multiple opportunities to learn the same skills, will give each child the correct number of guided instructional opportunities to master developmental benchmarks.

Starting with Tier 3 is a common place to build supports because students who are low academically are less likely engaged in class and are more likely disruptive, destroying the learning environment for everyone else. Students who externalize behaviors and present as a danger to themselves and others will require intensive interventions and support immediately. Supporting a healthy Tier 3 is also an equity factor for students with educational disabilities, and those with potential or unidentified disabilities. Students with the highest needs require individualized supports with progress closely monitored, which requires the most coordination of resources and regular communication between staff members.

Putting together a Behavioral and Mental Health MTSS team may seem like a good place to start in secondary school, especially in light of recent mass shootings and violence in schools nationwide. The recent urgency has cast the spotlight on the need for increased school safety measures; however, what is at the heart of prevention of school violence is a comprehensive and coordinated mental health model which includes proactive and crisis procedures to maximize school safety. Academic MTSS is a harder concept to sell at the secondary level because, while it is widely accepted, it is rarely implemented due to the many tasks that must be coordinated simultaneously that are not necessarily explicit, which causes confusion or paralysis of implementation and growth. *MTSS systems that are poorly understood, have many moving parts, and lack coordinated administrative vision or supervision required to build or sustain, will be less likely to be implemented.* Schools that implement Academic MTSS will already have a school culture that supports Behavioral and Mental Health MTSS and should find less resistance to new roles and responsibilities from educators.

School administrators and leadership teams must ultimately decide for themselves which issues to tackle first, from credit retrieval to social-emotional-behavioral screenings. There is no correct answer for where a school should get started on building MTSS, just that it should be "built to last" as part of a growing and sustainable comprehensive system. The superstar administrator might take action to add multiple new initiatives at once, while another administrator may find it difficult to take action to add more than one new initiative at a time knowing that every new piece added to MTSS requires active problem solving and supervision to begin and sustain. *Starting with low hanging fruit is often a good place to build success.* Increase educators' earning potential for motivation. Empower collaborative teams with leadership opportunities to grow under a distributed leadership model and reward problem solvers on your campus. Institute quarterly benchmarking to quickly identify underachievers, schedule reading and math intervention classes in the master calendar with researched-based curriculum, and monitor student growth over time. Make things easier for teachers by automating data collection with easy-to-use tools for decision making. Schedule regular team meetings in the master schedule to get school experts working on problems. The sooner stakeholders feel the positive benefits of new practices, the more likely new practices will be embraced and sustained.

Exercise 14.1

- What are your schools' low hanging fruit, easy-to-fix problems, or obvious solutions?
- Survey your staff, prioritize, and fix those small problems, while increasing motivation and positive support of all staff members
- List and rank your schools' problem priorities 1–5 (i.e., attendance, teacher retention, high rate of suspensions/expulsions, low academic rigor or achievement, lack of qualified educators/too many long-term subs, low morale, etc.).
- Pick one initiative at a time and let the problem solving with your smart teams begin.

Just Do It

When to start MTSS structures and functions is never as important as what or where to start. The beginning of the year is always a great time for new initiatives, but any time is a good time for best practices to occur. Schools need not wait for the beginning of the year to address a problem systematically. Schools are more likely to put things in place incrementally so as not to bite off more than can be chewed in terms of incorporating and managing new professional expectations. Some principals can systematically restructure a school all at once, in a dramatic turnaround fashion. For the high achieving, blue ribbon principals who will use this guide to affirm current educational practices already in place, or to reconsider different options and build or improve upon ideas, kudos to these superstars in education. Unfortunately, these superstar leaders may have inherent leadership skills and the transformative results they obtain may not necessarily be intuitive to others, which is why a framework or roadmap is needed to reach the same destination. See Table 14.1 for examples of the various components necessary at each tier. Many of the components, such as restorative justice and advocacy, should be embedded within each tier.

Every new initiative, program, curricula, agenda, activity, and mindset should align with the LIQUID Model if it is to be implemented successfully in a school. Evidence-based practices must be spearheaded and sustained adequately through the *leadership* lens: budgets, resources, human capital, staff motivation, systematic supports, vision, and supervision. Educational practices must be *inclusive*: equitable, equal access, provided in a culturally competent context, examining and challenging implicit bias, and making concerted efforts to improve relationships with people from all backgrounds. All practices must have *quality controls* in place to ensure implementation fidelity through data obtained by feedback looping. Ineffective practices must be replaced with effective practices. Quality control depends on the strength of leadership to monitor outcomes and revise curriculum factors, implementation factors, and human capital factors. Every practice in a school must be considered in the *universal* context. How does a practice impact all students? How can educational services have the best outcome for the most students? Do all students have equal access and do they get what they need when they need it? Universal screening helps target at-risk students quickly so that help starts immediately, leading to better short-term and long-term outcomes. Educational practices must be evaluated through the *implementation and feedback looping* lens which requires iterative analysis to engage in continuous improvement of practices. Implementation fidelity is essential to effective teaching and without it, outcome data may be skewed as it assumes that fidelity criteria were observed. Feedback looping provides guidance to school leadership for which quality control indicators must be addressed. Lastly, the *data* never lies. The wrong questions might be asked of the data that can lead to erroneous conclusions, but the data are objective, in and of itself, as long as the fidelity of standardized testing procedures are observed. Using the preponderance of evidence to lead and drive better practices, actively analyzed by relevant stakeholders on a regular basis to review and revise, results in better outcomes for all.

Table 14.1 Examples of Tiered Components for Academic MTSS and SEB MTSS

	Academic MTSS	Social-Emotional-Behavioral MTSS
Tier 1 Supports	• Evidence-based Tier 1 curriculum implemented with fidelity • Regular benchmark screening, summative and formative assessment • Block scheduling with opportunities for differentiation and enrichment • Support for accomplished teaching as outlined by the National Board for Professional Teaching Standards	• Evidence-based positive behavioral intervention supports • Universal school-wide and classroom management strategies • Universal social-emotional curriculum implemented • Regular benchmark screening • Advocacy for mandated social-emotional-behavioral curriculum K–12 • School counseling services • Family engagement and outreach • Culturally competent teaching practices • Restorative justice • Access to social services providing basic needs and housing security • Student-centered advocacy, communication, and leadership
Tier 2 Supports	• Extended school year in at-risk communities • Longer school day opportunities for at-risk students • Daily access to evidence-based Tier 2 curriculum implemented with fidelity in scheduled classes of reading/English Language Arts and math • Tutoring and homework assistance is available to all students requiring academic support on a volunteer (or scheduled) basis • Technological supports with instructional skills practice is used to generalize skills practiced with direct instruction • Students with higher needs in Tier 2 will require active case management to determine whether targeted needs become intensive over time • Progress is monitored monthly and rate of improvement analyzed • Consideration of 504 plan if warranted	• Targeted social skills curriculum in scheduled classes (anger management, empathy training, problem-solving, etc.) • School counseling services • Restorative justice • School social worker involvement • Check-in check-out, pressure passes, short-term accommodations, targeted communication between school and home • Incentive Plans • Referral to community services (i.e., Boys' Town or therapeutic counseling) • Consultation with school psychologist • Staff development in Life Space Crisis Intervention (Long, Wood, & Fecser, 2001) • Family leader–teacher–student conferences and contracts between home and school • Consideration of 504 plan if warranted

| Tier 3 Supports | • Case manager assignment for coordination of individualized supports
• Implementation of academic plans with discrete goals and supports defined which are monitored for progress weekly to bi-monthly
• Tier 3 intensive academic curriculum implemented with fidelity in scheduled classes in addition to core curriculum classes
• Intensive classes should have smaller class sizes and be counted for elective credit so that entry and exit out of remedial classes are based on need and rate of improvement (block scheduling allows for double electives and will allow for scheduling fluidity quite well)
• Technological supports with Tier 3 level instructional skills practice is used to generalize skills practiced with direct instruction
• The academic MTSS team is actively monitoring students for improvement
• The most intensive instructional resources are exhausted in documented poor response to instruction
• Referral to Multidisciplinary Team for educational eligibility consideration
• Individualized Education Plans and protections under IDEIA | • Case manager assignment for coordination of individualized supports, implementation of individualized behavior plans (requiring high ratio of positive reinforcement and data collection of antecedents, behaviors, and consequences, in addition to frequency, intensity, duration data in response to interventions)
• Trauma informed care, requiring trusting relationships with teachers engaging in repeated rehearsals of replacement behaviors
• Restorative justice
• Functional behavioral analyses
• School counseling services
• School social worker involvement supporting treatment at home and school
• Most often managed by grade level MTSS case managers
• Referral to the Behavioral and Mental Health MTSS team for active case management of most severe Tier 3 students (potential danger to self and/or others)
• Team is actively supporting families in community-based and school-based treatments for students
• Students are monitored for improvement at least monthly by the MTSS team or at least twice a month by Behavioral and Mental Health MTSS team
• The most intensive instructional resources are exhausted in documented poor response to instruction
• Referral to Multidisciplinary Team for educational eligibility consideration
• Individualized Education Plans and protections under IDEIA |

Final Words

Public education is at a crossroads. It is preparing some of our children for bright futures, while leaving others stranded in the middle of nowhere with little chance of moving forward. Regardless of school, socioeconomic area, or population, individual educators can make or break opportunities for students to succeed in academic rigor, independent living skills, mental and behavioral health, and social responsibility with respect for self and others. Every child should have the opportunity to learn how to be a productive member of society, to be independent and self-sufficient. *Educators must first and foremost make students partners in their learning.* Life is very complicated for children, and many are vulnerable to dangers, and have life traumas that are more horrific than any scary movie ever made. Educators must team up with students to inspire their young minds, challenge them to think critically while developing academic excellence, and nurture their ability to make healthy connections with others. When students want to come to school and look forward to that time-honored relationship between teachers and students, educators have excelled at the relationship piece of the learning equation. A master educator once said that there are no attention deficits, only deficiencies in making things interesting or motivating enough for students that they cannot help but to attend and learn. Learning has to be something students are partners in, not just something that is happening to them. Trust plus curiosity equals optimal learning conditions.

Not all children have the organic or environmental capacity to learn or perform at the same rate as typical students. Even so, educators must be able to connect student interests and potential to positive outcomes. Targeted and intensive learning opportunities need to be *more* interesting and motivating to attract curiosity of the students who have to work harder to succeed. Despite all the other variables that impact student achievement, positive relationships with caring teachers is the magic bond for students to remain invested in learning when things get difficult, rather than giving up. Since evidence-based practices clearly support positive relationships with educators, educators must feel more supported by administrators and systems in place to make their jobs possible. Educators who do not have financial security to pay for their own basic needs, those who do not have administrative backing and clear access to structures and functions that support at-risk students, and those who do not know how to effectively respond to and correct student misbehavior are being set up to fail. Positive relationships with students are a clear and obvious job responsibility for educators that should be part of educators' continuous training, performance evaluation rubrics, and valued as much as any other performance indicator.

American education has gotten off track, as deep-pocketed private interests have become more involved in the policy-making process, blurring the distinctions between public and private sectors in education (Lubienski, 2016). In the process, private interests are supplanting public education and student rights; educational access and equity are marginalized (Singh, 2015). "Education policy-making itself is being privatized through a significant shift toward private interests in the making of public policy for public education" (Lubienski, 2016, p. 192). This includes the promotion of implicitly biased, expensive, high-stakes tests that result in big business turning a profit while they simultaneously use propaganda to turn public opinion against the public's best interests. The use of propaganda to influence public opinion is nothing new (Wind-Cowie, 2014; Exley, 1949) and the unfortunate target of this new campaign for social control (Freeley, 2002) is our students. This destroys the civil right to a free appropriate public education (FAPE) and delivers socially unjust consequences when at-risk students, especially those of color or impacted by poverty, fail.

Big businesses have devised a business plan to prove that public schools are failing by developing tests that large segments of the population will never pass and will be disproportionality punished for not achieving. Minority students, students living in poverty, students with poor language skills, and students in the process of learning English as a second language will be significantly impacted by this test bias disproportionately (Au, 2015; Solórzano, 2008). These test biases only serve to promulgate racism under a so-called anti-racism wave of education reform (Au, 2015). Charter schools with little accountability are gobbling up public schools, while providing worse outcomes (Chingos & West, 2015), and giving families no choice under the guise of increasing school choice. There also exists a lack of democratic influence within charter school policies, and until these democratic principles exist, justice within charter schools cannot be achieved (Abowitz & Karaba, 2009). Private and charter schools do not have to pass the same tests or "rigor" public schools must endure, and public schools will always fail in comparison until all school types are held to the same standards. All schools that receive public monies should have to meet the same criteria, which should not be left up to the whims of state legislators who are often indebted to big businesses.

Public education currently spends much of its energies in teaching practices to pass tests that are funded by the very interests that wish to destroy it. Hens, meet the foxes guarding your house. How did these high-stakes tests take over the goal of public schooling? Marketing and public deception may be at the root of private interest's effectiveness in their big grab for monies dedicated to public education funding, playing on the public's fear (Cooper & Randall, 2008). Savvy local school districts are starting to hire public relations managers to counter the negative publicity bombarding the media largely promoted by a few well-endowed individuals and corporate entities who benefit financially by swaying public opinion against public education. When public opinion is swayed, then hawks can swoop in to institutionalize racism, abuse, and social injustice while maximizing corporate profits. Fortunately, public apathy is not a permanent condition, and defense of hard working educators in public schools can be rallied successfully by coordinated efforts of educators in solidarity with parent groups and community leaders, as evidenced by successes in recent educator walkouts nationwide.

Public educators and local communities must quickly figure out how to prepare our children for survival skills, vocational training, and consumer science, while providing social-emotional and behavioral regulation skills and relationship building in the technology age. They must also do this while meeting the required accountability standards. Public schools are inherent to the American way of life as we now know it; that every child can learn up because education is at the heart of democratic schooling and social justice. In the words of a prominent social justice advocate and researcher: "None of us created the racial and social injustice that is deeply rooted in U.S. society and none of us can solve these problems by ourselves" (Shriberg, 2016, p. 339). Educators must become intellectual soldiers in the army defending knowledge, research, and evidence-based practices, with the goal of a humane society. *Advocacy is the urgent call to battle for the survival of public education.* The civil right to FAPE is eroding quickly, and with public support from students, families, and communities, educators must step up and organize. Attention, current and retired educators and child caregivers: run for political office, help someone run for office, join a policy committee, show up and testify during public comment at public meetings such as State Board of Education meetings, legislative meetings, or meetings of other government entities. Additionally, submit written comments to these meetings, write letters to your representatives, vote, and make donations to candidates that support the value of education. Be a force and speak up at every opportunity. There are many partners who can help you achieve positive things for children, and having socially just, evidence-based practices, such as MTSS, memorialized in education policy and practice, at any level, is an incredible accomplishment.

References

Abowitz, K. K., & Karaba, R. (2009). Charter schooling and democratic justice. *Educational Policy, 24*(3), 534–558.

Au, W. (2015). Meritocracy 2.0: High-stakes, standardized testing as a racial project of neoliberal multiculturalism. *Educational Policy, 30*(1), 39–62.

Bialystok, L., & Kukar, P. (2017). Authenticity and empathy in education. *Theory and Research in Education, 16*(1), 23–39.

Bolman, L. G., & Deal, T. E. (2017). *Reframing organizations: Artistry, choice, and leadership* (6th ed.). San Francisco, CA: Jossey Bass.

Bryk, A. S., Gomez, L. M., Grunow, A., & LeMahieu, P. G. (2016). *Learning to improve: How America's schools can get better at getting better.* Cambridge, MA: Harvard Education Press.

Chingos, M. M., & West, M. R. (2015). The uneven performance of Arizona's charter schools. *Educational Evaluation and Policy Analysis, 37*(1), 120–134.

Cooper, B. S., & Randall, V. (2008). Fear and privatization. *Educational Policy, 22*(1), 204–227.

Creighton, F. P., Doub, G. T., & Scott, V. M. (1999). *Survival skills for healthy families* (2nd ed.). Holly Springs, NC: Family Wellness Associates.

Exley, D. (1949). The role of public opinion in the modern state. *Political Science, 1*(2), 14–19.

Freeley, M. M. (2002). Entrepreneurs of punishment: The legacy of privatization. *Punishment & Society, 4*(3), 321–344.

Grissom, J. A., & Loeb, S. (2011). Triangulating principal effectiveness: How perspectives of parents, teachers, and assistant principals identify the central importance of managerial skills. *American Education Research Journal, 48*(5), 1091–1123.

Long, N. J., Wood, M. M., & Fecser, F. A. (2001). *Life space crisis intervention: Talking with students in conflict* (2nd ed.). Charlottesville, VA: Pro-Ed.

Lubienski, C. (2016). Sector distinctions and the privatization of education policymaking. *Theory and Research in Education, 14*(2), 192–212.

Shriberg, D. (2016). Commentary: School psychologists as advocates for racial justice and social justice: Some proposed steps. *School Psychology Forum, 10*(3), 337–339.

Singh, K. (2015). Safeguarding education as public good and regulating private providers. *Social Change, 45*(2), 308–323.

Solórzano, R. W. (2008). High stakes testing: Issues, implications and remedies for English language learners. *Review of Educational Research, 78*(2), 260–329.

Song, S. Y., & Swearer, S. M. (2016). The cart before the horse: The challenge and promise of restorative justice consultation in schools. *Journal of Educational and Psychological Consultation, 26*(4), 313–324.

Stetler, C. B., Ritchie, J. A., Rycroft-Malone, J., & Charns, M. P. (2014). Leadership for evidence-based practice: Strategic and functional behaviors for institutionalizing EBP. *Worldviews on Evidence-Based Nursing, 11*(4), 219–226.

Wind-Cowie, M. (2014). Political vacuum opens up propaganda possibilities. *Index on Censorship, 43*(1), 74–77.

Appendix

Resources

Program Level

Models that Can Help Improve Low-Performing Schools (Center for American Progress, 2016): https://cdn.Americanprogress.org/wp-content/uploads/2016/03/01075517/NonCharterSchools-report.pdf.

Nine Characteristics of High Performing Schools (Shannon & Bylsma, 2007): www.k12.wa.us/research/pubdocs/NineCharacteristics.pdf.

Secondary Readings and References for MTSS (Shinn, 2013): www.tnspdg.com/pdf/RTItraining/2/Shinn%20Secondary%20Readings%20and%20Resources.pdf.

Turning Around Low-Performing Schools: A Guide for State and Local Leaders (U.S. Department of Education, 1998): www2.ed.gov/PDFDocs/turning.pdf.

Interventions

Blueprints for Healthy Youth Development: www.blueprintsprograms.com.

Evidence for ESSA: www.evidenceforessa.org.

Intervention Central: www.interventioncentral.org.

Positive Behavioral Interventions and Supports: www.PBIS.org.

Secondary Readings and References for MTSS (Shinn, 2013): www.tnspdg.com/pdf/RTItraining/2/Shinn%20Secondary%20Readings%20and%20Resources.pdf.

The Department of Education's What Works Clearinghouse: http://ies.ed.gov/ncee/wwc (Education).

The U.S. Substance Abuse and Mental Health Services Administration's National Registry of Evidence-based Programs and Practices: www.nrepp.samhsa.gov (Mental and Substance Abuse Disorders).

Family Programs

Promising Practices Network: www.promisingpractices.net.

STAR Parenting: http://starparent.com.

Strengthening Families Program for Parents and Youth 10–14 (SFP 10–14): www.strengtheningfamiliesprogram.org.

Survival Skills for Healthy Families: www.familywellness.com/programs.php.
Systematic Training for Effective Parenting (STEP): www.steppublishers.com.
Triple P-Positive Parenting Program: www.triplep-parenting.com/us/triple-p.

Additional Resources

California Evidence-Based Clearinghouse for Child Welfare: www.cebc4cw.org
(Child Welfare).
Coalition for Evidence-Based Policy: http://coalition4evidence.org (Social
Policy).
National Alliance on Mental Illness: www.nami.org/Find-Support/NAMI-
Programs.
National Association of School Psychologists: www.nasponline.org.
U.S. Department of Justice's CrimeSolutions.gov: www.crimesolutions.gov
(Criminal and Juvenile Justice).
What Works in Reentry: http://whatworks.csgjusticecenter.org (Re-entry).

Glossary

Alingual is the classification of students who are not proficient in any language.

Ask is a specific request made from one individual or group to another.

Automatization is the result of processes that have been converted from loose implementation to automatic implementation.

Base funding is the amount of money a state sets aside to cover the basic costs of education.

Behavioral and Mental Health MTSS is comprised of highly trained individuals tasked with school safety, student behavioral health, and emotional well-being of students in a school and community setting.

Benchmarking is conducted at set intervals throughout the year to provide a snapshot of a student's performance compared to grade level.

Braided funding is the weaving of funds from multiple sources and is useful in maximizing impact without relying too heavily on any one funding source.

Case manager model is student-centered and assigns a specific educator to advocate for the students they are assigned to represent.

Case notes are supplemental data that are entered into the MTSS Student Database that are not otherwise captured in one of the pre-determined columns.

Categorical funding is reserved for a very specific program or purpose.

Change agents influence innovation and make decisions that align with the central entity.

Commissive is a manner in which a state policy is written that commits itself to action.

Communitycentric is the sense that a broader community influences and promotes student success, not just the immediate family.

Connector is someone with high social capital who can put a group in touch with other like-minded individuals or with individuals who have a specific skill set that can benefit an initiative.

Contagion effect   refers to a replication of a particular behavior by others, due to proximity or social media exposure.

Controlled chaos   is a term borrowed from the biology, engineering, and life sciences fields that recognizes some or whole segments may be disorganized, yet can be controlled within given parameters.

Counterintuitive cultures   arise when practices in the field are producing results opposite to that which is desired.

Cultural brokering   promotes culture as an asset that can be used to positively influence and bridge family and school relationships.

Cultural change   is the observable shift toward new standards, attitudes, and behavior.

Decentralized   is the transfer of power and decision making from central government to local government.

Dedicated funding   are monies dedicated for a specific purpose, such as teacher salaries, through a specific funding source, such as specific tax revenues.

Directive   is a manner in which a state policy is written that tells the local education agencies what to do.

Discipline   is the training of adherence to codes of behavior and may include punishments to correct noncompliance.

Discretionary grant funding   is monies that are awarded through a competitive application process.

Ecosystems   are the confluence and interaction of all social and environmental variables that influence students growth, development, and functioning.

Education malpractice   is the preventable adverse impact on a student through educator negligence or incompetence that goes against evidence-based practices.

Ethnic match   occurs when a student's teacher and family both identify with the same ethnic background.

Feedback looping   is when the outputs of a reflection or outcome are used as inputs to inform and improve upon the next phase of the cycle.

Fidelity   is trust in the accuracy and quality of the overall implementation process.

Formula funding   is the dollar amount assigned from the state to each district based on various computed factors.

Gerrymandering   is when the geographic boundaries are manipulated to benefit one party over another.

Growth model   is comprised of rich data points that measure student growth, or lack thereof, over time. It is well documented as more effective at determining a student's performance than high-stakes tests in high-risk schools.

Human capital   includes the competencies, value, and knowledge the professionals on campus bring to the table.

Implementation science   deals with the integration, application, and refinement of evidence-based practices in the field.

Implicit bias   are the underlying beliefs, stereotypes, and attitudes that unconsciously impacts a person's decision making.

Infrastructure   is the foundational framework that supports data-based decisions about students on campus.

Intermediate organizations   are typically not practitioners and their involvement can either impede or facilitate implementation depending on resources and motivations.

Internal validity   is the extent to which a causal relationship between the interventions provided and the outcomes obtained can be attributed to or determined.

Intervention graph   is the visual representation of scores obtained during progress monitoring data collection cycles.

Intervention log   tracks the date, type, and duration of intervention provided.

Intervention plan   defines the student's area of difficulty, targets a discreet skill for baseline to enable goal setting.

Iterative   refers to a repeated process that occurs at regular intervals with the purpose of achieving an established goal.

Leadership fidelity checks   are the review of all aspects of implementation procedures conducted by administration or a member of the leadership team that occur on both a random or as needed basis.

Legitimization   occurs within an organization when an act or process becomes entrenched in its values and norms.

LGBTQ+   students are those who identify as being lesbian, gay, bisexual, transgender, questioning, or gender diverse.

Linchpins   hold various elements of complicated structures in place to keep students from sliding off into an abyss of school failure.

LIQUID Model   is represented by the non-negotiable variables of Leadership, Inclusiveness, Quality Control, Universality, Implementation and feedback, and Data-based decision making to guide teams through all phases of the MTSS process using critical exploration and problem-solving.

LIQUID Theory   explains the process, constructs, and intersectionality necessary for successful MTSS implementation and sustainability: Leadership, Inclusiveness, Quality Control, Universality, Implementation and feedback looping, and Data-based decision making.

Logic models   can be used as an effectiveness framework to ensure inputs are leading to desired outputs in the short and long term.

Master schedule is the calendar and timetable to support the hourly, daily, weekly, monthly, and annual activities on a campus and is essential for successful program implementation.

MTSS is a socially just framework to providing equitable access and support to all students in the educational setting.

MTSS case managers are responsible for researching and documenting student history, collecting data from multiple sources, presenting data at meetings, communicating changes to student instructional interventions to relevant stakeholders, and getting feedback from student teachers on efficacy of interventions.

MTSS chairs communicate MTSS meeting dates, record meeting discussions, lead meetings, problem solve MTSS functions and processes, and liaise with stakeholder groups.

MTSS Evaluation Frequency and Intensity Framework outlines that some practices must be evaluated universally, or on a regular basis, while others must be evaluated on a targeted basis, such as during benchmark windows; and others will require intensive, in-depth and thorough investigation, such as through an annual reporting of the program.

MTSS extension opportunities are programming options or incentives for students outside the traditional school offerings.

MTSS meeting logs are the official dated documentation of the MTSS Student Portfolios and case notes discussed at MTSS Team Meetings and are updated during or after each meeting.

MTSS Student Database is the storehouse that archives all data for students who are discussed at MTSS team meetings, and is achieved by creating and maintaining a running record of at-risk student history, interventions implemented, school performance, current needs, and recommendations for school success.

MTSS Student Portfolios are comprised of the artifacts to present to the MTSS team when making decisions about a student and help support the MTSS Student Database.

Neo-institutional theory is a sociopolitical lens in which to view how organizations interact and how they impact society.

Outside evaluator is an impartial person hired to collect data and report out on the program's progress toward their stated goals and may include information about resource utilization, efficiency, effectiveness, and fiscal allocations.

Overcorrection is the explicit repeated practice of a desired behavior.

Physical capital includes the tangible tools necessary to implement an MTSS program and includes materials needed to execute the research-based interventions as well as the computerized assessment tools necessary for benchmarking and progress monitoring.

Positive class culture is a learning environment based on trust in which the students are encouraged and empowered to make and learn from mistakes.

Progress monitoring   is conducted at regular intervals, such as weekly, to build into the overall portfolio of student progress in response to the interventions provided.

Protective factors   are conditions that positively contribute to student well-being and include factors such as having their basic needs met as well as having resilience skills, strong social connections, social-emotional skills.

Rate of improvement   is the student's actual rate of improvement and is contrasted against their goal rate of improvement to make decisions about adequacy of progress.

Reliability   is the consistency of the implementation and delivery of the intervention procedures as a treatment each time the classes meet.

Resource allocation   is part of the school's overall school improvement plan linked to fiscal management, and is a puzzle to be assembled by administrators in school settings.

Responsive adaptability   is the ability to quickly and seamlessly adjust to ever-changing environmental demands.

Role   is a function assumed by a particular person; it is duty or skill specific, not title specific.

Schoolcentric   is when the narrative is framed around how parents can help schools to promote student education.

School counselors   provide academic, personal, social, and career support to students.

School psychologists   are uniquely trained individuals on a school campus who conduct psychoeducational evaluations, provide mental and behavioral supports to students, assist teams with intervention planning, and help school administration implement evidence-based policies and programs.

Smart teams   are comprised of a group of individuals who equally contribute and are savvy at understanding and identifying the emotional states of others.

Social-emotional and behavioral (SEB) programming   is a combined framework of supports under the MTSS model that provides identification, intervention, and progress monitoring of social-emotional learning and positive behavior intervention supports.

Social-emotional regulation   is the ability to control and negotiate emotions, thoughts, and behaviors effectively and efficiently.

Social justice   occurs when all children, from all different backgrounds, regardless of socioeconomic background or demographic characteristics, are valued in a school community and have access to a relevant education.

Specialists   are often teachers on special assignment and are one of the most adaptable resources on campus, fulfilling any role or function that is required to support administrators looking to accomplish a wide range of responsibilities for students on campus.

Stakeholder networks are a complex web of stakeholders with a shared understanding who can be called upon in times of need to maximize impact.

Strategic opportunism is a term borrowed from the business world that simply means the leader is able to adhere to the long-term vision, for example higher student achievement, while remaining flexible enough in the short-term to take advantage of opportunities that arise to support and help meet the long-term vision, for example implementing a model of support consisting of multiple tiers.

Student Led Informational Conferences are a powerful evidence-based method to encourage students to take responsibility for their own learning and require self-reflection, identification of strengths and needs, goal setting, self-monitoring, organizational practice, and communication skills.

Teacher efficacy is a teacher's perceived level of ability to impact student learning through their instruction, data analysis, motivation, and organization.

Teacher-student relationships fuel the efforts of students, which can persist despite challenges and are resilient in times of adversity, with the right level of support.

Three As of Awareness, Access, and Action are all necessary components of inserting the school psychologist's perspective into a school and community's ecosystem.

Three-Pronged Motivation Approach consists of including students in the data collection and analysis process, increasing student buy-in through teacher motivation, and incentivizing achievement at all levels.

Trauma-informed care is an organizational framework that can be used to guide responsiveness to various types of trauma.

Triangulating data across multiple sources helps teams validate a student's need for intervention and provides insight into what type of support best meets the student's need.

Unfunded mandates are statutory requirements or regulations imposed without funds provided to carry out the directive.

Unicorns are mythological creatures with unique talents and characteristics who can make extraordinary impact.

Unintended consequences are outcomes that are realized without purposefully working toward them.

Universal screening is administered to all students to determine their current level of performance in any given domain.

Validity is when the data collected can be used meaningfully to create inferences and make decisions about the students from the scores collected.

Why is the individual's purpose or motivations behind their actions.

Index

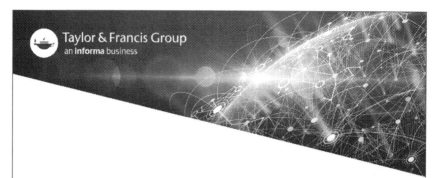

Printed in the United States
by Baker & Taylor Publisher Services